Jennifer Overha...

C000225590

Juggling
the BIG
3

Business

Brand

Leadership

for Lawyers

A career-building plan to develop your
personal brand, client business, and leadership mindset

ProvechZiel

Published by ProvechZiel Ltd.
P.O. Box 50486
London W8 9EN
England

www.provechziel.com

publisher@provechziel.com

Copyright © 2009 by Jennifer Overhaus

No part of this publication may be reproduced, stored in a retrieval
system or transmitted in any form or by any means including photocopying,
electronic, mechanical recording or otherwise, without the prior written
permission of the rights holders, application for which must be made
to the publisher.

All rights reserved.

Printed and bound in Dubai by Oriental Press.
Book design and layout by Pentacor**big** www.pentacorbig.co.uk
Illustrations by Julia Langran www.jules.net
Back cover photo by Virginia Grey www.virginiagrey.co.uk

This book is designed to provide accurate and authoritative information and while the
author has tried and achieved success with the advice given, neither she nor the publisher
accepts responsibility for any inaccuracies or omissions, and they specifically disclaim
any liability, loss, or risk that is incurred as a consequence, directly or indirectly, from
the contents of this book. Further, the author's extensive reading in the areas of personal
development and psychology has made exact citations a challenge. The author has made
every attempt to reference all materials sourced from a third party and sincerely regrets
any omissions. If you believe any other reference or authority influenced the content of
this work but was not cited, please advise the publisher.

Juggling the Big 3 for Lawyers

To my husband Marcus, whom I love very much
I'm so grateful to have you in my life

Publisher's Note

This is a "work in progress," which will be revised as necessary to keep it current with the legal market and to include viewpoints and stories received from readers. We want to know what you think and hear about your experiences and perspectives, even if (especially if!) they differ from those of the author. Also, any review would be much appreciated.

You can email us at: comments@provechziel.com.

Otherwise, please feel free to email the author directly at:
Jennifer@jugglingthebig3.com.

Author's Note

In writing this book, I grappled with the gender issues common to many modern authors. The world of law long since ceased to be a male bastion, and it will be apparent from the stories told throughout the book that I had female colleagues, bosses, and clients in abundance throughout my career in the law. To make this manuscript entirely gender-neutral, however, would have been extremely cumbersome, so I've made the decision, for simplicity's sake, to use masculine pronouns in most cases where I refer to lawyers and clients in the abstract. I hope this doesn't offend any of my fellow females.

Acknowledgments

This book has benefited hugely from the life experiences of many of my fellow lawyers and people in the legal world, to whom I am most grateful.[1] In the course of my research, they've provided me with feedback and lots of stories—some funny, some inspiring, but all beneficial. To each of you: Thank you.

For a lawyer, writing a book felt almost natural (much like drafting a long, complex contract), but after a while the words began to feel stale. Fortunately, by that point I had Alice McVeigh (www.alicemcveigh.com) to add a touch of finesse and make it all flow. Her input to the process was invaluable as an editor, friend, and champion of the project. I also thank Alice for bringing Katharine Shaibani on board. Kathy completed the final edits with proofreading precision and a terrific eye for detail.

In the early stages of developing and writing the book, I had the wisdom of my friend, coach, and mentor, Jim Hever, who was instrumental in helping me work through my ideas and ensure the integrity of my propositions. His guidance and championship have been invaluable.

Last, this book only came together at all because of the support of my wonderful husband. He admits to sometimes longing to shove my computer out the window, yet it was he who proposed that I leave the practice of law to fulfill the next stage of my journey: this book. Without his support and encouragement, I could have never done it.

---

[1] Where appropriate the names have been changed, and some (or all) of the context has been changed in those stories that could be construed as negative toward an individual. However, all stories are based on true accounts.

The Look and Feel of the Book

When the idea of this book first came to mind, I knew it had to be supported by illustrations and diagrams—and color! So I was fortunate to find some exceptional people who helped me implement my concept.

My wonderful illustrator, Julia Langran (a.k.a. "Jules"), has worked with me almost from the very beginning, bringing to life my ideas and concepts. She has been a delight to work with and a tremendous partner. Without her artwork, the book would simply be incomplete. Based in the UK, Jules is a freelance illustrator and animator who has worked with clients such as BBC Digital, Celador, and The Monster Factory. She has also been published in various DGV books, magazines such as *Computer Arts* and *Digital Arts*, and participated in art shows as far afield as Florida and Singapore. You can see more of her work at www.jules.net.

Unlike most lawyers (who covet words), I love using diagrams—for me, the cliché fits: a picture is worth a thousand words. For the book, however, I could no longer call upon the wonderful assistants I had had in the past to turn my sketches into clear and comprehensible graphics! Instead I found Tia Seifert, who artfully took my ideas and developed the diagrams I envisioned (tia.seifert@gmail.com).

Last, Pentacor**big** (www.pentacorbig.co.uk) created the book cover, inside layout, and design. The whole team at Pentacor was fantastic, encouraging me and helping me every step of the way.

Preface

I have been lucky enough to enjoy an incredible law career that has brought me satisfaction, recognition, world travel, the opportunity to live abroad, transatlantic homes, and wonderful friendships. Having started off as an eager, naïve associate, I worked hard to achieve my goal of partnership and eventually became the global head of a practice group of an international firm. Along the way, I learned some unexpected lessons: about myself, about people in general, and about the practice of law. Without doubt, my most surprising discovery was the realization that legal talent and superior intelligence, even when combined with dedication, will not guarantee success. Worse still, I found that the critical factors—such as character, mindset, people skills, and presentation—generally go untaught.

I was fortunate to have both wise mentors and an innate desire to develop the necessary traits. But in today's ever-growing and hugely demanding firms, young lawyers aren't usually offered the close mentoring relationships that benefited me, or the one-to-one associate/partner arrangements that were typical in the past. Further, the fact that firms today expect long hours (and brilliant work) from their lawyers tends to encourage an insular focus, and leaves the new lawyer with little time or energy to pursue anything beyond raw technical skills. Yet the irony is that the softer skills, so critical long-term, can only be developed by acquiring broader interests and subtler priorities.

To make matters worse, clients increasingly demand that lawyers excel in these softer skills as well; technical talent is no longer enough. So the means for young lawyers to develop such skills have decreased, while the need to demonstrate them continues to escalate, and law firm training programs (for the most part) have failed to fill the gap. I find it extremely paradoxical that so many firms aspire to be the "McKinsey" of the law but fail to do the key thing that has brought McKinsey & Company (the consulting firm) its success: that is, developing their people beyond mere technical and intellectual skills. This remains the case despite the fact that following the McKinsey model would result in far greater long-term gains for individuals and law firms alike. Instead, firms ignore such training until it is too late, and then try to "fix" the problem of underperforming lawyers!

So, by giving lawyers the awareness and tools they need, I hope to compensate for some deficiencies in our professional training and to provide the foundation that lawyers need for long-term success. (I'm not implying that the fault lies solely with the law firms; individual lawyers must take responsibility for their own careers. Looking back on my own journey, I realize that I would have been better prepared if I had shown more initiative myself—and that my lack of resourcefulness transpired despite being surrounded in each of my firms by some wonderful mentors, role models, and friends.)

But before moving into the book's introduction, let me explain how this book came about.

I believe there comes a time in life when all our past experiences, preparations, and decisions come together in some significant change or opportunity. The circumstances leading up to that moment may not have been uniformly positive (or even completely understood at the time), but they still tend to guide most people down paths that ultimately fit together as neatly and inexorably as two puzzle pieces. And when we find our purpose, we realize that all the journeying (the unsuccessful parts as well as the scintillating parts) has particularly, and even uniquely, qualified us to pursue the new challenge opening up before us.

This purpose can be world-changing or merely life-changing; it can affect masses of people or only one person; it can be practical or abstrusely theoretical; and it can sometimes appear pretty crazy (one friend starts up a law firm, another moves to the wilderness to "find himself"). The nuances are infinite, and surely no purpose is intrinsically "better" than any other. The one constant is that our purpose derives from each of the special gifts, talents, skills, and abilities acquired on our journey so far—and, of course, as our journeys change, so may our purpose.

I feel incredibly lucky to have found my "moment" and my purpose: alerting you, the young lawyer, to the *real* things that will make or break your career, and showing you how to succeed. Fueling me is my belief in personal development and my frustration that so many lawyers (as well as others) are not equipped to realize their innate potential.

My path began when my parents instilled in me the belief that I could do just about anything I set my mind on. From an early age I was told to dream and that my success was limited only by my own actions (or lack of action!). Only later in life did I realize what a rare gift self-belief is; it took a few terse comments from friends, who had seen my parents' attitudes first-hand, to make me realize just how lucky I'd been.

In my teens, my mother used to give me books to improve myself, or to help me deal with particularly difficult situations—even sending me on courses and taking me to conferences. I must admit that some of the books went unread and that I had to be coerced into attending a few of those events, but as I got older I learned to appreciate the strength of their lessons, and, as an adult, I came to relish discovering my own channels of personal growth.

Another major factor for me was that, while only in my twenties, I was diagnosed with cancer and spent the better part of two years zigzagging in and out of hospitals, facing not only operations but also radiation and chemotherapy. I realize now that my mental outlook and positive beliefs (inculcated by my family) were critical to my recovery. I was probably very naïve, but it certainly never occurred to me that I wouldn't get better—and, miraculously, I did! The experience left me with a greater conviction in the power of the mind and the belief that any of us can change and shape our situations by altering our mental outlooks. Since then, I've absorbed huge amounts of information—scientific, medical, and spiritual (not a lawyer's typical reading matter!)—that have reinforced my convictions. Recently, I've become particularly fascinated by neuroscience: discoveries about how the structure and development of the brain affects behavior and how this knowledge allows us to enhance our own development.

It's always been important to me to share my advantages and awareness. Again, my parents taught by example, as they were always involved with education and always keen to give the less fortunate the tools to do better. My particular passion has been working with young children through charitable organizations, community projects, and mentoring programs. This has been a source of tremendous gratification, and I've felt truly inspired by seeing others discover their own talents. Mentoring has convinced me that the single best way to influence others is through teaching and empowerment. This conviction, too, spurred me into writing this book.

Obviously, the greatest single contributor to this new purpose has been my legal career. It's only through my own experiences that I feel equipped to guide anyone. And since my own career didn't exactly launch as spectacularly as I had envisioned, I know first-hand that setbacks are merely temporary and that we can all achieve our ambitions!

After graduating from Emory Law School, my dream job fell through. Left with a significant level of debt and no employment, I went to visit my parents, and while there unexpectedly found a position in a small "boutique" firm specializing in technology law. (Actually, back then it was referred to as "computer law." Don't ask me the year!) It wasn't exactly where I'd anticipated starting my career, but I realized that technology law could be a unique niche, and it turned out to be a solid foundation for my future. From day one I was taught that being a lawyer is a business, and that your only business asset is yourself, along with the perception people have of you and of what you deliver. An analogy from my first day has stayed with me. My boss asked, "If you go to the world's best neurologist and the plaque on the door reads 'Brane Surgeon,' wouldn't you think twice before going inside?"

My next job was in a larger firm in Atlanta, Georgia: Morris, Manning & Martin, which had a groundbreaking technology practice. Again, I was lucky in my mentors. My boss there, John, remains my role model in how to use networking to generate business and how to bring people together to create synergistic benefits for everyone. (I reveal many of his techniques in this book.) The partners I worked with at Morris, Manning & Martin instilled in me at an early stage the belief that successful law careers have to be carved out; they don't just happen.

With the guidance of these people, I made myself into a well-known IT lawyer. At the time this was a novel specialty, so I was sought after by other firms wanting to develop technology expertise. I'd always yearned to travel—in fact, my dream was to live abroad—and eventually I made it happen, moving from America to London to work at Freshfields, a "magic circle" firm.[2] While the Americans and the English may ostensibly speak the same language (not!), I discovered that subtle differences in mindset between English people and Americans can create very different intentions and methods of working. Learning these particular "English lessons" was an invaluable experience, and I developed some wonderful friendships in the process.

While at Freshfields, I was lucky to work with some great lawyers on a wide range of mega-deals but realized more and more that outsourcing gave me a special enthusiasm. So when the pioneering outsourcing firm of Shaw Pittman approached me about helping to set up their London office, I was thrilled. Suddenly I was, in essence, an entrepreneur—no longer reliant on the steady work generated by my previous magic circle firm. (This was both a daunting and an exciting prospect!) It was a fantastic time in my career, because I truly loved the sense that my colleagues and I were building something from scratch, and I felt real ownership of what we were cultivating. I finally began to under-stand for myself what my early mentors had sought to teach me: I was not just practicing law, but building a business. After only a year of setting up the London office, we won the Legal Business IP/IT Team of the Year Award.

---

[2] The "magic circle" is a brand associated with a handful of elite global law firms that were originally based in London. The magic circle firms are renowned for advising the most coveted clients on their highest-profile deals.

I enjoyed my years as a partner with Shaw Pittman, but when Pillsbury Winthrop approached me to head their global outsourcing group, I made the move. (Ironically, Pillsbury Winthrop later merged with Shaw Pittman.) Again, it was a great firm with some gifted lawyers, and even though I had been a partner for some time at this point, I continued to glean beneficial lessons from many of my colleagues there.

I was lucky during my career to have been rewarded with my dream legal job, working on global deals involving hundreds of millions and billions of dollars, many of which became headline news. I spent much of my time traveling between London, New York, California, and Asia, sometimes not entirely sure myself where "home" was! (This might seem torture to some, but I found it thrilling!) But regardless of the size of any deal, location, or client, what remained constant was my passion for my work. I thought this should have been enough to ensure consistent success, but it wasn't, and it's been an enlightening experience to sit back and analyze my legal career in the context of this book and to consider the reasons for every success and failure. The luxury of time—something few practicing lawyers can contemplate—was crucial in allowing me to really analyze the factors that can propel a young lawyer toward a more successful and satisfying career.

My hope now is that my research and my experiences can help you.

How to Benefit Most From This Book

This book is not designed to be skimmed and then cast onto a bookshelf. It's really more of a course, and to *really* benefit, you should read it methodically, making notes and doing the exercises. I suggest using a notebook to keep track of any new ideas or problem areas that emerge; then re-read the book, using your notes and your understanding of the entire step-by-step process to show you what you most need to work on. (At that point, one hopes, the book's "process" will have become a comprehensively understood methodology for success.)

Optimally, you should also work through the *Juggling the Big 3 Tool Kit*, which provides a framework (in an in-depth workbook format) for creating your personal strategy. (Originally the Tool Kit was designed as an appendix to the book, but as the book grew to over five hundred pages, this became impractical.)

You can obtain the *Juggling the Big 3 Tool Kit* at **www.jugglingthebig3.com.**

TABLE OF CONTENTS

▦ Acknowledgments   v

▦ The Look and Feel of the Book   vi

▦ Preface   vii

▦ How to Benefit Most From This Book   xii

Introductory Chapters

▦ Introduction   1

▦ **Chapter 1:** The Valley of Death and Other Hazards   5

▦ **Chapter 2:** The Juggling Act   11

▦ **Chapter 3:** The Secret Knowledge of the Master Juggler   25

The Awareness Building Blocks

▦ **Chapter 4:** Awareness Building Block 1: Personalities   35
(Working with the personalities around you—including your own!)
     APPENDIX 4.A: Questionnaire: Preferred Behaviors   70
     APPENDIX 4.B: Table of Strengths   78
     APPENDIX 4.C: Table of How Extreme Strengths   82
         Can Become Liabilities
     APPENDIX 4.D: Practical Application: Managing   89
         Behaviors in Relation to Others

▦ **Chapter 5:** Awareness Building Block 2: Motivators   99
(Understanding your motivators to enable them to fuel your goals)
     APPENDIX 5.A: List of Motivators   114
     APPENDIX 5.B: Exercise   116
     APPENDIX 5.C: Rebecca's Example   117

▦ **Chapter 6:** Awareness Building Block 3: People Skills   123
(Learning how to connect)

■ **Chapter 7:** Awareness Building Block 4: Thinking   155
(Optimizing your thinking and generating confidence)

■ **Chapter 8:** Awareness Building Block 5: Positive Impact   185
(Understanding how impressions are made)

An Introduction to the Three "Balls"

■ **Chapter 9:** Brand: The Beginning   193

Ball 1: Brand

■ **Chapter 10:** Brand "You"   203
         APPENDIX 10.A: Table of Brand Attributes   215

■ **Chapter 11:** Adopting the Core Traits of a Superior Brand   217

■ **Chapter 12:** Brand Creation   241

■ **Chapter 13:** Enhancing and Marketing Your Brand   261

■ **Chapter 14:** Public Speaking   287

Ball 2: Business

■ **Chapter 15:** Networking: The Reality   307

■ **Chapter 16:** Expanding Your Network   341

■ **Chapter 17:** Winning and Developing Business   371

Ball 3: Leadership

■ **Chapter 18:** The Three Dimensions of Leadership   417

■ **Chapter 19:** Self-Leading   433

■ **Chapter 20:** Leading Within Relationships   457

■ **Chapter 21:** Leading a Team   481

Conclusion

■ **Chapter 22:** Streamlining the Juggling Act   517

Introduction

Lack of awareness can be the greatest impediment to success; knowledge enables the preparation necessary for future greatness.

T he immediate trigger for this book was a routine performance review for one of my associates. She asked me a pertinent (and simple) question: "What do I need to do to succeed? How did you do it?" I responded, bluntly, by telling her that very few of the criteria upon which she was currently being measured—and that we had just spent close to an hour discussing—would have much bearing on her ultimate success. Since she was a committed and high-performing associate (by standard benchmarks), this was a major blow to her belief that she had been pursuing a well-marked, near-infallible route to her goal of partnership.

Later, recalling our conversation, I had an epiphany—or, more accurately, a crystallization of what I already knew at some subconscious level: Most lawyers are poorly prepared for partnership because they fail to lay the groundwork for advancement at the inception of their careers. To make matters worse, in most firms the criteria for success at partner level are rarely emphasized and may even be implied rather than explicitly stated. Thus, young lawyers are immediately "wrong-footed" and can flounder for years before realizing what they should have been taught from the start.

I had always tried to mentor the young lawyers who worked for me (as well as those I encountered through alumni groups or other contacts), but now I began to focus far more intently on helping them with the subtler skills that would be crucial to them in the long term. And although I initially encountered some resistance, I persisted, and was delighted to observe initial skeptics first concede my points and finally flourish.

I began to make extensive notes regarding my mentoring efforts and to discuss my observations with everyone around me. One day one of my colleagues flippantly asked if I was planning to write a book. "You've got to be kidding," I said. "At the moment I have to schedule time to breathe!" I was a full-time lawyer and partner and was also busy writing a technical book on my principal topic of expertise, so the probability of my writing another book was not exactly high. But when I discussed my observations (jokingly) with partners and colleagues, everyone said the same things: "How I wish I'd known this stuff in the beginning!" "If only someone had told me!" When I mentioned the book to young lawyers, they all chorused, "When can I get a copy?"

Over time I realized that my passion for legal practice had transitioned, and that educating young lawyers had actually become more important to me than doing another deal or engaging the next big client. In other words, I finally began to burn to write this book! And this is why:

- To provide the ambitious young lawyer—you!—with sufficient awareness of (first) the transition process from associate to partner and (secondly) the skill set that must be developed along the way. (In short, lawyers immersed in client work find it all too easy to ignore the warning signals and procrastinate.)

- To set out the tools of enablement needed to achieve sustained success. Law firms and senior partners tend to demand and reward short-term achievements—such as meeting a client's immediate needs, winning the next pitch, or increasing this month's billable targets. Those initiatives are necessary, of course, but young attorneys also need to invest in their own futures, whether or not they hope to make partner.

- To share insights from my experiences. We can always learn from the successes and failures of others. I want to give you the benefit of my "20/20 hindsight" so that you can avoid at least some of those hardships on your own career path.

■ To motivate you to take responsibility for your career as a lawyer and to consciously commit yourself to new ways of thinking that will bring you success.

■ To inspire you to set goals that will provide optimal satisfaction, to take them seriously, and to keep yourself on track to achieve them.

■ To instill the confidence that you are capable of developing the necessary skills and that your professional journey, while challenging, will be both enjoyable and rewarding.

■ To ignite your enthusiasm and passion for your career.

You may actually discover that the career path you're currently on is not the right one for you, or that making partner is not the right goal. On the other hand, if partnership is not your current career objective, you may discover that it should be. This book could even take you in an entirely different direction, away from private practice or the law. Whatever the outcome, the broad principles of this book will help you achieve your goals.

I want you to see me as your mentor and to use this book as a systematic exposition of the tools that will help you achieve your goals. It contains both the information I wish I'd been provided with—and the information I should have known myself.

No matter where you are in your career, the principles of my program can help you. It's never too early to start applying them!

So let's take a long, keen look, first of all, at the skill set needed to succeed as a partner.

Chapter One

The Valley of Death
& Other Hazards

Had I been asked, some years ago, "What does it take to become—and succeed as—a partner," I might have responded as follows:

- Superior intelligence;

- Top academic qualifications;

- Innate legal talent;

- An exceptional ability to drive deals or win cases;

- Proven expertise in a specialist area;

- A depth of experience, along with a strong track record;

- Ambition, hard work, and a provable history of strong billable hours; and

- The ability to deal effectively with clients and colleagues.

And it's true that these qualities have traditionally been the standard by which lawyers are judged. (Of course, there have always been those rainmakers who can generate clients and business in a way inexplicable to others—the few with a certain magic touch. But they're no longer the exception.)

The point here is that, fortunately or unfortunately, the attributes I've listed above no longer guarantee success in the law (not even in combination!); instead, today's extremely competitive legal market requires lawyers to demonstrate much more than technical expertise. We *all* need the "magical skills" that in the past made a partner exceptional or a rainmaker! Such attributes are crucial for any lawyer aspiring to partnership—as well as for most senior lawyers, whether they are in-house, in a law firm, or otherwise employed.

The problem is twofold: First, too many young lawyers are busily pursuing their goals without reference to the (new) realities. Many simply don't understand the new ground rules—and who can blame them? They, naturally enough, aspire to resemble their role models—and those role models probably succeeded through technical expertise, combined perhaps with driving ambition or inspiring intellect. Thus, some young lawyers are enthusiastically (and naïvely) choosing to follow an outdated system.

Second, law firms are failing to adequately encourage lawyers to develop the right skills, and this only exacerbates the problem. For example, many firms still pay bonuses purely on the basis of billable hours, a practice that can actively undermine the development of those aspiring to the top tier. These law firms thus reward ambitious and technically gifted young lawyers, and give them the impression that they *are* doing all they need to do to succeed. So why would these lawyers think otherwise, and why would they seek to develop themselves further? (And where would they find the time to develop themselves, anyway?)

So today's lawyers need to understand and master *new* criteria for success. Let's examine what happens when this reality is ignored or overlooked.

NEW CRITERIA FOR SUCCESS

As lawyers, most of our training is focused on technical ability, and in our junior years we are mainly rewarded for working hard and for delivering fast, first-rate work. However, after satisfying those standards over many years, upon approaching partnership, we are suddenly confronted by a new reality: the benchmarks for success that we've come to understand and expect abruptly disintegrate. Intense commitment and the delivery of exceptional work—in short, technical performance—have become so routine that they no longer guarantee success.

The new success criteria rely on things that may have previously seemed unimportant, at least when compared to technical performance—things like sociability, likeability (?!), and marketability. Even more problematic, it's vital to have outside interests and access to an extensive network of contacts (hands up, all lawyers who've found the time to create all that?!). Further, success today requires an understanding of how to *really* manage and lead others. Very few lawyers are born with such skills, and they're not likely to be developed through total immersion in technical training.

This change of objectives is so immediate that some sense a drop in performance, which can undermine their confidence. To compound the problem, many lawyers' immediate instinct, especially if they have been superb performers to date, is to carry on as before and hope for the best—a strategy that can prove fatal! (The sad irony is that it's often super performers, or the ones who truly love the law, who are at greatest risk.)

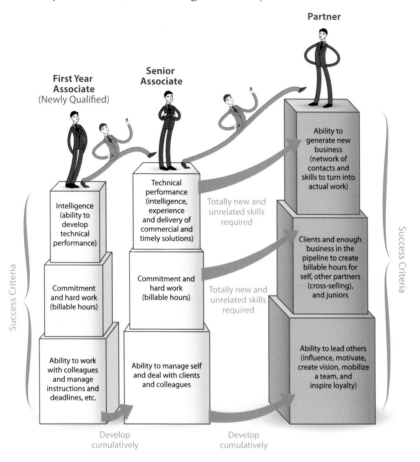

Lawyers who learn only the skills of technical performance (the white boxes) cannot make the final leap.

> *As a partner, intense commitment and exceptional work are now presumed to exist and no longer represent an accurate measure of success.*

The diagram above sets out the criteria used by most firms to measure the performance of each tier of lawyers. Here it becomes obvious that, in the jump from senior associate to partner, technical performance no longer factors in. Without a deeper skill set, the partner with "only" technical ability will never generate the required results.

8

Realizing this, I made an immediate decision to better prepare the young lawyers around me. Yet when I communicated the advice of this book (and even sought to teach the skills that long-term success would require), I routinely encountered initial resistance. These were some of the objections:

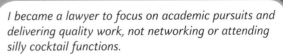

But that can't be the case! The most important thing about a lawyer has to be basic intelligence, right?

I work really hard to excel at my client work and don't have time for that other stuff.

I became a lawyer to focus on academic pursuits and delivering quality work, not networking or attending silly cocktail functions.

Frankly, I'm working really hard to be the best lawyer I can be. If I'd wanted to be a salesman I wouldn't have spent all those years training to be a lawyer!

You may have a point, but marketing activities are sooooo boring.

Sure, but I'm an expert in my field and that should speak for itself, shouldn't it?

I don't care about leadership. My goal is to be a profitable partner, not lead the firm.

Hang on, I have to meet my billable targets, right? There are no rewards in my firm for non-billable pursuits.

Believe me, I understood what they were saying! I too had enjoyed the challenges of my associate years, when each project seemed to draw out a new and exciting dimension from my evolving abilities; I'd felt confident in my work and valued by both my superiors and my clients. But when I became a partner, I realized that I had to adapt or perish—and so do you.

I firmly believe that it doesn't have to be difficult. After all, the things we must learn are very basic and easy to implement; they're skills every lawyer should have the necessary qualities to master.

IT ALL STARTS WITH AWARENESS!

We all have the necessary skills and qualities. The trick is knowing when we need to employ them, making the decision to do so, and not giving up!

THE VALLEY OF DEATH

As I studied the training and performance of advancing lawyers, I became aware of a strong trend—something I had always been aware of, as a partner, but had never really focused on. (Have you ever bought a new car and noticed suddenly how many clones there are on the road?!) The trend was this: The billable hours of new partners tend to plummet dramatically, or, as my friend Jim calls it, they enter "the Valley of Death."

Once I began discussing the Valley of Death with colleagues and friends, I realized that it is common to most firms. Its casualties are good lawyers, and its cause is simple: New partners are not prepared for the transition from associate to partner. Their workload as an associate is dependent on others, but once they make partner they must generate work for themselves—a task for which most of them simply lack the skills.

As I researched the Valley of Death, I observed yet another trend: the two-to-three-year partner, or partners who stumble into the Valley of Death and fail to climb out. After failing, they somehow persuade another firm to hire them, only to fall into the Valley again. These lawyers may even fail repeatedly, convinced each time that the fault lies with the firm rather than themselves. They weren't "appreciated," their superiors or other departments were "against them," the firm's client list was "inferior," there were Machiavellian types conspiring against their success, and so on. Now, no one who knows anything about human nature or law firms can deny that some of these things do occur, but the two-to-three-year partner (especially the repeat offender) should seriously consider that he or she may have stumbled into the Valley of Death.

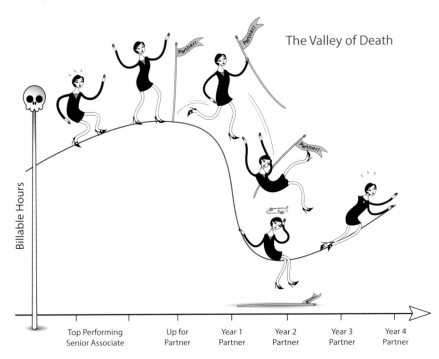

The Valley of Death

Billable Hours

| Top Performing Senior Associate | Up for Partner | Year 1 Partner | Year 2 Partner | Year 3 Partner | Year 4 Partner |

Caveat: Does the casualty actually climb out of the Valley of Death, and her billable hours increase again, as the graph shows? Or, for some, is the Valley endless?

The Valley of Death is nobody's goal, but some very good lawyers end up there. Some are naïve and don't realize that they should be focusing on a new skill set; others demonstrate an obstinate refusal to adapt. Whatever the reason, it's tragic that so many lawyers end their previously flourishing careers in that canyon! Yet the solution is surprisingly simple, so let's move into the next chapter to discover the advancing lawyer's strategies for success.

Chapter Two
The Juggling Act

Life is often described as a juggling act. Most of us are juggling various balls—careers, personal relationships, leisure time, and health—and if we can keep them all flying, life feels great.

But with age, our juggling act can become more complicated. New balls are constantly being added to the mix (kids, promotions, health issues), and no one ball can stay up in the air forever. If one slips through our fingers—we get sick, we lose our job, our marriage collapses—things get tougher, but we usually manage to pull through. If two balls falter, we struggle that much extra, and if more (or even all) drop, life can feel pretty bleak.

Sometimes a ball just falls—our partner leaves, or we have a run of bad luck at work. At other times (if we're honest), losing control of one ball or another is really our fault. We can get so enthralled by the perfect motion of one ball that we disregard the others. We've all seen lawyers who work too hard at the expense of their personal lives or their health. A reality check may be needed to help us evaluate priorities and get all the balls back up in the air.

But just as we juggle in life, we have to juggle at work. And when we are able to deftly handle the several balls that make up a legal career, we get the greatest satisfaction and reward—at least from the "work" part of life.

THE LAWYER'S JUGGLING ACT

When we first launch our careers as lawyers, we're generally dealing with only one ball (technical ability), and such a task can feel straightforward enough. The technical ball begins to feel comfortingly familiar in our hands, and we gradually learn how to maneuver it smoothly. We learn our craft and become increasingly competent in our chosen discipline. Clearly, this is the right focus and the right place from which to start our development.

Gradually we sharpen our skills and make progress. Drafting a document that previously seemed complex becomes a piece of cake. We add new tricks to the mix, perhaps replicating a negotiation tactic we saw a partner use, or maybe spotting a legal argument or loophole and finding enough self-assurance to exploit it. Confidence increases day by day, yet basically we are still only dealing with that single, well-grooved ball: technical performance.

What young lawyers may not realize is that some day technical ability will no longer be the only aspect of performance that matters and that a new set of seriously slippery (and more advanced) balls will be heading their way. Ideally, they would be forewarned and forearmed, easily able to assimilate each new requirement. In practice, however, this rarely happens.

So, what are these new balls? There are **three**, each with multiple layers and different components: brand, business, and leadership.

Brand

First of all, each of us needs to determine what we want to represent (our "brand") and then figure out the most efficient and effective way to project it. To succeed, we must lose—overnight!—the mentality of being an associate in "X" firm (which in today's competitive market and among some firms can even equate to a commodity) and instead think of ourselves as someone individual and different—something more than an intellectual asset and a creative problem-solver. We want to compete on uniqueness. Too many lawyers (and law firms, for that matter) try to compete on the same dimensions: technical expertise, depth of experience, breadth of capability—and in doing so fail to really differentiate themselves. *Being forced to compete on fees should act as a signal that we have failed to compete on the unique value of our brand.*

We must first choose exactly what brand we want to project, and then do everything we can to support and market ourselves in this role. Our personal brand must be conveyed unmistakably with each first impression. Our reputation communicates our brand, and our brand must be something we walk and talk constantly. Yet maintaining its ethos and integrity is not enough! We also have to get out there and strategically advertise and communicate it. In short, we need to "sell" ourselves.

Toby's Brand

Toby was a promising young tax lawyer in my firm. Hugely intelligent and extremely able, he knew the ins and outs of the regulations better than any of his peers. He routinely impressed his boss, and (for that matter) everyone in his department, with his ability to spot issues and provide clever solutions. Toby was fast becoming a master of legal technique.

On the other hand, Toby could be arrogant and even wickedly irreverent toward his colleagues, even to their faces, especially when they couldn't immediately grasp something he understood effortlessly. This attitude eventually caused so much friction that Toby's boss became concerned. Tax lawyers are heavily dependent on other groups within the firm, and Toby's behavior was effectively undermining the entire department. So his boss hauled him in for a chat. "Listen, you're a superb technical lawyer, as everyone knows. But if you want to truly succeed in this department, you're going to have to be even more than that. You have to be known as a positive person to work with, and you can only do that by developing your people skills and managing your relationships better."

Toby was genuinely shocked by this feedback, and he resented the advice. Deep down he thought that his superior attitude was justified. (After all, he had graduated top of his law school class, hadn't he?!) Secretly he thought, "It's not my fault that my colleagues are stupid!"

Toby was certainly building a brand—"intelligent but extremely difficult to work with"—but it wasn't quite the one most clients or colleagues are looking for.

Pause for thought

- What kind of brand are you creating for yourself?
- Does it support the career you're really seeking?
- How do your day-to-day activities and relationships with your colleagues, clients, bosses, or even rivals, enhance (or damage)

Business

The second ball we have to deal with is developing business, which means cultivating clients, both for ourselves and on behalf of our firm. The truth is that there will come a point at which your entire career is dependent upon your network of relationships and your ability to feed yourself (and others) work.

We all know that the key to a financially secure future is to plan, and that only fools wait until the verge of retirement before building up an investment portfolio. What is less obvious is that precisely the same principle applies to business development. The sooner we start building up a portfolio of clients, the more impressive will be our contributions to our firms—and the greater the potential for promotion, distinction, and growth. And if we wait too long, enjoying the youthful pleasure of having work fed to us, we'll have to do that much more to catch up. So we must constantly ask ourselves...

> ■ How much business will I have when I really need it in the future?
>
> ■ What will the revenue be from that portfolio of business (both for me and for my firm)?
>
> ■ Will this be enough to support my needs and fulfill my ambitions?

After all, investing in business development is the most important part of career planning. Are you sure that you're doing enough?

Mark and Catherine

I had an associate working for me called Mark who anticipated the areas of his career that would eventually become pivotal and routinely discussed these things with me (his immediate superior). He was particularly concerned about building a strong foundation that would ultimately bring him the business that he would some day need to generate. With this in mind, Mark nurtured relationships with contacts and clients and spent much of his free time enhancing his network.

In contrast, his colleague and office-mate Catherine almost entirely ignored this side of her career. I understood her reasoning: An excellent technical lawyer, Catherine had built herself a stellar reputation of driving projects through to completion, and both clients and colleagues admired her work. She was succeeding in her career, so why would she need to do anything more?

Whenever I encouraged Catherine to consider handling the more advanced "ball" of business development, she hid behind her other talents: "I'm far too busy with client work, which is much more important anyway." Once, when I questioned her absence at a marketing function, she even implied that I was devaluing her client commitments. "OK, fine," she said (heavy irony here), "Next time I'll just let the client down and prioritize networking instead!" Yet Catherine was smart enough to know that I wasn't really telling her to drop her existing (golden!) ball; instead, I was suggesting that she add another—crucial—ball to her already glittering repertoire.

Had Catherine been unequivocally honest, she would have acknowledged her avoidance of client development for what it was—her dislike of leaving her comfort zone. (The irony is that when Catherine first started working with her preferred ball of technical performance, she hadn't felt entirely easy with that, either. Each professional phase requires new skills.)

While Catherine had an excellent track record of project work and high billable hours, when the time came for senior advancement and partnership, Mark was streets ahead of her. In fact, at that critical stage, Mark had clients of his own and on that basis was made partner; Catherine had never built herself a network or developed the tools that would bring her business, and so was forced eventually into a different type of role within the profession.

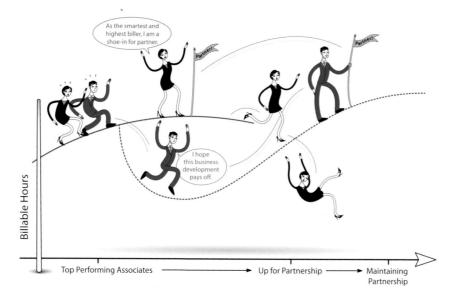

Early investment in client development can make a crucial long-term difference.

Pause for thought

■ Are you thinking about your future and putting the right framework in place to generate your own clients?

Leadership

The third ball we must learn to deal with is leadership. If you are currently junior, please don't be put off from considering this aspect of your career. Leadership is not entirely about a position within an extant hierarchy. I'm convinced that you probably have partners in your midst whom you do not really perceive as true leaders, and (if you accept my views) you'll probably find juniors among you who are already managing themselves as the genuine article.

There are many ideas of what constitutes a leader. Some focus on personal characteristics; some look at strength of influence; some emphasize purpose and values; some only consider results achieved. Still others use a combination of these factors. Throughout this book we will consider most of these things.

But first, let's agree on a definition of a leader. For me this is someone who has vision: someone able to mobilize and inspire others so that everyone is working steadfastly to achieve the same goal (a "shared purpose," "part of the team," "singing from the same hymn sheet"—whatever image works for you). Even—or especially—during times of turmoil, such a leader inspires his followers to stay the course and maintain integral loyalty not only toward himself, but also toward the shared purpose.

Put like this, leadership might seem like a distant and even unattainable goal, so it can prove beneficial to consider leadership in terms of three incremental levels: self-leading, leading within relationships, and then leading others (a team) toward a shared purpose.

First, we must **self-lead**. This means that the same principles of shared purpose must apply to us as individuals. We must have a vision for our own future and, despite setbacks, must consistently and unwaveringly maintain our commitment and our belief in ourselves. Leaders who hope to inspire and motivate others must also first drive themselves. This level of leadership applies equally to newly qualified lawyers and to senior partners: From the inception of our careers, each of us should be developing our personal vision of ourselves. This vision is embodied in the "brand" I referred to earlier, which we should be constantly trying to strengthen.

Second, we must learn to manage ourselves as leaders in relation to other people. To be a leader we must have followers, which requires motivating and influencing others to support us. Stunning ideas and scintillating intellect are great assets, but without followers we simply *cannot* (by definition!) lead. So I suggest that there is a critical stage between the first level of leadership (self-leading) and the third level (leading others). Between these two steps, we develop ways of behaving in relation to others (clients, colleagues, and superiors), and we learn how to influence—and how to motivate. In essence, we learn to **lead within our relationships**. This is how we build our "brand": by cultivating the respect of others and by developing our support network (clients, sponsors, alliances, and followers).

Of course, it's only once we are able to manage ourselves, both individually and in relation to others, that we can hope to **lead**...and **inspire others (a team) toward a shared purpose**.

Leading a team
(toward a
shared purpose)

Leading within
relationships
(influencing and
motivating others)

Self-leading
(commitment
and self-belief
in vision)

Regardless of our current level within a firm, we must seek to act as leaders. In practice this may mean different things, depending upon our seniority and what stage we are in the process, but a set of core behaviors and mindsets still provides the strongest foundation on which to build most aspects of leadership. Leadership skills are cumulative, and we must begin developing them from the start of our careers.

This is another idea that Toby (our sensationally gifted tax lawyer) didn't really grasp. Leaders are people-focused and know that they build their strengths and successes primarily through relationships. By treating his colleagues with disrespect and condescension, Toby was proving himself unfit for leadership.

Pause for thought

■ Are you acting like a leader every day, managing yourself in relation to your vision and creating support from the people around you?

THE MASTER JUGGLER

Throughout my career the lawyers who have ultimately achieved the greatest success are the ones who handle each of these balls—brand, business, and leadership—with such celerity as to basically create a blur where one ball begins and another one ends! In essence...

- They are continuously building their brand, and as leaders maintaining a vision for that brand.

- Leadership qualities and behaviors are core to their brand, and it is their leadership brand that interfaces with clients and colleagues (influencing, inspiring, and motivating) to generate business.

- As part of developing business they communicate and market their brand—promoting themselves as leaders, cultivating positive relationships, and fostering trust from their current and potential clients (business).

- They work toward their vision every day (self-leading), and achieving that vision means constant and careful brand building and marketing (business development).

- Their personal brand inspires respect and trust, generating in turn both clients (business) and followers (leadership).

These Master Jugglers are building their legal practice in the same way that entrepreneurs build their businesses. Most entrepreneurs start with an idea and turn it into a successful company by building a brand for themselves, developing business, and leading with vision.

They have to become multi-dimensional, and so do we. Past generations may have attained success with an employee mindset, relying for work on their firm name and their colleagues, but luckily or unluckily, those days are over. Today's competitive environment requires that we all work to become multi-dimensional Master Jugglers: owners and entrepreneurs of our individual practices, each of which must be driven and controlled by our distinctive personal vision.

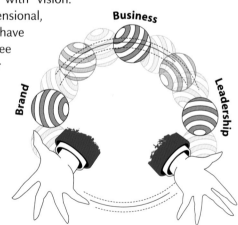

A Proactive Mindset

At this point you may be saying to yourself, "Yeah, OK. Those are the three balls: brand, business, and leadership. And so? Tell me something I don't know!" I agree. It *is* obvious; you might even say mind-numbingly, brain-batteringly obvious. That said, how often do you actually sit back and analyze these three major aspects of your career, and what you are doing on a daily basis to make each of them happen for you? If you're like most of us, you'd probably have to answer, "Well, not often enough...not every day...well, not even every week, if I'm honest..."

Our goal is to handle these three career facets while maintaining the technical ability that will always remain intrinsic to everything we do. If we don't perform technically, our more advanced balls will eventually plummet out of control.

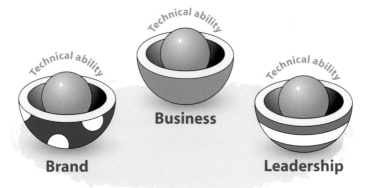

Technical ability must be at the center of our brand, business, and leadership. It's intrinsic to the integrity of our performance.

Our first challenge is to get into a mindset of proactivity. This means removing ourselves from the comfort zone of insular thinking and creatively contemplating our career options, considering our choices, and determining which actions will best propel us toward the Master Juggling goal.

Believe me, I know how difficult this can be! We face demands from clients and colleagues, unexpected challenges, sometimes-unreasonable deadlines, and plenty of thinking-on-your-feet situations. But alongside these professional demands we must never lose sight of the importance of setting our own agenda and seeking to influence our own situations.

This means prioritizing, or determining the things that are truly important rather than merely accomplishing the task in front of us. By "important," I mean those pursuits that are going to help us achieve our ultimate goal—i.e., developing our brand, business, and leadership.

Our daily activities can be classified as follows:

Urgent/immediate and **important** (1)	Not immediate but equally **important** (2)
Immediate but not important (3)	Not immediate and not important (4)

Obviously, if a task is urgent/immediate and also judged important, it must be done ASAP!!!!—otherwise we run the risk of being considered able, yet not completely reliable, which is a damning verdict for any legal career, and not a positive attribute for our brand. I suggest that most technical delivery activities fall into this urgent/immediate and important category (quadrant 1). On the other hand, most activities required of us to develop our brand, in terms of business and leadership, fall within quadrant 2 of the chart—not immediate, but still important.

Of the four categories, the activities in quadrant 2 will certainly yield the highest rate of return to our career, and if left undone may eventually even turn into a career crisis. But as rushed-off-our-feet, time-poor lawyers we mistakenly procrastinate on these, tending, with charmingly youthful optimism, to assume that in the next days or weeks we will certainly find the time.

This could prove a serious error! Regardless of immediate pressures, it's up to each of us to plan and control our commitments so that we're accomplishing tasks in strict order of importance. In his book *The 7 Habits of Highly Effective People,* Stephen Covey calls it, succinctly, "putting first things first." The commitment made toward quadrant 2 activities (in contrast to time spent on quadrants 3 and 4) correlates directly to our professional development. So to optimally organize our time, we should give less attention to quadrants 3 and 4 and instead devote that focus to (you guessed it) quadrant 2. (Well, OK, some days you simply HAVE to spend an hour on the phone with your best friend, but we're talking *general* rules here.)

Now I'd like you to think about your last week's work, and consider exactly how much time was spent within each of these four quadrants.

■ Were you basically just fighting quadrant 1 "fires"? If so, it's time to prioritize the things in quadrant 2. Remember, some of us thrive on quadrant 1, deadline-driven pressure (count me in!), but failing to think about the future can cause even the most ambitious types to lose out in the long run.

■ Did you spend time in quadrant 3, probably thinking that it was quadrant 1? In other words, did you find yourself dealing with immediate demands, questions, and problems that will probably result in no long-term benefit? If so, you need to deliberately move outside that quadrant—however secure and comfortable you might feel within it. Here are your choices:

- Just say "no" to those activities.

- Alternatively, transform such interactions into quadrant 2 activities. For example, if you absolutely can't get out of some boring and trivial meeting, then use it to convey your confident, deeply professional, and organized "brand." Be on time. Be prepared. Engage. Offer outside-the-box ideas. Take notes detailing action items, and at the end offer a summary. Show yourself to be a leader—as opposed to being late, looking bored, writing emails, and basically disconnecting from the other people in the room.

Being proactive also means focusing on the people and activities that can be influenced, rather than wasting precious resources and emotions on things that are not really controllable. Concentrate on possibilities and solutions (as a potential Master Juggler should) and, in each situation, consider how you can use that moment to positively communicate your "brand." In other words, you may not be able to control your circumstances, but you *can* control how you react to them.

For example, one morning, having just flown in overnight from abroad, I called one of the associates working for me on a project, intending to leave a message, on the assumption he'd be there within the next few hours. I was shocked to hear his enthusiastic voice answering, "Hello. This is Thomas!" Had I gotten my time zones wrong? No, it was definitely 5:00 a.m., and yet Thomas was in his office—where he'd been all night long!

It turned out that one of the paralegals had checked out some documents she was working on (something she wasn't in fact authorized to do), only to face a family emergency. Since Thomas couldn't access the documents, he'd elected to spend the whole night re-creating their content so that the work could still be delivered on time. Further, throughout our conversation, Thomas never once blamed the paralegal. He took full responsibility—the attitude of a born leader. In addition, he was upbeat and positive despite his lack of sleep, saying, "Oh, well, we do what we have to... Anyone would have done the same in my place." "No," I thought to myself (reminded of one particular associate also working on the same project), "and, *if* they had, they certainly wouldn't have done it in such a gracious manner."

Thomas's exceptional attitude in what can only be described as a supremely exasperating situation conveyed the positive, can-do, people-focused brand of a Master Juggler. I was convinced that he would make that journey with ease—and he has!

Juggling the Big 3 for Lawyers

Technical delivery activities

Client and deadline-driven work; important meetings; unexpected projects and challenges; responding to client and colleagues on critical matters.*

Master Juggler activities: brand, business, and leadership

Planning, strategizing, and implementing goals; making connections with people; building relationships within the profession; client development; self-marketing; networking; self-development.

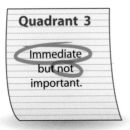

Meetings (not qualifying as truly important); doing work that should be delegated (whether admin- or client-related); fighting "fires" which could be left to smolder indefinitely, or which are not important; some phone calls, email, and correspondence; people dropping by and taking up crucial time on relatively trivial matters.

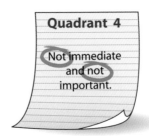

Idle surfing of the Internet; mindless activities and escape time; excessive socializing; gossiping; purely social phone calls, email, and correspondence irrelevant to the work in hand or to the greater goal.

*Note: Things *can* become urgent because we didn't manage time properly: Filling in time sheets or doing client bills should fall within quadrant 2, but if not addressed on a regular basis can become hair-pullingly, head-bangingly urgent!

I was taught this matrix as a time management tool by various people but later came upon a similar one in Stephen Covey's book *The 7 Habits of Highly Effective People,* which I believe is the original source of the idea.

RECAP AND SUMMARY

As we increase in seniority, our performance as lawyers is judged by much more than technical delivery. Instead it is evaluated on overall performance, including the successful juggling of several new balls, as represented by these three goals:

■ To convey a distinct and widely respected brand;

■ To encourage and develop new streams of business; and

■ To act as (and to be perceived as!) a natural leader.

If we fail in the more advanced elements of the overall production, our "audience" of clients and colleagues will be left (relatively) unimpressed, regardless of our technical expertise.

Only when we learn to handle the higher facets of our career simultaneously—brand, business, and leadership—can we make the transition from a technically competent lawyer into an exceptional leader and business performer. We become the Master Juggler—which is what we set out to be.

EXERCISE

In the coming week, document your own activities and determine whether the focus of your work-time is in the critical quadrants.

Chapter Three

The Secret Knowledge of the Master Juggler

In my introduction I promised you a systematic exposition of the tools for success, and I assured you in Chapter 1 that the skills you must learn are simple to implement—and that every young lawyer, including yourself, possesses the necessary qualities to make it happen. Yet you may still be thinking, "Hang on, how can she promise this when there are so many (amazingly able) lawyers around who have yet to learn the Master Juggler skills?" After all, we've all heard comments like these: "Well, she's a great technical lawyer, but just not so hot with the other stuff"; "Sure he's exceptional, but simply lacks the right qualities to lead others"; "He's a hard worker, but just isn't going to make it." Doesn't this suggest that there is a certain type of person who is able to become a Master Juggler and another who simply lacks the right qualities?

My answer to this is an unequivocal "No!" The ability to Master Juggle is not about molding ourselves into a certain persona. You wouldn't try to replicate *every* quality of someone you admire! Instead, it's about learning some simple skills—skills we can all implement regardless of personality, style, strengths, or weaknesses. It's not about education or intelligence—you obviously have *enough*, if you've gotten this far. Your firm's "name" or lack thereof doesn't guarantee (or preclude) success, either.

The message here is that there is no ideal profile that enables some lawyers to succeed. Instead, our level of success is determined by how effectively we work within our own mental makeup. To do that optimally requires a high level of awareness about ourselves and about the way we impact others. This is the **foundation** for the skill sets we need to reach our goals.

As for colleagues who have yet to become Master Jugglers, they have almost certainly failed for one of two reasons: Either they've not even attempted to acquire the requisite skills, or (more likely) they *have* tried, but without the necessary self-awareness and knowledge. Lacking this comprehension—what I call the **"awareness building blocks"**—they were pursuing a near-impossible objective.

Ollie was oblivious to the foundation that he should be building.

26

THE AWARENESS BUILDING BLOCKS

So let's look at these awareness building blocks and the knowledge that prepares us for (a) developing our brand, business, and leadership and (b) learning the skills of the Master Juggler. There are five awareness building blocks:

1. Working with the personalities around you—including your own;

2. Understanding your motivators to enable them to fuel your goals;

3. Learning how to connect;

4. Optimizing your thinking and generating confidence; and

5. Understanding how impressions are made.

Each of them is addressed in more depth in later chapters, but I think a brief overview at this point is helpful.

1. Working with the personalities around you—including your own

It's critical to understand yourself so that you can effectively use your unique strengths and better develop your weaker areas. This is especially important later in your career when you'll be required to work with a different set of personality traits than those you exploited in the early years. Knowing your own personality will help you design a strategy suited to your distinctly personal makeup, and this is what will optimally propel your success.

But there's more to this self-perception than the touchy-feely "know yourself" of pop psychology! By understanding ourselves we are able to interact optimally with others, intuitively recognizing how our personality might work in conjunction with theirs. We can

- Perceive situations more accurately instead of selectively through our own (biased!) viewpoint;

- Read, interpret, and anticipate the motivations of other people; and

- Correctly identify decision-making patterns in both our colleagues and our clients.

By learning how to "read" clients and fellow lawyers, we will better understand their perspective and can better inspire their enthusiasm for our vision.

In our profession we are constantly being tested, and competitors are always on the *qui vive* for signs of error or weakness. An opponent worthy of our steel will understand personality types and may well be capable of identifying our limitations. If we aren't aware of them ourselves, we may be exposing ourselves to manipulation, sublimation—and defeat.

2. Understanding your motivators to enable them to fuel your goals

If we analyze our underlying values and motivators, we should be able to set achievable goals that satisfy our ambitions and passions. As lawyers, most of us have extrinsic motivations—recognition, status, admiration, and financial reward, to name a few!—which will probably drive us for much of our careers. But each of these incentives tends to run its natural course, and when that happens they will need to be bolstered with new motivators. This will maintain our commitment and persuade us to "go the distance." This is what purpose is all about.

3. Learning how to connect

In the junior years success is all about work, but as a Master Juggler it's really all about people. As we advance up the career ladder our ability to create valuable relationships will impede or enhance our careers *more than any other single factor.* Surprisingly, though, most lawyers don't cultivate even the most basic people skills, thereby limiting their potential for success. I will outline to you the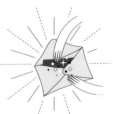

secret of how to get people to like as well as respect you, which will help you to motivate and influence others.

Once you've learned the formula, you should be able to instantly identify those (rare!) people around you who have also mastered these techniques. You'll probably find that they'll be the people you most admire—because they'll have used the techniques on *you*.

4. Optimizing your thinking and generating confidence

There is no more valuable tool than your mind to help you propel your vision forward, but if used improperly, the mind can also quickly bring defeat. This is because it is through the mind that we generate (or crush) our self-belief—the biggest arbiter of our success. The most successful athletes know that it's their thinking that makes the difference, and most of them have used mental techniques for years as part of their standard training. As lawyers, we can similarly benefit from such performance techniques. If the power of the mind is a new idea to you, examine this tool with openness. It can bring amazing results to your career—and your life.

5. Understanding how impressions are made

We want to convey an image consistent with our desired "brand"—right? Clearly, if we believe we're projecting one thing while the outside world sees something else, we're not exactly authenticating the image we're after. In later chapters I will introduce some data about communication and image—data that may be surprising, especially to lawyers who think the best way to come across as credible is by saying something clever.

■   ■   ■

It is only by working through the five building blocks listed above that we can equip ourselves to begin the pursuit of brand, business, and leadership development. Just as the performance juggler has to work on his coordination and concentration (building blocks) before he can attempt to work in yet another ball, so we require underlying technique and tools to cultivate our growing skill set.

A few years ago Jack Welch gave a lecture at MIT's Sloan School of Management. When asked, "What should we be learning in business school?" he told those aspiring leaders to concentrate on their "softer skills"—connecting with people and learning how to build relationships and influence others. He concluded, "Everything else you need to know, you can learn on the job." Subsequently, MIT (along with many top business schools) began adding self-awareness and interpersonal courses to its program, affirming their importance in the marketplace. Similarly, companies, banks, and consulting firms invest in self-management and relationship development courses as part of their training for new hires and rising stars. Yet, remarkably, these patterns of thinking have still not made their way into the general law curriculum, either in law school or in law-firm training programs.

It's not as if the concepts are new: In the 1930s Napoleon Hill was so inspired by Andrew Carnegie that for over 20 years he studied the factors that contributed to Carnegie's success as well as to the achievements of other outstanding businessmen, like Charles Schwab and John D. Rockefeller. Then Hill wrote *Think and Grow Rich*, which listed what he called the "Carnegie Secrets" of personal achievement. In the book he delineated certain "soft skills" that were common to the business geniuses he had studied. Since Hill's book, other studies of successful entrepreneurs have revealed the same common thread—not a specific personality type or a superior business model, but a similar set of skills to those observed by Hill. In short, it is the soft skills that lead to great business achievement.

The softer skills required in business are just as important to us as lawyers. Remember, we are entrepreneurs of our own practices, and as such should be accessing and applying the same skill set as business leaders. Fortunately, the skills in question are all learnable, and they are set out for you in this book.

BECOMING THE MASTER JUGGLER

As we work through this book together, I am going to help you achieve three things:

1 You'll develop an awareness of yourself and a way of thinking and interacting with others that will enable you to face most of the challenges of your career with optimism, confidence, and the right set of tools. We'll do this by working through the "awareness building blocks," which make up the first chapters of this book and embody the softer skills I referred to above.

Chapter 4 Personalities
Awareness BUILDING BLOCK 1
(Working with the personalities around you—including your own!)

Chapter 5 Motivators
Awareness BUILDING BLOCK 2
(Understanding your motivators to enable them to fuel your goals)

Chapter 6 People Skills
Awareness BUILDING BLOCK 3
(Learning how to connect)

Chapter 7 Thinking
Awareness BUILDING BLOCK 4
(Optimizing your thinking and generating confidence)

Chapter 8 Positive Impact
Awareness BUILDING BLOCK 5
(Understanding how impressions are made)

2 You will gain insight into the dynamics of the three "balls": Brand, Business, and Leadership.

Chapter 9   Brand: The Beginning (An introduction to the three "balls")

BALL 1: BRAND

Chapter 10   Brand "You"

Chapter 11   Adopting the Core Traits of a Superior Brand

Chapter 12   Brand Creation

Chapter 13   Enhancing and Marketing Your Brand
Chapter 14   Public Speaking

BALL 2: BUSINESS

Chapter 15   Networking: The Reality
Chapter 16   Expanding Your Network
Chapter 17   Winning and Developing Business

BALL 3: LEADERSHIP

Chapter 18   The Three Dimensions of Leadership
Chapter 19   Self-Leading
Chapter 20   Leading Within Relationships
Chapter 21   Leading a Team

3   Last, in Chapter 22 ("Streamlining the Juggling Act") you will discover how to handle and leverage the different balls to achieve your career objectives, ultimately juggling them all with ease. This must be our ultimate goal—to achieve the status of a Master Juggler.

Chapter 4: Personalities

(Working with the personalities around you—including your own!)

Chapter 5: Motivators

(Understanding your motivators to enable them to fuel your goals)

Chapter 6: People Skills

(Learning how to connect)

Chapter 7: Thinking

(Optimizing your thinking and generating confidence)

Chapter 8: Positive Impact

(Understanding how impressions are made)

Awareness Building Blocks

Chapter Four

Awareness Building Block 1: Personalities

(Working with the personalities around you—including your own!)

You may look at the title of this chapter and think to yourself, "Hang on, I ought to know my own personality, at least! Sounds like psychobabble to me." But our success as lawyers depends upon gaining the loyalty of clients and colleagues, and intelligence and technical skills are of limited use if we can't deal with people. The best way of working with others is through a clear-eyed understanding of ourselves—along with a working knowledge about what makes different personality types "tick."

You'll have noticed even within your own law firm that very different types of people coexist, and that X (compared to Y) will:

- Communicate differently;

- Work at his or her highest level under different conditions;

- Interact with people differently;

- Derive stress from different things;

- Handle heavy workloads in different ways; and

- Value different things (signaling different motivations).

You may have thought at times, "Guess it takes all types to run a law firm," "If it's a tight deadline I'd better not give it to A, but B will be sure to deliver," or even, "Spare me C's management style!" After reading through this chapter, you should be able to...

1. **Know the four primary personality types (patterns of behavior)...and *why* B is more likely to deliver than A**

2. **Know your own personality type**

   a. Understand your personal strengths and weaknesses

   b. Leverage your strengths strategically at work

   c. Either convert or mitigate weaknesses that have the potential to undermine your goals

3. **Learn how your own type generally interacts with other types so as to...**

   a. Maximize positive relationships

   b. Use others' strengths for your own (and the firm's) benefit

   c. Develop greater impact and influence

4. **Use this information to work for you and help you achieve your goals**

Current leadership experts believe (and study after study has proven) that a direct relationship exists between self-awareness and superior career performance. By reading this chapter you will learn to adapt your behavior to your colleagues' personality styles to obtain your desired outcomes.

When we are focused on technical ability we are leveraging the aspects of our personality that deal with analysis, logic, and task completion. As we transition into the next phase of our careers, however, we are increasingly called upon to deal with emotions, motivation, and influence. Understanding our personality gives us a framework for developing and working with these new elements of our behavior.

It can be tough for any professional to undergo the process of self-examination. ("Am I *really* a procrastinator? Can I think about that tomorrow?") However, when we become willing to scrutinize temperament and become self-aware a huge array of benefits flows back to us. The process reveals our strongest points as well as our weakest, and this in turn gives us the ability to leverage ourselves both positively and professionally. Simply reading this chapter should immediately put you miles ahead of the many lawyers who are unaware of the impact their behavior can have on others—and ultimately, on their own careers.

Remember: Lack of awareness is an impediment that can prevent you from reaching your highest potential.

EXERCISE: Your Personality

Before going any further, I suggest you move immediately to the end of this chapter (Appendix 4.A) and answer a few questions about yourself. This exercise will make obvious some of your behavioral preferences and give some indication of your personality type. Remember, there is no "right" or "wrong" personality type, and no type has an inbuilt edge with regard to building a brand, developing clients, or evolving into a leader. Each of us has to balance some of our preferred behaviors with new ones to achieve what we're after.

I URGE YOU TO DO THE EXERCISE NOW, AS READING FURTHER MAY SUBLIMINALLY INFLUENCE HOW YOU ANSWER THE QUESTIONS, THUS MAKING THIS CHAPTER LESS USEFUL TO YOU.

PERSONALITY FRAMEWORKS

Before explaining the categories of personalities and the meaning of your results, it's probably worthwhile to consider what we mean by a personality type. There are various frameworks and tests around for figuring out personalities; some are quite straightforward, while others (such as the psychometric variety) can reduce the sanest person to a gibbering wreck.

However, each of these tests creates a framework by labeling and classifying behaviors. People tend to do this naturally: When someone's personality is described as "outgoing," the reference is to his or her preferred or customary way of interacting—behavior that has been routinely observed. Keep in mind that personalities are about overall patterns of behavior and that everyone is capable of modifying his (or her) patterns. Also, we're not attempting to put anyone into a personality "box." Certain personality traits do tend to prevail together, and we're simply determining as well as we can what those patterns are, both in ourselves and in the people around us. Understanding our own patterns helps us (a) better direct our behavior to achieve our goals and (b) figure out how our own styles interact with other behaviors and personality types.

Let's now look at the four categories of personality types represented in the questionnaire at the end of the chapter. If you have examined personality types before, you will realize that my categories are based on various personality philosophies and frameworks. However, the patterns I suggest are specific to us as lawyers.

The Connecter—Category A

The Connecter is the most extroverted of all the temperaments; he's someone who thrives on interaction with other people. The Connecter's style is casual, and you know his office door is always open for a chat. One of my early bosses comes to mind: He greeted everyone with warm enthusiasm, no matter how busy he might be. "Jennifer, come in!" he'd say, waving his arms and beckoning me into his office. "Just the person I wanted to see! Pull up a chair!" (Finding a chair in his office was always a challenge because—in common with most Connecters—his room was in constant chaos. Despite this, he somehow always managed to put his finger on whatever it was he needed.) "What can I do for you?" he would ask, as he sent an email and called his secretary. Multi-tasking is a true talent of the natural Connecter.

The Connecter gets his or her energy from people and activity, so the more the better. They gladly take on projects—turning something down is difficult, if not impossible—and of all the personality types, they indeed multi-task the best. Part of their ability to do so is their casual approach. Doing something "well enough" is more acceptable to the Connecter than to any of his peers. He (or she) "doesn't sweat the small stuff"—which may mean, of course, the Connecter falls short in detailed work.

Connecters love fun and have an innate ability to create it; in the midst of tension or conflict, the Connecter is likely to offer lighthearted distraction. A serious and intense friend (not a Connecter!) learned the value of this approach from his colleague Jason. During late-night negotiations that were going nowhere, Jason suggested taking everyone down to one of New York City's all-night diners. My friend was annoyed at the idea. He was determined to continue hammering away until the other side caved in—even if it took all night! But Jason's enthusiasm proved persuasive. Over burgers and fries Jason entertained everyone, telling one amusing story after another, including one that my friend loves to recount about the history of ketchup(!?). Like most Connecters, Jason always had a relevant story—even in a diner! By the time they headed back to the office, the two sides felt as though they had had a night out with their mates rather than dinner with adversaries. To my friend's amazement, Jason's personal approach had broken down hostilities, and the deal-breaker points were resolved within an hour.

I've never met Jason, but he sounds a lot like one of my former colleagues, Chris. Within a month of joining the firm, Chris became our unofficial social planner. Now some partners might have viewed this as a frivolous skill, but it was actually one of the key sources of positive feeling and drive in the office. I know it's a cliché to say "a team that plays together stays together," but in our case, thanks to Chris, it was true.

> Have I ever told you the story about...

Connecters just let things happen, and if things don't go quite as anticipated, the Connecter rolls with the punches and deals with surprises as opportunities. He is typically able to spot the bright side no matter what the situation. If I had to do a really boring job—tedious data discovery in the dark basement of some isolated building—I'd choose a positive Connecter to do it with. Rather than complain, he would make it a memorable event, and I'd probably have more fun doing that job than I've had at parties with other colleagues! I once went on a brutally scheduled roadshow across the U.S. with a fun-loving Connecter client, and despite near-constant sleep deprivation and some extremely challenging presentations along the way, he made it feel like being on vacation.

Connecters naturally draw people to them, and because Connecters are so likeable they seem to get away with things that most people couldn't. For example, one of my colleagues once invited a group of us (his fellow lawyers) to a ceremony where he was receiving an award. Now, as none of us particularly liked this person we each quickly decided to find an appropriate excuse. But Richard—

a true Connecter—found it hard to say "no." He saw the positive—a party opportunity! With his abundant enthusiasm and great ability to inspire, he convinced a few of us to accept the invitation ("We'll have a great laugh; it will be fun"). Of course, like a typical Connecter, Richard hadn't quite thought it through—or considered that his wife might be less than pleased with his plans to attend a party with work colleagues instead of being with the family. Once she made her feelings clear, Richard abandoned us to follow through on his grand idea without him. We were all annoyed but couldn't help laughing—"Only Richard could have gotten us into this!"—and only Richard wouldn't have had it held against him!

Like Richard, most Connecters can inspire others to do almost anything—even things they don't really want to do. In this lies the secret of their leadership abilities. But because they are big on ideas and enthusiasm, and not so hot on detail and focus, they don't always follow through reliably. In fact, in keeping with his sanguine nature, the Connecter sometimes manages to avoid doing the actual work. One of my clients and I once had the opportunity to present together at an industry conference. Now James, a typical Connecter, was fizzing with ideas when we first met to discuss the project ("Hey, listen to this!... And wouldn't this be great?"). However, as the deadline loomed I began to realize that getting James to do any solid work would be almost impossible, and that it would probably be my job to do it for both of us. Then, out of the blue, I received a phone call from Tracy, James's colleague. James had inspired her to help us. Tracy and I worked hard over the next few weeks. James stopped by on a few occasions, and his enthusiasm was contagious, but he never did—er—contribute to the actual *work*. On the big day, though, James knew his part and delivered it with flair and magnetism in the way only a Connecter can. Our presentation was considered the highlight of the conference—but only because of James's delivery! All the hard work in the world couldn't have achieved what James could do almost effortlessly.

I would make a bet that the most serious intellectuals in your firm are not Connecters; however, the top rainmaker types probably have a significant amount of this personality type. Connecters engage others easily and have figured out how to turn those interactions into relationships and clients. Interestingly, the Connecter's client base tends to choose him or her as their lawyer primarily based upon the relationship they have with the Connecter, not the Connecter's stellar reputation, the firm's credentials, or any superior client development scheme. The bottom line is this: Connecters make their clients feel good—and who doesn't like that?

The Driver—Category B

The Driver is also extroverted, but in a very different way. The Driver thrives on activity and tangible accomplishment, and because this can only be obtained through the outside environment, the Driver must be extroverted. However, this does not mean that the Driver is necessarily a "people person," and, in fact, he can seem to be just the opposite. Drivers typically make decisions with the head, not the heart, and tend to disregard personal feelings. For them, it is all about the goal.

Drivers are purposeful in their activities, and are great doers and achievers. But unlike more introverted personalities who get joy from the process, Drivers are motivated by accomplishment and the associated (external!) recognition that goes with success. Without that, the process is meaningless to them.

Their working styles are intense and fast-paced, as if a crisis might erupt at any moment. If you knock on Drivers' doors, they will probably let you know, rather bluntly, that they're too busy to be disturbed. Drivers have little time for niceties and tend to "say it like it is," especially when immersed in a project.

Unlike Connecters, who can skip from project to project, Drivers have a single-minded determination and do not let anything get in the way of completing a project. If necessary, they will shut their doors, skip lunch, and ignore frivolous phone calls to meet a deadline. In light of their ambitious nature, you can just imagine how annoyed they are when, in the middle of a negotiation, the Connecter suggests a coffee break! Fun is not high on the list of Drivers' priorities, and this can make them less than popular. Drivers will naturally sacrifice personal and social life for the sake of work, and there can be significant conflict when they expect others to do the same. If colleagues don't oblige, Drivers become angry and resentful; and if co-workers do cooperate, anger and resentment will be directed toward the Driver in question.

By now you should have gathered that the Driver is the most determined (and demanding) of all the personalities. However, Drivers are also by far the most competent. For them, "good enough" is just not acceptable. At this point I must confess that I am by nature a Driver, and have suffered the inevitable consequences of this temperament—including many late nights in the office long after my colleagues have called it a day.

As part of their need to succeed, Drivers are strong-willed and decisive. Drivers make a decision on the balance of evidence, and don't fret or falter. This enables them to find solutions quickly and move forward, but their conviction can cause them to believe that their way is the only way—which has the potential to cause conflict. Drivers are natural leaders and organizers of projects and people. They know what to do, how to do it, and how to make it happen. They are extremely efficient—quick to identify problems and swift to delegate as necessary. If they haven't been appointed the leader, they tend to become so.

As a young intellectual property/technology associate I was often called in on large corporate transactions to work on discrete IP/technology aspects of the deal. On more than one occasion, once involved I began identifying issues (related to my discipline) and offering solutions, gradually taking over more and more of the deal until what was originally a corporate transaction became increasingly a technology deal run by me. This was never my intention, but it was a consequence of my natural propensity to see issues, take control, and get them resolved. There were obvious rewards, and more work came into our practice as a consequence of my expanded role. However, in the process I sometimes allowed myself to tread on the toes of my corporate colleagues, who naturally resented any assumption of seniority.

Even now, it's still my instinct to be in control. Just last week I was persuaded by a friend to attend an acting class. As part of the program, we were separated into groups and told to develop our own original sketch, which we would then perform for the rest of the group. Now acting and playwriting are *not* within my skill set (not at all!!), but after five minutes with my group I could tell that we needed direction. So I began soliciting their opinions, making decisions, and forming our sketch. I delegated the parts, choreographed, and directed. My group was astounded that I had never been involved in the performing arts before and concluded that I had a natural talent for it. In fact, I only have a talent for project management, and very little (if any) for the stage. The group was so grateful for the organization I provided that they failed to notice the reality!

Being a Driver is a two-edged sword. On the one hand, Driver qualities combine to make them natural, confident leaders. You've no doubt seen this personality type at the top of your own firm—probably at each level of seniority. The top performing associates—those with high billable hours, exceptional delivery, and ambition for partnership—are typically Drivers. Many partners will have gotten to their position by virtue of this personality. However, the need to succeed above all else can cause Drivers to be careless of others' opinions and feelings. They can even be perceived as bossy or arrogant. And in today's consensual environment, where "control and command" is no longer a sustainable leadership style, the same characteristics that have taken Drivers to the top can help to bring about their downfall.

The Perfectionist—Category C

Perfectionists are the ultimate introverts and natural intellectuals. These are the talented and serious academics drawn to a legal career for love of analytical pursuits. They naturally flourish in academia and can flounder in private practice, where personal interaction is critical. However, when willing, and when able to come out of their shell in the law firm environment, they can become the intellectual stars of the firm.

Perfectionists, like Drivers, are focused and task-oriented, but they tend to be much slower and more methodical. Producing fine work is very important to them, but Perfectionists get intrinsic pleasure from the overall process as well. Their working style is formal and you will typically find them with their doors closed, quietly focused on the task at hand. Of all the personalities, Perfectionists are the happiest to work alone.

Perfectionists are typically neat (a rare quality in a paper-filled law firm): Their desks will be organized, without the usual mess all over the place. Unlike the Connecter, who will have pictures and personal things studded around his office, Perfectionists tend to be very private and their offices reveal very little.

While the Driver will do just about anything to achieve a task or a goal, Perfectionists are extremely honorable and follow all the rules. They believe in doing what is right, and define that by the rules and regulations of the organization and those in authority. In fact, the Perfectionist can even be fussy about procedure, and will expect others to be equally meticulous. They are dutiful, conscientious, and professional, and if there is work to be done the Perfectionists see it as their responsibility to help.

Above all, though, as the name implies, the Perfectionist cannot stand for anything less than perfection. Doing something right takes precedence over any other consideration. It doesn't matter how long it takes or whether the benefit objectively justifies the burden; if something is worth doing, it's worth doing right!

To some people the phrase "significant detail" is an oxymoron, but to the Perfectionist every detail is significant. Maureen is a busy, time-pressed lawyer but so meticulous that she finds it difficult to delegate anything, from legal drafting to household chores. She has learned from experience that others will overlook details that she views as essential. While Maureen humorously acknowledges her compulsion, trying to be more flexible just stresses her out. So she shapes her lifestyle around her perfectionism, and does *everything* herself—from her legal practice to her household cleaning. Maureen's argument is that it actually saves time and, more importantly, anxiety—because she doesn't have to worry about re-doing someone else's less-than-careful work. Perfectionists like Maureen, who are unable to lighten up, sentence themselves to long (and lonely) hours of doing everything themselves, yet their standard of work is second to none.

Perfectionists not only set high standards for themselves, but they do the same with the people around them. They expect others to be just as methodical, and (sadly!) truly believe that that is what the other person wants as well. They don't get the message that sometimes the rest of us just don't care!

This may be why Perfectionists are pessimists. It is their natural temperament to see and focus on problems, in contrast to the optimistic Connecter (who doesn't even identify the issue, because he is concentrating on the positive) or the confident Driver (who will see the issue, but has already determined how to fix it).

Organization and planning are key characteristics of Perfectionists. They are compulsive about schedules and love routine; they generally have lunch at the same time every afternoon, happily eating the same preferred foods day after day. Other personalities might become bored with repetitive tasks, but Perfectionists rarely do. I once had a Perfectionist associate, Sophie, take on the job of developing some precedent documents for our practice group. She is the only associate I've ever charged with this onerous responsibility who actually enjoyed it! Everyone else either refused the task or found it impossibly monotonous, but not Sophie. She could plan her schedule, confident in being able to keep it because her task was not subject to out-of-the blue client interruptions. She relished working through the detail, and when she encountered problems with some of the precedent clauses used in her analysis, she would politely raise the issue with the relevant author—who did not always welcome the criticism!

Her fellow associate, Tom, was an assertive and fast-paced Driver who viewed any critique of his work as a waste of time. Sophie truly believed that everyone wanted the same perfect precedents that she did, and that every colleague shared her diligence. She persisted in viewing Tom's hostility as a lack of comprehension. Over and over again she patiently attempted to walk Tom through her detailed analysis—until one day Tom, tested beyond endurance, rose from his desk and shoved her bodily out of his office. It's *very* difficult for Perfectionists to understand that other people do not share their values!!

Perfectionists tend to be reserved and extremely cautious with people. They may seem cold, but other personality types must remember that the introverted Perfectionist finds it most difficult to engage and open up. Further, Perfectionists' high standards mean that they are repeatedly let down by others, and each disappointment reinforces their behavior, affirming that they were right to be cautious. The whole process of working with less-stringent souls can cause disillusionment, and Perfectionists may begin to expect disappointment, rather than a positive experience, when working with others.

When Perfectionists do engage, they work hard to ensure that everyone knows the overall purpose, follows the rules, and operates to appropriate standards. Because they have sharp and unbiased discernment, they often notice things that others have missed. Though their constantly critical viewpoint can be annoying, it is based on a genuine concern for the greater good.

Since most of us go to law school in pursuit of intellectual accomplishment, we tend to assume that the genius-prone Perfectionists in our academic midst will be the highest achievers. Ironically, in a law firm environment it doesn't always work out that way. Most firms do rely upon Perfectionists for their intellect and their detailed solutions, but unless they develop more extroverted skills these people are rarely the firm's front-end business generators. I am reminded of a Perfectionist partner I know, "Lawrence," who early in his career happily supported his more extroverted colleagues and loved nothing more than being called upon to solve the most difficult challenges. His group's reputation as a preeminent authority grew as a result of Lawrence's skills—and the analytical articles he wrote on his topic of expertise. But Lawrence's colleagues were disproportionately benefiting from his talents, and although he was the expert, his business was significantly inferior to theirs. To be more than an intellectual asset, he had to improve his people skills—dealing with clients, marketing, maneuvering himself through law-firm politics, and managing and motivating other lawyers. By working with a more extroverted and open mindset, Lawrence was able to capitalize on his strengths, and he did (in the end) cultivate a thriving practice. This is not to imply that Lawrence became as extroverted as his colleagues (he will always, and rightly, be considered an introvert), but it does demonstrate the significant benefit to him of doing things slightly differently. Developing people skills can be challenging for the Perfectionist, but the result can be extremely powerful.

Perfectionists who can develop an extroverted streak become credible business developers because their formidable intellect is integral to their brand, and this is what they market. They are likely to be the preeminent authorities in their fields, authoring books and articles, and have enviable scholarly reputations. Their clients are certain that they have retained the best lawyer available because the Perfectionist is *the* authority. This is the Perfectionist's unique weapon.

The Moderate—Category D

Of the four personalities, Moderates are probably the hardest to identify because their style is low-key and less extreme than the other three. They are naturally introverted, like the Perfectionist, but when involved or when among people they like they will engage more easily than the Perfectionist does. And unlike the Perfectionist, the Moderate tends to have many friends, and is very good in social situations.

In fact, Moderates have the best one-to-one people skills of all the temperaments. They are agreeable and cooperative, and prefer to avoid conflict. They're good at listening to the ideas of others and believe the best way to get something done is through amicable teamwork.

So the mild-mannered person who just seems to get on with things, without seeking attention or creating conflict, is probably a calm, cool, and collected Moderate. These people lack the highs and lows of the other personalities, but typically march steadily along. Sometimes Moderates are so apparently unemotional and stoic that they are impossible to "read." One of my partners had this personality. When a group of lawyers from our team abruptly announced to him that they were resigning, I asked one of them about this partner's reaction. He said, "Well, you know X, he never reacts to anything! Why would our leaving be any different?" From my own knowledge of X, I knew that he would certainly have been upset, but he kept it completely to himself, both at the time and afterwards. Had I not known him better, I would have thought him completely indifferent to what had happened.

Moderates' working style can be characterized as laid back, and they are usually friendly, down-to-earth people. Because they do their work without any fanfare, their dedication can go unnoticed, and if they lack backbone they can be taken advantage of. But when sufficiently determined, Moderates can rise to the top in such a gracious way that they have only supporters in their midst, which gives them unparalleled power.

The best way for me to describe the Moderate is to describe "Frank." He was part of a new office of a large firm, and had joined at the same time as several other new partners. Now, as the most experienced partner, and the only one with previous management skills, it would have been reasonable for Frank to demand the role of office managing partner. In fact, he was perceived by almost everyone as such, and it was assumed that the title had been formally bestowed on him. However, in his unassuming way, he neither demanded nor claimed the role; he modestly took on most of the related responsibilities, and ultimately all the administrative and management tasks fell on his desk.

While Frank's partners were focused on what would bring them clients and billable credits ("what's in it for me"!), Frank did things that would benefit the office as a whole, and he did them without fanfare. Ironically, there were times when his fellow partners took the credit—even, on occasion, telling the press and clients that *they* were the managing partner. Frank was completely unbothered, and thus only gained more respect from everyone.

Because of his approach, Frank has many friends and is well respected in the marketplace—in fact, no one who's dealt with Frank has a negative thing to say about him. He is on good terms and in regular contact with his previous colleagues, law school friends, and old clients—even Frank's "adversaries" like him! His connections are significant and far-reaching, so he always seems to have work while his partners have to pound the pavement to bring in equivalent business.

One final thing about Moderates: They may appear passive, but they can be extremely stubborn. Once they come to a decision (typically without fuss), they tend to stick with it, and changing their minds can be frustratingly difficult. I should know, having grown up with a Moderate sister!

While they don't wear their ambitions on their sleeves, Moderates, with their likeable and nonaggressive style, can be the most successful of all the personalities. In fact, Moderates succeed in large measure from what they *don't* do. They never act aggressively and antagonize people, like the Driver. They never talk too much or monopolize the limelight, like the Connecter. And unlike the Perfectionist, they instinctively know when excessive detail is not warranted.

Moderates can have the best people skills of all the temperaments, and this brings them business and helps to develop them into leaders. Their diplomatic approach makes them ideal managers. Some of the most respected heads of departments and firm-managing partners are natural Moderates.

ALL PERSONALITIES ARE LAWYERS!

Remember, all the personalities have to be taken in the context of the legal profession. If we were to study temperaments outside this narrow framework we would almost certainly discover behavior much wider, and much more extreme, than my descriptions. Because my types are based on how lawyers behave, they all share a core level of ambition, efficiency, capability, intellect, detailed perfectionism, and people skills. In the diagram below, note where the personalities are similar, where they are complementary, and where they potentially conflict with each other.

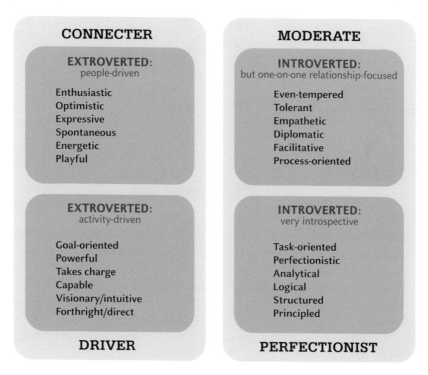

CONNECTER

EXTROVERTED:
people-driven

Enthusiastic
Optimistic
Expressive
Spontaneous
Energetic
Playful

MODERATE

INTROVERTED:
but one-on-one relationship-focused

Even-tempered
Tolerant
Empathetic
Diplomatic
Facilitative
Process-oriented

EXTROVERTED:
activity-driven

Goal-oriented
Powerful
Takes charge
Capable
Visionary/intuitive
Forthright/direct

INTROVERTED:
very introspective

Task-oriented
Perfectionistic
Analytical
Logical
Structured
Principled

DRIVER

PERFECTIONIST

Obviously, two people of different personalities will have diverse objectives and patterns of behavior, and there can be friction. If the lawyers concerned are not aware of the cause, the potential for dispute and relationship breakdown increases.

Social Orientation: Extroverts Versus Introverts

Connecters and Drivers are both extroverts, although they demonstrate this in different ways. Connecters seek social situations (they like nothing more than to entertain and be entertained), whereas Drivers seek activity and purpose (which usually requires social interaction, although socializing in itself is not the objective). Verbose and fast-paced, both types are uninhibited and tend to act on their desires. On the other hand, Moderates and Perfectionists are both introverts, and are typically reserved, quiet, and much calmer than their counterparts.

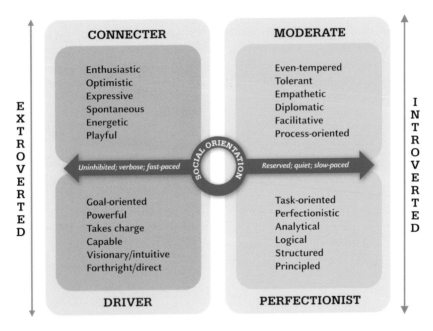

Connecters and Drivers can overwhelm Moderates and Perfectionists with their fast pace and their need to interact, and conflict is most likely to arise when the extrovert is not sufficiently sensitive to the introvert's need to be quiet or alone. In addition, because extroverts share information (without necessarily first thinking about it!), introverts may tend to perceive them as unreliable and less credible than they are themselves. Introverts need to understand that the extrovert may just be tossing ideas around, without any serious intention of following through.

Extroverts can become extremely frustrated with slower-paced introverts, yet pushing introverts can only create further conflict and may even encourage them to retreat. When extroverts and introverts fail to appreciate each other's differences, conflict is certain to arise.

Planning and Organization

Neither Connecters nor Moderates are long-term planners. Connecters like to keep their options open, in case something better comes along; Moderates avoid planning because they tend to be indecisive.

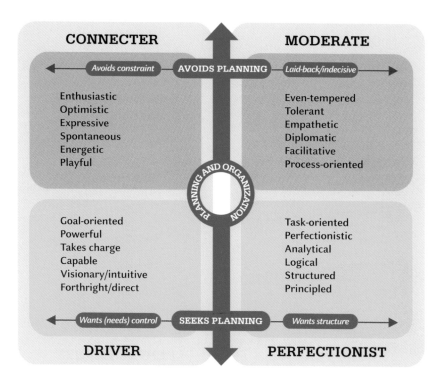

CONNECTER		**MODERATE**
Avoids constraint — AVOIDS PLANNING — Laid-back/indecisive		
Enthusiastic		Even-tempered
Optimistic		Tolerant
Expressive		Empathetic
Spontaneous		Diplomatic
Energetic		Facilitative
Playful		Process-oriented
	PLANNING AND ORGANIZATION	
Goal-oriented		Task-oriented
Powerful		Perfectionistic
Takes charge		Analytical
Capable		Logical
Visionary/intuitive		Structured
Forthright/direct		Principled
Wants (needs) control — SEEKS PLANNING — Wants structure		
DRIVER		**PERFECTIONIST**

Thus, conflict is likely between these two types and the types who like to plan—Drivers and Perfectionists. (Drivers want to be in control, while Perfectionists need structure.) Imagine a project where one personality wants to plan the process and the other thinks planning itself a difficult, annoying waste of time!

Project Priorities

Again, Connecters and Moderates are similar in their priorities when managing a project. Both are process-oriented, meaning that they may care less about the result of a project than about the way the project is managed. To the Connecter, a successful project or meeting is one involving fun; to the Moderate, success means that people work together harmoniously and share ideas without conflict. To these types, those *are* results! (In essence, the Connecter and Moderate care most about the people perspective of any activity.)

Conversely, Drivers and Perfectionists aren't too bothered about fun or harmony (the people aspects) as long as the project achieves a successful result, although they may define "success" in different ways. Drivers, with their extroverted personalities and fast pace, want an expedient result; Perfectionists are slower and more meticulous, and only value the result if it is perfect.

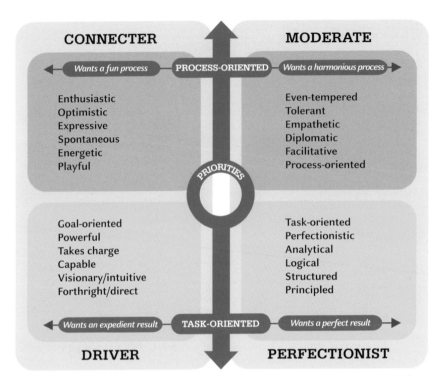

Naturally, a representative of each of these four personalities on one project can create a huge amount of conflict, because each is trying to achieve a different objective from the other.

The Greatest Opposites

The greatest conflict occurs between the most opposite of personalities: the Connecter versus the Perfectionist, and the Driver versus the Moderate.

The Connecter and the Perfectionist just don't understand each other.

Connecters have enthusiasm and energy, but having to maintain focus on one thing for too long makes them bored and anxious. This can cause fireworks! Conversely, Perfectionists are the least-enthusiastic personality, and working methodically on a task comes naturally to them. So when Connecters lose focus, Perfectionists become frustrated with their lack of discipline and (perceived) lack of substance. Unfortunately, most Perfectionists fail to acknowledge that Connecters' enthusiasm (even if short-lived) is a valuable asset to any project.

Similarly, Connecters think Perfectionists are clever but *sooo* boring. When Perfectionists identify and raise problems (they always do!), Connecters, who are excessively optimistic, view Perfectionists as unduly negative time-wasters, sublimating the whole to the details. The more deeply Perfectionists focus on the issues, the more problems they perceive, which only creates further tension.

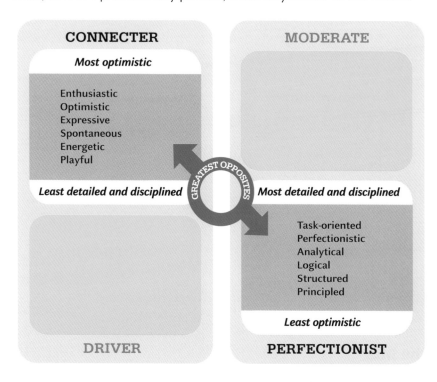

When these OPPOSITE personalities work together without an understanding and appreciation of other temperaments, conflict is frankly inevitable.

Similarly, Drivers and Moderates are also extreme opposites.

Drivers, because of their aggressive style, tend to lack empathy; their focus on the goal tends to override any one individual's feelings or perspective. And as the most empathetic toward others, Moderates expect empathy in return. When they don't get it from the Driver, they sometimes feel personally attacked—even abused. This may cause them to retreat into themselves and feel resentful toward the Driver. Meanwhile, Drivers are likely to decide that Moderates are ineffective and may label their lack of ambition (in comparison to the Driver's) as laziness. What's worse is that the Driver may have no respect for the Moderate's empathy, and may view his understanding and tolerant approach as "weak."

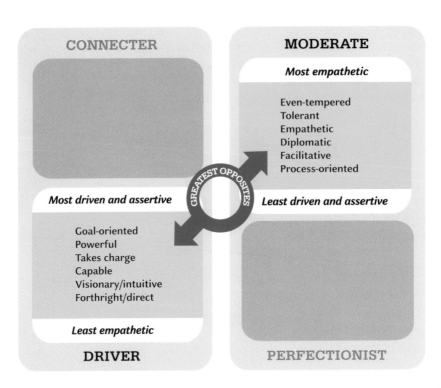

CONNECTER

MODERATE

Most empathetic

Even-tempered
Tolerant
Empathetic
Diplomatic
Facilitative
Process-oriented

Most driven and assertive   GREATEST OPPOSITES   *Least driven and assertive*

Goal-oriented
Powerful
Takes charge
Capable
Visionary/intuitive
Forthright/direct

Least empathetic

DRIVER

PERFECTIONIST

All of this results in animosity between these two
OPPOSITE personalities.

The Mix

Thus far, you have probably thought to yourself, "I know somebody just like that!" or "Oh, that's me!" or "Now I understand why X bugs me and why we never see eye to eye." But you may have also thought, "Wait a minute, I can relate to personality A but I also act quite frequently within personality B." "Y is primarily personality C, but I also see personality B in him and even fractions of personality D." This is because rarely does anyone fit perfectly within one behavior pattern. Most people find that they are a mix of two (or more) different patterns, taking bits and pieces from each. One pattern may dominate, or the traits may be pretty evenly distributed. I describe myself as a Driver because no matter what the task, if I decide it is my goal, I am tenaciously determined, and this is core to my personality (and something I will probably never change). But that doesn't mean that I embody only Driver characteristics! Much of the time I'm outgoing and fun-loving, and I can be extremely perfectionistic (especially in my work). Further, I frequently make decisions on the basis of my heart rather than my head—which is hardly characteristic of a Driver.

We all have a certain amount of each pattern within us, and we create our own unique blend as we access different attributes. There is also a certain amount of overlap between the personality types: For example, the Connecter and Driver personalities are both extroverted, energetic, optimistic, and talkative, so often someone who has one of those types will also have a touch of the other. When the mix of the two is right, and the outgoing Connecter blends with the Driver's capable ambition, we will probably see the most dynamic and influential partners in our firm—because this combination is the foundation for the most powerful of all rainmakers. However, it's a rare and difficult combination to get right, and these people can easily seem desperate to hog the limelight, the conversation, and the credit for themselves.

As introverts, the Perfectionist and Moderate personalities also overlap, and thus many introverted people will have a mix of the two. Ideally, this combination will produce a dependable, highly intelligent, and deeply consistent lawyer, but this personality may still need to exhibit some of the other traits to succeed in a competitive environment where client development (an extrovert activity) reigns.

Similarly, the mix of the Driver and the Perfectionist can be a natural combination because both personalities are task-oriented and desire control. An optimal blend can result in the most capable lawyer imaginable—a combination of extroverted ambition, serious ability, and superior intellect. However, lawyers with these traits must become sensitive to the feelings and opinions of others to truly attain success and to avoid becoming tyrannical "intellectual supremacists"—a type most of us know only too well.

Although the Connecter is an extrovert and the Moderate is an introvert, these two personalities can create a wonderful mix because both are people-oriented (although in different ways). My good friend Rachel is a wonderful combination of these two temperaments. On the one hand, she is energized among people and always shines, telling amusing stories and "connecting." However, she balances her extroversion with the Moderate's strength of facilitation, which means that she can step back from the limelight and empower others. (As we will examine in later chapters, this is a huge asset to a leader!)

You may have noticed that the natural blends of personalities are adjacent to each other on our diagram.

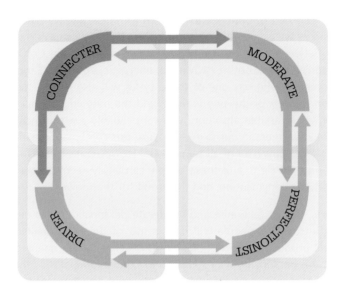

In my case, as a core Driver, I have Perfectionist and Connecter tendencies (those personalities adjacent to me on the diagram), and naturally draw the least from the Moderate attributes (my opposite personality, across from me on the diagram).

THE GOOD NEWS: WE'RE ALL ADAPTABLE!

Our behaviors can be affected by manipulation, circumstances, or the people we are with. I draw upon different aspects of my personality when I am at work and in my private life: I'm intense and focused in the office, but more relaxed (and less meticulous) at home. Similarly, my personality can vary depending upon whom I'm with. My husband and my friends all cause me to behave in distinct ways (sometimes silly, sometimes very serious; sometimes introverted, other times the life of the party!), and of course when I go home to visit my family I quickly transition back to the daughter who needs looking after and (truth to tell) the know-it-all older sibling to my unlucky sister.

I am the same person in each of these circumstances, but in different situations I seem to emphasize distinct aspects of myself. And each gives me an equal, yet different, sort of satisfaction. We are all adaptable, probably much more so than we imagine. In different situations I'm sure you, too, modify your preferred behavior, or exploit a different side of yourself. Keep reminding yourself just how versatile you can be as we work through the rest of this chapter!

Judgments

Whether we realize it or not, we make judgments about people in the blink of an eye, based upon our preferred types. Each of us tends to assume that our way is the right way, and this is the filter that we use to take in information, make decisions, and consider the behavior of other people. When we decide someone has "idiosyncrasies," what we're probably saying is that they have a different temperament from our own. One of the key benefits of understanding personalities is realizing that there is no "right" way, just different ways, and this knowledge allows us to interact with people on a more useful and insightful level.

Attracted to—While Resenting!—Our Opposites

What's paradoxical is that many of us are seriously attracted to people with different personalities from our own because we see something in them that we don't perceive in ourselves. The irony is that we may later begin to resent those same people for not being "enough like us"! For example, my friend Brandon (a tax lawyer) is a typical Perfectionist. This fact, coupled with his long working hours and dedication to his career, has meant that he's had very few personal relationships. So I was thrilled when he called me to rave about his new girlfriend, Kelly (also a lawyer). He described Kelly as vivacious, outgoing, and lots of fun—basically, his opposite. They had just returned from the U.S., where they had attended a legal seminar together—something he hates doing, because it requires so much small talk. However, on this trip Kelly (a "people person") had worked the room for him and made the whole thing a delight. Brandon couldn't sing her praises enough, and he urged me to come to his country house the following weekend to meet her for myself.

When I arrived, however, Brandon was tense and frustrated with Kelly's high energy and need to talk. As he put it to me privately, "This was the final straw— she introduced herself to the neighbors and even invited them over!" Brandon had come to the country to *get away* from people, not meet new ones!

As we discussed the situation, Brandon acknowledged that he couldn't have it both ways, appreciating Kelly's positive attributes when it suited him and then resenting those same qualities in a different context. Since that time, he and Kelly have both made some adjustments, and because they were willing to do this, they actually make a great team! Kelly brings sparkle and lightheartedness to the mix, while Brandon is a stable and practical influence.

Realizing how his willingness to adapt has benefited his personal life, Brandon has since committed himself to doing the same thing professionally—and has been amazed by the results. His working relationships have improved, and he's working hard to understand people of different temperaments. When he thinks it will bring a better outcome, he even adapts to their style.

We all have relationships—both personal and professional—with people of opposing temperaments to our own, as well as with people we instinctively feel are on our "wavelength." Yet we still have a choice in how we choose to deal with our opposites. We can try to change them (which almost always fails), we can decide to resent them for not being more like us (which is a waste of energy), or we can choose our last option: to appreciate their strengths. If we work with those strengths to our own advantage, we can usually realize optimal results from the collaboration.

Synergize With Your Opposites

You may recall Mark and Catherine, last mentioned in Chapter 2 ("The Juggling Act"). Mark had focused on building his client base, whereas Catherine had concentrated on her project work and had never built up enough of a network to support her future business. Early on, Mark and Catherine had worked well together and had combined their strengths and weaknesses, excelling much more than either would have done alone. Catherine, an intense Driver, had pushed Mark and balanced his "good enough" approach to his work; the more people-oriented Mark had helped ease Catherine into social and networking situations that she considered difficult, or even a waste of time. But after a while, Catherine began to resent Mark's "frivolity" in leaving the office for business development functions, instead of appreciating his contributions. She would sigh, "There he goes, off to some party. As usual, it's me ensuring the work gets done!" Unfortunately, Catherine wanted appreciation for behaving nobly, when she was actually electing to stay within her comfort zone!

By not working together with Mark to improve her weak area, Catherine lost a great opportunity to develop herself and her future business. On one occasion she received notice from a client (who viewed her as an exceptional lawyer) about some other work he had in the pipeline. Competing for it, however, still required Catherine to contact the right people in the client organization, make connections, and really sell herself. As these tasks were all distasteful to her, she decided that she didn't want to follow up. If, instead, she had asked the outgoing Mark for help, they might have pursued the opportunity together, probably winning the work and learning new skills from each other in the process.

Being Attracted to Our Own Type (and Trapping Ourselves)

While many of us are naturally attracted to our opposites, we also lean toward our own type. (Notice the professional ego at work: "I'm so great, so someone who's like me must also be great!") We often value in others what we most like in ourselves. Have you ever rushed home after a first date to tell your friend how wonderful it was and how many things you have in common with your new flame? We do this at work as well. We hire a colleague, or include someone on a project, because he or she has the same strengths that we recognize in ourselves. It sounds perfect, right?—but, actually, there are two problems with this approach.

First, a team of two lawyers of the same personality type may become too extreme, lacking the balance and softening influence of other traits. Consider the following scenarios:

- Two outgoing, fun-loving Connecters may move so fast in the same direction that they don't stop to think about where they are going. And once they achieve their goal, they typically lose interest fairly quickly.

- Two Drivers can become extremely competitive, losing their personal touch with clients in the process.

- Two Perfectionists, consumed in detail, may lose the big picture. Since they tend to be distrustful of new ideas and ways of thinking, their approach may also preclude casual brainstorming.

- Two Moderates might focus so much on making the process harmonious that they lack sufficient direction and postpone crucial decisions.

Second, in spite of similar strengths and approaches, differences between two lawyers of the same type will eventually arise, and when that happens we will be disappointed. Our natural instinct to "fix" those differences may well kick in, and then we return to wanting to change the person who is not sufficiently "like us."

A QUICK RECAP

At this point in the chapter we have examined the four personality types (Connecter, Driver, Perfectionist, and Moderate), and with luck you should have developed some awareness about your own behavior preferences and how these preferences influence your interactions with other people—a crucial step in gaining control over events. During the remainder of the chapter we're going to examine more closely some of the behaviors within each of the usual patterns and see how increasing reliance on some attributes (and sometimes decreasing dependence on others) can help us transcend our natural preferences and become the optimal blend—the Master Juggler.

Strengths

Whatever your personality type (or combination), you have many strengths. Even if you haven't analyzed your temperament before now, you have probably been made aware of your own aptitudes to some degree. Probably perceptive friends have said, "Gosh, I wish I had your memory for detail!" "But didn't you get nervous before the presentation?" "Frankly, I couldn't be bothered with it. I can't believe you got it done!" "How do you deal with him so diplomatically? I end up starting an argument every time"—or any combination of these!

However, the question for each of us is whether we are leveraging ourselves effectively by

- Building on our strengths, whatever they may be;
- Converting (or balancing out) our inherent weaknesses; AND
- Directing our behavior patterns to better achieve personal goals.

It's when we direct our strengths strategically that we can achieve great things—because this is the source of our talents, accomplishments, and greatest gratification. When we work within our strengths we're almost certain to excel, and thus get the most enjoyment possible out of the work. In comparison, when we are working in one of our weaker areas, we often feel frustrated and insecure because it's so much harder, so much less natural—and it doesn't help that at least *some* of the people around us are likely to pursue it with less difficulty or none at all!

Let me give you a concrete example. One day I asked one of my employment partners to brief my group on some regulations relevant to many of our transactions. My employment partner cleverly elected to use this as an opportunity to give two of his associates speaking experience and name recognition.

The first presenting associate, an obvious Connecter and strong performer, came across as both knowledgeable and confident, while the second associate stumbled through his presentation and appeared to convey an inferior intellect. In fact, it was the *second* presenter who possessed superior knowledge and depth, but his presentation suffered because of his comparatively ineffective communication skills—an area of weakness. My partner had known this when he gave the associates their assignments, and had offered each of them assistance in developing their talks. The first associate accepted the offer, so my partner helped him formulate his talk and went through some presenting tips with him. This help, on top of the fact that he was working in an area of strength, resulted in a very strong performance. The second associate, accustomed to recognition for his analytical talents, declined my partner's offer on the grounds that he was too busy—doubtlessly thinking that he didn't need help. This associate had not realized that he was working in a (rare) area of real personal weakness and that, without extra effort, he was bound to struggle.

We all have to do things in a law practice that are not necessarily within our areas of natural aptitude. This is why it's so important to recognize such occasions and compensate to avoid failure, either by working a little harder or by leveraging one of our strengths. If we know ourselves, we can avoid being defeated by a weakness—because we realize that, to balance each potential handicap, we all possess distinct strengths.

61

Having said that, it's very easy to lose sight of our strengths and imagine that our offering is no better than anyone else's. We evaluate our attributes on the basis of rigid guidelines acquired through our training: academic measurements, technical abilities, and law firm reviews. But these fail to take into account the fact that each of us has deeper strengths, both instinctive and innate, which we may not fully appreciate—or even use.

When Sarah was appointed head of her department, her priority was to create business for the group. So she developed a strategy and worked with her team members to implement it—spending the majority of her time outside the office, networking and developing business. One of her more junior partners, Adrian, took over day-to-day management of the group. After a few months Sarah sensed that the cohesiveness of her team had dwindled and stepped back to assess the reasons why. After talking to everyone involved, Sarah realized that she possessed a crucial strength which Adrian lacked: empathy. Her associates told her that they had appreciated the way she managed the department, that she made each of them feel valued and understood, and that this was critical both to their motivation and their development. This management style had seemed so natural to Sarah that she had never considered her inclination toward empathy a particular strength, and had never thought to capitalize upon it.

In light of this realization Sarah decided to reconfigure the group's strategy so that she supported the activities of the group while Adrian (and others) took on more of the out-of-office networking responsibilities. Almost immediately the associates became happier and more productive, and the work of the group improved overall. And by working with her strength, Sarah not only excelled, but also felt increasingly confident and content with what she was doing. In fact, she felt relief at relinquishing some of her networking activities and happy to focus on her real passion: developing the juniors in her group.

The ironic thing about Sarah's story is that her firm appreciated her bottom-line delivery—a more productive group and increased business development—but never recognized her for the source of her success—her empathy. Fortunately for Sarah, she was smart enough to capitalize upon her uniqueness, rather than trying to achieve results by the more traditional approach of single-handed networking.

Your next task is to check out the table in Appendix 4.B and to think how the strengths listed within it apply to you, prioritizing those that you feel you should be using in a more conscious and advantageous way.

Extreme Strengths Can Degenerate into Liabilities

While our strengths are (obviously!!!) our greatest assets, if we fail to control them they can actually turn into liabilities. As an associate, I exploited my driven personality and became a top performer. Yet while my boss, Andrew, appreciated my fervent commitment, he also stated in one of my reviews that my positive attributes of "dedication, drive, and perfectionism" could also "be perceived as negative when I expected the same of others, and that I could be too demanding when my standards weren't met"—in other words, I didn't suffer fools lightly. Clearly I was allowing my strengths to become handicaps!

Consider the table in Appendix 4.C, which shows how the strengths we examined in the previous table may become liabilities. How do you measure up?

The Power of Developing Your Latent Traits

We can consciously work with our strengths and address our weaknesses, but we only become Master Jugglers (and achieve exponentially improved results) when we transcend our instinctive inclinations and improve in areas that don't come naturally. Every Master Juggler needs strengths from each of the four personality types to build a successful legal career. Here are a couple of examples:

Susan

Susan is an extroverted, fun-loving, and naturally spontaneous woman who worked in one of the big City firms. While she sometimes got fed up with the heavy workload, she thrived on the camaraderie she had within her team. By intertwining work and fun Susan counterbalanced the downsides of late nights spent at work. In fact, she might never have left the firm had not her husband been transferred abroad. When they eventually returned to London, Susan made the decision to set up on her own.

The easy part was making contact with her old colleagues and clients and drumming up business through personal contacts. Susan actually enjoyed the process, including the somewhat difficult task of asking for work. But to make her practice successful Susan has also had to master less congenial modes of behavior. After winning the work, she has had to get it done—and by herself, without the motivating factors of a supervising boss or a lively office environment. She has been forced to focus and to delve into detail—things she had gladly delegated before. Susan also has had to learn to be strategic, rather than impulsive, about bidding for work, and has carefully checked the accounting aspects of her practice, to ensure that all her projects are profitable. None of these things appeal to her natural temperament, but that hasn't stopped her from learning them—which is why her personal practice has become so successful.

Stephen

Conversely, I was extremely surprised to hear that my friend Stephen had left his large Chicago firm to "go it alone." While extremely likeable, Stephen is an introverted person whom I would have expected to prefer the structured environment of his firm, and his reserved personality doesn't naturally lend itself to getting a business off the ground. Stephen makes decisions slowly and tends to facilitate rather than lead. And he is the reverse of outgoing—which is, let's face it, exactly what starting a law practice most requires.

It was hard at first, and Stephen had to exert himself daily to get in touch with people, make contacts, solicit opportunities, and ask for meetings—doing lots of talking in the process. Yet over the ten years since Stephen took the plunge, he's managed to build up a strong business in an extremely competitive environment.

He's developed a good network and has excellent relationships with his clients, all on the basis of drawing on various (not-especially-innate) extrovert skills.

Susan and Stephen set off with the same objective but with very different personalities, and both of them had to dig deep (and modify their natural tendencies) to succeed. Similarly, each of us could probably achieve better results by doing things "the hard way" at times.

One of my most effective partners had a brilliantly instinctive ability to tap into his different personality traits when needed. One day we emerged together from a very intense meeting where he had been extroverted, articulate, and decisive. As we headed toward his office to debrief he was suddenly confronted by one of his associates, who had a serious problem. My colleague immediately transitioned into an introverted listener as he turned his attention to the associate. He didn't throw out ideas, lay down his opinion, or tell the associate what to do: He just listened empathetically. Eventually, the associate solved his own problem through the one-sided discussion and left with new vigor. We then encountered another of our associates—again, a person with a problem, seeking advice. But this time my partner turned to her and said, "Listen. It's your problem; deal with it." She looked surprised at first, but quickly rediscovered her determination and resolve. (At first I took this to be a clear case of "compassion fatigue," but it later transpired that her problem had occurred many times before and that they had had continual discussions on how to handle it.)

Later, I realized that my partner had quickly transitioned through three distinct styles:

- He had been extroverted and expansive in our meeting (his natural preference);

- He had seemed both introverted and empathetic with the first associate; and

- He had been terse and bracing with the second associate.

When I asked him about this, he acknowledged that he understood his own preferences but had learned over time to develop the other sides of his nature as well. He had realized that achieving the best results often requires transcending one's preferred ways of communicating to better meet the needs of another person or situation. Looking back, I realized that in each of those encounters my partner had quickly calculated the appropriate approach and effectively became into what the other person most needed him to be.

This has to be our goal: to break out of the limitations of one personality pattern and exploit the most advantageous behaviors of the others. We all have the ability to accomplish this, as each of us possesses at least some of the qualities that make up all four types. However, some of us have to work harder than others to develop certain traits!

Most people who know me describe me as a people-focused extrovert and someone who engages easily—natural behaviors of a Connecter. But I wasn't always that way, and it can still surprise me when I am referred to as such. So let me tell you how I transcended my more introverted self. When I moved to London I knew no one, and found it difficult to meet new people and to develop new relationships. One week my good friend Debbie came to visit me from the States, and at first I wasted a lot of time moaning to her about how lonely I was. Now Debbie is an *extreme* Connecter—and I mean extreme! Sometimes I've had to literally drag her out of a social gathering because she just can't get enough of people and activity—and of course she can talk forever. Yet thanks to Debbie's sociability, I met and connected with many more people during her visit than I had during all the previous months.

When she left, I decided that Debbie's attitude worked better than mine. I began to dare myself to approach new people and to engage in casual conversations with strangers, starting with nonthreatening situations and slowly advancing into trickier ones. At first it felt uncomfortable, but over time it became much easier. Eventually I found myself instinctively reaching out to people and making connections in the same manner as Debbie. Accessing those behaviors started to feel natural—although they'll never be as natural to me as they are to her!

Check out the diagram on the next page, which is similar to the ones we examined previously.

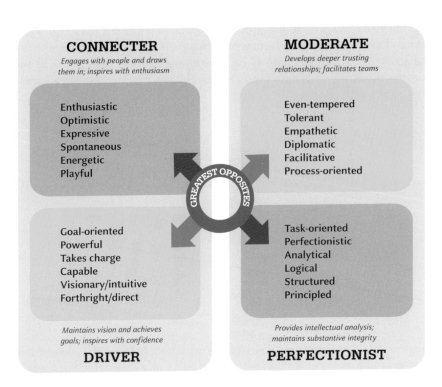

CONNECTER
Engages with people and draws them in; inspires with enthusiasm

Enthusiastic
Optimistic
Expressive
Spontaneous
Energetic
Playful

MODERATE
Develops deeper trusting relationships; facilitates teams

Even-tempered
Tolerant
Empathetic
Diplomatic
Facilitative
Process-oriented

GREATEST OPPOSITES

Goal-oriented
Powerful
Takes charge
Capable
Visionary/intuitive
Forthright/direct

Task-oriented
Perfectionistic
Analytical
Logical
Structured
Principled

Maintains vision and achieves goals; inspires with confidence
DRIVER

Provides intellectual analysis; maintains substantive integrity
PERFECTIONIST

Each personality type has distinct strengths, so the goal is to cut across the different behavior patterns and intelligently select the best one for the situation. Then we'll have a strong foundation for moving from the comfort of technical ability into the skills required for developing business and becoming a leader.

For example, consider the following goals:

- Engaging with others (a Connecter strength);

- Once engaged, developing deeper one-on-one relationships (a Moderate strength);

- Establishing a vision and pursuing goals (a Driver strength); and finally,

- Maintaining the intellectual and substantive integrity of one's legal work and greater goals (a Perfectionist strength).

For each of us, certainly one (possibly more!) of those strengths will be a distinct nonpreference and therefore demand conscious development. The most important (and difficult!) modification usually sits within our opposite personality. For example,

- The Connecter probably most needs to develop Perfectionist strengths;

- The Perfectionist probably most needs to develop Connecter strengths;

- The Driver probably most needs to develop Moderate strengths; and

- The Moderate probably most needs to develop Driver strengths.

You may have read this section and thought, "Great advice, but just not realistic. This is the way I am, and there's just no way I'll change." If that is the case, I urge you to reconsider—no matter how stuck in your ways you think you might be. First, practice will bring improvement, and over time the thing that you thought was impossible can become automatic. But apart from the empirical argument that "practice makes perfect," there is a second scientific basis to the ability to change behavior (i.e., "personality") through actions. When you put a new behavior into practice, you actually change the structure of your brain, strengthening the physical elements used in the activity. As they strengthen, you increase your ability to perform the act, and, in fact, change yourself. (It is the structure of the brain that determines how we think, feel, and behave, so as it changes, so do we. We will examine the science behind this concept, called neuroplasticity, in more depth in chapters 6 and 7.)

Your Original Temperament: The Foundation

Understanding your own behavior gives you an appreciation for others' personalities and motivations, and how theirs compare to yours. This can provide you with invaluable insights—especially if you use this new knowledge to anticipate possible actions of clients and colleagues, and to understand how to best influence them. Appendix 4.D sets out some practical ways for making the best impression on clients (and bosses) and for working optimally with different personalities. Have a look and consider how you might do things differently within your circle of relationships.

Bear in mind that although you can develop yourself, your natural temperament will always underpin things—much as a building's foundation is the basis of everything erected above. Even though whole rooms can be added or modified, and the outside of a building can be revamped, the foundation always remains the same. Similarly, you can improve in different areas, but if you operate for too long without those things that remain core to your personality, you may find yourself dissatisfied—and even, conceivably, depressed.

For me, challenges and rewards are essential, and I need to feel as though I'm always on the path toward achieving a worthwhile goal. I'm the *last* person who would be happy winning the lottery, or retiring and sitting at home planting my garden—unless planting my garden became a passionate project that included real challenge and a tangible objective (and, if I'm being super-honest, probably some sort of prize at the end of it!).

So I shouldn't have been surprised at waking up one morning with an empty feeling in the pit of my stomach. You see, I had recently left my job, and before putting myself 100 percent back into my work, I had determined to simply spend some time with my husband—traveling, relaxing, and having fun. My new life was picture-perfect, and just what I'd always longed for. So why did I feel so empty? Because I was not experiencing the thing *most* central to my personality: a sense of achievement and of working toward a clearly-defined goal. Travel and spending time with my husband were tremendous joys, but I still needed a challenge!

Other people would have been blissfully satisfied with my lot. In fact, I have a good friend whose core requirement is the opposite of mine: time by himself for deep reflection and peace. This is how he recharges, and without it he becomes highly stressed and even unhappy. He recently gave up his fast-paced city life to spend a significant amount of time planting a beautiful garden. When I visited I was so impressed with his achievement that I started waxing lyrical with ideas: for him to create a garden-based business, or to enter a competition with his innovative designs. Then he turned to me and said, "I'm sorry, Jennifer, but you just don't get it... I love creating and appreciating the beauty of my garden. All the other things you've just described would completely depress me." Feeling a bit deflated—but also recognizing exactly where I'd gone wrong—I assured my friend that I did, indeed, "get it!"

Core needs are sparked by one's principal personality and are what I call *motivators*. We will examine motivators more thoroughly in the next chapter and will consider how they propel a personal vision.

RECAP AND SUMMARY

The purpose of this chapter is not to put anyone into a personality box with a little red label on it, but instead to use the behavior patterns of each of the personality types to better understand our preferences. With this in mind, let's recap:

Each of us has a distinct personality, which is a blend of behavior preferences. The process begins with understanding your own psychological makeup and then acknowledging the following: (a) each of us is adaptable; (b) each of us has the necessary traits to function in accordance with every personality type (we merely have to work harder on our weaker areas); and (c) excuses ("That's just the way I am") don't cut it.

1. Remember that no personality is "better" or more "right" than any other—all types have separate strengths and are uniquely optimal for different aspects of overall objectives.

2. Continue to develop and work with your natural strengths without allowing them to become so marked that they degenerate into liabilities.

3. Acknowledge that your own ways of behaving are no better than (only different from) those of other people; this reduces frustration and helps you to work better with all kinds of people (which is part of the job!).

4. Try to understand someone else's temperament, whether colleague, client, or boss; this enables you to align tasks and incentives to meet needs and maximize productivity.

5. Take the personalities of your superiors, colleagues, and clients into account. You'll deliver a better work product (in their view) and also put yourself in the best possible light. (You make yourself even more valuable to your boss when you capitalize on a trait you possess that he may lack.)

6. Learn to access less instinctive ways of behaving; then you can select the best action in light of your objective and move an enormous step forward toward the ultimate goal—communicating your brand, developing your business, and becoming a leader.

7. Although we are all adaptable, we each have a core personality that is fundamental to us. Don't operate outside those key behaviors for too long, or you're likely to become dissatisfied. The key characteristics of your personality are bound to be the foundation of your enthusiasms and passions.

In short, understanding your personality is the first step to self-awareness and frees you to make your best choices and achieve your goals! So let's move on to the second step and look at how understanding the things that bring you satisfaction builds on your new-found personality awareness and increases your chances of success.

APPENDIX 4.A

QUESTIONNAIRE: PREFERRED BEHAVIORS

In the questions below, rate yourself on a sliding scale of 1–5, with 1 meaning that *you never act in this manner or feel this way* and 5 meaning that *you always, or almost always, act or feel this way* (give yourself a 5 if you emphatically say "yes" to the question). Where possible, avoid choosing 3, which is "on the fence"!

QUESTION #1: PEOPLE AND PARTIES

A. If someone suggests a party, even if I am tired, I feel a desire to go because I prefer being with people to being by myself.

   1   (2)   3   4   5

B. I like situations where I can feel in control, so my choice of whether to go to a party or not is somewhat dependent on feeling in charge of the situation.

   (1)   2   3   4   (5)

C. I would rather be alone than go to a party—especially if there are a lot of people I don't know. In that case, it would take something quite significant to make me go.

   1   2   3   (4)   5

D. I would not choose to go to a party of people I don't know, but if a friend asked me to go with him or her I would have a difficult time saying No.

   1   (2)   3   4   5

QUESTION #2: PROJECTS AND DETAIL

A. I think having a discussion about the issues is much more beneficial than drafting a detailed document—and clearly more enjoyable than getting into technicalities.

   1   2   (3)   4   5

B. I like to be in charge of projects, and doing the best job possible is the most important thing to me—detailed or not, I excel at it.

   1   2   3   4   (5)

C. I am very detail-oriented, and often can see problems others do not.

1   2   3   (4)   5

D. I take instruction well and can implement the task I am given.

1   2   3   (4)   5

QUESTION #3: ACTIVITY

A. I am always busy; I seem to move easily between projects and am able to change my focus of activity very quickly.

1   2   3   (4)   5

B. I have very little patience. Doing long-term monotonous tasks bores me. I like a challenge.

1   2   (3)   4   5

C. I don't enjoy doing anything unless I can do it perfectly. Even if it takes a lot of time, I will work steadily to finish a given task.

1   (2)   3   4   5

D. I don't take the initiative much, but if someone asks me to do something I will ensure it gets done.

(1)   2   3   4   5

QUESTION #4: TEAMWORK

A. It is important to me that people on my team have a good time.

1   2   3   4   (5)

B. I demand a lot of myself, and I expect the same of the other members of my team.

1   2   3   (4)   5

C. I work best alone rather than as part of a team.

1   (2)   3   4   5

D. Being part of a team is important to me.

1   2   3   (4)   5

71

QUESTION #5: TOP CHARACTERISTICS

A. Above all else, I consider myself outgoing and fun. People generally like to be around me.

1   (2)   3   4   5

B. Above all else, I consider myself an ambitious achiever. People generally respect my success.

1   2   3   (4)   5

C. Above all else, I consider myself analytical—a problem-solver. People generally respect my analysis.

1   2   (3)   4   5

D. Above all else, I am easy-going and empathetic toward others. People often disclose their problems to me.

1   2   3   4   (5)

QUESTION #6: DECISION-MAKING

A. I like to keep all my options open in case something better comes along.

1   (2)   3   4   5

B. I am decisive and like to be organized and in control.

1   2   3   4   (5)

C. I can be slow at making a decision, and I like to plan well in advance. Once a plan is made, I like to stick to it.

1   (2)   3   4   5

D. I don't initiate plans, or like to be in charge, but if someone else does the planning I am usually glad to be included and happy to go along.

(1)   2   3   4   5

QUESTION #7: EMOTIONS

A. I openly express my emotions; I'm demonstrative.

1   2   3   (4)   5

B. I sometimes express myself and then realize that I've unwittingly offended someone. For me, getting something done can be more important than just being nice.

(1)   2   3   4   5

C. I often feel estranged from others and don't "click" with them emotionally.

(1)   2   3   4   5

D. I don't usually get emotional; I may not seem overly enthusiastic, but I rarely get really angry, either.

(1)   2   3   4   5

QUESTION #8: APPROACH

A. I like to get things done quickly; sometimes my approach can be haphazard.

1   (2)   3   4   5

B. My approach is usually the best one, and I am confident of this most of the time.

1   2   3   (4)   5

C. I have a methodical and systematic approach to most things.

1   2   3   (4)   5

D. I can be accommodating. If someone suggests a certain approach, I will take that on board.

1   2   (3)   4   5

QUESTION #9: HUMOR AND FUN

A. Having fun is high on my list of priorities, and I love being in the midst of laughter—especially if I can be the one telling the joke.

1   (2)   3   4   5

B. I am not really a joke-teller.

1   2   3   (4)   5

C. I prefer deep introspection rather than mindless humor.

1   (2)   3   4   5

D. People say I have a dry humor. I can usually come back with some quick-witted one-liners.

1   (2)   3   4   5

QUESTION #10: ON THE JOB

A. Ideally, work should be fun all the time—there's no point doing something if it's not enjoyable.

1   (2)   3   4   5

B. I am a leader, and find it difficult to let others take over. I usually think I'm the best person for the job.

1   2   (3)   4   5

C. Ideally, I'd spend my time on the job doing interesting and quality work, with enough time to thoroughly analyze all the issues.

1   2   3   (4)   5

D. I am a good manager of other people, and I empathize with others in an environment where this quality can sometimes be overlooked.

1   2   3   (4)   5

QUESTION #11: LEISURE TIME

A. I love adventure and spontaneity. I don't really plan my leisure time, and sometimes I can be impulsive (such as impetuously charging off on a weekend trip with friends).

(1)   2   3   4   5

B. I don't really relax on the weekends. I typically fill my time pursuing challenging activities, or trying to master a new skill.

1   (2)   3   4   5

C. I enjoy spending leisure time quietly alone—e.g., enjoying music or the arts, or just reading a book.

1   2   3   (4)   5

D. I like to spend my leisure time with friends and family; I don't usually initiate plans but like to be asked.

1   2   3   (4)   5

QUESTION #12: THOSE WHO REALLY KNOW ME

A. The people closest to me accuse me of being too talkative and not letting them get a word in.

1   (2)   3   4   5

B. The people closest to me accuse me of being stubborn and headstrong.

1   (2)   3   4   5

C. The people closest to me accuse me of being overly critical about details.

(1)   2   3   4   5

D. The people closest to me accuse me of being too easygoing and not taking enough initiative.

(1)   2   3   4   5

QUESTION #13: PERCEPTION BY OTHERS

A. At work I am perceived as very sociable.

1   2   (3)   4   5

B. People see me as a workaholic and very ambitious.

(1)   2   3   4   5

C. Others perceive me as intellectual—and perhaps somewhat withdrawn.

(1)   2   3   4   5

D. At work people think I am dependable, and as such I tend to get stuck with lots of jobs.

1   2   (3)   4   5

QUESTION #14: NETWORKING

A. Networking is a positive aspect of the job. What's not to like about a social occasion and a glass of wine?

1   2   (3)   4   5

B. Networking is a necessary aspect of the job, and it's something I have to do to accomplish my ultimate goal of success.

1   2   3   4   **(5)**

C. The thought of networking makes me nauseous. I hate small talk.

1   **(2)**   3   4   5

D. I don't always choose to go to a networking event, but once there I usually find someone nice to talk to.

1   2   3   **(4)**   5

QUESTION #15: PROBLEM-SOLVING

A. I solve problems emotionally (with my heart) and can usually see a solution relatively easily.

1   2   **(3)**   4   5

B. I don't spend a lot of time analyzing my problems; I just tackle them head on. I probably use my head more than my heart, but above all else I'm decisive.

1   2   **(3)**   4   5

C. I definitely analyze and think through my problems very thoroughly before making a decision. I am extremely logical with my solutions.

1   2   **(3)**   4   5

D. I tend to avoid thinking about my problems.

(1)   2   3   4   5

YOUR SCORE

The four statements within each question above correspond to a particular personality type, each of which we will discuss at length in a moment, beginning on page 38. All A statements are associated with one personality, all B statements with another, etc. To determine which category you most identify with, add up your total score for all of your A, B, C, and D answers. You can have a maximum of 75 for any one of them, but only if you circled a 5 for every answer that corresponds to that letter. The category (or categories) with the highest score(s) are the one(s) most relevant to you.

TOTAL SCORE:

A STATEMENTS   40

B STATEMENTS   44

C STATEMENTS   39

D STATEMENTS   40

Don't worry about the makeup of your scores; there's absolutely no right or wrong, or (for that matter) a normal or an unusual mix. And certainly no personality type best exemplifies the ability to build a brand, develop clients, become a leader, or succeed in law.

Some people find that one category stands out from all the others, while other people see a clear balance of two categories, and others have a haphazard, eclectic mix. And whatever your particular makeup, you'll also find that you will have *some* of each of the personality types. Now return to page 37.

APPENDIX 4.B

TABLE OF STRENGTHS

The strengths below correlate with the key traits of each of the personalities. List the ones that most apply to you and determine how you could be using them more advantageously.

Chapter Four: Personalities

78

Juggling the Big 3 for Lawyers

TRAIT AND TEMPERAMENT	STRENGTH
THE CONNECTER	
Extroverted (thrives on people)	Engages effortlessly with others; influences easily.
Enthusiastic	Persuasive and fun; influences and inspires through enthusiasm.
Optimistic	Inspiring; confident; resilient; looks for and finds opportunities and workable solutions.
Expressive	Emotionally demonstrative; passionate and funny; great storyteller; draws people in; excellent brainstorming capabilities; stimulates communication and ideas; a good "performer."
Spontaneous	Risk-taking; innovative; adaptable; easily able to respond and switch gears; open to new situations and ideas; seizes today; doesn't procrastinate (makes decisions quickly); works with large and immediate energy; accepts the situation; enjoys (even thrives in) the moment.
Energetic	Volunteers for projects; multi-tasks; handles stress of heavy workload.
Playful	Makes things fun for others; can make a stressful situation less so; doesn't take situations or self too seriously.
Decision-making style: emotional (makes decisions with the heart rather than the head)	Perceives the effects of issues and situations on people and their emotions.

TRAIT AND TEMPERAMENT	STRENGTH
THE DRIVER	
Extroverted (slightly different from the Connecter because the Driver thrives on activity more than on people)	Gets things done; energetic and enthusiastic; influences easily; engages straight away and immediately gets to the point.
Goal-oriented	Ambitious; hard worker; successful; results-focused; action-oriented; welcomes competition; thrives on challenge.
Powerful	Definitely able to impose order and to organize others; a natural leader; inspires people; doesn't waste time worrying or blaming self; gets on with things.
Takes charge	Good in a crisis; thinks quickly; resolves problems; plans both for the process and for the outcome.
Capable	Confident; influential; dependable worker; produces quality outcome; inspires others to emulation.
Visionary/intuitive	Sees the big picture; looks for possibilities, improvements, and new ideas; often an innovator and idea-generator; creative; insightful; understands subtleties; discovers meaning when not necessarily evidenced by facts; reads between the lines.
Forthright/direct	Honest; creates an aura of confidence and ability; provides beneficial feedback.
Decision-making style: impersonal on the basis of the goal	Impartial and results-focused.

TRAIT AND TEMPERAMENT	STRENGTH
THE PERFECTIONIST	
Introverted	Deep; reflective; creative (especially artistically, culturally, and academically); well-thought-out content; excellent depth of concentration; good attention span; calm.
Task-oriented	Prioritizes the task; always gets the job done; cares about and enjoys the process; rarely loses focus.
Perfectionistic	Disciplined, organized, thorough; always delivers quality; reliably tests ideas and information for accuracy; challenges others to do better.
Analytical	Thinks through all the issues before making a decision; reviews all the information; makes reliable judgments; good at developing ideas (as opposed to generating ideas); probes deeply and always concentrates; intellectually stimulates others.
Logical	Practical; sees the bottom line; accurate; impartial; literal and precise.
Structured	Reliable; plans and adheres to schedules; provides orderly progress on projects; gives a clear sense of direction.
Principled	Does the right thing; follows the rules; minimizes risk.
Decision-making style: based on tangible evidence	Observes accurately because focuses on facts and experience; inherently practical; will question ideas to ensure they are based on reality; terrific memory for detail (very focused).

TRAIT AND TEMPERAMENT	STRENGTH
THE MODERATE	
Introverted (though rather less so than the Perfectionist because of the ability to focus on people and make decisions more on that basis)	Contented; self-contained; patient; calm; quiet; reflective.
Even-tempered	Consistent; easygoing; stable; balanced; inspires confidence; dependable.
Tolerant	Patient; adaptable; welcomes spontaneous challenges; open-minded; gives other people room (vs. stipulating parameters).
Empathetic	Good listener; helpful; considerate; good mentor; naturally recognizes the contributions of others and shows appreciation; loyal.
Diplomatic	Cooperative; helps people get along and work together; creates stability and harmony; good team player; resolves conflict.
Facilitative	Can inspire commitment and generate consensus; willingly takes on projects; likes to give to and support others; empowers others to succeed.
Process-oriented	Enjoys the process of a project; facilitates decision-making and consensus.
Decision-making style: considers the impact on people	Empathizes with others' perspectives; makes decisions and interprets events based upon their impact; good relationship-building skills; naturally motivating.

APPENDIX 4.C

TABLE OF HOW EXTREME STRENGTHS CAN
BECOME LIABILITIES

Now take your list of strengths from the previous exercise and consider how
they can become liabilities.

TRAIT AND TEMPERAMENT	STRENGTH	IN EXTREME FORM, DEGENERATES INTO THIS LIABILITY	RESULT OF DEGENERATION
THE CONNECTER			
Extroverted (thrives on people)	Engages effortlessly with others; influences easily.	Insensitive to the needs of others who may also want to talk or simply voice an opinion; impulsively shares what can be rather undeveloped ideas; always on the go; lacks calmness and introspection.	Others may feel overwhelmed and may retreat.
Enthusiastic	Persuasive and fun; influences and inspires others through enthusiasm.	Can be impetuous; impulsive; may wildly exaggerate; may not follow through.	Loss of trust from others.
Optimistic	Inspiring; confident; resilient; looks for and finds opportunities and workable solutions.	Unrealistic; doesn't always learn from mistakes.	Not taken seriously.
Expressive	Emotionally demonstrative; passionate and funny; great storyteller; draws people in; excellent brainstorming capabilities; stimulates communication and ideas; a good "performer."	May monopolize conversations; probably interrupts; rather attention-seeking; relies too much on charm rather than on preparation and substance; may be overly emotional.	Perceived as egotistical, self-centered, even melodramatic.

TRAIT AND TEMPERAMENT	STRENGTH	IN EXTREME FORM, DEGENERATES INTO THIS LIABILITY	RESULT OF DEGENERATION
Spontaneous	Risk-taking; innovative; adaptable; easily able to respond and switch gears; open to new situations and ideas; seizes today; doesn't procrastinate (makes decisions quickly); works with large and immediate energy; accepts the situation; enjoys (even thrives in) the moment.	Not a serious completer/finisher; lacks introspection; too motivated by short-term gains; finds routine tasks boring and loses focus; undisciplined and neglects planning; far too impulsive; places too much emphasis on pleasure and enjoyment of the moment.	Seen as unreliable; not trusted to deliver.
Energetic	Volunteers for projects; multi-tasks; handles the stress of a heavy workload.	Takes on far too much; normal response to stress can be to take on yet more work (which only contributes to the problem!). Tendency to lose focus compounds the potential for disaster.	Over-promises and under-delivers, thereby losing trusting relationships.
Playful	Makes things fun for others; can make a stressful situation less so; doesn't take situations and self too seriously.	Easily bored; lacks depth.	Not perceived as a serious leader; can be a distraction to those trying to accomplish something important.
Decision-making style: emotional (makes decisions with the heart rather than the head)	Perceives the effects of issues and situations on people and their emotions.	Allows personal feelings to both persuade and to distort perception and reality.	Irrational decision-making.

TRAIT AND TEMPERAMENT	STRENGTH	IN EXTREME FORM, DEGENERATES INTO THIS LIABILITY	RESULT OF DEGENERATION
THE DRIVER			
Extroverted (slightly different from the Connecter because the Driver thrives on activity more than people)	Gets things done; energetic and enthusiastic; influences easily; engages straight away and immediately gets to the point.	Never relaxes; sets a pace too aggressive for others to follow; somewhat insensitive to needs of others; impulsively shares ideas and takes action; not introspective enough.	Others can feel overwhelmed or outgunned; they may either retreat or avoid.
Goal-oriented	Ambitious; hard worker; successful; results-focused; action-oriented; welcomes competition; thrives on challenge.	Aggressive; manipulative and self-serving; drives others too hard; workaholic; over-competitive; insensitive and judgmental of others.	Loses support; may have no followers or clients.
Powerful	Definitely able to impose order and to organize others; a natural leader; inspires people; doesn't waste time worrying or blaming self; gets on with things.	Arrogant; demanding.	Perceived as bullying or tyrannical.
Takes charge	Good in a crisis; thinks quickly; resolves problems; plans both for the process and for the outcome.	Impatient; possibly too controlling; makes hasty decisions; desire for control can become a compulsion.	Can fail to motivate and take colleagues along; may restrict participation and contributions of others.
Capable	Confident; influential; dependable worker; produces quality outcomes; inspires others to emulation.	Intolerant and hypercritical of others' failures or inadequacies; may be overconfident.	May be perceived as overbearing and intimidating. Can fail to develop promising juniors.

TRAIT AND TEMPERAMENT	STRENGTH	IN EXTREME FORM, DEGENERATES INTO THIS LIABILITY	RESULT OF DEGENERATION
Visionary/ intuitive	Sees the big picture; looks for possibilities, improvements, and new ideas; often an innovator and idea generator; creative; insightful; understands subtleties; discovers meaning when not necessarily evidenced by facts; reads between the lines.	Insufficient focus on reality or facts; too conceptual; impractical; unrealistic about the detail or implementation of ideas.	Loses credibility when implementation fails.
Forthright/direct	Honest; creates an aura of confidence and ability; provides beneficial feedback.	Argumentative; needs to be right; quick to point finger and blame others; can become forceful and confrontational.	Others may feel intimidated or even attacked. Loses credibility when wrong.
Decision-making style: impersonal on the basis of the goal	Impartial and results-focused.	Indifferent to what others are doing or feeling.	Fails to notice negative impact felt by (or generated toward) others.
THE PERFECTIONIST			
Introverted	Deep; reflective; creative (especially artistically, culturally, and academically); well-thought-out content; excellent depth of concentration; good attention span; calm.	Detached; alienated; estranged; boring; too serious.	May be perceived as arrogant, secretive, and hard to trust; difficult to engage; possibly lacking the relationship skills needed to garner clients and foster support.

TRAIT AND TEMPERAMENT	STRENGTH	IN EXTREME FORM, DEGENERATES INTO THIS LIABILITY	RESULT OF DEGENERATION
Task-oriented	Prioritizes the task; always gets the job done; cares about and enjoys the process; rarely loses focus.	Insensitive to people issues (probably because overly focused on the task in hand).	Lacks necessary relationships to cultivate clients and support.
Perfectionistic	Disciplined, organized, thorough; always delivers quality; reliably tests ideas and information for accuracy; challenges others to do better.	Inflexible; negative; fussy; pessimistic; hard to please; too detailed; spends too much time on a task; doesn't sufficiently prioritize deadlines; too careful; overexplains; asks too many questions.	Others may feel overcriticized, intimidated, and even stifled.
Analytical	Thinks through all the issues before making a decision; reviews all the information; makes reliable judgments; good at developing ideas (as opposed to generating ideas); probes deeply and always concentrates; intellectually stimulates others.	Paralysis through analysis(?!); lacks commensurate spontaneity and instinct; comes across as rather negative due to determination not to be overtly positive until all conceivable data has been examined.	Frustrates others when they want progress.
Logical	Practical; sees the bottom line; accurate; impartial; literal and precise.	Relatively unfeeling: does not evaluate human emotions or relationships well; can lack empathy.	Others may feel misunderstood, unappreciated, and unrecognized.
Structured	Reliable; plans and adheres to schedules; provides orderly progress on projects; gives a clear sense of direction.	May not deal well with interruptions or spontaneous demands; unforeseen challenges are unwelcome.	Does not adapt quickly enough.

TRAIT AND TEMPERAMENT	STRENGTH	IN EXTREME FORM, DEGENERATES INTO THIS LIABILITY	RESULT OF DEGENERATION
Principled	Does the right thing; follows the rules; minimizes risk.	Judgmental; cannot view things in terms other than black and white—there is no gray.	Disliked as a faultfinder and viewed as an irritating impediment.
Decision-making style: based on tangible evidence	Observes accurately because focuses on facts and experience; inherently practical; will question ideas to ensure they are based on reality; terrific memory for detail (very focused).	May lack imagination; not brilliant at brain-storming; can miss the big-picture viewpoint; cannot deal with ambi-guities; will not take on a view without tangible evidence; relies on personal experience too much; may be too keen to reject new ideas and stick to tried-and-true methods.	Can miss opportunities for lack of substantive evidence.
THE MODERATE			
Introverted (though rather less so than the Perfectionist because of the ability to focus on people and make decisions more on that basis)	Contented; self-contained; patient; calm; quiet; reflective.	Disinterested; detached; unenthusiastic.	Hard to read; may be viewed as secretive and untrustworthy. May be perceived as independent, rather than a team player.
Even-tempered	Consistent; easygoing; stable; balanced; inspires confidence; dependable.	Unemotional; too reserved; indifferent; dispirited; lazy; not sufficiently ambitious; unable to motivate others; lacking in enthusiasm.	Difficult for others to evaluate; perceived as uncaring or even uninvolved.
Tolerant	Patient; adaptable; welcomes sponta-neous challenges; open-minded; gives other people room (vs. stipulat-ing parameters).	Permissive; directionless; can wait too long to see which way the wind is blow-ing; indecisive.	Creates anxiety in others due to innate inability to give direction.

TRAIT AND TEMPERAMENT	STRENGTH	IN EXTREME FORM, DEGENERATES INTO THIS LIABILITY	RESULT OF DEGENERATION
Empathetic	Good listener; helpful; considerate; good mentor; naturally recognizes the contributions of others and shows appreciation; loyal.	People-pleaser; too generous.	May be taken advantage of; may feel under-valued and even resentful.
Diplomatic	Cooperative; helps people get along and work together; creates stability and harmony; good team player; resolves conflict.	Avoids conflict; unable to provide negative feedback, however deserved.	Unable to develop others or to influence; may stifle ideas (because they usually arise from different opinions/conflict).
Facilitative	Can inspire commitment and generate consensus; willingly takes on projects; likes to give to and support others; empowers others to succeed.	Unable to give overall direction or demand control; unable to challenge others or motivate them to reach higher potential; overly accommodating; feeble.	Lacks credibility as a leader; risks burnout due to tendency to overextend.
Process-oriented	Enjoys the process of a project; facilitates decision-making and consensus.	Prioritizes process over task; seeks premature consensus; desperate to keep people happy; may lose focus on actual results.	Colleagues may belittle him or her as lacking ambition and drive.
Decision-making style: considers the impact on people	Empathizes with others' perspectives; makes decisions and interprets events based upon their impact; good relationship-building skills; naturally motivating.	Gets overly caught up in other people's problems; allows the "people factor" to blind or distort perception; can be indecisive or overaccommodating.	Distorted judgment; may lack credibility as a decision-maker; may induce anxiety in followers due to lack of firm direction.

APPENDIX 4.D

PRACTICAL APPLICATION: MANAGING BEHAVIORS IN RELATION TO OTHERS

Understanding personalities helps us to work with clients and colleagues in the best way possible. If we understand how various personalities (including our own) behave, different types can be brought together to create optimal results. Let's see how this works in practice.

THE BOSS

You might imagine that the best-case scenario is when a Connecter boss works with a Connecter associate, or a Driver boss hires a Driver, but this is normally not the case. Complementary qualities work much better than two people with the same temperament, which is often too much of a good thing. But whatever type of boss you have, understanding his or her personality will help, and even when (or *especially* when) the boss possesses an opposite temperament to yours, you can choose to use that to your advantage. *You can even provide the missing component to his personality*, thus making things much easier for him. (Oddly enough, in some cases we may achieve more recognition for doing this than for anything else we might do!)

1. The Connecter Boss

Connecter bosses typically talk a lot, see the big picture, and refuse to get bogged down in detail, so the associate who is savvy to behavioral preferences will present the boss with solutions suited to his working style—straightforward, high-level, executive summaries. Long, technical emails are never the way to interact with a Connecter. (If you are a Perfectionist, take note!) Scheduling a five-minute face-to-face meeting achieves more. In that short period you can make it abundantly clear that you've taken from the Connecter boss the burden of the detailed analysis *and* provided a beneficial result. He will be relieved and grateful!

If you're self-aware and boss-aware, you won't sit back and wait for direction with regard to timing: you'll know that detailed scheduling is not the boss's strength. Further, realize that Connecters are natural chatterers (they may even work best that way), so you will need to accommodate his preferences and communicate with him comfortably. (If you are introverted and accustomed to getting on with your work quietly and diligently, this can be a challenge.)

A Connecter boss is likely to come up with ideas and storm into the associate's office full of enthusiasm, leaving him or her with the burden of delivery. Juniors (especially Drivers and Perfectionists) take all assignments seriously and will work hard to perform. Yet many times you may find your work sitting forgotten on the boss's desk, because his enthusiasm has—er—moved on. This is one reason why communication with this type of boss is crucial: It ensures that your efforts remain aligned with his focus and that you actually get credit for the work you do!

Dos	Don'ts
1. Meet in person	1. Don't give more detail than is absolutely necessary
2. Give him an opportunity to talk about himself (ask questions to show interest)	2. Don't get upset when a) he gets sidetracked b) he does not follow through *(instead, be prepared for it!)*
3. Engage in small talk	3. Don't be too formal
4. Be open to opportunities to connect on a personal level	4. Don't hold back comments or opinions—Connecters enjoy communication
5. Provide high-level, on-point analysis	5. Don't voice only negatives; look for ways to support his ideas
6. Be prepared to move quickly and make decisions	

2. The Driver Boss

If a boss exhibits a Driver temperament, achievement is uppermost in his or her mind. Be sure to update him about progress on every single project and everything you have completed. It doesn't have to be formal reporting, but it must be regular, brief, and to the point. Drivers enjoy sticking to business. If there are problems with a project, this style of boss needs to be informed as soon as possible, for several reasons. First, it allows you to emphasize what you *have* done, and second, it prevents him from pointing the finger in the future. (Remember that this personality does *not* enjoy taking responsibility for mistakes!) Unexpected failure is the last thing the Driver boss wants, and excuses are unacceptable because results are all that counts. Bear in mind that the Driver can appear to be both brusque and impersonal—which can be hard for other types to take. This is nothing personal; it's just his way of dealing with business and accomplishing more.

Dos	Don'ts
1. Get to the point	1. Don't be upset by a brusque manner
2. Keep to business	2. Don't challenge him or try to prove him wrong (but don't withdraw completely or you will be viewed as weak)
3. Expect a fast pace	
4. Talk about projects in terms of goals and objectives	
5. Begin assignments straight away so you can report progress	3. Don't cut corners
	4. Never give excuses
6. Understand delivery requirements and then meet them	5. Never, ever let him down
7. Show willingness to do whatever it takes to get the project done, and done well	6. Don't expect him to understand personal problems or be emotional
8. Let him (or her) have the last word	

3. The Perfectionist Boss

Having a Perfectionist boss can be rewarding and frustrating in equal measure. A Perfectionist boss tends to be highly academic, so you can learn a lot and be challenged from working with him. He or she will also welcome any desire on your part to explore intellectual issues and solutions. However, when you have to deliver work to him, your task is likely to be more intensive than with other superiors. You can never "wing it" with a Perfectionist boss: If you try, you will almost certainly fail, and you may even discredit yourself forever in his eyes. Instead, be prepared with all the evidence and present it in an organized way, so that no detail is left uncovered. Inspiration is not enough for the Perfectionist boss. Provide logical and factual evidence, and avoid any attempt at persuasion. Unlike the Driver (who only wants workable solutions), the Perfectionist wants us to mention problems and then make it clear to the meanest intelligence how they've been sorted out. All this may seem overly meticulous to some, but to the Perfectionist boss it's nothing less than essential. And don't even *think* about being late or casual about meeting with a Perfectionist superior!

Dos	Don'ts
1. Be on time	1. Don't wing it
2. Be prepared	2. Never break the rules
3. Provide concrete and factual evidence	3. Don't get emotional
4. Be willing to provide background and thorough detail for any argument/analysis and an explanation of how you arrived at the solution	4. Don't digress into personal matters or small talk
	5. Don't wait for him to come to you
5. Give the highest and detailed quality time to the work	6. However, don't barge into his office unannounced
6. Create agendas for meetings and schedule them well ahead of time	7. Don't give an unsupported bottom-line answer, unless asked for it
7. Show keen interest in the boss's analysis and be prepared for questions	

4. The Moderate Boss

Having to rely on a Moderate boss to provide direction can prove extremely frustrating, because he or she can't always be counted on to deliver it. This can create anxiety among associates, who aren't sure what they should be doing. When dealing with a Moderate boss, regularly seek both direction and feedback and make sure that you ask the right questions to receive both. Otherwise, you may find yourself falling behind the peers and competitors who get much more guidance from their Connecter, Perfectionist, or Driver bosses. With that said, however, the Moderate boss can be the most generous personality with help or support, and he is the most likely to serve as a coach and mentor—although you may need to take the initiative and ask for the help.

Dos	Don'ts
1. Engage personally with him or her (Moderate bosses are relationship-focused)	1. Don't talk too much
	2. Don't be aggressive or confrontational
2. Be patient if you are not receiving enough direction—and do ask for it	3. Don't create conflict
3. Look for opportunities to plan and schedule (when he doesn't)	4. Don't over-do facts and logic
	5. Don't be frustrated by the boss's passivity; use it as an opportunity to show your own initiative
4. Talk about ideas, analysis, and decisions in terms of actual impact on people	
5. Ask questions to get adequate and helpful feedback	

The Client

When dealing with clients, the rule is simple: Deliver what the client wants in the form in which he prefers to receive it. Once you recognize his personality type, you should be able to tailor your knowledge to meet his needs. Even though we are the lawyers (and thus the experts on what should be delivered), we must constantly deliver *to* our client's personality—not *from* our own. Clients unfortunately don't come with labels ("Perfectionist with Driver tendencies: every detail counts!"), but every moment spent assessing their signals and reading their "style" will be amply rewarded when you deliver what they want the way they want it. That means a glowing reputation and repeat business, which, inevitably, results in success!

The Connecter Client

The key to dealing with extroverted clients is to give them what they most need—the limelight. Whatever you do, don't fight them for it! You are there to support their desire for attention. By sitting quietly and supportively in the clients' shadow, you make them look good and do your job effectively.

Of all the personalities, Connecters like schedules and deadlines the least, and of course, as lawyers, structure is our job. So when dealing with Connecter clients, try to impose structure in a way that doesn't stress them out. Give them lots of warning before deadlines, and don't be afraid to remind them if one is pending. Be alert for opportunities to lighten the atmosphere and initiate small talk—the Connecter likes to talk about anything. And if you're a Driver, remember that the Connecter wants to have some fun—even at work!

Dos	Don'ts
1. Allow him center stage (especially in front of others)	1. Don't overanalyze
2. Engage, by letting him talk about himself and by responding with personal items about yourself (connect on the same wavelength)	2. Don't allow yourself to get bogged down in detail
3. Address things immediately (Connecters are in-the-moment people)	3. Don't be too formal and stuffy
4. Be enthusiastic and upbeat	4. Don't dictate procedure or react too rigidly, as this may create stress and resentment
5. Keep up with his natural fast pace	
6. Return messages and respond quickly, even if it's just to say, "I'll get on to this soon..."	

The Driver Client

An overconfident Driver can often put projects at risk through unwillingness to listen to legal advice or objections. The more we try to tell him the error of his ways, the more he will tend to get defensive and fight back. One strategy is to present him with strong and irrefutable evidence as objectively and impersonally as possible—ideally from a third-party expert. Another method is to provide information in such a way that the client can work out the answer for himself, without having to admit to having been mistaken. Remember, this personality will rarely apologize or give credit to others, so our job is to make him look like the winner he needs to be.

Dos	Don'ts
1. Acknowledge his accomplishments	1. Don't waste his time
2. Allow him to think of himself as the leader	2. Don't take critical or blunt reactions personally
3. Give him solutions and results, proposed in objective, unemotional ways	3. Don't try to overpower him or prove him wrong
4. Put things in writing—this personality does not easily admit mistakes	4. Don't make mistakes
5. Allow him to make decisions	5. Don't approach anything casually
6. Show commitment to his projects	
7. Give him closure on tasks and inquiries	
8. Show him ways to achieve optimal results	

94

The Perfectionist (Highly Introverted) Client

If a client is naturally introverted, think long and hard before putting him or her into the spotlight without considerable advance notice. The introvert prefers to think carefully about his answers and make a plan before providing an opinion. Further, an introvert may view spontaneous ideas as irrational and brainstorming (without serious preparation) as a waste of time. Consequently, consider carefully before offering your opinions to the introverted client.

Dos	Don'ts
1. Maintain things at a slower speed than usual (especially if you are extroverted); take the time to pause and pay attention to the client	1. Don't spontaneously put him in the spotlight or ask him to brainstorm ideas unless you are sure he is comfortable with this
2. Ask questions—introverts do not easily volunteer things	2. Don't overload him with small talk and unnecessary chatter
3. Allow him time to think about his answers	3. Don't interrupt
	4. Don't assume that his silence means consent
	5. Don't just throw out ideas; make it clear that they're possibilities, not necessarily solutions
	6. Don't invade his physical space

The Moderate Client

The first thing to remember when dealing with a Moderate client is to start on a personal level because Moderates view everything in terms of relationships. In addition, bear in mind that they typically don't want to be viewed solely as having a role within the project, but want to engage on a personal level (as opposed to Drivers, who may actually prefer keeping things detached). The best plan is to make an early connection and then to continue to develop the relationship. Second, with the Moderate client's innate distaste for conflict, it's crucial to ask his opinion along the way and to be sensitive to any misgivings you may sense. Remember that the Moderate client may never verbalize disagreement, even when he feels it strongly. If his views differ from yours, your Moderate client might quietly disappear without your ever understanding quite why.

Dos	Don'ts
1. Engage warmly with him	1. Don't create conflict
2. Make the process as harmonious as possible	2. Don't allow the mood to become hostile
3. Take upon yourself the task of keeping the desired result in constant focus	3. Don't force him to make decisions
4. Maintain structure and provide specific tasks and deadlines	4. Don't treat him impersonally
5. Ask questions along the way to elicit his thoughts and emotional state	
6. Be proactive to resolve conflict	
7. Allow him to support ideas rather than analyze or decide on them	

LEADING

As leaders, whether as part of a project or as manager of a practice group, we are constantly called upon to create direction or to motivate our team. We do this best through an intelligent understanding of the individual personalities concerned.

Let's take a look at this in practice.

Tony had recently moved to a new firm as a partner and had taken four associates with him: Connecter Cathy, Perfectionist Peter, Driver David, and Moderate Melissa. The first week in their new firm, an opportunity to land a new client came up. As Tony discussed the work with his team, Perfectionist Peter provided a lengthy discourse on the regulations that would come into play, thus proving that his knowledge of the subject was superior not only to Tony's, but also to everyone else's on the team. Tony decided he'd have to take Perfectionist Peter with him to pitch the deal.

After the meeting, Connecter Cathy went straight to Tony's office, petitioning to go to the client meeting (as an extrovert, meetings were definitely her favorite part of the job!). At the same time, Tony received a call from an events organizer asking if his team could host a seminar the following week. (Normally Tony wouldn't have agreed to this on such short notice, but the events organizer had [correctly] surmised that Tony, having just switched law firms, would be eager for an audience filled with potential clients.) So Tony said, "We'll do it." Since Cathy was already in his office, he immediately asked her to take responsibility for administering everything that needed to be done.

Before leaving with Perfectionist Peter for the meeting, Tony realized that he was supposed to be going to a networking function that afternoon. So he stopped by Driver David's office to ask him to attend in his place. Hearing this request, Moderate Melissa came out of her office to ask Tony what she should be doing. Tony hadn't yet considered her contribution, so—off the cuff—he told Melissa that she could present one of the main talks at the seminar.

And with that Tony departed, having brilliantly misused every lawyer in his office!

Now, you might think I am making up this story, but I'm not! Tony told it to me one time when we were talking about the personalities on our respective teams. (Yes, I did change the names.) Tony is usually very perceptive about temperaments and motivators, but on this particular day, he was under stress because of his recent move and therefore rather distracted. You can imagine the consequences of those four assignments on each of Tony's associates!

Perfectionist Peter. Perfectionist Peter attended the client meeting but rambled on with far too much detail about the regulations, boring everyone to tears in the process. Tony had to gently shut him up, only for Peter to barge in again. Tony became short-tempered and began to wish that he'd brought Connecter Cathy to the meeting instead. They failed to get the deal, and Perfectionist Peter knew that he had somehow been part of the reason.

Connecter Cathy. Cathy was deeply frustrated with her assignment as administrator. She was relegated to her desk doing tedious organizing while David was at a networking event and Peter got to go to the client meeting.

Driver David. David wondered why he hadn't been asked to make a real contribution as opposed to chatting at an afternoon networking event. He understood the need to connect with clients, but twenty minutes into the event he had already concluded (wrongly) that there was no real benefit in his being there.

Moderate Melissa. Moderate Melissa was not naturally one to complain, but she still needed to feel appreciated and Tony's neglecting to include her in the assignments had made her feel insignificant. Yet Tony's next move—casually throwing her the task of presenting a key talk—was even worse. A typical Moderate, Melissa routinely tried to avoid the spotlight. Having to make a public presentation with such short notice was her worst nightmare.

After fretting over losing the client pitch (and realizing his mistake in taking Peter to the meeting), Tony thought about how he could fix the situation. As part of the process, he recognized his horrific delegating choices. Meanwhile, the client reconsidered and gave Tony another chance at the project. Together, Tony and his team assessed the best way forward for both the client work *and* the seminar.

1. Driver David and Moderate Melissa jointly took over the organization of the seminar. (David's ability to accomplish things quickly and efficiently made him the only one of the four who could complete the task in such a short time.) David decided what everyone had to do to make the seminar happen and organized a schedule for everyone to meet. Melissa facilitated the process and was asked to go around to each office to ensure that everyone was meeting his deadline. (David's aggressive style could have caused antagonism in such a role.)

2. Connecter Cathy took over Melissa's responsibility of giving one of the presentations at the seminar, which also meant that she was able to spend two full days at the seminar networking with the other speakers and attendees. Cathy was thrilled with the idea!

3. Connecter Cathy and Perfectionist Peter went together to meet the client. This time Peter followed his mandate of conveying in-depth knowledge *without* going into excessive detail. In combination with Cathy's extroverted personality, the meeting went exceptionally well. Peter then followed up the meeting with an impressive document explaining the complicated regulations governing the situation.

In short, understanding personality types is essential for effective teamwork. However, please note that it's not always possible to hand out tasks on that basis, nor is it in the best interests of team members themselves. Every lawyer should occasionally move outside his comfort zone, improving a weak area in the process. As a leader, it's crucial to evaluate when a job requires a certain talent and when it's appropriate to ask one's associates, as part of personal growth, to work outside their most obvious strengths.

Chapter Five

Awareness Building Block 2: Motivators

(Understanding your motivators to enable them to fuel your goals)

In Chapter 2 ("The Juggling Act"), I introduced you to the three vital facets of your career—brand, business, and leadership. We also examined the concept of incremental leadership development, beginning with self-leading—which means forming a clear personal vision and working toward it in a consistent way. However, if we truly want our vision to propel us toward our ultimate goals, the vision must generate three things:

- a long-term, passionate motivation to achieve those goals;

- an inner satisfaction from their accomplishment; and

- a sustained happiness in living the life we're aiming for.

A personal vision—always a long-term endeavor—can only deliver these outcomes when it incorporates what really matters to us. So understanding—*really* understanding!—what we want is the first (and most critical) step toward success.

Reading this chapter and analyzing what most motivates and satisfies you should equip you to develop your own personal vision. If you skip this step, you risk building your career around a goal that may well prove unsatisfying and unsustainable in the long run.

I've seen it over and again (and so, I suspect, have you): the talented associate who burns out long before his time because of the burden of incongruous expectations—perhaps doing what motivates his partner (or his parents), or doing what he thinks he *should* do, rather than what he really *needs* to do for himself. The trouble is that setting goals that don't "set us on fire" gradually atrophies the will to move forward. The casualty of such flawed goal-setting will be the cornered lawyer: listless, tired (even ill), and perhaps blighted by the burden of expectations.

We cultivate sustainable success when what drives our personal lives and career goals is in alignment with our needs, wants, and values. Let me define what I mean by each of these.

NEEDS—TWO TYPES: CORE NEEDS AND HIGHER NEEDS

Core Needs

These are the essentials that are critically important to happiness—even, in extreme cases, to survival. In his theory of hierarchical motivation, Abraham Maslow suggests that we are all motivated by a succession of needs, starting with the most basic physical needs (such as food, water, or air), and ascending through the progressively more sophisticated needs of safety, love, esteem, and (finally) self-actualization.

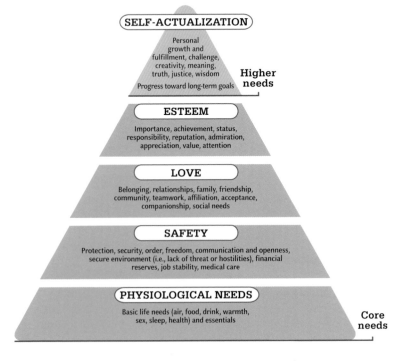

Maslow's hierarchy of needs, adapted from Motivation and Personality *(1st edition, 1954; 2nd edition, 1970)*

The needs leading to self-actualization are what I call "core" needs. These motivate all of us, although the level and strength of each of those needs may vary from person to person. For example, we all need esteem—both self-respect and admiration from others—but some of us crave it to a deeper extent. However, happiness *always* requires satisfaction (to some level) of each of the core needs.

Maslow's categories of needs are broad descriptions and may be defined differently for each of us. (Exactly how we develop our own definitions might well derive from the personality types examined in Chapter 4.) For example, Maslow's need for "love" represents, among other things, the necessity for relationships, belonging, and teaming up with others, yet different personalities are likely to define those things in very different ways. A Connecter's definition of love probably includes many close relationships and being near those people most (even all) of the time; the Perfectionist will probably be satisfied by fewer close relationships, and may even want to keep some (if not all) of those people at arm's length. (In fact, the Perfectionist might view the Connecter's definition of "love" as more like torture!)

It's important to recognize that progress may be sporadic and that we're unlikely to ever feel that all our needs are fully satisfied. If you're enjoying a successful life and career when your partner suddenly leaves you, your instinct is usually to regress and to focus on filling the space left by your loss. This is because physiology, safety, love, and esteem are "deficit" needs: if one or more is inadequately met, we immediately feel the need and are strongly motivated to fill it.

Tiffany's bucket was overrunning with love. It was esteem that was in deficit.

Most of us normally have our core needs met to a reasonable level, but when this is not the case we tend to feel anxious and defensive. I'm sure you've experienced dispirited colleagues who are anger-prone, paranoid, opportunistic, self-serving—or all of those things! Their actions are almost certainly the direct result of a core deficiency, yet chances are they're completely unaware of this lack. Hence, they adopt inappropriate behaviors under the mistaken belief that such actions will somehow bring them some kind of satisfaction. (Anger, especially, can be intensely satisfying in the short term—even if it's not addressing the underlying cause of the problem.) If these people were to focus on what they *really* need, they might find ways to meet the deficiency and would no longer need to relieve their anxiety or lack of contentment.

> *Core needs are the things essential to us and important to happiness—even, in extreme cases, to survival.*

Higher Needs

I categorize the need of self-actualization (Maslow's last and most fulfilling need) as a "higher" need. It is different from the others because it motivates us to grow and to fulfill our unique potential. In Maslow's words, "A musician must make music, an artist must paint, a poet must write, if he is to be at peace with himself... It refers to man's desire for fulfillment...to become everything that one is capable of becoming" (A.H. Maslow, *A Theory of Human Motivation*, Psychological Review 50 [1943]: 370–396).

Core needs have a relatively obvious level of satisfaction (we fill the deficit!), but self-actualization is a process, so its pursuit is—arguably—never-ending. We can always be better, do more, and improve at whatever it is we want to be. This particular quest will of course be unique to each of us, with the common thread that we each must discover the right path for ourselves and fully commit to it. Yet because self-actualization is about realizing innate potential, it uses our strengths, and (like the core needs) it derives naturally from the heart of our personality, the part we can't change.

> *Self-actualization is about realizing innate potential.*

I believe the progression of satisfying needs is variable and unique. Some people may even choose (consciously or not) to prioritize higher needs over lower ones. We've all seen those who strive for achievement and career status at the expense of such basic human needs as sleep and food—and who even (bizarrely enough) feel good about their choice! For some, the needs that Maslow categorizes as self-actualization can in fact *be* core needs. An artist may need to paint as much as—or even more than—he needs love. In such a case, art may be a core need more than a means toward self-actualization.

Painting renews the artist's energy, and without it, what he values most about himself might be lost.

> Core needs have a relatively clear level of satisfaction (we can fill the deficit), but self-actualization is a growth process. That said, the needs that Maslow categorizes as self-actualization can in fact be core needs when they are essential to our happiness.

It's up to each of us to discover what constitutes our core needs and what form our higher needs should take.

We all possess a primal instinct when it comes to satisfying basic needs, and that instinct results in extraordinary energy. We're "on fire," and that fire fuels us.

In Chapter 4 ("Personalities") I discussed my need for challenges and goal attainment, noting that a fast-paced—and even a stress-filled—day can bring me significant satisfaction. For me, goal attainment is a need, as well as a significant source of energy. Yet I've worked with many lawyers who find that having to endure such pressure seriously depletes their spirit and enthusiasm. Their core personalities are different from mine, and their needs and sources of energy are consistent with *their* makeup.

WANTS

Sometimes we pursue things in excess of, or even inconsistent with, our requirements, going after "wants" rather than needs. Some people might argue that in relation to the core needs there is a universally defined deficit to fill, making the definition of a "need" and a "want" the same for everyone. I choose instead to define these terms in relation to each of us as individuals. Some people may define a magnificent home as a core need (possibly because of a need for security, possibly because they need/desire/wish to show off!); others would consider such a house an obvious "want," preferring to spend any excess income on their kids' education, family holidays, charity fundraising, or the violin/car/stud pig of their dreams.

There are two further aspects to my personal definition of a "want." Most wants bring us incremental pleasure in excess of our core need satisfactions, but we still maintain the ability to *recognize* them as wants, and (if pressed) could take them or leave them without undermining our overall level of happiness. For example, in common with most women I have many more shoes than I need, and I still get a thrill out of each new purchase. But this doesn't mean that I'd lose sleep (not much, anyway!) if a tightening budget made me rein in my shoe habit; my want is pleasurable and harmless, and I haven't confused it with a need.

The trouble begins when wants are mistakenly pursued as core needs. Some people imagine that money will bring happiness but find themselves increasingly dissatisfied and miserable after attaining the income they had worked for. In such a case, either wealth was never the real need in the first place, or else they exceeded their need requirements, in the process creating a deficit in another area. This type of want can be extremely dangerous, undermining the alignment of what truly motivates (and satisfies) us in our lives.

Unlike needs, which come to us intuitively, wants are things that we typically absorb from our environment, our experience, or our relationships. (At times we may slave away to accomplish something that—if we're completely honest—was never our personal aspiration at all, just to please someone else or support another person's ambitions.) In short, our *wants* lack the inner motivation associated with our *needs*. As a result, the desire to satisfy them is almost always less powerful, and the results less satisfying and meaningful.

Let me give you an example. When I was young I joined the swim team and was driven to excel at it (that "Driver" instinct again!). When I finally achieved my goal of state champion, I was thrilled beyond expectation; realizing my goal brought me true satisfaction. Meanwhile, my younger sister decided that she would get a similar kick from swimming, and joined a team. But for her, early mornings in (icy!) cold water were anything but appealing, and even winning her own awards failed to bring her the same gratification I had found. In other words, the blue ribbon was a need for me; it was merely a want for my sister—nice to have, but something she could take or leave.

Unlike needs, which come to us intuitively, wants are things that we typically absorb from our environment, our experiences, or our relationships. They may even be something we pursue to meet the needs of another person. Since wants lack the fiery fuel of motivation associated with needs, our desire to achieve them is less powerful, and our satisfaction from the result is less meaningful.

VALUES

The last thing we have to consider is what we really believe in: our values. Something only qualifies as a value if we are sincerely dissatisfied without it and seriously willing to sacrifice to attain it. One example: We all want a clean environment, but it's only of real value to me if I'm doing my part to make it happen, choosing to support this cause over my own comfort and convenience. Similarly, many of us claim to value our families, and (by implication) the time we spend with them—but then we travel a lot, work late nights, and socialize excessively with clients. The bottom line: Our actions reveal our true values.

When our values become critical to our inner satisfaction, they become part of our core needs, and take on a similar power and energy.

■   ■   ■

All these things—needs (core and higher needs), wants, and values—drive our actions and comprise what I call our "motivators." When our goals are in proper alignment with our motivators, we are energized, and reaching our goals brings us tremendous satisfaction.

MOTIVATORS
inspire us to act

WANTS (not intuitive, but learned)

- Desires in excess of our needs (e.g., taught to us by society or pressured upon us)
- Desires inconsistent with our true needs
- Other people's needs/wants that we feel compelled to meet

LEAST PRIORITY

Although these can be beneficial, we don't usually realize inner satisfaction or sustainable happiness from achieving them

HIGHER NEEDS

- Self-actualization; filling unique potential; becoming greater self
- Values we are working toward

SECOND PRIORITY

Working toward these is necessary both for our growth and our ultimate happiness

(To some degree we can work toward first-priority and second-priority motivators simultaneously)

Passionate Motivation (Energy)

CORE NEEDS

- Our unique definition of Maslow's core needs —physiology, safety, love, and esteem
- Self-actualization needs that are essential to happiness
- Values critical to inner satisfaction

FIRST PRIORITY

Acting on and fulfilling these purposes brings satisfaction critical to our present happiness

So, what are your needs? Are you allowing them to propel you in the right direction, or have you permitted them to slip to the back of your mind? It's incredibly easy to get caught up in a law career, with its everyday demands, competitive environment, and prestigious trappings, without stopping to think about whether our day-to-day activities are actually in line with our true needs. *We set goals and achieve things that are outwardly impressive yet, for many, are not satisfying. This is because we haven't aligned our goals with our personal motivators.*

Take the case of Tim, an outgoing guy who gets his energy from being with people, having fun, exploring new places, and playing sports. (You guessed it—a Connecter!) Tim was lucky: He obtained an in-house role that enabled him to travel with project teams, work with sales and marketing, and pitch deals to prospective clients, in addition to conventional lawyering tasks. When on the road his days wrapped up reasonably early, leaving the evenings free for socializing. Since the company didn't have a "punch the clock" mentality, Tim could arrange his schedule to accommodate his love of sports and a lively social life. Yet rather than appreciate the benefits of his position, Tim focused on the fact that his counterparts in private practice were advancing far beyond him in salary. So when the opportunity to join a firm came along, Tim took it without really considering how he would fit in.

The change proved almost unbearable: long, rigidly imposed hours, a heavy workload, and increased billing pressures, not to mention being cooped up in an office all day with people who generally failed to share his lighthearted view of life. One morning he just couldn't face it and decided to work from home, only to have a partner call up and order him to come into the office. Tim felt belittled, degraded, and caged. The days of flexible working were long gone, and his rewarding social life felt like history. However, Tim pushed through the transition and, surprisingly, has stuck it out in private practice. In fact, he's now a partner in his firm. On the plus side, and consistent with Tim's original motivator (money), his income is surely far beyond what it would have been had he remained in his previous position. Tim has used his salary to buy an expensive home and a top-of-the-line Porsche, and he's invested in all the other trappings his current salary offers. However, I suspect that this is just to cover up the fact that he still feels dissatisfied with his job and longs for a more social and relaxed working environment. Tim admits that he still thinks of his in-house days as the best of his career, and every time we get together, Tim talks of finding his dream job again—which, oddly, resembles the one he used to have...

Conversely, consider Darren, a highly respected lawyer in his field. Having signed with one of the top New York law firms, he was reckoned certain to make partner, with an extremely bright career ahead of him. However, one day Darren took a step back to think about whether making partner was going to fulfill his real priority—which, after careful analysis, turned out to be quality time with his family. (No, *not* the "quality family time" used by failed politicians as an excuse for early resignation—the real thing!) As part of his evaluation, he realized that the time required by his firm was inconsistent with his true priority, so he chose to leave and strike out on his own. While his decision has meant far less financial reward, the benefit of having more control over his time has proved a powerful motivator, and Darren is flourishing because he is nourished on a daily basis by the things that bring him the most personal satisfaction. Although he recognizes that his choice was very unconventional—to some people, even crazy—the days when he's able to walk his kids to school validate his decision.

Unlike Darren, Tim never stopped to consider what really drives him. His ideal day would probably involve working in the morning, playing golf with his mates, and hanging out afterwards over a few beers. Ironically, his in-house role gave him plenty of time to do this, but each career decision since that time has moved him further away from his favorite things. Tim may have lots of money and executive toys (clear "wants," in his case), but those things don't satisfy him.

Obviously, there's no gratification in meeting a goal if we're not achieving our innate potential or, worse still, not meeting our needs. When our goals are out of alignment with our personal drives, the joy of victory will be less sweet, no matter how successful we may be. Just as an architect must know the parameters of the building he hopes to design, we must know the parameters of the course we're pursuing. If we don't ensure that our course is the right one, we might end up "achieving" the wrong thing.

Take Colin, a man I've long admired. Colin was a bio-tech lawyer who developed a strong idea (in conjunction with one of his clients) and became passionate about building his own company. When he finally realized his dream, Colin surrounded himself with a team of great and trustworthy people and worked hard to build his business. In the process, he fulfilled most of his core needs—challenge, passion, people, and teamwork. Colin's company was his "baby," and the people in it were like his family, so with its growth, Colin flourished. Ultimately the company became prosperous, and Colin was rewarded with the final things that had always motivated him—success and recognition. For many years Colin continued to run his company, and I've never met anyone more obviously fulfilled.

However, the day came when Colin was made an offer he could not refuse (lots and lots of money!), and he sold his company. Unfortunately, he did this without really thinking through his real values and needs, and he quickly found himself very rich but completely unsatisfied. Since then Colin has involved himself in various business ventures, each of which has been "a dismal failure" (his own words). Only recently has he recognized the reason: He's pursued these schemes only to leverage his money, which is a poor motivator compared to his real convictions and passions. Colin needs a new goal where he can create something that meets his core needs, and then he'll again succeed and feel enriched.

Okay, let's admit it: We'd all like to have Colin's problem (too much money!). But that's not the point of the story. Colin achieved a goal that many business owners happily pursue (selling a company for lots of cash), but in his case it was the wrong goal.

We all need to assess our objectives and think long and hard about whether or not they're really the right ones. And don't forget that the principles that motivate us can change: Events in our personal lives, for example, can totally reconfigure our priorities (having a baby can do this—fast!). Similarly, factors beyond our control can affect our financial needs, and, in turn, our professional lives. However, core needs are likely to remain consistent, and the only real difference will be in how we elect to fulfill those needs. For example, I met my need of goal attainment through my legal career, but deciding to stop practicing certainly didn't mean that this core need was no longer relevant to me; I just had to find a different way to satisfy it.

WHAT ARE *YOUR* MOTIVATORS?

When you ask yourself this question ("What are my motivators?"), be totally honest, remembering that there is no right or wrong answer. Don't identify the things you wish were important to you or the things that should motivate you; focus on the things that actually do!! Appendix 5.A provides examples of what I mean by motivators. Many could be categorized as a benefit, and some as a trait or a behavior, while others are more of an activity. Regardless, they all derive from an underlying need, want, or value.

Identifying motivators is no easy task because most of us don't know ourselves as well as we think we do. If we honestly examine our motivators and the things that bring us satisfaction, we might well discover unexpected traits. If you struggle with the exercise, use the following questions to guide you:

■ How are Maslow's needs defined for me?

- ■ Physiological needs: home environment, sleep, and health

- ■ Safety: security (for myself and for my family), home, quality of life, and employment

- ■ Love: relationships, friendships, romance, family, and sense of belonging

- ■ Esteem: self-esteem, confidence, respect, and admiration from others

- ■ Self-actualization: growth and fulfillment

■ How are these defined for me in terms of work?

- ■ Physiological needs: working conditions and environment

- ■ Safety: pay, job security, and the acquisition of skills (those that help to develop my career); certainty of advancement and/or career path

- ■ Love: friendships, sense of belonging, feeling of being part of a team; satisfying work/client relationships

- ■ Esteem: my own self-respect in doing what I do well; praise and recognition from people I respect; advancement and financial recognition for achieving something outstanding or unusual

- ■ Self-actualization: Am I growing and fulfilling my greatest potential at work? How can I do better?

■ What do I enjoy doing the most?

■ When was the last time I felt elated or excited by something? What was the source of that enthusiasm?

■ What is most resolutely core to my personality, without which I'd feel dissatisfied?

■ What engages me to the point that I divert all my resources and attention toward it? When am I energized and fueled by real fire?

■ What are my greatest strengths and how do they work?

Dig deep and spend time considering these questions. Then try the exercise below.

EXERCISE

Step 1

Using the table in Appendix 5.B, write down your motivators. There is no "right" number, but between five and ten is most workable, and at least some of them should be attainable through work. The more specific you can be, the better. For example:

■ If your motivator is money, give your reasons. What do you want it for? Why does it drive you? Be honest!! If you get the hots only when a Maserati whizzes by, say so!

- Don't just write down "family"—specify what is involved. Luscious holidays with your wife, or the kids' private education? Perhaps you enjoy particular activities with your partner or kids, or maybe your first concern is raising moral, intelligent, and well-rounded children in a stable home environment.

- If you're motivated by being the best—why? Is it self-respect? A need for the admiration of others? Subliminal parental pressure?

- If you list a hobby or activity, understand your motivation. If you love playing rugby, is it because of the camaraderie (sense of belonging), or is it the long evenings socializing after the match? Is it a love of challenge and competition, the satisfaction you get from using a natural talent, or a need for admiration?

To assist with this exercise I've given a real-life example in Appendix 5.C of a fifth-year associate.

Step 2

Determine whether each of your motivators is a need, a want, or a value. Then determine which ones qualify as a core need—that is, as something that is essential to your happiness.

Step 3

Consider whether you're meeting your needs and living your values in the right order, with the priority being *core needs first—and wants last!!!* The reality is that we are all driven by wants, and society pushes us remorselessly along this path. This becomes a problem, however, when we prioritize our wants above our needs, without recognition of the consequences (or the potential cost). Concentrating on our wants means that we are risking not only our present situation but also our future.

Thinking about your own situation, answer these questions:

- Do my daily activities meet my core needs?

- Do my work/time commitments dovetail with my core needs?

- Do the resources I expend, such as money or energy, go (to some degree) toward meeting my core needs?

If at this point you find yourself feeling a bit anxious, you're not alone. This exercise makes most of us identify some sort of divide between our core needs and our current commitments. If this is the case for you, ask yourself, *Am I sacrificing my core needs for a bigger goal (or higher need)? If so, is that acceptable over the long term?*

Let me give you two examples.

First, there were periods in my career when my core needs for leisure activities and relationships outside of work were clearly not being met, due to long office hours and significant amounts of travel. I acknowledged the situation but thought it acceptable for the short term because other important core needs were being satisfied—my passion for my work in general, for being challenged, and for camaraderie with colleagues and clients—and because the sacrifice *was* necessary to achieve my greater goal of partnership. However, had such sacrifices been expected of me indefinitely, I would have found myself increasingly dissatisfied. A second example would be the friend in the previous chapter who recently left his city job to live in the country and work on his garden—for him, the ultimate state of self-actualization! For many years he suffered in the hectic business world (where he was denied many of his core needs) so that he could eventually afford his higher goal and experience the satisfaction he now enjoys.

The second question to ask when we discover a gap between our needs and our focus is, *Am I sacrificing my core needs (at a long-term cost) because I am in pursuit of a "want" that will not bring me inner satisfaction?* If your answer to this—be honest!!—is "Yes," then you might need to make some changes.

In general, when denying our core needs, we must monitor the situation to make sure that our focus is not misguided and that we maintain a workable balance. Note that this is the *only* context in which I encourage you to create balance in your career—and I use the term in a very specific way. I think the phrase "finding balance" in regard to one's career—any career—has been overused to the point where it has lost all meaning. When I talk of balance, I mean that our energies (time, money, resources) should be expended in the right proportion toward meeting our core needs. If 80 percent of my core needs (say) are satisfied through my achievements at work, then spending 80 percent of my time focused on my career is the right balance for me. My mother may (and doubtless *will*) think my ambitions wildly out of control, but if that is where my fulfillments lie it's the right balance *for me*. For me, and for most people, passions derive from core needs, and I contend that passions need no balance.

Remember that in Chapter 2 ("The Juggling Act"), in relation to achieving our ultimate goals, we examined the necessity of prioritizing the important over the immediate (the tasks in front of us)—that is, putting first things first. When our daily activities are aligned with our motivators, we feel nourished and energized. With regard to our careers, each of us needs to regularly ask ourselves, "What is my goal?"—examining our *own* motivations, not those of a spouse, partner, or parent. What do we want to achieve for ourselves? After that, ask two things:

> ■ *Is what I am doing now completely consistent with that objective, and is it nourishing my core needs today?* We will never succeed if we leave our core needs behind as we enter work each day. Our goal is to align the daily activities of our career with those core needs. While attaining this objective is not always easy, striving toward that balance brings immense reward: (a) Rather than merely doing our jobs we look for stimulation, challenge, and enjoyment at work, and (b) our day-to-day responsibilities provide satisfaction, making us happier, more positive people. This is the source of our ability to convey optimism in our brand and our leadership: They are essential to our success and *cannot* be faked!
>
> ■ *Is my career goal consistent with my future needs and ultimate satisfaction?* This is the key to sustainable success. Success is usually the by-product of passionate commitment, and we gain a sense of freedom when our drive is not just about status, titles, or income.

These questions are tough, and the process is very personal, but it's critical to resolve any discrepancy you find, whether that means downsizing, upscaling, moving into a different area of specialty, or setting up on your own—whatever it takes.

To reach your goals, and to be happy when you get there, requires integrity toward what matters most—whatever that means to you as an individual. In later chapters we will look at developing your personal vision. The information gained by working through this chapter will support that process.

APPENDIX 5.A

LIST OF MOTIVATORS

PERSONAL NEEDS (CORE TO YOUR PERSONALITY)		CAREER-RELATED NEEDS
Adventure (new challenges; thrills)	Independence and autonomy (the ability to make one's own decisions)	Advancement (promotions, partnership)
Ambition	Integrity (honesty, sincerity, standing up for yourself)	Competence
Being a role model	Loyalty	Dedication, commitment, hard work
Being clever	Optimism	High service, responsiveness
Being the best	Order, stability	Support from superiors and working environment
Candor, openness	Originality	
Challenges (having goals and a purpose)	Passion	
Compassion, fairness	Persistence	
Control	Personal development	
Creativity, innovation	Pleasure (fun and enjoyment)	
Excellence	Recognition (status; acknowledgment from others)	
Freedom (the right to manage one's schedule and personal time)	Responsibility, accountability	
Friendliness	Self-respect (pride, personal identity)	
Generosity	Teaching	
Helpfulness	Wisdom, learning (discovering and understanding knowledge)	
Humor		

SOCIAL NEEDS	LEISURE NEEDS	COMMUNITY INVOLVEMENT NEEDS	OTHER NEEDS
Affection, love	Arts	Community service	Beautiful things
Being around people (talking, sharing ideas, etc.)	Cultural activities	Philanthropy	Culture or race (strong racial or ethnic orientation)
Collaboration, teamwork	Entertainment	Stewardship (charitable causes; improving society)	Diversity, equality
Family	Hobbies		Environmentalism
Involvement (belonging to a group, becoming involved with people)	Home		Fitness
Relationships (close bonds with others; friendships)	Leisurely lifestyle		Gender (strong identity to gender)
	Playing sports		Health
	Shopping		Inner harmony (being at peace with oneself)
	Personal time with .... ?		Money (economic security, getting rich, or just having "stuff")
	Personal time to do .... ?		Politics
	Watching sports		Religion
			Sexual orientation (strong identity in sexual orientation)
			Spirituality
			World issues, peace

APPENDIX 5.B

EXERCISE

	MY MOTIVATORS	TYPE	MET	IF YES, EXPLAIN. IF NO, ASK "WHY NOT?" IS THIS AT A COST TO ME? WHAT CAN/WILL CHANGE TO MEET THE NEED?
1				
2				
3				
4				
5				
6				
7				
8				
9				
10				

APPENDIX 5.C

REBECCA'S EXAMPLE

Rebecca is a fifth-year associate in the London office of a U.S. law firm. Her motivators generally relate to her work, but are also inseparable from her personal life.

	MY MOTIVATORS	TYPE	MET	IF YES, EXPLAIN. IF NO, ASK "WHY NOT?" IS THIS AT A COST TO ME? WHAT CAN/WILL CHANGE TO MEET THE NEED?
1	Challenge: facing new tests, learning different skills, and self-developing in the process; being placed in situations that take me outside of my comfort zone and give me the opportunity to grow.	Higher need; and YES = Core need	Yes	This is being met through the projects I'm getting at work—and by my boss's support in allowing me to take on greater responsibilities. I'm also beginning to stretch myself into some marketing and client-development activities. I'm starting to work with clients in a way very different from my normal lawyer- client relationships, and I feel a sense of accomplishment knowing that I am able to interact in a broader capacity.
2	Involvement with people; teamwork: being part of a group of people who are working toward a similar goal; sharing ideas and a common purpose.	Core need	Yes	This is also fulfilled through my work; I really enjoy the camaraderie of my team, and our partners help to make it feel that way. I've realized how important working with other people is to me because last year my biggest and longest assignment involved lots of research. It was a solo project; there were very few people I could even discuss it with! By the end of the project I found myself bored and frustrated.

	MY MOTIVATORS	TYPE	MET	IF YES, EXPLAIN. IF NO, ASK "WHY NOT?" IS THIS AT A COST TO ME? WHAT CAN/WILL CHANGE TO MEET THE NEED?
3	Writing music: time alone writing music, which brings me happiness and makes me feel calm again after a stressful day. It also lets me be creative in a different way from work.	Higher need; and YES = Core need	No	I haven't been committed to making this happen; instead I've found myself staying out late with colleagues. The only time I seem to write is after a late night out and when I'm not really focused or able to give my best. I can feel myself tensing up without the release of working on my music—work seems less satisfying and much more stressful without the balance and calmness music brings to me. I think I was treating music as something "nice to have" (i.e., a "want") when in fact this exercise has revealed to me that it's really a need, and a core need at that! I will consciously commit time toward my music by scheduling time alone for it, and not feel guilty about that.
4	Advancement: a sense of success and comfort that my commitment and hard work is rewarded, and that it will pay off in the end.	Core need	Yes, for now	I feel that I am advancing appropriately in my firm and with each step upwards I get a renewed sense of reward. However, as I get more senior I'm not convinced that my career path will remain so certain.
5	Friendships: quality time spent one-on-one with friends; having fun with groups of friends; doing activities together; maintaining and nurturing friendships.	Core need	Par-tially	I get along well with my colleagues, whom I consider friends; however, I have friends outside of work who share different and broader interests and I really haven't been maintaining those relationships as much as I did in the past. I miss their input in my life! I need to consciously commit time to see friends who are outside of law work.

	MY MOTIVATORS	TYPE	MET	IF YES, EXPLAIN. IF NO, ASK "WHY NOT?" IS THIS AT A COST TO ME? WHAT CAN/WILL CHANGE TO MEET THE NEED?
6	Health and fitness: being healthy and having time to work out is important.	Core need	Yes, but not optimal	Not as much time as I would like, but sufficient; some yoga and going for runs. However, just "fitting this in" will not be satisfactory forever!
7	Love, intimacy, personal relationships, family: intimacy is important to me, but I am not currently in a relationship; I'd like more time with family (parents, siblings, and nieces).	Core need; and a "want" —if I'm honest	No	This is a hard one. Do I lack a love interest because I commit no time to looking? Or because I haven't met the right person? (But how do I meet the right person if I have no time?!) Maybe spending more time with non-work friends and doing other things will broaden the kinds of people I meet and interact with. That said, if I'm honest, right now my career takes precedence—and that feels OK for now. I admit that I need to spend more time with my family—but (again, completely truthfully) at times that can actually be draining and anything but a need ... more of an obligation!
8	Money: I don't need a lot, but I want security (and a hedge against future surprises!); I recently bought a new flat, so I want to pay off the mortgage. Would like more money to decorate new flat (a want!).	Core need, but also a want	Yes	The money I earn satisfies my core needs and some wants; I still have many wants, but I can live with that! The fact that I go out a lot with friends and spend significant money on nice meals and drinks might suggest that I'm not "valuing" money—but that social time is more important to me at the moment than saving money or decorating my flat.

	MY MOTIVATORS	TYPE	MET	IF YES, EXPLAIN. IF NO, ASK "WHY NOT?" IS THIS AT A COST TO ME? WHAT CAN/WILL CHANGE TO MEET THE NEED?
9	Charitable work: I spent a summer traveling (which is the next motivator) and doing charity work—the best time of my life! It was enjoyable and provided significant gratification. I've since gotten involved in a few charitable activities, but it's very sporadic, and it's nothing that has generated long-term meaning.	Higher need; value of giving back	No	I haven't been sufficiently committed to seek out an avenue to fulfill this—primarily because work leaves me too little time. Maybe I could talk to my firm and look for a way to do this with their support, and involving other people from the office.
10	Adventure/travel: I enjoy traveling and adventure; I try to plan action-packed holidays (which goes back to number 1 above—challenge).	Core need; higher need and a bit of a "want"	No	My last big holiday had to be postponed due to work commitments. (Also, I'd just bought the flat so I was a bit relieved to save the money.) I really need to make some plans for weekends away (which are more manageable), rather than rely on a few big holidays to recharge my batteries. Perhaps I should think about organizing activities with friends and colleagues, or even clients. Maybe I could suggest a client event built around an adventure, like rock climbing?? Or I could combine that with a charitable event and get clients involved.

REBECCA'S CONCLUSION:

Overall, I feel satisfied with my job, as I'm stimulated by the people and the projects and feel very lucky to be part of a team that works so well together. I'm also learning new things and developing as a person and a lawyer. For the most part my motivators are fulfilled, and I see that continuing as I pursue my current course. Having said that, this exercise has really helped, because it's made me focus more on those things I've let slip and made me think creatively about what I can do to put them into the right alignment in my life.

Chapter Six

Awareness Building Block 3: People Skills

(Learning how to connect)

There are two unavoidable facts about being a lawyer in a private-practice firm: First, strong working relationships are critical to one's success, and second, they don't just happen—great relationships are built up step by step. They often take root in unexpected circumstances, but they always grow from the same foundation—*making an initial connection.*

The challenge is that we can only establish a connection by creating a positive and uplifting experience for the person in question (not necessarily ourselves!). If the initial opportunity is missed, we lose our first (and best) opportunity to connect, and sometimes that particular chance will be gone forever. So with *everyone,* follow one straightforward rule: Focus on the other person's experience, and make it positive for *him or her.* "No problem," you may be thinking, "I do that already. I've got good manners, and I'm pretty easy to like. I'm not an insensitive clod like A, or a boorish geek like B."

You may be right. But first answer "Yes" or "No" to the following statements:

> ■ This morning, as I paid for my coffee, I smiled at/thanked/and even made a remark to the (Starbucks) barista: YES (or NO, I blindly handed over my change. In fact, to be honest, I couldn't even tell you who served me my coffee this morning).

> ■ Today, as I traveled to work, I noticed the people around me, and even acknowledged someone by a nod, a smile, or even a word or two: YES (or NO, I was frankly too occupied with my own thoughts).

■ When I met my colleague most recently, I asked about something of particular value or concern to him or her: YES (or NO, actually, I preferred to tell my colleague about something that had happened to *me*).

■ In my last meeting with a potential or existing client, I thought beforehand about his (or her) personal issues and perspective, and asked at least a few questions about those issues: YES (or NO, I showed how experienced and knowledgeable *I* am—I'm sure I was pretty impressive!).

■ When I meet people for the first time, I usually like to figure them out and ask them all sorts of questions: YES (or NO, the last person I met was really quite boring/shy/difficult, and I found that I had to do most of the talking myself).

■ I tend to learn a lot of information about my clients: YES (or NO, I believe in sticking to business issues with my clients).

■ I showed appreciation to at least one person yesterday: YES (or NO, in fact, I probably criticize people much more than I compliment them. I don't like to criticize, but most of the people around me tend to make a lot of mistakes).

■ The last time I made a mistake, I admitted it and apologized: YES (or NO, I became quite defensive, even though I don't often make mistakes).

■ When I want to impress someone, I first make it clear that I respect his abilities: YES (or NO, I prefer to tell him things about myself).

Now if you answered "Yes" to all, or even most, of these statements, I commend you as one of the rare lawyers who naturally and instinctively understand the foundation of relationship-building, and I admit that you don't need this chapter to the same extent as the rest of us. On the other hand, if you didn't quite match that standard, you might just discover from this chapter the single most critical factor you need to take you forward. By the end of this chapter, you should be ready to create a positive and uplifting experience for anyone around you—which is the beginning of surrounding yourself with the strong business relationships on which your career will depend. And even if parts of this chapter may at first strike you as merely common sense, I urge you to read on. Common sense itself, ironically, can be quite...uncommon.

*By the end of this chapter, you should be ready to create a positive and uplifting experience for anyone around you— which is the first and critical step to **making connections** and surrounding yourself with the strong business relationships on which your career will depend.*

■   ■   ■

The biggest single factor in a successful career in law is how we deal with people. This ability (or lack of it) pervades every aspect of our practice, from dealing with clients to interacting with secretaries. In today's law firm environment, the likeability quotient can be more important than one's intellect and carefully chosen specialties *combined*, which makes it all the more surprising that so few lawyers choose to develop people skills. But I promise that if you DO master them, people skills will take you very far. In fact, all three goals of this book—brand, business, and leadership—are dependent on such mastery.

The biggest single factor in our success as lawyers is how we deal with people. All three goals of this book—brand, business, and leadership—are dependent on mastery of people skills.

THE RULES OF HUMAN NATURE

There are two main rules of human nature that concern us here.

First, *people want to feel important*, and this provides the primary motivation for many of their actions. Remember from the previous chapter that under Maslow's theory of hierarchical motivation one can only reach the highest and most satisfying level of true self-actualization by first recognizing one's own importance. And, as discussed, the things that make each of us feel important are dependent upon core needs and values—on the things that matter to each of us individually. Does this not apply to you?

Second, *people want appreciation* for how they look, what they do, and how they perform. Most of us actually crave appreciation to satisfy the core need of self-esteem (of which Mark Twain famously wrote, "It may be called the master-passion: the hunger for self-approval"). But ironically, while wanting appreciation ourselves, many of us still routinely fail to give it to others. Instead of accentuating people's positive qualities we often focus on their weaknesses and mistakes, sometimes even bringing gaffes to the attention of friends, family, and colleagues. (The little aside you "didn't think" your Perfectionist colleague heard, the joke that the Driver was supposed to "get" but didn't, will sting long after you have forgotten them.)

This is short-sighted. Overt appreciation is the easiest way to earn colleagues' admiration and support. Parents, teachers, and work colleagues routinely fall afoul of this principle by criticizing rather than expressing appreciation. One of the most famous teachers I know calls the best method "a sandwich of advice surrounded by the bread of compliment." Criticism almost never motivates, but appreciation arouses both enthusiasm and a desire to do still better. I've never met anyone (no lawyer, at least) who didn't try harder or work with more gusto if highly rated.

When we satisfy people's desire for importance and appreciation we fulfill a core need in them, and we then receive some measure of goodwill in return. This is as true of a grumpy taxi driver as of your boss's unforthcoming spouse. It may sound ridiculous, or ridiculously simple, but it is virtually foolproof.

So, how do we go about it?

Be Interested, Not Interesting

When you first meet someone, do you try to convince him how clever, funny, or cultured you are? Do you find yourself worrying that you won't have anything worthwhile to say, or (still worse) that what you do say will sound stupid? Well, fear no more. I'm going to give you a new and better approach: *Be interested—not interesting!!*

By this I mean that you should listen, ask questions, solicit information, and involve yourself in the feelings of the person you're addressing. This is the easiest way to make a good impression. Even if you happen to be one of those rare and lucky people with a knack for entertaining anecdotes, the tragic reality is that other people are inevitably more interested in themselves than in anyone else. (In fact, many lawyers consider a moment not thinking about themselves as a moment lost.)

For example, you've almost certainly at some point had a friend who's been dumped by a boss, spouse, or partner. You acted very sympathetic and supportive, but you certainly didn't see it as the end of the world. Your friend might suffer a bit—always a shame—but you felt sure, secretly, that he (or she) would eventually find a new job or a better relationship. In short, at least a part of you didn't really understand why he (or she) was wasting quite so much time and energy feeling sorry for him- or herself. S*** happens. Life is like that. People get fired; relationships can end.

Now, compare this to how you feel when the same thing happens to you! Suddenly you're the only person in the world who has ever had to face such unfairness, opposition, and ingratitude. No one understands your unique circumstances, and the universe has crumbled on top of you.

Let's face it—people are most interested in what's personal to them, and would far rather talk about their recent virus or house purchase than global warming or poverty in Africa (most people, anyway!). By the same token, other people don't really want to hear us drivel on about something that doesn't affect them at all.

In addition, interactions become more enjoyable and much less difficult when we take a genuine interest in others. We no longer have to worry about where a conversation is taking us, and those uneasy pauses disappear like magic. When we take a sincere interest in someone else we are (subconsciously) telling him, "You interest me. Tell me *your* story." The truth is, most of us are desperate for someone to listen—really listen—with bona fide eye contact and without bullish interruptions. (Try this simple, and quite discouraging, test: the next time you're talking with someone, check out whether the other person is truly listening to you or whether he is just waiting for a suitable place to insert a personal opinion, joke, or story.)

When we become the sincere and intelligent listener, we become a rare and valued person—and without the nervous strain of perfecting our comic timing, or figuring out how far our witticisms can dare to go!

Many years ago I was starting a project with a new client. The person who had hired me was not directly involved, and I'd never even met the project manager, Steven. In fact, Steven had openly opposed me as the project's lawyer, instead pushing hard for a firm he'd worked with before. In the end, he reluctantly OK'd my involvement, subject to meeting me before the project kick-off and (in his words) determining that I was "sufficiently qualified." I was under real pressure to impress him, or risk losing the work—and a beneficial contact.

Steven and I met in his office, and from the very beginning his brusque attitude suggested that, whomever he was going to ask on his next long walking holiday, it wasn't going to be me. I was beginning to wonder how on earth I could convince this human glacier to employ me when I noticed a picture, behind the desk, of Steven scuba diving. Before launching into my credentials showcase, I decided to ask him where the photo had been taken. (As a fellow diver I did feel some genuine interest in the question, but I wanted to focus on something of interest to Steven.) That single question opened the door for him to tell me about his scuba diving—and tell me he did! There were moments when I longed to interject—an avid diver myself, I was bursting to share my personal adventures—but I was careful to keep the conversation on Steven's experiences, knowing that my job-of-the-day was to listen.

In the end, Steven gave me much more time than he had grudgingly promised, even if most of it was spent discussing his scuba-diving passion. Somehow I never got around to my (perfectly planned, exquisitely calibrated) sales pitch, but by the time I left Steven's office he was certain that I was more than qualified for the job. That meeting set the tone for both our ongoing working relationship and our friendship, and to this day Steven often mentions how much I impressed him at our first encounter. (It's fascinating to note that when I recount what really happened, he refuses to believe me, having convinced himself that I captivated him with my résumé.)

Even as I tease Steven about his rationale for choosing me as his lawyer, I must admit that I've fallen into the same trap. At one point I had all but accepted a new position, except for having one last partner to meet (Margaret). I had made my acceptance of the new job contingent upon my liking her personally, so I went to our meeting armed with a list of questions, ready to conduct *my* interview.

Two hours later, I couldn't believe where the time had gone! At that point, Margaret looked over at me and quipped, "Is that enough? Will I do?" and I could only laugh. I left our meeting certain that Margaret had passed my stringent test, only to realize later that I'd failed to ask her a single question! In fact, I'd spent the whole time talking, while Margaret had listened intently, asking *me* leading questions. No wonder I'd had such a good time! She'd appeared really interested in that most amazing creature: *me!* Margaret turned out to be an exceptional boss, a consistently good listener, and—ultimately—a very good friend.

In fact, when my husband-to-be and I were working out the arrangements for our wedding, we were stumped over seating the only guest who had nothing in common with the rest of the party. Whom could we put next to her? Simultaneously, we decided on Margaret. She can chat to anyone, on any occasion, because she naturally focuses on others. After the wedding our friend mentioned how much she'd enjoyed sitting next to Margaret and what a lovely and entertaining person she was. When we thanked Margaret, she too said what a pleasure it had been, and began telling us all sorts of things about our friend that we'd never known—because, of course, Margaret had inquired about her and listened to her story. (It later transpired that Margaret had *said* almost nothing...ironic, considering that our friend had referred to her as "entertaining"!!)

In our profession, people love to talk. So if you want to be hugely popular with almost everyone you meet, cultivate the art of listening, asking questions, and soliciting information. Then sit back and watch how esteemed you become.

> *Be interested—not (yes, I said not!) interesting. Listen, ask questions, solicit information, and involve yourself in the feelings of the other person. This is the easiest way to make a good impression.*

Search for Commonality

If you feel someone likes you, don't you automatically warm to him at least a little? And if you're convinced that someone dislikes you, isn't it commensurately difficult to acknowledge her strong points? Likewise, the people you meet actually want you to like *them*—and if you seem to, it's much more likely that you'll be liked in return. And there's

no better way to convince someone that you like him or her than to reveal something in common.

Mutual interests create friendship. Have you ever learned, in the course of a casual conversation, that you and your contact came from the same city, or attended the same university? Didn't you feel that a bond was instantly created? There's no doubt in my mind that Steven's first impression of me was much enhanced by the fact that we shared a passion for scuba diving. It's our job to ferret out these common interests, and they don't have to be incredibly meaningful; even the simplest thing can create commonality.

> **He/She:** "This buffet is delicious. I'm vegetarian, and I've noticed that they normally serve loads of meat hors d'oeuvres at these events."
>
> **You:** "You're so right. I don't eat much meat myself, and I really appreciate it when they remember we're not all red in tooth and claw!"

If you look for the thread of common interest—something that can propel the conversation forwards, and potentially form an important connection—you can usually find it.

Respect and Admire Differences

When searching for that common ground, we inevitably come across differences. Highlighting them is always the wrong approach, and creating opposition out of differences is completely useless. Here's a conversation cut off at its very roots:

> **She:** "I'm going on a skiing holiday next week."
>
> **You:** "I can't stand skiing. I broke my leg my first time in Switzerland and I've loathed it ever since."

The above response might well be truthful, but what it communicates to the other person is that you have nothing (zero, zilch) in common; even her opinion is somehow devalued. Also (well done!), you have managed to kill further conversation stone dead. Where can it go from here, except to showcase obviously opposite viewpoints?

Instead, you might come back with something like, "Oh, lucky you. I was never any good at skiing because I have all the coordination of a brain-damaged warthog." This response is still accurate—you can't ski—but by being admiring and open-minded, you've revealed that difference in a way that potentially boosts your acquaintance's self-esteem. And although it doesn't create the common ground you are looking for (you still disagree about skiing), chances are that the other person won't notice, and will probably enthusiastically tell you about something that, in comparison to you, she is knowledgeable about (skiing). You have turned her, effortlessly, into an expert—and, better still, you have made her feel important.

Stand in Their Shoes

People want to be understood. When a situation comes up with your colleagues, respect their perspective and attempt to empathize with their situation. As someone who is not a parent but who over the years has managed many associates who are, I've had many conversations in this vein:

> **He:** "I'm so sorry I'm late, but my four-year-old woke with a temperature and I had to find a sitter."
>
> **Me:** "I really appreciate your making the effort. It must be really difficult when these things happen."

Obviously, understanding the father's perspective achieved far more in terms of his cooperation, and because I was empathetic I probably gained his respect. The outcome could have been very different if I'd lashed out, "There are no good excuses for being late!" or even, "Fine, but you really need to work out a system which doesn't penalize the rest of us when your child gets ill, as children do." When we "stand in the shoes" of others, they are always grateful.

Further, bear in mind that for all of us the key question (alas) tends to be, "What's in it for me?" Generally speaking, if there isn't any benefit, we probably won't do it. Even the most altruistic action has a benefit. When people donate money to charity, for example, they're subconsciously looking for a reward—even if it's only the warm, fuzzy feeling of knowing they've done something good for someone less fortunate. If they were under some pressure to donate, and they decide to unbelt, they've still effectively chosen to alleviate the pressure rather than keep their money. In short, the question for most people is whether the benefit of action is enough (in relation to the comfort of inaction) to make it worthwhile.

Many law-firm marketing schemes, client-development activities, and associate-motivation programs fall foul of this basic principle because they don't stop to think about others' points of view. Normally, we lawyers are too focused on what we want others to do: buy our services, give us more work, produce more billable hours, and so on. So if we want someone to do something for us, we need to align that action with a definite benefit—and to know what that benefit is, it's necessary to understand the other person's perspective.

Humility Begets Admiration

Still worse than disagreeing with someone is playing the one-upmanship game. People who do this are the biggest turn-offs in law (or any) circles. You know the type:

"So how did your firm do last year?—Of course, those smallish firms are always in danger of getting crushed in the cross-fire... Good Lord. Do you mean to say that it's not included in your benefits package? I thought everybody got Holmes Place membership these days... Of course, they'd really like him to retire, but they don't want the aggro. Instead they keep on paying the rest of us more and keeping him on the same rung of the good old ladder..."

Ugh! These people think they're impressive, but in fact they leave the vast majority of us feeling angry and resentful.

A conversation with this kind of person normally goes something like this:

You:	"Sorry, I can't; I'm just off on a skiing holiday tomorrow."
He:	"Oh, I just got back from mine. I was taking on the same black runs as [insert name of current world-class skier] and [insert name of Olympic athlete]. In point of fact, I was told some years ago that I could have been a professional skier myself, but instead I decided to focus on other talents... After all, those black runs—one mistake and you're history!"

Some of these people actually believe everything they tell us, but just as often they're only trying to convince themselves. Boasting only emerges out of insecurity, and braggarts generally have to advertise their accomplishments to drown out the undercurrent of worry beneath. But many people do eventually figure out the emptiness behind the mask.

I have a friend who is the resident expert, no matter what the situation or the subject matter. Music. History. Art. Literature. Economics. Almost anything! In fact, the first time we met I was extremely impressed. She struck me as highly intelligent, extremely well-educated, and hugely confident. I began to wonder what I'd been doing with my own life, as she rattled off all her achievements. But gradually I've come to realize that my friend has a problem. Rather than assume that people might like her for herself, she is driven first to boast of her accomplishments and knowledge, even exaggerating in the process. Her tactic is self-defeating, as people like me tend to walk away feeling less-than-wonderful about themselves, or (after a while) just plain irritated. It's unfortunate, because underneath (like most of us!), she just wants to be accepted.

When we try too hard to make an impression, it works against us because we make ourselves, rather than the other person, feel important.

When I turned my potential nemesis, Steven, into a friend by engaging him in a discussion about scuba diving, I was very careful to mention just my interest in the sport, not my own diving qualifications. I was actually a much more advanced diver than Steven, at that point, and could have tried to impress him with stories of my shark encounters and perilous wreckage dives. I chose not to, electing to approach our conversation as if I was the comparative novice. This made Steven feel important, and positive toward me.

It's Okay to be Wrong

I have always been argumentative—especially when I was young. Whatever the topic of discussion, I had to be right—and if I couldn't convince my opponent instantly, I'd go to great lengths to prove it, gathering evidence and pursuing the issue until the other side either admitted his comparative ignorance or died of boredom. It's only as an adult that I've recognized the intrinsic idiocy of this approach and accepted that many arguments simply can't be won. This is a more complicated notion than it may seem at first blush. If you lose the argument, then (obviously) you've lost; yet if you win, you may still have lost something important. The gratification you may feel in being right might well be tempered by the realization that, in being "right," you've managed to make the other person "wrong."

How does that make him feel? Not good. And by making the other person feel bad you certainly haven't endeared yourself to him. In winning an argument, you may have lost an incredible friend, connection, or client.

As lawyers it's sometimes worth being labeled wrong just to avoid an argument. I was once at a celebratory dinner with some clients and two of my partners, following the closure of a successful deal (I was an associate at the time). The World Cup final had only just ended, so the conversation inevitably turned to soccer. Now, as an American, I enjoy an almost limitless lack of interest in this subject, but I still remember the sequence of events. One client was discussing a particular play, when one of my partners butted in: "No, no! That wasn't X, but Y!" (I charitably assume that he did this to look knowledgeable.) However, rather than settle the issue, he initiated a stormy debate with the client. They finally submitted the dispute to the judgment of my other partner, Lucas, also a soccer enthusiast. Lucas wasn't sure, but he indicated that he thought that the client's version sounded right, and then he quickly changed the subject.

On the way home in a taxi, the other partner turned to Lucas and said, "You knew I was right! Why didn't you support me? You made me look stupid in there." Lucas responded by saying that making a partner look stupid was not his intention but that it was still a rather better result than making a very important client look wrong. He went on to point out that the client had only been telling a harmless story, and that turning that story into an opportunity to make the client look bad was also pretty stupid. Listening to Lucas, I learned a crucial lesson: *Pick your battles intelligently*; don't let them result in a lost connection.

Remember, the objective is to make the other person feel important. If you contradict that person, you're proclaiming (in essence) that you're smarter than he is—especially if it's done in a "Just let me tell you, buddy," sort of way. If you must pursue the argument, do it much more subtly: "I'm probably up a creek without a paddle here, but I thought it might be Y. Maybe you could tell me a bit more about how you saw it." Oddly enough, there's power in being confident enough to admit that you just might be wrong!

Although as lawyers we are trained to argue and prove our points (thus demonstrating intelligence and worth), sometimes we gain more by saying nothing—or even by being labeled wrong.

Admitting That You Don't Know the Answer Instills Confidence

A lawyer's job is to give advice, so it is peculiarly distressing to us when we lack the answer. However, no one will think any the less of us if we honestly state we don't know something—in fact, people are more likely to respect us because they know where we stand, and they feel that they can trust us. There's no falseness, no pretense.

As a senior associate with a new firm, I once traveled from London to some of our U.S. offices. As part of that trip one of the senior partners in my group invited me along to a client meeting and negotiation. Now this particular partner was a legend in our industry, and I was honored to have the chance to see him in action. Extremely impressive and immensely knowledgeable, he commanded the room with every point. However, on more than one occasion he admitted his own ignorance, asking for elucidation both from the client and from the other side. This was a revelation to me. If even the leading expert in his field doesn't have all the answers (in his own particular subject!), why should the rest of us feel that we've somehow failed when we need more information?

When you don't know something, your best solution is to ask. This actually signals self-confidence, because ironically, only the truly self-assured are willing to admit their unfamiliarity or inexperience. Self-conscious types will instead try to hide behind a barrier of bravado and self-importance, and when that illusion breaks down it's obvious to everyone that they didn't really have the knowledge they pretended to have. If this happens to you, you really do look stupid—and (even worse) dishonest.

> As lawyers, we tend to take ourselves too seriously. People will like (and ultimately respect) the humble person who can laugh at himself and admit the occasional mistake. In the context of leadership, the most successful leaders are not the larger-than-life "know-it-alls" but the humble ones who never allow ego to undermine their goals—or other people's.

Criticism Creates Resentment

Sometimes criticism is meant constructively and we eventually (and correctly) interpret it as support, but these cases are rare. Mostly criticism is delivered without any tangible benefit, and only serves to make us feel defensive, ill-used, or angry. We then naturally project those negative emotions back toward the speaker. In the end, what most critics achieve is nothing but resentment.

Depending on personality type, different lawyers have very different ideas about what merits criticism. Perfectionists often think punctuality is paramount and may erupt in disappointment when other people are even a few minutes late. A Connecter may find tardiness acceptable but will expect everyone to contribute, and will often criticize anyone who appears to lack either ideas or enthusiasm. If your boss is a Driver, he may view all meetings as a monumental waste of time and could criticize you for not prioritizing client work instead. It all depends on what is perceived as important.

It would be naïve to suggest that we should never criticize—especially in a law-firm environment, where some guidance is necessary to ensure the development of each lawyer and the delivery of the best possible product. But it should be done in a constructive and beneficial manner. And just like arguing, which should be done sparingly (again, choose your battles!), make sure it is worth it before you criticize.

Everybody Wants a Compliment

Regardless of whom you're dealing with, you can rely on the simple fact that people crave appreciation. So as you focus outwards and attempt to take a genuine interest in others, don't withhold praise and positive comments. I don't mean sickening instances of insincere flattery ("I could not BELIEVE how brilliant you were... I felt as if I should have been taking NOTES in there! How could you just WORK them around to a completely different point of view?!"). What I mean is being willing to genuinely acknowledge people's good points.

You would be surprised how many lawyers overlook this statement of the obvious. Bob's a great sportsman. He knows it—he's got a cupboard full of golf trophies, hasn't he?—but he still likes to be told! Sue landed three of our best clients this year through zeal, sincere charm, and a touch of genius. She must realize that everybody thinks she's fantastic, right? But actually, she doesn't. She can only see the clients who got away. People can never be praised enough, especially with regard to the obvious. Recognize talents or achievements, and watch your colleagues' faces light up.

Try it for yourself—especially if you have a partner or children at home. For a full day, say nothing to them but positive and encouraging things. You might be amazed at the results! By the end of the day, most people who do this exercise can't believe the affection they've received in return. (If criticism is instinctive for you, be forewarned that doing the reverse will feel awkward at first. The rewards, however, are well worth the effort.)

Personalizing Makes People Feel Important

Giving a compliment or expressing thanks is always a good thing, but if the comment is personal and specific it will have much greater impact. Imagine receiving a holiday card from a friend you haven't spoken to in ages, only to discover that she's just exerted herself sufficiently to sign her name at the bottom. Of course, it's nice to have been remembered, but a personal message would have increased the pleasure beyond all calculation.

This is why names matter: Using people's names tells them they're important. My husband and I eat out most of the time, and when we find a restaurant we really enjoy, I've made a habit of thanking the maitre d' on the way out and praising the meal or the service. As part of that conversation, I typically ask for his name and make sure to use it subsequently when making another booking. By making it personal I've made him feel special, which makes it much more likely that he will go out of his way for me. As a result, my husband and I have access to some of the best tables in London, even when those restaurants are (supposedly) "fully booked."

Sometimes it may feel awkward to ask for a name, but this is one question that no one ever resents. The tricky part is *remembering* names. When you ask for it, repeat it back. If it's complicated, write it down. Do whatever it takes to remember it and use it again. In the event you do forget, immediately admit your error, and ask again. This is far better than forever afterwards saying "Hey, uh, hi..."

All great networkers know the importance of names, but I know a very successful business consultant who does something even better. He will somehow discover your birthday—perhaps by mentioning astrological signs or someone else's birthday in conversation, and then bringing the discussion around to you. However he does it, once he's wriggled the date out of you, he then plugs it into his database, and when your birthday arrives—long after you've forgotten the conversation—so does a birthday card, generally amusing or neatly tailored to your character. You can't fail to be touched by such thoughtfulness (even your family sometimes forgets—right?).

Generosity Creates Prosperity

If we put ourselves out there for other people—doing things that require time, energy, and selfless acts—we're never disappointed. Of course, some people will return our generosity while others won't; that's just the way it works. But if we act out of sincere generosity, because we want to, then even when the favor is not repaid we tend not to notice. Remember, "what goes around, comes around"—it's not always immediate, or when remotely expected, but the universe does seem to work this way.

My grandmothers illustrate this principle. Grandmother Fox, 95, is still with us and very much "with it"; Grandmother Mattingly, sadly, passed away several years ago. Grandmother Fox grew up without much money and worked very hard all her life. By most people's standards she was never wealthy, but she always seemed to have a surplus—she helped my cousins through college, paid for vacations and summer camps, and even managed to help a relative start a business. Grandmother Fox always gave away more than she kept for herself. And her efforts weren't limited to money—whenever anyone had a problem, she was there. When I had cancer, Grandmother Fox was one of my main comforts. Nor was her generosity limited to her family—she formed deep and significant relationships with many people, because she cared for them. Because of this my Grandmother Fox is still surrounded by people, family, and friends who love and take care of her, and even those of us on other continents keep in contact with her and visit her as much as possible.

Unlike Grandmother Fox, my Grandmother Mattingly was well-off and even privileged throughout her life. My grandfather spoiled and adored her, and she in turn was very loyal to him. However, when he passed away she was left on her own because she had never really bothered to reach out to others. My grandmother expected people to do things for her; when a neighborhood girl who ran errands for her was in a car accident, Grandmother Mattingly's primary concern seemed to be who was going to do her shopping! I still loved her, and I cherished memories of childhood times with her, but as an adult I couldn't help seeing her selfishness for what it was. In short, unlike my Grandmother Fox, Grandmother Mattingly didn't spend her final years surrounded by a small army of family and friends because she did not put love out for it to be returned.

The principles personified by my two grandmothers apply not only to our personal lives but to our professional ones as well. In our work, if we don't help others, give credit where credit is due, and make sacrifices of time and support, then sooner or later we'll find that no one (at least, no lawyer!) is going to do the same for us. And trying to achieve success alone is a near-impossible task in our profession.

Now, if you happen to be a young associate, you may be thinking, "Yes, sure, but you just don't understand the environment I'm in. The only way to get ahead in my firm is to look out for myself and nobody else. Believe me, that's how most partners operate, not to mention my immediate boss!" For a start, you can't be privy to everything that's going on behind your partners' doors, and they may be more cooperative than you think. But second, even if it looks that way from where you are, most older or more experienced lawyers will tell you that while self-serving, arrogant, and egotistical behavior may have short-term rewards, in the long run it catches up with almost everyone.

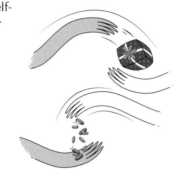

Many of us commit the same fatal error when dealing with colleagues, clients, and contacts—the mistake of thinking "What can they do for me?" instead of "What can I do for them?" The most successful people know that if we *give* first, the *getting* somehow takes care of itself. Generosity creates prosperity!

That Feel-Good Factor

People want to be around those who make them feel good, so when you engage with others you should try to transmit that feel-good factor. If what you convey is "I like/respect you... I'm really glad to see you... You're admirable/important/special to me," people can't help but match your own positive mood.

This is not just the unspoken law of the universe, but it also has some basis in scientific research—a phenomenon called *mirroring*. Brain researchers have shown that one person's brain can transmit signals to another's, changing the second person's physiology, body language, and even emotions. It's based on the phenomenon of "parallel circuitry" discovered by neuroscientist Giacomo Rizzolatti, M.D., and his colleagues in 1995 when they were mapping the brains of monkeys and monitoring certain neurons.[3] One of the neurons would fire

---

[3]Neurons are a type of cell in the brain and spinal cord that sends and receives electrochemical signals between the brain and other parts of the body. In essence, the brain is an extremely complicated signaling system, and the brain's neurons form the basis of that system.

when the monkey raised its arm; however, the remarkable (and unanticipated) revelation was that the neuron also fired when the monkey merely *observed* the same action—meaning that it fired (causing all the similar sensations) as if the monkey were itself raising its arm, mirroring what it saw.

This discovery may be one of the most significant revelations in neuroscience because subsequent research has shown that the same pattern occurs in humans. As we observe, our parallel neurons fire, and this specifically applies when we perceive the emotions of others. Mirror neuron research proves that one person's emotions will influence another's, and it's even been shown that the positive feelings of warmth and friendliness have the most powerful impact of all the emotions. This is why laughter can be contagious, and why, according to several studies, a smile has the best chance of all the expressions of being mirrored (returned), regardless of culture.

We don't need neuroscience to prove emotional contagion; we see it in offices, at social gatherings, and around the family dinner table when we observe energy from one person spread to the others. However, for us lawyers (or at least for me), there is something particularly intriguing about solid evidence to back up what could otherwise be dismissed as coincidence.

So on that basis—that of science rather than conjecture—we can have a positive impact on others merely by conveying the emotion we want to arouse.

Being Positive Draws People In

People want to feel positive because then everything around them looks and feels better. If I go out with a colleague and spend the whole time complaining about the people and the politics in the office, my guest may agree wholeheartedly (and even commiserate), but he or she won't recall the evening with positive feelings. And if mutual gloom is the only bond, the friendship will eventually wear thin, like a rope worn down by too many knots, and it may even break under the strain.

When I attend a conference I'm often surprised to observe how many attendees concentrate on making disparaging remarks—about the speakers, the accommodation, or (most often) the food! These people exude a mist of negativity, superciliousness, or cynicism that acts as a repellant. It's those with something positive to say who are attractive.

I had a roommate in college, "Becky," whom I liked immediately. I never tired of being in her company—and this set her apart from some of my other roommates, who sometimes drove me to the library! She was one of the most popular girls on campus, so our phone rang constantly (primarily for her), and our room was always crowded with visitors. While Becky was far from ugly, she certainly wasn't the most beautiful or talented girl around, but she was bombarded with dates and always had a party to attend. Initially the extent of her popularity was a mystery to me, and I remember during my first weekend home discussing with my parents (with a touch of jealousy!) why Becky received so much attention. Over time, however, I realized that Becky's secret was rather simple... She was just naturally positive.

Our physics professor once gave us an unusually left-field and out-of-the-blue question on an exam, and told us it would factor heavily into our final grade. Most of the class spent the week waiting for the results, despondent and certain that they had failed. Everyone, that is, except Becky. She spent the week in an upbeat mood, certain that the question had a purpose, and that she, as well as the rest of the class, would have satisfactory results. Her assurances gave us hope that we might survive the exam, too. In the end, Becky was right: Our professor was not looking for us to answer the question correctly, but wanted to examine our analysis in trying to find a solution. The rest of us had wasted time, energy, and sleep worrying, and a few classmates had even allowed the tension to turn into the flu! By contrast, Becky, who had maintained her high spirits, glided through the week well-rested and radiant.

In short, Becky's optimism helped her in various ways, but it was also the source of her popularity. Because other people (unconsciously) relied on her energy to uplift them, she became a magnet for their attention.

Again, we can trace the reason to the brain, which (believe it or not) is the social organ of the body. Emotions are controlled by the brain's limbic system, which does not merely react to external sources but actually relies on such stimuli for its regulation. In other words, we need emotional exchange for psychological stability. (This is called *interpersonal neurobiology*.) The brain deliberately seeks output (from other people) to emulate and integrate into its own process of emotion generation, with the goal of achieving balance. So where emotions are concerned, mirroring is not an inadvertent or passive occurrence but a necessary, proactive function. And when we encounter people with particularly strong expressive emotions (such as Becky's positive ones), we tend to eagerly integrate with them, and we become biologically drawn to that person.

The contagious, magnetic, and repellant nature of emotions

When your brain integrates on a two-way basis with that of another person—that is, his brain takes in your output, and yours takes in his—your neuron activity adjusts to his, and you can even synchronize, matching each other's profile. When this occurs in a positive way, you are usually in a high state of rapport. In fact, this is thought to be the scientific basis for friendships, and even love. So if, like Becky, you emit positive emotions, you are bound to transfer them to others, and your chances of rapport are naturally increased.

Enthusiasm Generates Enthusiasm

Enthusiasm tends to be received with enthusiasm. When we greet people in person or on the phone with energy and *joie de vivre*, they receive the impression—however erroneously—that we're glad to hear from them.

Now if you live in London and have ever bought or sold a property, then you'll probably feel the same way I do about estate agents (need I say more?!?). I've had estate agents tell me blatant lies, give me a falsified survey report, and even put me in a bidding war with a (non-existent) buyer. I now assume that they'll do anything, including sell their children, just to make a sale. So I have to grit my teeth as I write that I actually warmed to my last estate agent, despite my gut feeling that he was no different from the rest. Why? Because every time I called him, he sounded genuinely pleased to hear from me. I can hear his voice in my head as I write. "Jennifer!!" he'd exclaim with wholehearted zeal, as if I were his long-lost childhood buddy, "Great to hear from you! What can I do for you?" As I rattled off my issues, he would respond with such enthusiasm that I was certain he was on my side, sincerely supporting me. Clearly, a person so interested in me was genuine, right? Yes, I was a sap—but his enthusiasm got me every time!

Once my husband and I got into a huge argument and he dashed out the door for work without kissing me good-bye. I felt terrible, because I have a hang-up about never parting on bad terms, but at the time I was just plain mad. I knew my husband would eventually call because we had a few time-sensitive issues that couldn't go unaddressed. At first I planned to hammer home to him how wrong he had been (in scintillating terms!), but later I decided that it would be better to keep my negative thoughts to myself. When he called I quickly indicated how pleased I was to hear from him. At first he said curtly, "We need to decide on those flight times." "Of course," I said. "I'm so glad you remembered—this trip is going to be fantastic; I'm really looking forward to it!" Whereupon my husband immediately relented, forgot his bad mood, and eagerly joined in planning our weekend away.

Everybody Responds to a Smile

The effect of a smile is powerful. If you don't think smiling can make a difference, try this: Start off your morning with a smile when you look in the mirror, and for the rest of the day, smile at anyone you come across, even people who come to you with complaints or grievances. You'll find that most people smile right back at you—even the fed-up people—and your day just became that much easier.

What if you don't feel like smiling? Smile anyway. If you act as if you're happy, psychological research suggests that your mood is likely to improve. Feelings typically prompt action, but the two are so intertwined that action can actually affect our feelings. Just acting as if you feel OK might help make you so. We will talk about this concept much further in Chapter 7 ("Thinking"), but for now take my word for it, and (as Nike says), just do it! Smile, and make yourself happy!

I once had a young associate who was clever and appealing but extremely introverted. Despite her secret longing to be part of the social crowd who went to lunch together, or hit the pub after work, she secluded herself in her office all day. She privately admitted that she envied their easy camaraderie, but she still continued to sit and work in her office. One day I told her that she couldn't expect them to come to her out of nowhere, and that she had to make an effort. "But I don't know what to say!" she protested. I shook my head. "You don't have to say anything at first. Just smile." The next time she saw a few of the bright young law team by the coffee machine, she went over and made herself a cup she didn't want, and gave them a big smile. Immediately her smile was returned and a conversation initiated. When she later thanked me for my advice, she told me that she'd been shocked to learn that her new friends had penciled her in as a snob. She'd changed their minds with a single smile.

Your smile conveys the feel-good factor, and there's no (zero) tax on it. So what do you have to lose?

Shower everyone you encounter with the feel-good factor—
focus on the positive, be enthusiastic, and SMILE!
—and watch the results unfold.

It is, of course, easier to say this than to do it; we all get caught up in bad moods and emotional outbursts at times. However, I hope that giving you some awareness of the potential impact your feelings can have on others will encourage you to express your emotions better.

Even if optimism is not your strength and does not come naturally to you, it can still be learned. In the next chapter we will examine how our beliefs impact our feelings and how, through the way we think, we can manipulate that inter-action to achieve a better outcome. However, since we've been examining the function of brain neurons in this chapter (in the context of generating positive emotions in others), let's examine how we can use neuron functioning to gen-erate our own positive instincts.

Scientists used to believe that the adult brain was pretty much "wired" and didn't really change. However, recent neuroscience has proved this wrong, and neuroscientists now know that structural and functional changes in the neural networks of the brain happen all the time. These alterations occur when we are learning, thinking, behaving, and experiencing (and doing a few other things not relevant to our purposes, like taking psychoactive drugs!). These changes are referred to as *plasticity*. When the brain's neural networks are changed by plasticity, there is a corresponding change in the behaviors managed by those connections. It becomes a circular process.

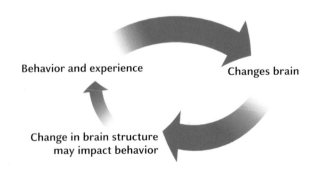

As we considered earlier, the brain is made up of individual neurons. They connect with each other to form networks, and the spaces between those connections are called synapses. The narrowness of this slender gap enables neurotransmitters (signaling molecules) to pass rapidly from one cell to the other, and these communications determine the brain's activity. In essence, the particular pattern of *synapses* in your brain is the key to who you are. Synapses are created (or strengthened) when we are learning, behaving, or experiencing, because when we do these things the neurons transmit to each other. This, then, is the underpinning to the circular process.

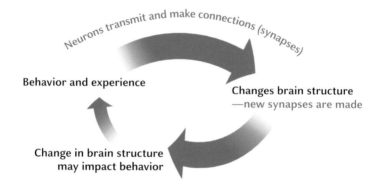

Neurons transmit and make connections (synapses)

Behavior and experience

Changes brain structure
—new synapses are made

Change in brain structure
may impact behavior

Each of us is born with a unique neural system and set of synapses that predispose our starting point (i.e., genetics). However, as we take in new information or experiences we create new connections (a new neurological structure of synapses!), and if we repeat an experience the new synapse "roots" to the synapse created previously. Thus, repeating an experience strengthens that particular neural network of synapses. (In terms of behavior, this means that we are strengthening the behavior supported by that neural network.) This is how habitual behavior is developed.

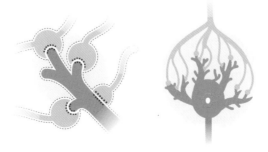

Conversely, if we don't use an existing connection, the brain will eventually expunge it (there are just too many to maintain them all!). Multiplication takes place in dramatic fashion: Each neuron in the brain of a newborn baby has approximately 2,500 synapses (connections with other neurons), but by age two or three each neuron has twice the connections of a typical adult's (about 15,000). Thereafter, regardless of our education or how much we learn, we begin losing connections through a process called *pruning*. Synaptic pruning eliminates the weaker connections; those that aren't being used die off, and those that are activated most frequently survive. As Joseph Ledoux writes in his book *Synaptic Self*, "use it or lose it." A connection, once lost, can be recreated, but (as you would expect) this requires more effort, especially if the opposite behavior is our natural instinct and a strong set of synapses is pulling us in that direction.

Controlling our behavior and the situations that develop our neural networks (thinking, training, learning, experiencing) can be extremely powerful, and the natural functioning of our brain (and the changes we make to its neural pathways) can affect personality and emotions. Admittedly, it is easier to rewire at certain periods of life than at other less-malleable times, but it is still possible.

So if you want to become more positive, make a conscious choice to behave that way. You really can rewire the brain and create (or strengthen) the synapses that support positive behavior and emotions. You can wallow in pessimism (or misery or anger) if you prefer, and if that is your habitual behavior, existing synapses will strongly encourage you to continue. However, if you choose to be positive you can create a new synapse, and if you keep repeating the positive behavior you might just build up a new strength.

You'll recall from the previous chapter that we examined strengths and weaknesses. You doubtless now realize that each unique strength is supported by a strong neural network of synapses and, conversely, that areas of weakness enjoy a far less powerful network of support. In terms of brain function, we instinctively behave in accordance with our strengths because robust neural networks pull us in that direction, due to reflexive modes of neural firing that have been built up over time. These powerful networks make working with our strengths the easiest way of achieving success. In addition, the skills built using our strengths are easier to generate because they produce new synapses that interact with, and connect to, the related ones already in place. To put it another way, creating a synapse in which the connecting neuron forges toward and intensifies an already-strong network is easier than creating one that lacks such direction and foundation.

But this doesn't mean that we can't rewire the infrastructure at least a bit better! By consciously acting in a new way we can alter previously automatic modes of neural firing and enable new patterns of neural synapses and behavior.

CASE STUDY

A transaction I once handled illustrates many of the principles of this chapter. I was negotiating a multi-billion-dollar project in which my client was outsourcing the bulk of its global IT department to a service provider—the company on the other side of the deal. Before the contract stage and final negotiations, the two sides' project teams spent several months together in an effort to understand the service requirements from each other's perspective so that we could define them contractually to everyone's satisfaction. We probed each other's motivations for putting something on the table; "Why?" and "How?" were popular questions. I suspect that every one of us at some point wanted to put a little-known Asian poison in the other side's coffee, but everyone knew that getting it right (for both parties) was critical to a successful long-term contract, and that a good outcome was contingent on everyone around the table showing respect.

For this phase of the project the service provider did not employ outside counsel but used its own in-house lawyers, which is not unusual. Because it was such a critical transaction, however, the service provider did decide to bring in outside counsel at the contract negotiation stage, choosing to hire a partner from a prestigious international firm.

Unluckily, as it turned out, this impressively intellectual lawyer had all the people skills of a cocktail peanut. Before our first in-person negotiations, we received a marked-up contract from this lawyer. The revisions were so extreme and unreasonable that we could only assume that they had been made by a young associate with limited understanding of the commercial aspects of the deal, and that, when the partner came along in person, he would be far more amenable and sensitive. But we were wrong! The mark-up had been made with his direct involvement, and he arrived with the intention of arguing to the death for every revision—whether or not this was in the best interests of his client.

When he arrived I welcomed him warmly, knowing that the first moments would help to set the tone for our ongoing working relationship. However, he was brusque and arrogant in return, indicating that he had no time to spare for chit-chat. He then opened by telling all of us that he had been brought into the project by his client's top management. Although he intended to reinforce his status by this remark, he succeeded instead in turning everyone against him; his comment even suggested to his own team (his client!) that he was the most important person present. (Isn't that supposed to be the client?)

After these opening remarks, this lawyer began railroading my client, pushing each of his positions down the client's throat. He treated the negotiation like a contest in which winning was measured by prevailing on each of his positions and arguing was the only means to victory. The crucial consideration here was that the two project teams had already been working together for many months. So when this new lawyer tried such aggressive tactics, even his own client team became uncomfortable.

Now just because he didn't care to ask about my client's perspective didn't mean that I gave up trying to understand his. Throughout the process I remained calm and asked questions in an attempt to understand his positions. He displayed a serious lack of commercial reasoning, but he maintained his views tenaciously until his own client, at length, was forced to overrule him.

This lawyer failed to focus on the interests of his own client or on the underlying perspectives of each of the parties. His only priority was intellectually superior legal arguments, and we all concluded that he just needed to show us how intelligent (and important) he was.

After far too many frustrating weeks locked in a room "negotiating" (not!) with this lawyer, he was finally "uninvited" by his own client. It's ironic to note that he had actually made some good points in the negotiations, but the good points were discarded along with the bad because everything was delivered so unpalatably.

Emphasizing status and brilliance without an appreciation for people skills can sabotage a lawyer's career (without the lawyer even being aware of it).

In addition to the obvious (his failure to see any perspective but his own excessively legal position), let's recap a few of his other mistakes.

1. *He was arrogant.* His unrestrained ego was apparent from his initial introduction. The lawyers who were retained to replace him presented quite a contrast: They were gracious, and anxious to become part of a negotiation that they recognized had been going on for some time before their appearance. They were conscious of being the "new kids on the block" and introduced themselves by saying, "We apologize if we're behind the curve a bit, as all of you understand the underlying services much better than we do at this point. We may have to ask a lot of questions along the way, but we hope to get up to speed very quickly." Don't you think that everyone—even we, their "adversaries"—did our best to help them catch up?

2. *He took no interest in people.* In daily negotiations, people straggle into the meeting room at varying times, pouring themselves coffee and checking their emails before starting work. During this period, people take an interest in each other. ("How was your weekend?" "Did you make it to your son's football game last night?" "Good journey in?") But not this lawyer! He thought himself too important to "waste his time" on "meaningless" small talk.

3. *He avoided making anything personal.* It was a surprise when he happened to use someone's name, and he routinely called Ewan "Ian," even after being corrected more than once. If we hope to have influence, we have a much better chance if we first put things on a personal level.

4. *He was routinely negative.* When sandwiches were brought in for lunch one day, he remarked that we really should have held the meetings in his offices because his firm provided superior meals from a rated chef—thus neatly managing to egregiously insult his host (my client). I couldn't help contrasting this with a different negotiation in which I was involved where the lawyer on the other side complimented my client as a host, and probably even won a few negotiation points for that reason.

5. *He never admitted when he was wrong or when he didn't know something, and therefore lost credibility.* Even when his positions were legally correct or even astute, his arguments weren't commercially viable within the context of this project. To make matters worse, he refused to back down—even when he realized that his views were

not workable. (One of my colleagues contended that he would have refused to change course even if caught driving the wrong way on a one-way street!) Furthermore, he had not consulted enough with his own client, and therefore lacked sufficient information. Instead of trying to understand the situation, and admitting his ignorance, he always tried to mask his deficiencies with argument.

In my years of negotiating I've come across plenty of lawyers who've made these errors, but this lawyer stands out in my mind for two reasons: He succeeded in committing all of these sins within a single negotiation, and further, he did so in the midst of two project teams that were, by contrast, successfully using their people skills both inside and outside the negotiation room. While the rest of us were making connections with each other, he alone seemed incapable of being personable while negotiating a deal.

I've gone into detail on this case for a few reasons:

■ The rules of people skills should be used with your family, friends, colleagues, clients, and other people you meet, but they can also be used to better your influence as a lawyer, and as part of any negotiation. Doing this, rather than just arguing, will normally produce better results.

■ We later had to renegotiate aspects of the contract, for reasons unrelated to the project itself. In doing so, I realized the strength of the terms we had negotiated, and the CFO of my client publicly acknowledged that I had saved them a considerable amount of money because the contract was so well-honed. I was especially pleased to recollect that I'd achieved this, not by aggression or hard-nosed tactics, but by talking through the issues and genuinely seeking the other side's perspective.

■ Because I dealt with the lawyer on the other side with respect and refused to respond to his arguments with similarly unreasonable counterattacks, people listened to what I said and assumed my positions were justified. By showing respect I received respect, and in the end, I gained authority.

Ironically, when this deal was concluded I was hired by the opposition, and their consultant referred me to several big projects as well. You never know where your connections might lead you! Never discount the importance of gaining respect from your adversaries.

THE CHARISMATIC YOU: THE ELEVATOR MISSION

Most of us have heard people say, "Oh, he's got such charisma!" and secretly thought, "I wish I did." And it's true that a few lawyers do seem to have a natural ability to draw people in and arouse delight and admiration—natural Connecters, for the most part. However, based upon what we learned about ourselves in Chapter 4 ("Personalities") and in this chapter, I hope you'll agree that most of the elements of charisma and influence can be learned.

John, one of the first partners I worked with, was one of the most charismatic and people-focused persons I've ever known. When I asked him his secret he said, "Jennifer, with every person I meet, I have the opportunity to lift him up or take him down. I see it as my personal mission to lift him up." I now refer to John's secret as the Elevator Mission. With each person you meet, think of the elevator doors opening to that person. It's up to you to press the button to lift him up or send him down. As lawyers, each of us has the tools to ensure that the elevator goes up.

So I challenge you to implement your own Elevator Mission and give everyone around you a positive (and uplifting) experience!

To summarize:

1. To make the initial connection you may have to initiate contact, and if you're not naturally extroverted this may be difficult at first. But after reading Chapter 4 ("Personalities"), you know it's possible! Some of the subsequent chapters will help you with practical suggestions.

2. From this chapter, you know that the easiest way to lift someone up (and inspire admiration in yourself) is to make people feel IMPORTANT and APPRECIATED.

    a. *Take an interest* in them (not, repeat *not*, by being interesting yourself). You can listen, ask questions, solicit information, and involve yourself in others' interests—the things that personally affect their lives.

        i. You can ask them to *tell you their story*. And then you can *listen*.

        ii. You can choose to look for things of *mutual interest*. Commonality creates an instant bond, and thus rapport.

        iii. When you discover differences...

            ■ You can decide not to highlight them, unless you can use them to elevate the other person into the position of storyteller or expert. "Really? I know nothing about it; tell me more."

            ■ You can stand in his shoes empathetically: "That must have been so difficult." When you stand in someone else's shoes you can discover that person's "What's in it for me?" and obtain more influence.

    b. *Don't be arrogant.* This is not an opportunity to highlight your own accomplishments. Your mission is to elevate the other person.

    c. *Don't argue.* Better to be labeled wrong yourself than to make someone else feel lousy.

    d. *Admit your lack of knowledge.* By doing this, you elevate the other person and display innate confidence in yourself.

    e. *Refrain from criticism.* We know that people will make mistakes, but try to focus on the positive. Sometimes what you don't say is just as important as what you do.

f. *Take responsibility.* When you make a mistake, rather than defend yourself, show confidence and admit your error. When you do this, the other person respects you and is much more likely to forgive.

g. *Show your appreciation by complimenting and acknowledging the other person's good points*—even if you think those points are blindingly obvious. No one can ever be complimented too much. For most people, compliments are rare and precious.

h. *Personalize* everything you do, making your compliments, courtesies, and conversations both specific and personal. Whenever possible, use people's names.

i. *Maintain a generous attitude.* Put yourself out for other people in terms of time, energy, and actions, while expecting nothing in return. The boomerang effect means that generally, what you give out will be returned—and that goes equally for the positive and the negative.

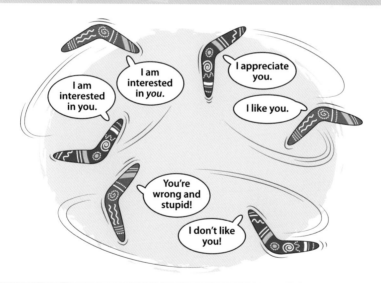

3. The "elevator" automatically goes up when you transmit that feel-good factor to another person by being *positive, enthusiastic,* and *smiling.* Through the mirroring phenomenon, you transfer your buoyant emotions onto him or her. If you don't feel good yourself, act as if you do, and you'll be surprised how much better you'll feel. In some cases, you may even alter the neural network of your brain in such a way as to support your more positive behavior.

Chapter Seven

Awareness Building Block 4: Thinking

(Optimizing your thinking and generating confidence)

In Chapter 3 ("The Secret Knowledge of the Master Juggler") I mentioned that if you do nothing other than read *this* chapter with an open mind, you would learn enough to achieve amazing results. The contents of this chapter are critical, and it both frustrates and motivates me that this information is almost entirely ignored throughout the education system—at all levels.

You see, most people make the mistake of assuming that life's biggest challenges are external. We kid ourselves that some challenge is too difficult, that our situation is intrinsically unfair, or that we lack the requisite resources, skills, or support to succeed. Actually, the real problem is internal, based on a lack of self-belief and a shortage of positive thinking. Most obstacles arise from our own attitudes, including a failure to develop, nurture, and sustain high levels of self-belief and self-confidence.

It's no surprise that we rarely develop these inner strengths naturally. It has been estimated that by the age of eighteen most of us will have been told "no" (or, "No, you can't," "That's impossible," "No/get lost/No, you're bugging me," or even, "You're a loser") well over 100,000 times, either from our parents or from other adults in authority. Even if we receive enough encouragement to override such defeating words, it still takes a much greater proportion of positive reinforcement to remove or lessen the imprint of negative messages.

So most people are so conditioned to negative thinking by the time they reach adulthood that it has become habitual, their "default" attitude. However, the good news is that you have in your hands the tools to eradicate such negative influences. You can choose the positive, can-do mindset that study after study has shown to be the core shared trait among great achievers. In fact, that's what this chapter is all about!

My aim here is to help you see the amazing potential that exists within *you*. If you've never been exposed to some of the concepts I champion here, you might either doubt them as too simple to be true or suppose that "if these ideas really worked, I'd have learned them years ago!" But stick with it! Remember that most of the *really* great achievers of our time—and even of all time—believed in these ideas and techniques, which reroute the inner mapping of our minds.

First, I plan to explain how our modes of thinking are the greatest predictor of success, and how we can use thought patterns to generate optimal emotions, behaviors, and results. Most people unwittingly harness the power of their minds to their own psychological detriment, despite the fact that the brain's processes allow us to manipulate it for our benefit. You should find here a new, and better, way of thinking.

Second, I hope to teach you how to use the subconscious to improve both creativity and decision-making. This intuitive skill is generally believed to be the "spark" for most works of genius.

Finally, I'll explain the mind's connections to a still-greater source of inner power: the mind's inbuilt computer program. By visualizing our goals, we can hugely improve our chances of achieving them.

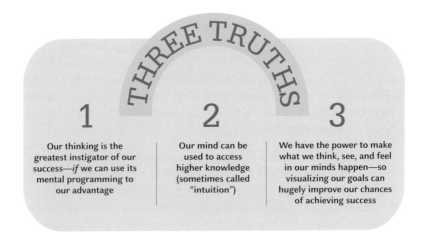

THREE TRUTHS

1

Our thinking is the greatest instigator of our success—*if* we can use its mental programming to our advantage

2

Our mind can be used to access higher knowledge (sometimes called "intuition")

3

We have the power to make what we think, see, and feel in our minds happen—so visualizing our goals can hugely improve our chances of achieving success

THE FIRST TRUTH: OUR MENTAL PROGRAM

If we think back honestly to our greatest successes and failures—or even just to those things we seem to be good at, or not so good at—we soon realize that our *thinking* has affected the results of our efforts. Normally our successes were the result of positive thinking, while our failures were linked to negative beliefs at the time. (If you don't agree, I urge you to read this chapter very carefully and then reconsider my assertion!)

I was very young when I first heard the words "Think positive" from my parents. As our car hurtled toward the state swimming championships, I remember wondering to myself, "Now, how exactly can *that* help the situation?!" Little did I realize that my parents were actually giving me the best possible advice—advice which, had I taken it on board, could very likely have helped me win the state swimming title. However, I had overheard a casual comment by a friend that my rival "couldn't possibly be beaten," so I was too busy concentrating on the possibility of losing to her, and far too focused (in a broader way) on deep-seated fears of a negative outcome. Consistent with those thoughts (yes, you guessed it), I came in second! Only some time later, after many other such failures, did I come to realize just how astute my parents' advice had been.

Our success (or lack thereof) is completely dependent on the programming we choose to give our minds, and failure is generally a result of mental conditioning, whether direct or indirect. The process follows a consistent set of steps (the "mental program"), which always starts with cognitive input and finishes with a predictable outcome, depending on the data presented to it. In between, very little is left to chance or luck. In other words, things don't just happen to us, as a rule; they happen because of mental programming.

We all possess only one mind, but that mind is itself divided into two parts—the conscious and the subconscious—which function quite separately but constantly interact with one another. Our conscious mind represents our rational, objective side. This part of the brain observes, analyzes, interprets, and validates the world as presented to us. It enables us to reason, weigh evidence, and calculate decisive judgments. On the other hand, and simultaneously, the subconscious continues to "beaver away" behind the scenes, perceiving truths through intuition to a far deeper level than the conscious mind does. For example, some things that the conscious mind doesn't even register will be picked up automatically by the subconscious mind. Most people aren't even aware of the actions of their subconscious, yet it remains the source not only of instinct but also of our every creative idea.

Our conscious mind is only a minor nugget in comparison to the gigantic power of our subconscious, which is constantly working—even while we sleep. In fact, it's reckoned that over ninety percent of our thinking is done with our subconscious mind, which some scientists believe can outperform our conscious mind on a scale of ten million to one! Take just one example. Have you ever been driving down the road, deep in thought, and suddenly been shocked to realize that you had reached your destination? Your subconscious mind can work on several different levels without involving conscious thought at all!

1. First, your subconscious drove the car (though, initially at least, your conscious mind had to teach it how).

2. Second, your subconscious navigated your journey, making sure that you drove safely and according to traffic laws. Again, your conscious mind determined the route—but it was your subconscious that enacted it.

3. Simultaneously, without your even being aware of it, your subconscious was taking in all your surroundings, from Dr. Phil's radio show, to traffic data, to a solution to your primary problem of the day—but we'll get to all that later on.

Just as in this example, most things we do are powered by the subconscious. Right now, while (consciously) reading these words, your subconscious is doing much of the work for you—although admittedly your conscious mind is also analyzing, interpreting, and intellectualizing. Your subconscious is recording all the sounds and sources of information that you're otherwise not processing: the blare of the car horn from outside the window, and the screams of delight from the kids next door.

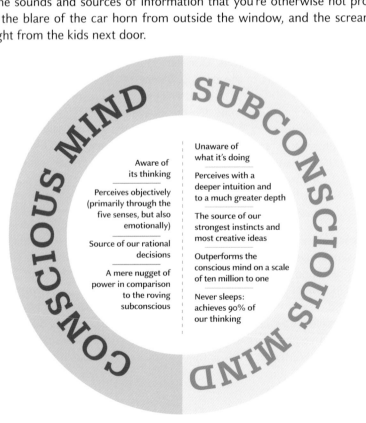

CONSCIOUS MIND

Aware of its thinking

Perceives objectively (primarily through the five senses, but also emotionally)

Source of our rational decisions

A mere nugget of power in comparison to the roving subconscious

SUBCONSCIOUS MIND

Unaware of what it's doing

Perceives with a deeper intuition and to a much greater depth

The source of our strongest instincts and most creative ideas

Outperforms the conscious mind on a scale of ten million to one

Never sleeps: achieves 90% of our thinking

Although it's difficult for rational and intellectual types (including most law-yers!) to immediately comprehend, it's actually our *subconscious* that outlines or limits our successes and failures—not our objective, conscious mind. Once we grasp this, and begin to understand how the two sides of the mind col-laborate to create our version of reality, we are empowered to succeed in ways we may never have thought possible.

Let's look at how the mind works:

- *The subconscious records everything.* The subconscious records every word uttered and every single event occurring around us. Most of it will appear to pass us by, yet our subconscious captures it. (The conscious mind is, for the most part, limited by what it can take in through the five senses; the subconscious works on a much higher and deeper level.)

- *The subconscious stores and remembers.* Once the subconscious records something, that information is irrevocably filed into its database and is thus made potentially accessible *forever*! In short, everything we've ever read, thought, heard, or imagined is in there somewhere. (By contrast, the conscious mind can retain only a limited number of facts at any one time, so much information is discarded.)

STEPS	CONSCIOUS MIND	SUBCONSCIOUS MIND
1 RECEIVES DATA	Limited by what it can take in through awareness.	Captures and records everything happening around us (most of which we're not even aware of).
2 STORES DATA	Can only hold a limited amount of information.	Stores all information forever.
3 REMEMBERS (ACCESSES) DATA	Can only remember and access what is held (and sometimes even that can be forgotten!).	Recalls forever (with some, but usually very few, exceptions). Note: Even things consciously forgotten (e.g., as being too painful to recall) are accessible through the subconscious.

Taking all this information together, we can see how differently the two sides of our minds actually operate. However, there remains one last, critical, distinction.

The conscious mind, our rational and objective side, which interprets and validates, is constantly asking, "why?" and "how?" In short, it can *reason*. The subconscious mind lacks this crucial capacity. It has no ability to evaluate the information it receives; like a computer, it is entirely dependent on the input it is given. If a blind man says you look sensational, your subconscious doesn't evaluate whether his words are credible or not; it simply files the statement as a fact. So the subconscious, powerful though it is, is unable to discriminate, filter, or rationalize.

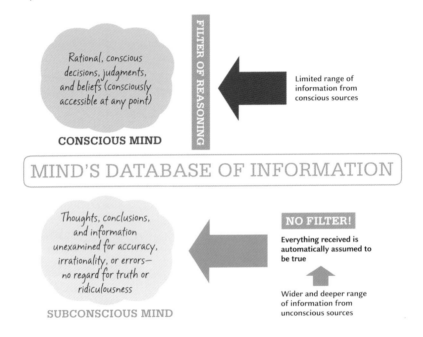

The Creation of Our Beliefs

One of the most crucial things the mind does with its enormous database is to create a personal system of beliefs. Many of our beliefs are affected by the mind's subconscious processing, as the subconscious possesses not only tremendous quantities of information but also great emotional power. But if our beliefs are derived *solely* from flawed, undiscriminating, subconscious programming, they may be partially (or even wholly) irrational.

Since conscious thoughts represent only a small percentage of input received, we may not even be aware of the information selected by the subconscious in the formation of our beliefs. In fact, a single belief may have been founded on a piece of data that the conscious mind has long since forgotten or disregarded, or even on something the conscious mind never perceived in the first place!

The tendency to form beliefs early in life explains why modern psychology focuses so much on things said to us at an early age. As bizarre as it may seem, one casual, unrecalled comment from childhood could prove to be the basis of a belief held decades later.

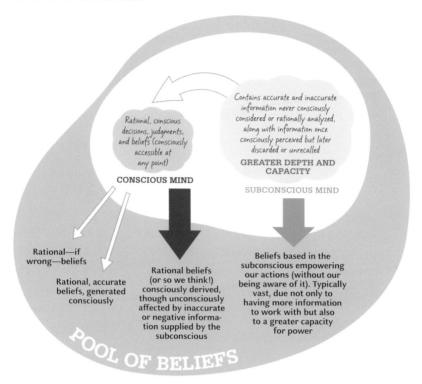

Beliefs are powerful because they are directly linked to our success or failure. Albert Bandura, arguably the greatest living psychologist, proved that a person's intrinsic self-belief with regard to his capacity to achieve something (whether accurately derived or not) is the highest significant predictor of whether or not he can make things happen.

Let's look briefly at how this works.

1. Beliefs create attitudes and feelings

Our beliefs about the outside world, about other people, and about ourselves form the foundation of our attitudes and feelings.

- If I *believe* I make friends easily, then I'll tend to be enthusiastic about social events (attitude); being in the company of others will make me happy (feeling).

- If I *believe* people don't like me, I'll feel pessimistic about meeting new people (attitude); social events will probably make me anxious (feeling).

- If I *believe* I have a good figure then I'll want to go to the beach and wear a swimsuit (attitude); when there I'm likely to feel confident (feeling). (NOTE: This is only a personal belief; I may in fact look completely revolting. Haven't you seen someone on the beach strutting his stuff while you think, "Wow. Where does he get *his* nerve from?" The answer probably lies in his underlying self-belief, from which self-confidence springs.)

- If I *believe* I have a lousy figure I won't feel good wearing a swimsuit in front of others (attitude); I'll probably feel self-conscious when I do (feeling). (On the other hand, how many times have you heard a slim, attractive woman— or man—proclaim that she feels "ugly" or "fat"? Again, this is all due to an underlying subconscious, and sometimes irrational, belief system—because consciously we can see the truth.)

2. **Attitudes and feelings determine actions**

Every action we take, or fail to take, is determined by underlying attitudes and feelings. If we feel positive about something we tend to gravitate toward it, do more of it, or work harder at it. Conversely, if we feel negative about something we'll tend to avoid it, sometimes without being aware of what we're doing.

- If I'm excited about meeting new people (feeling and attitude), I will tend to go to lots of social events (action). I'll feel confident around others (feeling and attitude) and as such will make lots of introductions (action).

- If I feel negative about meeting new people (feeling and attitude), then I'll almost certainly avoid doing so (inaction)— or else feel inadequate when I do.

- If I feel confident in my swimsuit (feeling and attitude), then I'll go to the beach more often (action).

- If wearing a swimsuit makes me uncomfortable (feeling), then I'll avoid doing so whenever I can (inaction).

3. Actions bring results

It's really only through action (or inaction) that we realize results.

- If I go to lots of social events and make many introductions (action), then I'll wind up with significant contacts and connections (result).

- If I don't go out and meet people (inaction), then my range of contacts will inevitably be limited (result).

- If I wear my swimsuit to the beach (action), then I'll have the pleasure of soaking up some rays and developing a good tan (result).

- If I avoid the beach (inaction), then I miss out on the tan, the psychological benefits of sun, as well as on vitamin D (result)!

A person's belief about his capability to achieve something (whether accurately perceived or not) is the highest predictor of whether he in fact makes it happen.

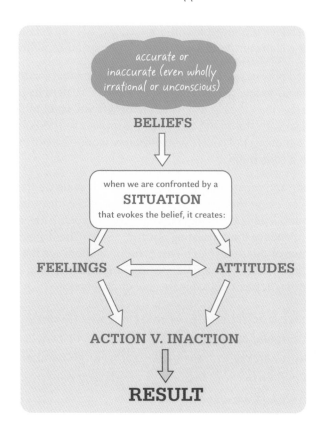

Most of us realize that the results we achieve are directly linked to the actions we perform, and that to succeed we must undertake the right initiatives. However, we tend to try to make changes by modifying our actions rather than by *examining our underlying beliefs*. To achieve a better result, we should instead manage (to every extent possible) our pool of beliefs. The only way to do this is by altering the mental programming outlined above.

First, we can use the conscious mind as a gatekeeper. We have the ability to control much of the information we deposit into our minds, but most of us fail to exercise this power. Instead, we allow negative, defeatist, and critical information in—so how can we expect positive results? Haven't you heard the old saying "Garbage in, garbage out"? Since we can't perceive what our subconscious is taking in, we must remain focused on our conscious mind.

Second, the conscious mind has the power to reprogram, through repetition, information sitting in the subconscious. Remember the driving-the-car example? We taught our subconscious to drive, mainly through conscious repetition and reinforcement, until it became almost automatic. The same principles apply to internalizing preferred beliefs. Bear in mind that as the subconscious takes in information it will invariably receive conflicting data. It has no way of knowing which idea is preferable or more accurate, so—by default—the dominant mindset will prevail. In this lies the value of repeating our instructions!

Third, as noted previously, there is a major flaw in the program: the inability of the subconscious to analyze information received. This permits us to manipulate the subconscious to help us create the beliefs we *want*. In short, we can be "economical with the truth" (or we can just plain lie!) to ourselves. "I *am* confident, I *am* doing brilliantly" will inevitably work—even if reality fails to support such a contention.

By consciously and repetitively giving the mind the evidence that we want it to have, we can cause the subconscious to accept those ideas and even make them automatic, "default" thoughts. Once this happens, the mind has no option but to produce the correlating positive results. There are many ways to do this, but two of the easiest (and best-proven) methods are through self-talk and affirmations. At the same time, it's also important to address any inner anxieties that might block our ultimate goal of confidence.

> To achieve a better result, we must manage (to every extent possible) our pool of beliefs by using our conscious mind as a gatekeeper, repeatedly reprogramming and manipulating the subconscious to create and reinforce the self-beliefs we want.

Self-Talk

Without a filter of reasoning, the subconscious really has no option other than to accept what we say as the truth and to use this information to form our beliefs. Unluckily, many of the statements people make to themselves throughout an average day are wildly negative. Here are just a few:

I'm so stupid.

Nothing ever works out for me.

I can't seem to do this.

I'm just not organized.

I hate my job.

This is impossible.

I'll never get this done.

I'm just no good at sales.

I have all the creativity of a roasted potato.

I'm so stressed. Even my laptop is tense!

(Not to mention: I hate my shyness/my looks/my baldness/my personality, etc., etc.—but we won't go there!)

We all need to take conscious control of our mental program through inner self-talk because we all have an ingrained habit of making negative statements. From now on, try to make anything that you say (or think) about yourself both encouraging and positive. (For example, don't say "I'm not nervous"—which is negative—but rather "I feel confident.") I know this may seem like nitpicking, but for whatever reason, the subconscious tends to miss words like "not," focusing instead on the negative word, "nervous." This is why you need to make your statements both affirmative and positive to create the belief you want.

NEGATIVE STATEMENT	POSITIVE STATEMENT	NOT LIKE THIS
I'm stressed.	I am relaxed.	I'm not stressed.
I'm stupid.	I am intelligent.	I'm not stupid.
I'm blowing this deal.	I am successfully completing this deal.	I'm not blowing this deal.

I have a friend, Anna, who has known and practiced the concept of positive self-talk for years. She happens to be an extremely accomplished and successful woman, as a direct result (she believes) of her mental programming. When Anna was recovering from a major operation, I visited her in the hospital. As I approached her bedside I said, rather hesitantly, "You're looking really good." (Admittedly, it wasn't true, but what else can you say?!?) She looked me straight in the eyes, and with total confidence said, "Yes, I know. I look great, don't I?" I was stunned and impressed—but then realized that I shouldn't have expected anything less. Whereas most people would have moaned about how pale they looked and how terrible they felt, Anna was busy feeding herself the belief that she was getting well. Not surprisingly, she recovered at a remarkable rate—stunning even her doctors.

I understand how this works from personal experience. In my early twenties I was diagnosed with a serious cancer. While I'd always been a naturally optimistic person, until that point I hadn't really realized the true significance of positive beliefs and self-talk. However, I had an innate tendency to welcome challenges, and I approached my diagnosis with the belief that I could win. I occupied my mind with thoughts of my recovery and all the things I was going to do when I was well. It was only later that I realized that my belief, although very naïve, had also been critical to my survival.

If we keep the conscious mind busy with productive and encouraging beliefs, they will eventually become natural to us and we will see results.

Affirmations

Similarly, we can create affirmations for ourselves and use them throughout the day. As with self-talk, we don't need to actually believe the encouraging statements as current reality, but by repeating them on a daily basis we can condition our minds to manifest the belief we want.

Keep your affirmations short: That way they are easy to repeat and simple to accept. And always state your affirmation *in the present as though it is a fact:* not "I will," but "I am." This is another trick we play on the subconscious. Depending on what you want to achieve, sample affirmations might be:

People like me.

I am a great communicator.

I am confident in everything I do.

I always achieve my goals.

I'm a motivator.

Remember, just a few words will do. ("I'll make myself a well-liked and confident communicator with a strong grasp of motivational skills who is adept at achieving great things" does *not* represent a great affirmation strategy!)

Once I was managing a major and extremely nerve-racking deal for which I had neither the requisite time nor the necessary resources. Any objective observer would have probably reckoned it "mission impossible." I found myself boring my partners with all its problems, as well as freely cursing my client and my own lack of organization. I even came home and continually expounded my frustrations to my husband. Then I suddenly realized that "I can't" or "I'm so stressed about" seemed to be all that I could think about, and that, not unnaturally, my results were beginning to reflect that belief. So I decided to imprint a new and positive impression into my subconscious. I began repeating to myself, *"I always make my projects come together. This project is successful. I am relaxed and focused. I am having fun."* It certainly wasn't always true—especially not the "fun" part—in fact, I've had loads more fun in traffic jams—but it worked. The project deadlines didn't change, but my attitude and expectations did. And the result was a successful project, a satisfied client, and a much happier lawyer—me!

Whatever your preferred affirmation, the key is to repeat it often—in the shower, on your way to the office, or standing in line to pay for your lunch. Just make your affirmation the prevalent belief in your subconscious programming and watch those positive results mysteriously (and wonderfully) unfold.

Now obviously there are some rational limitations to supporting our goals with positive beliefs, because the capability and the effort (practice!) we put into the activity also factor highly into the equation. But if we *start* with self-belief we will approach the challenge as something to be mastered and we will gain a sense of control over the situation. These attitudes inevitably fuel commitment, persistence, and resilience.

Alleviating Fear to Build Confidence

Our experiences play a significant role in bolstering self-belief, as tangible evidence of our abilities. If we've failed at something in the past, it's doubly difficult to override that information with positive suggestions—especially if we've developed the bad, yet amazingly common, habit of reliving the experience over and over again, each time imprinting the negative information deeper into our subconscious. Our failure then feeds into negative beliefs and spirals into anxiety and fear—a truly vicious circle that can only compound the problem!

Let's look at this in the context of our previous diagram on page 163.

We all face fears, whether based on a bad experience or on irrational or unconscious beliefs built up during our lifetimes. Do any of these fears feel familiar to you?

- *Fear of public speaking?*
- *Fear of failure?*
- *Fear of looking stupid?*
- *Fear of voicing an opinion?*
- *Fear of making a mistake?*
- *Fear of asking for help?*
- *Fear of rejection?*
- *Fear of not having enough money?*

The list could go on and on. Of course, nobody is immune to fear, but if we really want to be successful we have to acknowledge our fears and master them rather than allow anxieties to color our thinking and (effectively) control us. The first step is to abandon our toxic thinking processes. These include...

■ *"Awfulizing."* This refers to the tendency to imagine all sorts of disasters arising from a single, relatively minor event. Perhaps you're about to give a talk and you worry that you might mess up. Not content with that, you go on to imagine complete humiliation and a wrecked reputation for generations to come.

■ *Having an "all or nothing" mindset.* Here one setback becomes a complete failure and a major impediment to long-term achievement. You fail one exam in law school and totally write off your degree; you're rejected for one job so you gloomily decide that you'll never be employed. Your relationship ends and you imagine decades of coming home to a house solely inhabited by dust (and maybe a few cats).

■ *Making negative assumptions.* Perhaps you feel a little nervous approaching new people. So when you see someone you want to meet at a conference, you worry that if you engage him in conversation you'll feel anxious and stumble over your words— not to mention that he probably won't be terribly interested in meeting you anyway. So you neatly talk yourself out of taking a minor risk, which might very well have really paid off!

■ *Negative filtering.* Instead of feeling good about your strengths and the things you've achieved, you use a single setback as incontrovertible evidence of total failure. When I once had a "client catastrophe" (see Chapter 17), I forgot my multitude of satisfied clients and instead lapsed into toxic thinking ("I'm a failure"). Luckily, my lapse was only momentary, as I knew the slippery slope represented by that kind of thinking.

These mistakes cruelly sabotage our self-belief and either prevent us from acting to our advantage or (worse) lead us irresistibly to our most-feared destination. So we must eradicate and exterminate such toxic patterns of thought.

EXERCISE: Over the next week, each time you feel even slightly anxious about a situation, make an immediate note of it. Is your anxiety based on reality or fiction? Are you letting your mind work against you? Over the course of a week you'll probably discover certain patterns of thought that you need to consciously eliminate. If you push yourself to work on these with real self-discipline, you should gradually find your thinking becoming more positive and more confident.

Of course, even eliminating toxic thought processes doesn't necessarily remove the fear that started off the chain of bad consequences. The only way to do that is by *taking action*. Avoiding an anxiety-provoking situation simply compounds our fear, over time creating an ever-larger mountain to climb. (Some people like to use the acronym FEAR: Face Everything And Recover.)

As lawyers, we've all been in a sink-or-swim position of sorts at one time or another, but it's better to act on our fears in a manageable way. If we jump before completing preparations, we risk a negative experience. (If that does happen, however, remember that you can always reprogram the subconscious to repair the damage.) Studies show that graded exposure and gradual success over our fears optimizes the outcome, simultaneously reinforcing self-belief and reducing anxiety.

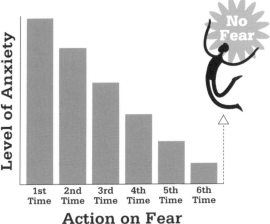

Action on Fear

In Chapter 4 ("Personalities") I mentioned my friend Stephen, who left the security of a big firm to work on his own. As a natural introvert, picking up the phone and establishing contacts was far from within Stephen's core personality—in fact, it was something he actively feared and detested. When he was setting up his practice he used every excuse in the book to avoid making those necessary phone calls until one day he realized that he had no choice but to sit down and face his fear. That day he made a list of his every contact and set himself a brutal timetable for getting through the list.

Making that first phone call took Stephen all afternoon, as he repeatedly picked up the phone, only to put it down again. He was convinced that his contact would never want to hear from him! But once Stephen did complete (and survive) that first call, the next phone call was easier, and the third easier still, until all his fear was gone. During the process, Stephen realized some things.

First, his toxic thinking—his skill at making negative assumptions—had been irrational *and* had eroded his self-belief. His feared outcome—rejection—did happen once or twice, but he found that it was manageable. (In her book *Feel the Fear and Do it Anyway*, Susan Jeffers suggests that every single fear we have can be boiled down to one anxiety: the fear that we cannot handle the situation or its negative circumstances.) In other words, fear of rejection really means, "I can't handle being rejected," and fear of ending a relationship really means, "I can't handle being alone." When we believe in our ability to handle a situation, we eliminate our fears.

Second, by taking action *every single day* Stephen gradually reduced his fear to a negligible level. If we force ourselves to confront our fears on a manageable and repetitive basis, then with each exposure we prove to ourselves that we *can* handle it. We therefore cultivate self-belief—and confidence.

> Success or failure is almost always the direct result of mental conditioning. This process follows a consistent set of steps, or mental program, which starts with our mental input and ends with a predictable outcome built on the basis of that data. In between, very little is left to chance or luck. In short, things very rarely "just happen" to us; they happen because of our mental programming.

THE SECOND TRUTH: INTUITION

While the conscious mind is closely linked to everyday knowledge and experiences, research has shown that the subconscious has far wider access to resources. Everything from a simple rock to a living being is made up of energy, connected by the interlocking web of the universe. Our minds are therefore mere bundles of energy, and it's really our subconscious that connects us to the greater universe of knowledge. This access is sometimes referred to as "intuition," "imagination," "super-subconscious," or even the "universal mind." Whatever we elect to call it, it's certainly the source of real genius—the place where artists and (especially) great intellects get their inspiration. Albert Einstein was a great believer in its power, saying, "The intellect has little to do on the road to discovery. There comes a leap in consciousness, call it intuition or what you will, and the solution comes to you, and you don't know how or why... I am enough of an artist to draw freely upon my imagination... Imagination is more important than knowledge. Knowledge is limited. Imagination encircles the world."

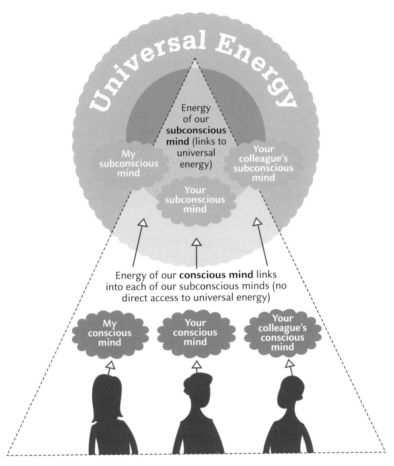

Therefore, if we actually allow the conscious mind to rest and rely on intuition, we might well discover better and more satisfying solutions. Of course, I'm not suggesting that we completely disregard logic, but instead that we allow our intuition to guide us. As Carl Jung wrote, "Intuition does not denote something contrary to reason, but something outside the province of reason." Similarly, Jonas Salk, the inventor of the polio vaccine, famously remarked, "I'm saying that we should trust our intuition. I believe that the principles of universal evolution are revealed to us through intuition. And I think that if we combine our intuition and our reason, we can respond in an evolutionary sound way to our problems."

Great leaders of today routinely talk about intuition or instinct as part of their success. Jack Welch, the former chief executive of General Electric (and widely credited with redefining business culture in America), believes that intuition plays a key role in success. The title of his autobiography says it all: *Straight From The Gut*. (In his subsequent book *Winning*, Welch refers to instinct as "gut calls.")

"Great," you may be saying to yourself. "But how can I *access* the terrific power of my intuition?" Well, it's not all that complicated. All you have to do is to let the mind sit quietly, optimally in an alpha-theta state, giving the brain time to digest and process information, and then do something creative with it. (And yes, I can guess your next thought: "What the hell is an alpha-theta state?")

As a long-time health-focused person (read: neurotic!), I'd often investigated the benefits of yoga, but had always dismissed it as inferior to "hard-core" exercise. My first yoga class only served to confirm my suspicions. "Give me a treadmill any day!" I thought to myself, as I sneaked out the back door midway through the hour. When a friend convinced me to try it again, this time in a more demanding Ashtanga class, I did at least find the challenge (and sweat) that I relished. However, sitting through the quiet meditation at the end was excruciating to me (I just *don't do* sitting still). Gradually, though, as I did more yoga, I became less averse to the meditation period and even began to explore its advantages. What I discovered convinced me to continue my efforts. While I still have difficulty sitting quietly for extended periods, I do it—if only five minutes a day—because everything I've discovered reinforces its benefits for a healthy system.

So what exactly is this alpha-theta state? There are four states of "being," as defined by the waves in our brains—beta, alpha, theta, and delta waves, measured by pulses per second (in hertz).

- ■ Beta—Represents active awareness.

- ■ Alpha—Represents relaxation, as when we're in deep contemplative or daydreaming mode. (Most people equate this state with meditation, but that isn't necessarily the case.)

- ■ Theta—Represents light sleep, as in Rapid Eye Movement (REM) dreams. In this state the brain is "working out," similar to what we do with our muscles at the gym—releasing tension and making the brain stronger and more efficient.

- ■ Delta—Represents deep (dead-to-the-world) sleep.

What fascinates me is that there is a range called alpha-theta, which is basically an overlap of two separate states.

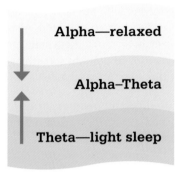

Alpha—relaxed

Alpha–Theta

Theta—light sleep

In this range the body experiences a partial theta and partial alpha state: We're conscious of everything around us, yet the body remains relaxed, almost to the point of dozing off. Because of the overlap of two states, the brain performs at optimal capacity, far beyond what it could achieve in either state alone. The wave pattern, a combination of alpha and theta, has dual benefits: The alpha wave serves as the bridge to the conscious mind (so that we can actually remember the contents of our brain activity), while the theta wave allows access to the subconscious inner space (which holds our highest creativity, insight, and intelligence; the source of intuition).

Albert Einstein meditated during his working day, probably putting himself in the alpha-theta state, to develop new theories. "The really valuable thing is intuition," he wrote. "Through meditation I found answers before I even asked the question." Now I'm *not* suggesting that you or anyone else will develop Einstein's genius by simply meditating(!), but it's more than possible that your productivity and creativity could improve.

Relaxing into the alpha-theta state does not mean being a Buddhist, a Zen master, a New Age follower, or even a remotely spiritual person. It can be as basic as finding some time to sit quietly and be aware of yourself—doing nothing, not attempting to solve the day's problems—your social life, your efforts to give up smoking, your kid's lost gerbil, or your upcoming tax bill. Instead, try simply *being*—allowing yourself to *be*.

THE THIRD TRUTH: OUR MINDS CAN MANIFEST RESULTS

Everyone's heard the phrase "mind over matter," but how many have considered its significance, or recalled that it's regarded as accurate by experts, including physicists, brain researchers, and important psychiatrists? These experts believe that the mind (our conscious thoughts) *can* have an impact upon matter (our physical reality). You don't need to understand the science involved to comprehend their conclusions: All universal energy is in constant motion and change, and when one piece changes, it automatically affects others. As humans, we're included within that chain of interaction, with our minds and bodies representing separate bundles of energy. In short, the energy of our thoughts can affect the energy of physical things around us.

Exactly how consciousness interacts with the physical world is still not fully understood. Some phenomena that were once accepted only in a spiritual context may now possess a basis in scientific proofs: It's now widely accepted that what we think and imagine—whether desirable or undesirable—will affect our preferred outcomes. Considering all the thoughts that go through our heads each minute, each hour, and each day, accepting and using this principle can harness tremendous mental power to help us achieve our goals.

Scientific research suggests that the connection between the mental and the physical happens something like this: When we think, that thought corresponds to a set of electrical impulses (energy) in the brain, within the neural system of the cerebral cortex. These impulses, through another process, establish the thought in the subconscious, which accepts it unquestioningly as reality. (Remember that the subconscious has no rational filtering system, so all thoughts are "truth" as far as it's concerned.) The energy of the subconscious is linked to the energy of the universe, and through this connection the subconscious attracts and forms those elements necessary for it to materialize our thought into its physical manifestation.

However, we have to be careful with positive and negative thoughts alike. A classic example of this is someone in financial difficulties. Obviously, his goal is—put bluntly—to have more money. But instead of moving positively toward that objective, he may instead focus entirely on his problems ("I can't afford my mortgage!" "What about my child's school fees?" "How can I possibly pay all my bills?"). Unless there is something stronger overriding these thought patterns, this person's entirely negative focus will probably only lead him into more—and greater—difficulties. Yet the irony is that such a person probably thinks that by focusing on his problems he's working to improve his situation!

On a personal level, people searching for strong relationships often make the same mistake, focusing on their loneliness and frustration ("Nobody available is right for me... How will I ever find someone who enjoys tuba-playing, steam trains, *and* Morris dancing?"). No wonder they fail to get the results they want!

Sports psychologists have been using these techniques for years in the form of visualization—a very powerful method used to nourish self-belief in the subconscious. Its power is based on the fact that something visualized is accepted as real by the subconscious just as readily as something tangible is deemed real by the conscious mind. In this case, the phrase "a picture is worth a thousand words" is actually true!

Jack Nicklaus is famous for his belief in the mind. In his book *Golf My Way*, he wrote, "Before every shot I go to the movies inside my head... First I see the ball where I want it to finish, nice and white and sitting up high on the bright green grass. Then I see the ball going there; its path and trajectory and even its behavior on landing. The next scene shows me making the kind of swing that will turn the previous image into reality. These home movies are a key... to every shot." In fact, Nicklaus attributes 50 percent of a successful shot to mental rehearsal, giving it equal billing with talent. Chris Evert, the former U.S. tennis champion, is another believer. Before every match she mentally pictured herself against her opponent, consistently overcoming her rival's best shots; then she visualized herself winning.

Weeks before the Olympics in which Mary Lou Retton won gymnastics gold, she suffered a knee injury that required surgery. As she lay in the hospital bed, she constantly visualized each of her routines and rehearsed the entire Olympic experience in her mind, including her elation at receiving the gold medal with "The Star Spangled Banner" playing in the background. (Obviously a productive use of her time!)

Visualization is key for today's great athletes as well:

> ■ Tiger Woods attributes much of his success to the visualization and mental techniques that he was taught from childhood by his father (who had a degree in psychology and Special Forces military training). When Tiger was 13, he began working with Dr. Jay Brunza, a psychologist who taught him relaxation and visualization techniques that became an everyday part of his training—and innate when on the course.

- Sir Clive Woodward, who guided England's rugby team to World Cup victory, sees mental preparation and visualization as every bit as important as physical strength. British tennis experts have turned to him to see how visualization could benefit Britain's top players, and today he is the elite director for performance with the British Olympic Association.

- Ron Dennis, the former boss of McClaren, one of the most successful Formula One racing teams, has said that most drivers visualize with such intensity that it all just becomes fluid in their minds.

Why shouldn't lawyers, too, benefit from these proven methods for success?

The subconscious accepts not only thoughts but whatever it "sees" (whether real or imaginary) as truth. Then it works hard to match our reality with what it believes its vision encompasses.

VISUALIZATION EXERCISE: Decide exactly what you want to accomplish, being crystal-clear about the specifics. To give your mind an accurate objective (i.e., a roadmap to the results you want), you must know exactly what that is. That's why we're so often told to write our goals down. We may *think* we know what we want, but only by writing our goals down do they become fully crystallized in our minds.

Second, give your mind the right information. Decide up front what sort of picture you want to imprint, and then focus your mind on that predefined, pre-determined image. Visualize yourself in possession of every characteristic required to accomplish the results you desire. Let's assume that you want to improve your communication skills and be more confident in the company of colleagues and clients. In that case, visualize yourself talking to those people, looking assertive, with strong posture and presence. Imagine these people listening to your every word while regarding you with admiration and respect. You might even imagine compliments and applause for one of your speeches. But don't only imagine big occasions: Picture yourself effortlessly excelling in the normal situations of your day-to-day environment. As you visualize, try to feel the joy of your accomplishment and the power of your communication just as if it was happening in real life. (Remember, by experiencing the success of your goal you increase the imprint of the visualization into your subconscious.)

My friend Anna, who starts thinking positively where most people leave off, goes one step beyond visualization by acting as if she's already achieved her desired result. Recently, she decided that she wanted a larger flat with a bigger garden in the same neighborhood as her home at that time. Considering that she already lived in one of the most exclusive areas of London and that homes there very rarely come on the market, I had little confidence in her realizing her wish. However, Anna began making arrangements for a move, and acting as if everything was happening in accordance with her plan. When I visited her one evening and saw piles of packed boxes, I frankly thought her mad. But then—out of the blue!—her dream home came on the market, and six weeks later she was enjoying her spacious new garden.

Now you might think this a lucky fluke, or that, for even recounting the story, I'm as crazy as Anna! However, many great achievers have supported their goals by acting "as if." Jack Canfield, the co-creator of the billion-dollar brand *Chicken Soup for the Soul*, advocates acting like a success before you are one (see *The Success Principles: How to Get from Where You Are to Where You Want to Be*). When he started with the goal of being an international consultant, he secured his passport, bought an international clock, and printed business cards featuring his desired title and details. After deciding that Sydney was his ultimate destination, he bought a poster of its harbor and hung it on his refrigerator. It was only a short while later that his dream became a reality, and his first assignment was in—you guessed it!—Australia.

In his book, Mr. Canfield also mentions a party he attended, with a theme of "Act As If." Guests were instructed to come as the people they aspired to be and to act in accordance with that status. Some people arrived in limousines, while the press interviewed others. Again, you may find this proposition weird, but a high percentage of the people at that party did in fact become what they impersonated that night.

The actor Jim Carrey wholeheartedly endorses visualization and acting "as if." Before he was well known, he used to drive himself to the top of Hollywood Hills and visualize his success. He wouldn't leave until he'd experienced the euphoria of (non-existent) adulation, and, while driving home, he'd feel as if it were reality. At one point he wrote a check to himself for $10 million, dating it November 1995. After that he secured his first major roles in several films, including the part in *Mask* that led to real fame. And in November 1995, he signed a contract for $10 million!

Carrey believes that everything that happens in life is first created in the mind, and that when you convince yourself of something, it will happen. He has said that he brainwashed both himself and the universe, and that this has been the source of his success.

If at this point you are still unconvinced—"Yeah, well, it still sounds like a lot of coincidences to me"—then consider the group of university basketball players who were tested to determine the impact that mental practice (as opposed to actual practice) could have on free-throw performance. They were first tested for proficiency and then randomly assigned to three groups. The first group practiced physically for an hour a day; the second group practiced only in their minds for an hour a day; and the third group did nothing. As expected, after one month the group that did nothing showed no improvement (duh!). But the group that practiced physically and the group that practiced mentally both improved—and at similar rates!

There have been over 100 scientifically monitored studies with similar results. (A few examples are Kolonay, 1977, free-throw shooting; Wrisberg & Anshel, 1989, free-throw shooting; Hird, Landers, Thomas, & Horan, 1991, landing an airplane; Bird & Wilson, 1988, conducting an orchestra; Palmer, 1988, gymnastics; and Isayama, 1992, swimming.)

In short, visualizing helps us not only for the reasons discussed earlier but also because of *symbolic learning theory*. This theory suggests that every action we take is first encoded like a blueprint in our minds, and that it's this blueprint that allows us to complete the action successfully. Mental rehearsing simply reinforces and clarifies the blueprint. Oddly, even when only visualizing an action we produce the same (somewhat miniaturized) muscle contractions used in that activity: In essence, the same neural sequence occurs when we mentally rehearse as when we physically execute, as the brain neurons fire the electronic

message to the appropriate muscles. The psychologist Richard Suin measured the electrical activity of downhill ski racers while they visualized skiing a course. The results showed the same muscle activity as when they were actually skiing, with the muscle activity level at its peak when the skiers were imagining the most challenging parts of the course. So by visualizing an activity, we strengthen the neural pathways controlling those movements.

This reinforces what we learned previously about the mind's mirroring behaviors: What the mind sees (either a real occurrence or a picture) becomes its own reality, evoking the same neural activity as if we were physically performing the action. By causing the neurons to fire in the brain we create new synapses related to that activity, and by virtue of plasticity (as discussed in Chapter 6) we create a strong neural network to reinforce preferred behaviors.

Further, whenever we visualize achievements, our brain believes we have actually performed well and uses this as evidence of success, which feeds into our self-belief (and our abilities!). In the study of basketball players mentioned previously, the free-throw skills of the participants were tested again a month after the end of the trial. The success rate of those who had physically practiced had dropped dramatically, but the players who had only visualized their performance actually maintained their levels of success. The study concluded that since visual practice involved only successful shots, the players' subconscious minds better maintained confidence in their abilities. In fact, the subconscious (having no contradictory information) was 100 percent confident! Envisioning "successes only" not only affected the players' beliefs but also created a powerful and permanent neural network to support the activity. (Remember the "use it or lose it" principle: Weak neural networks get expelled!)

SUCCESS IS CONTINGENT ON OUR THINKING

Having finished this chapter, consider again the "truths" I put to you in the beginning: Our success is the result of our thinking, and to succeed we must support all our actions with positive self-belief.

1. As advocated in the first truth, we can manipulate our mental programming by using the conscious mind as the gatekeeper.

    a. Eliminate any negative self-talk

        i. Consciously state encouraging beliefs, in the present tense and in a positive format ("I am confident," not "I am not nervous")

        ii. Repeat positive affirmations to reprogram the subconscious, in the present and as though current reality ("I am," not "I will")

b. Build confidence

    i. Develop the internal belief that we are capable of accomplishing our goals through the above steps

    ii. Reprogram the mind and override failures by visualizing new success stories—"movies in the mind"—and by *not* mentally replaying failures

    iii. Abandon toxic thoughts
- no "awfulizing";
- no "all or nothing" mindset;
- no negative assumptions; and
- no negative filtering.

    iv. Reduce anxiety with FEAR: Face Everything And Recover (create situations that engender manageable levels of anxiety and then prove to yourself that you can handle those situations)

2. As we learned in the second "truth," our subconscious is connected to universal energy, and is thus linked to a far greater depth of knowledge. If we can allow ourselves to relax and believe in it, we may find answers there that are more creative than our conscious mind has the depth to discover. We can best achieve this through the alpha-theta state.

3. The final truth is sometimes the most difficult to grasp—that our subconscious's connections with the universal energy give it the resources to manifest whatever reality we want, and that we have the power to consciously program it to do that. With this in mind...

    a. We should have a preconceived picture of what our success looks like: Then we visualize that image, use all the senses to really experience success, and manipulate the subconscious to accept it as reality

    b. We can override past failures or negative input with far more dominant positive beliefs (and images) of success

    c. We can act in a manner consistent with our goals—as if we are already achieving them

    d. When we practice (even just within our minds) we build and strengthen the neural network that supports the behaviors, skills, and mindset that we desire

ONE LAST COMMENT

When I first discovered the power of thoughts I was hopeful and skeptical at the same time. On the one hand I thought, "Wow! I think I've found that magical ingredient that will make all the difference to my success and my life!" But then my logical, cautious (read "lawyer"!) side kicked in, telling me: "Don't be ridiculous! Hard work is the only real secret to success. Besides, if it were that easy, everyone would be doing it." Fortunately, my natural curiosity and quest for knowledge propelled me to read every book I could find on the subject, attend any number of courses, and speak to a wide range of specialists. While much of the research came from different perspectives (from science to religion and everything in between!), it all boiled down to the same conclusion: Our thoughts determine our destiny.

Since my initial discovery, I've become more and more convinced of this truth. Of course, it has its limits. When I first discussed it with my good friend Gundula, a brilliant lawyer, she retorted cynically that, OK, if I'd just excuse her a second, she was off to imagine herself as a great opera singer! I'm *not* suggesting that if we just visualize something it will inevitably happen (especially given the quality of Gundula's voice!—SORRY, G.!!!). I'm just saying that if we combine daily action with supporting positive beliefs, we're still *guaranteed* better results than if we sabotage ourselves with negative thinking.

So if this is really the case, why isn't positive thinking a part of our lives? Why don't we grow up learning these simple techniques? It's a question I ask routinely. Authors including Napoleon Hill, Norman Vincent Peale, and Maxwell Maltz wrote about these concepts as early as the 1930s. (In Chapter 3 I mentioned Napoleon Hill and his book *Think and Grow Rich*, a book inspired by studying the "secret" positive-thinking mindset of the great financiers of his time.) In fact, since the '30s we've all been bombarded by self-help books on every aspect of positive thinking, along with many books derived or copied from the most successful of these. Perhaps many of us (lawyers by no means excluded!) tend to consider these ideas the work of self-promoting cranks. Yet in the 1990s Martin Seligman, then the newly elected president of the American Psychological Association, made waves by criticizing the entire focus of his profession, suggesting that it might be far more beneficial to focus on the positive mind than on the negative. Since then positive psychology has become a mainstream academic subject, and today even a number of governments are researching it with a view to improving quality of life for their citizens. Here in the U.K. we now have the Whitehall Wellbeing Working Group, which is even—finally!—examining how positive thinking can be taught in schools.

Despite the abundance of information now available, the main reason most people fail to access positive thinking is because they, like me, feel skeptical about something that sounds so simple. However, the reality is that thinking positively is *not* simple. We're all trained to think critically (a "good" thing) and pessimistically (a "bad" thing)—and we all live in a world where negativity dominates. Just watch the news or read a newspaper! So perhaps the real reason is that it's too hard rather than too easy, and—like going to the gym all the time or relinquishing a bad habit—we may all *know* we should do it, but find it difficult to commit for the long haul. In the meantime, while it's theoretically available to everyone, only the few who commit long term and persevere really take advantage of its enormous benefits.

So, what's your excuse? All I'm proposing is that, as an unquestionably well-educated, indisputably hard-working, and demonstrably able segment of the population, you should use to your advantage what is a proven ingredient to success. If not you, who? And if not now, when?

Chapter Eight
Awareness Building Block 5: Positive Impact

(Understanding how impressions are made)

Before going any further, I want to remind you of a few crucial facts about how we make an impression on people around us. Even if you feel sure that you know all the statistics already, they bear reinforcement.

POINT ONE: SADLY, IT'S NOT WHAT YOU SAY THAT MATTERS

Many studies have been done regarding how we form judgments about others. Depending on the report and the particular situation being analyzed, the statistics may vary—but only slightly. All such research seems to conclude that *at least* 90 percent of what people think of us depends on how we look and sound rather than what we actually say... Yes, the sad news is that *less than 10 percent* of how we are perceived depends on stunning content and mind-blowing erudition! In fact, the prevailing statistical data quotes percentages like this:

Verbal Content	7%
(Type/style of) voice	38%
Body language/image (non-verbal qualities)	55%

Note: These percentages were originally published by psychologist Albert Mehrabian in relation to studying communications involving feelings and attitudes.

Now, if you've never examined such statistics you might feel disposed to challenge them, but your time would be better employed in taking them to heart—because the same findings have emerged in study after study. Non-verbal qualities will always override the verbal, although this may occur at a subconscious level. Simply put, well-groomed and confident people will generally be perceived as cleverer than they really are. Conversely, the disheveled or unpolished instantly jeopardize any positive perception of their intelligence, competence, or charm.

Which door would you choose?

At this point you're probably thinking, "Yeah, sure, that's probably the case in some professions, but my job is all about providing insights; that's the real basis on which *I'm* judged." I completely relate to this point of view, because I thought similarly myself until, as members of a trend-setting practice, my partners and I attended a training course where we were presented with these statistics. I was willing to accept that the way people look and sound could somewhat enhance or damage their image but still privately thought, "These guys don't understand that, for lawyers, content will always have a much more significant role to play."

As the course progressed we practiced being interviewed in media situations and were shown various techniques to improve and exploit our delivery, choice of language, and communication skills. We were also constantly reminded that a powerful presence is more important than the substance of our responses. In fact, the trainer dared us to go still further by noting, "Even if you give a totally unrelated answer to a specific question, if you manage to look confident and sound articulate most people won't even notice, while many others—despite realizing that you've dodged the query—will still automatically conclude that you must be brilliant."

Ridiculous, I thought. How could any lawyer possibly be perceived as competent—let alone brilliant—without providing an answer to the question asked? But as we worked through the exercises I became increasingly convinced that there was something in the trainer's advice, especially during the mock interview exercises—all of which were videotaped and subjected to later scrutiny. Some of these exercises involved topics familiar to any lawyer; others focused on areas in which we had no expertise, forcing us to demonstrate our (fake) "know-how" anyway (in my case, not very well!).

Probably what made the strongest impression was the session in which—regardless of what question we were asked—we were to communicate a particular, completely unrelated, message to the audience. Lawyers with confident body language and persuasive voices were almost always accepted as providing superior answers, even though the audience (of lawyers) should really have been capable of far deeper analysis. One partner in my firm was especially capable; in fact, it was only later, while examining the videotaped interviews, that the rest of us realized the meaninglessness of his answer! Each of us had perceived him as extremely credible—based upon everything *except* the substance of his comments. (How depressing is that?!)

Historically, there may be no more powerful example of this phenomenon than the 1960 presidential debates between John F. Kennedy and Richard M. Nixon. These were the first televised political debates and are remembered because the way the candidates were perceived proved to be decisive in the ensuing election.

Most historians agree that Richard Nixon's verbal content, political experience, and policy overview were more appealing than Kennedy's. However, the vast majority of those who watched still selected Kennedy as the winner because they focused on what they saw rather than on what they heard; fascinatingly, most people listening to the debates on the radio actually favored Nixon. As it happened, Nixon had been seriously injured two weeks before the debate and arrived in an ill-fitting suit looking pale, tired, and underweight. Kennedy, on the other hand, appeared tanned, well rested, and impeccably groomed. In other words, it was Kennedy's smooth delivery and appealing image that persuaded people that he was the one to vote for.

The public perception of the debates and the fact that viewers saw them as a significant reason for the swing toward Kennedy have stoked argument regarding the impact of television (and image) on political campaigns ever since. No one can deny that Ronald Reagan's strong visual presence and ability to appear poised on camera (learned in Hollywood) benefited his political career. (Reagan himself, when asked whether acting prepared him for the presidency, once quipped, "I don't see how any fellow who wasn't an actor could do this job!") In fact, his charismatic persona was key to his 1980 debate victories over Jimmy Carter, who had hoped to overshadow Reagan with his stronger intellect. In the 2008 primaries Hillary Clinton's evolving styles got as much press as her politics, and the emergence of Barack Obama from relative obscurity to a Presidential candidate, and then the overriding victor, would suggest that being telegenic and a gifted communicator is more critical than ever to political success. Regardless of where one stands on the issue of image versus substance, one fact remains: Image can make or break a politician. In fact, these days the public perception of a politician seems to have more impact on his or her success than any number of policies and opinions.

If image can so affect today's politicians, then imagine what one's public persona can do for a legal career, encompassing such areas as client development, networking, public speaking, and the ability to convey a strong brand. However, stressing the importance of image doesn't mean that content no longer matters. Instead, I'm urging you to consider how a really positive image could enhance your knowledge, delivery, particular expertise, and other skills.

POINT TWO: FIRST IMPRESSIONS COUNT (A LOT!)

Once again, many studies have been conducted on how terrifyingly quickly people tend to form personal impressions. These studies conclude that it takes about four minutes in all, but that around *90 percent* of that impression is determined within the first 90 seconds.

FIRST IMPRESSION takes four minutes

90% OF THAT IMPRESSION happens in the first 90 seconds

Bear in mind that the chance to make a good first impression, by definition, comes only once, and that dropping the ball at this stage means that our best opportunity is almost always lost. First impressions are nearly impossible to retract, and they have the power to influence the way new acquaintances will view us from that point on. This is because the information they initially take in tends to act as a natural barrier to any later input. Scientists have proved that when the brain downloads subsequent information it first searches for similarities that can be reconciled with knowledge it has already stored, and that it therefore automatically emphasizes ideas that successfully match pre-received data. The brain can resist—even disregard—ideas intrinsically inconsistent with what it has previously assimilated (a process called *homeostasis*).

Another fascinating aspect to this *first impressions theory* is this: Once people perceive a particular personality trait in someone, they tend to assume that that person is likely to possess other (related) characteristics (the *implicit personality theory*). If I meet you for the first time and express warmth and interest in you ("Oh, yes; great to meet you! You must tell me all about your amazing deal with CNN!"), then from that initial encounter, you're likely to emerge with the impression that I'm a thoughtful "people person." However, the interesting part is that you're also overwhelmingly likely to assume that I'm also intelligent, generous, delightful, attractive, and a trustworthy and supportive friend, even though you have almost no evidence to support these theories. Even if I happen to be distracted and self-absorbed the next time we meet, you will probably filter this information out simply because it is inconsistent with your first impression, which (luckily for me!) has already become embedded in your mind.

Conversely, should you arrive for our first meeting and discover me screaming at my personal assistant, you might decide that I'm arrogant, bad-tempered, and acrimonious. Again, this may not actually be the case—I might have been involved in a rare dispute due to a highly volatile situation, and my fury might be either justified or totally out of character. Yet these ameliorating circumstances probably won't register (should you come to know about them), because your brain forevermore is likely to associate me with bad temper. I will have an uphill task afterwards to demonstrate my positive character qualities—if you even let me try! It will almost certainly take many more meetings and overwhelmingly positive interactions to erase that deep-rooted first impression.

MAKE A POSITIVE IMPRESSION

If we understand and work with these truths about how others form their first ideas about us, then we can do our best to start off relationships on the right foot. And remember, by making a positive impression you'll have a better chance to achieve your goals: conveying a confident and distinctive brand, developing your own business, and being perceived as a leader.

FIRST IMPRESSION STATISTICS

- Verbal content accounts for *only* 7 percent of first impressions

- Type/style of voice accounts for 38 percent

- Body language/physical image (non-verbal qualities) account for 55 percent

- People draw their first conclusions within four minutes—and 90 percent of perceptions are made within 90 seconds

- It's hard to overturn a first impression because of homeostasis; the brain subsequently rejects inconsistent data

- First impressions have such a significant impact because of implicit personality theory (people assume that you possess related characteristics)

Chapter 9: Brand: The Beginning

An introduction to the three "balls"

Chapter Nine
Brand: The Beginning
(An introduction to the three "balls")

Having now worked through all five of the awareness building blocks, you should have an optimal foundation from which to begin working with your three "balls"—brand, business, and leadership. In Chapter 2, in the context of becoming the Master Juggler of your practice, I suggested that your goal is not only to handle each of these balls individually, but to simultaneously manipulate them so smoothly that they become indistinguishable. (In essence, they each leverage off the other.) Achieving this result begins with building your brand in terms of the other two balls. Let me explain how this works in practice.

BUSINESS

Do you ever wonder why one of your colleagues always seems to get the most clients or reel in the best deals? Do you ever wonder why he (or she) is the unquestioned rainmaker, consistently outperforming more competent and dynamic colleagues? Is it phenomenal sales prowess, or just being in the right place at the right time?

Dig deeper, and you'll discover that most successful rainmakers have no greater talent for sales than anyone else. What they *do* have is a finely-tuned proficiency in connecting with people and an innate understanding of how relationships can turn into business.

Most successful rainmakers have no greater talent for sales than anyone else. What they do have is a finely-tuned proficiency in connecting with people and an innate understanding of how relationships can turn into business.

In the next chapters I'll show you how you too can achieve the results of a rainmaker by first creating (and marketing) your brand (ball number one) and then by using your brand to help you deal with your second ball—generating business. When leveraged one after the other, these two balls should complete the sales process for you and bring the business you'll need for long-term success. Here's how it works...

Clients engage us (their lawyers) primarily on the basis of trust, and this trust is a direct reflection of the relationship we've cultivated with them. By definition, our clients' trust in us must be founded on our reliability, truthfulness, and ability, as evidenced either first hand (over time) or through a credible source. So the goal of any client-development activity or sales process is to create that trust.

The Ultimate Goal (to Sell) = Establish Trust

The starting point is to determine the underlying principles of trust. What is it that you can offer?

- Who are you?

- What is your skill?

- What do you promise to deliver?

- How will you add unique value?

- What is your experience and track record?

Essentially, these elements make up your brand. The goal is to deliver a powerful message of who you are and what you do and then convince your clients that they can trust you. Do this *by demonstrating and being your brand at all times.* You can't turn on your brand Monday morning and turn it off when

Time to go home and be the real me.

heading home at night—unless you want to pursue the mentally exhausting route of projecting a fraudulent brand! The truth is that developing confidence and self-belief in your brand requires living it, being it, breathing it, and believing it every single day.

The next step in the sales undertaking is to create brand awareness, which means marketing and publicizing your brand by introducing yourself to people. When you first connect you make a pivotal breakthrough in the continuum of the sales process, but if you try to sell at that point you risk the possibility of rejection, and aborting the exercise altogether. This is the key aspect to selling and cultivating business that most successful rainmakers viscerally understand.

Before attempting to sell anything it's critical to bond with the person and nurture your relationship with him so that he has confidence in your brand. This *is* a part of networking, but don't allow yourself to be confused by negative connotations. Networking isn't merely cocktails and small talk; it's also strengthening relationships and establishing trust. It's about communicating and sharing ideas, information, and resources with the people who are now— at least peripherally—in your network.

It's only when we've developed the requisite trust that we can embark upon the final stage of the sales process. At this point the prospective client should know that we can deliver, and our networking activities ought to have generated a bond. Having cultivated that level of relationship, very little *selling* should be necessary. All the previous steps should have removed any need for self-promotion. Instead, we've created something far more valuable: trust, which makes up most of the sales decision process anyway. Now all we have to do is close on the details!

Sometimes we have to make a pitch or sell our services *before* we have the opportunity to develop a trusting relationship with a prospective client. It's on these occasions that our ability to sell is more essential and a positive outcome is rather less certain. That said, if we've gotten that far on the basis of a strong brand, that brand should still do some of the selling for us.

And remember, once a sale is made and a connection becomes a client, the marketing and networking process isn't done and dusted! Clients are the integral component to our network, and we must continuously nurture relationships with them.

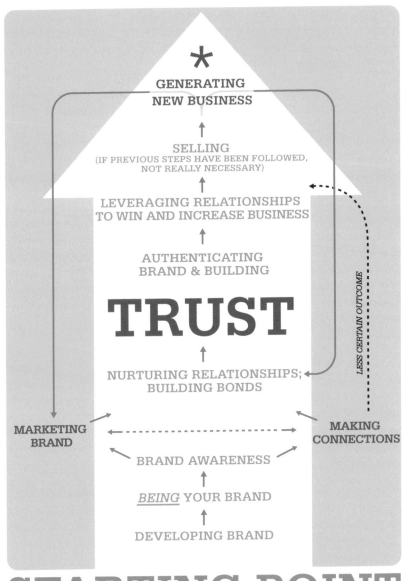

STARTING POINT

LEADERSHIP

Just as we begin the process of mastering the second ball (winning business) by initially succeeding with the first one (establishing an authentic personal brand), the third ball (leadership) also relies upon the first step of brand building.

Recall our definition of a leader from Chapter 2 ("The Juggling Act"): It's someone who has vision and is able to mobilize and inspire others, so that everyone is working steadfastly to achieve the same goals (shared purpose). As we considered briefly in Chapter 2, you cannot lead others unless you first lead yourself, and this boils down to creating (and working toward) your own personal vision. This vision should highlight both your natural strengths and your inner motivations, and when it does, you can build a truly authentic brand around it. If, for example, your personal vision is to become a corporate lawyer doing mega-deal transactions, then dealing with high-level, demanding executives in a fast-paced, high-pressure environment will be a source of (positive) adrenaline for you, rather than a source of stress. Such genuine passion will allow you to build and demonstrate a brand that is both credible and authentic, which in turn will help you achieve your goal (master of mega-deals!).

In addition, an authentic brand positions you for leadership because working with your true self brings contentment. This mindset tends to generate a positive outlook, a focus on other people, a genuine commitment (to your vision), and real integrity (reinforced by self-fulfillment). When acting on this basis, you are automatically in the optimal position to lead: In fact, an authentic brand is key to unlocking your leadership potential.

IT ALL STARTS WITH BRAND

The purpose of this chapter is to demonstrate how the first step toward developing business *and* leadership is to convey a brand that fosters respect and trust from others, and—from that basis—creates the relationships we need to fulfill our goals.

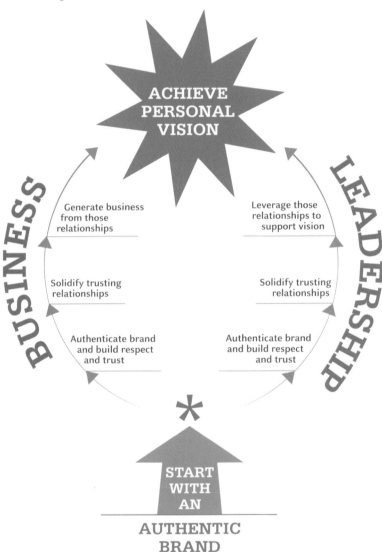

ACHIEVE PERSONAL VISION

BUSINESS

LEADERSHIP

Generate business from those relationships

Leverage those relationships to support vision

Solidify trusting relationships

Solidify trusting relationships

Authenticate brand and build respect and trust

Authenticate brand and build respect and trust

START WITH AN

AUTHENTIC BRAND

So let's move on to our three balls, beginning with our first ball—building and marketing a personal brand.

- We will examine how your brand must be developed on the basis of your true self—the only way it can be both authentic and distinct (Chapter 10).

- In addition to those things that make your brand unique, there are certain behaviors and skills common to *all* strong brands, which you may need to adopt (Chapter 11).

- In Chapter 12, we will put everything together to create your authentic, distinct, and superior brand, which will demonstrate how you deliver unique value—whatever that means for you.

- Finally, I'll discuss some ideas on how to enhance and market your brand to maintain superiority in a market that is both increasingly competitive and in a constant state of flux (Chapter 13). One of the most effective methods is public speaking, which is discussed in Chapter 14.

In Chapter 15 we will begin working with our second ball—business!

- Many lawyers have misconceptions about networking. If you're uncomfortable with the whole idea, Chapter 15 will introduce you to a new approach.

- Winning new clients requires making introductions and connections, which means getting out there: meeting and greeting. This can be one of the most intimidating parts of networking, so Chapter 16 is a step-by-step guide to ease the process—and even to make it enjoyable!

- In Chapter 17, we'll look at some strategies for leveraging your network, winning new business, and strengthening relationships with existing clients.

Finally, we'll move into our third and final ball—leadership.

- Chapter 18 sets out the most effective ways leaders influence others and teaches you how to use these methods in your own leadership journey.

The next three chapters detail how to move through the three dimensions of leadership and ultimately inspire others to help you toward your goals.

- *Self-leading.* In Chapter 19 you'll consider your personal vision and how to lead yourself with a positive mindset and real perseverance.

- *Leading within relationships.* In Chapter 20 we'll look at how we lead within relationships. In essence, we'll learn how to create the *right* relationships and then generate followers.

- *Leading a team.* After mastering the first two dimensions of leadership, we can finally build upon all the skills of the previous chapters and use them to motivate and empower a team toward a shared purpose (Chapter 21).

Let's begin!

Chapter 10: **Brand "You"**

Chapter 11: **Adopting the Core Traits
of a Superior Brand**

Chapter 12: **Brand Creation**

Chapter 13: **Enhancing and Marketing
Your Brand**

Chapter 14: **Public Speaking**

Brand

Chapter Ten

Brand "You"

T he world's most successful individuals (Richard Branson, Madonna, Oprah, Beckham)—in common with the world's most successful companies (Coca Cola, Google, Starbucks, Nike) each have a strong identity—something that sets them apart. As you read each of these names I'm sure that you felt a strong emotion: not necessarily a positive one, but at least *something!* And unless you have personal knowledge of these people (or companies), that emotion emerged from a montage of their appearance and style, personality, behaviors, values, and attitudes. In a word: their brand.

So, what's *your* brand?

- What experience do you create for your clients and colleagues?

- What emotions do you invoke in others?

- How do your skills and characteristics mesh? Do they accurately project the person you want others to see, reflect your values, and communicate a consistent message?

- What do people say about you (especially when you're not in the room)? Is it what you want them to say?

If not, you're willfully depriving yourself of one of the most effective marketing tools there is. Perhaps you're too anxious trying to be all things to all people to *have* a personal brand. If that's the case, you need to figure out exactly what you're about and create an image that will optimally present and sell *you*.

Before the personal branding seminar

INCORPORATE YOURSELF

Sometimes, especially if we've worked hard to become part of a firm, we can temporarily allow that role to define us. ("Nice to meet you. I'm an associate with the firm Hugely Exclusive & Important.") Even if the firm *is* impressive (and others are in fact impressed by your association with it), letting the firm define you over the long term drastically limits your ability to distinguish yourself, not only from colleagues but also from the competition. Each of us must at some point relinquish that employee mindset and instead consider ourselves to be an individual corporation, with a distinct identity and a personal mission statement. Bear in mind that as lawyers we're surrounded by hard-working and intelligent individuals (well, hey, that's the theory!), so those qualities alone are unlikely to set us apart.

After the personal branding seminar

It's important to realize that self-incorporation does not mean being disloyal to the firm or having objectives inconsistent with its interests. It simply means taking control of your own career. Think of your brand (including you, its main asset) as a venture partner with your law firm. If, at any time during the partnership, your personal company is not performing, the firm can terminate the arrangement (and it will!). But by the same token, if at some point you're no longer satisfied with the deal, make sure that your balance sheet is such that you have the leverage to do something about it.

Keep in mind that incorporation doesn't negate all the other things that I advocate—and it certainly doesn't imply either isolationism or egocentrism. We all know the unloved (and unlovable) members of the firm: the ones who are out for themselves. Maintaining good relationships with colleagues is paramount, and accepting the concept of self-incorporation doesn't alter that fact. So if you want your brand to thrive, be sure to partner with your colleagues on a daily basis and follow the rules of generosity.

WHAT IS YOUR BRAND?

But to get back to the point, try asking yourself three questions.

"What's my ideal brand?"
When pondering this, you might want to dig a bit deeper. What are the emotions you want people to feel when they see or think about you? How would you like your clients or colleagues to describe you to others?

"Is my ideal brand really in line with me?"
Think back to the chapters dealing with personality and motivators. For everything to work optimally, your core values and your brand should reflect your new understanding of yourself. (Also, as mentioned in Chapter 5 ["Motivators"], make sure you're not setting yourself up for disappointment by trying to live out someone else's dreams for you—perhaps your parents' dreams or your spouse's dreams.) Then consider:

"Is my brand attainable?"
Others' advice can be handy here. Don't panic if there is some doubt on this point, because your brand should be ambitious; the nature of a strong brand is that it *should* set you apart from the herd. However, its attainability will depend, in large part, on how well it fits the real you. A goal that doesn't drive you or suit you will be almost impossible to achieve.

So take the time to modify your brand so that it's in line with your true personality and values. It's time well spent, because otherwise your brand will never be entirely credible or sustainable. No amount of packaging or cover-up can suppress your true identity over the long term. If part of you yearns to wow the Supreme Court with an intricate devastation of the defense case, but your heart pounds with nerves when lodging a complaint at the dry cleaner's, this is not a sustainable goal for you.

The Warren Buffett Brand

Everyone has heard of Warren Buffett, one of the world's richest financial investors. His brand is equally well known: conservative and patient. He doesn't rush to invest in businesses or take undue risks; instead, he waits for market corrections or downturns to buy solid businesses at reasonable prices. He then manages them with the considered objective of long-term profits and solid market share. It is this approach that has safely propelled Buffett through various financial crises.

Buffett's brand is wholly consistent with who he is. He's not your average flamboyant, risk-taking, hotshot financial guru. He's unlikely to star in a television program, nor is he routinely accompanied by Hollywood "arm candy." Buffett has never tried to be anything but himself, and from the beginning of his career he leveraged his strengths of patience and practicality—neither of which is necessarily the norm in high-profile finance. Yet over the years he has become his own unique brand, now popularized as the investment style of "economic moat."

The David Cameron Brand

I recently had the opportunity to hear David Cameron, the U.K. Conservative Party leader, speak to a group of London leaders. In his speech he emphasized the importance of leading within the boundaries of one's own personality and not attempting to emulate someone else's style. He mentioned, for example, that he doesn't live and breathe politics 24 hours a day, that when he comes home at night he is merely a husband and father, and that without that "down time" he strongly feels that he would be much less effective in his job. I have no doubt that Mr. Cameron was emphasizing his authenticity here, and even possibly differentiating himself from the most successful post-war Conservative leader, Margaret Thatcher, who prided herself on her extreme work ethic and on sleeping (at most!) four hours a night.

The Al Gore Brand

At the same event, I also heard a speech by Al Gore. Now no one can deny that Al Gore has one of the strongest brands either inside or outside of politics, a brand based almost wholly on one of the things he values most: saving the environment. The result is a brand of superior and passionate authenticity.

Your Authentic Brand

If you think your true self is not the brand of the typically successful lawyer, don't despair: Instead, follow Warren Buffett's example by leveraging your particular personality strengths to create your own unique way of achieving success. (Most lawyers never get the chance to wow the Supreme Court anyway, but that doesn't mean they're not successful!) Like David Cameron, take your own path to your goals, and as Al Gore has done, guarantee brand authenticity by letting your brand proclaim what you really value.

DETERMINING YOUR BRAND

As you read through the following hints, think about how you should incorporate them into your brand, and then make some notes. (Keep the notes handy for the Chapter 12 exercise, when you'll put everything to do with your brand together.) Keep in mind that the objective of the exercise is to create a brand that is authentic, distinct, and superior.

Attitude

The first place to start is the attitude of your brand, or the emotional impact you want to have on others. How would you like to be summed up, using only a few words? Keep in mind that you're aiming for consistency of message, and that by achieving distinctiveness you may have to reject some things you might prefer. In terms of fashion, for example, you can't be classic (think Audrey Hepburn) and trendy (Madonna in the '80s) at the same time; however, you *can* just choose to be stylish, which possibly embodies both. (Although I certainly wouldn't recommend Madonna's "cone bra" look for a lawyer!)

How would you like to be summed up, using only a few words?

Of course, this goes beyond mere appearances. Consider how you speak, which emotions you tend to show (and to what extent), and whether (or how) you choose to use humor. You may have a witty, Churchillian aura, or a southern charisma worthy of Bill Clinton; you may choose to emphasize your innate resilience, or your volatile brilliance. In relation to your colleagues, you could be considered either a team player or an assertive star. Obviously, the attitude you're trying to convey should align with the characteristics and motivators you discovered in the previous chapters. Be honest with yourself, and determine your brand based on the strengths and tendencies you've observed.

If you still need help, Appendix 10.A provides some ideas related to the personality types examined in Chapter 4. From that list, figure out your key behavior traits and give yourself points on a scale of one to ten for all the traits listed. As noted before, most of us are a wonderful mish-mash of personality types, so your brand can authentically be a "mix and match"... However, if you identify strongly with one personality type, it's far less likely that you'll possess a core trait from that personality's opposite. A strong Driver, for example, is unlikely to exhibit the Moderate's modest qualities, but IS likely to score a 10/10 on "assertive"!

First Impressions

The initial impression you make on someone, even if no words are exchanged, is your first chance to convey who you are. So you must also demonstrate your brand through your personal image. What does your brand look like? Do you cultivate the wild artistic-tie look (the zany creative?) or the sober-sides ("rely on me")? Do you seek to look authoritative, or do you prefer to be perceived as cool? If female, do you emphasize your femininity or downplay it? The right choice depends upon you and the objective of your brand—but if you're looking to be the head of a traditional firm, trust me, a conservative style is preferable to body piercings!

A technology lawyer friend of mine incorporated Converse tennis shoes into her brand. She had them in all types (and almost every color) and was known as "the lady lawyer with hip shoes," which proved a popular message with her young, entrepreneurial clients. Yet when the technology boom came crashing down and her clients were no longer the cool, young, "in" crowd, she was smart enough to know it was time to invest in some Jimmy Choos and retire her Converse collection.

I had another colleague who had developed a brand as a geeky technology lawyer, which went over quite well with most of his clients, who were also (surprise!) geeky technology types. This lawyer conveniently decided that looking like a crumpled mess was simply consistent with his chosen brand. However, many of his colleagues—and those clients who didn't fall in the super-geek category—were put off by his wrinkled shirts, ancient socks, and general lack of good grooming. In short, by taking his brand too far, he actually compromised his image.

The Elevator Mission

Regardless of anything else about your brand, make sure that it generates a positive and uplifting experience for others. Everyone is subconsciously seeking to feel good, and giving people an emotional lift is the first step in making a connection. Refer back to all the things we discussed in Chapter 6 ("People Skills"), and think about the experience you want to generate.

How does your brand make people walk away feeling more positive, both about themselves and about you?

Who You Are

One key to success is how well we incorporate our character into our brand. What do you regard as most important in your work (i.e., your motivators)? Ethics? Quality? Helping others? Having a blast? Whatever it is, it should play a significant role in your brand. How do your interests and lifestyle fit in? This could be anything from your second home in Spain to your passion for jazz, playing a mean game of badminton, or being nuts about a football team.

In short, our brand should be so in sync with who we are that it applies in our personal lives just as much as it does in our profession. Of course, there may be distinctions—most of us leverage different traits in different aspects of our lives—but there should be an overall consistency. Similarly, our lifestyle and the environment we create around us must support our brand. Here are a few examples of when this fails:

- Noel's brand emphasizes organizational reliability—but Noel's office is such a chaotic mess that he couldn't find a paper clip without the aid and comfort of his secretary (who is prematurely gray!).

- Susan's brand is cool and cultured (she works mainly with media), but she hasn't managed to catch any of the latest shows or exhibits for at least a year. She is becoming uneasily aware at networking events that she can't keep her end up in conversation.

- John works as a divorce lawyer, and his brand includes being a caring, sensitive, avuncular family man. That's why it came as such a shock to his colleagues when he was spotted in a singles' bar flirting with three different women.

- Kim's brand is cautious and conservative (as one might expect for someone who deals with wills and testaments), but she just bought a flashy red Maserati.

- Randall's brand is enthusiastic, competitive, and sporty—one of the boys—but lately he's put on a lot of weight and looks pasty-faced, almost bloated. Could he have lost his competitive edge?

Experience and Achievements

Our backgrounds are "what got us to where we are today," and can tell people a lot. So don't be afraid to publicize things you want others to know about (*not* that naked bicycle ride at midnight around your college campus, but definitely your early passion for gymnastics!). This doesn't have to be limited to your school (yawn) or your job experience. Your brand should reflect your family and history, where you grew up, places you've been, your achievements (both professional and personal), and even funny anecdotes (preferably self-deprecating). *Don't* be the bore bragging about your award-winning chess-playing son, or the idiot driveling on about how he won the moot court competition in his second year of law school.

Your story—old hat though it may seem to you—provides opportunities for connections. If you have a specific narrative that can be woven into your brand to foster your objective, then use it. I have a divorce-lawyer friend who endured her own, extremely harrowing, marriage breakdown. She now uses that as part of her brand—she's the divorce lawyer who really *does* understand what you're going through.

Your brand should also incorporate your strengths, talents, and skill set—the resources you have to offer. Ask yourself the following questions, and then analyze whether or not your answers are adequately advertised by your brand.

- What are my strengths?

- What do I do best?

- What are my special and distinct skills?

- Where does my experience really lie?

- What do I most enjoy doing?

Oddly, we have strengths and skills that seem so natural to us that we lose sight of their value. We tend to think that something we do well is simple and easy for everyone—which isn't necessarily the case! Don't underestimate your talents, and do advertise them as a resource ingrained within your brand.

FINDING A SPECIALTY

Every field is becoming more specialized these days, and law is no exception. Rarely today is someone just a corporate or litigation lawyer: Instead, most of us are targeted to a particular sector or industry—technology, property, pharmaceuticals, oil, gas—or we find some other way to distinguish our practice. Having a specialty improves our ability to market ourselves, both within the firm and with prospective clients.

However, there are some important factors to consider when deciding on a specialty. What are the economics of that specialty? What about the potential for growth—or for saturation? How competitive is the market, and what is the makeup of the strongest lawyers in that specialty? (Is the profile a good match for you?) Consider, too, the cyclical nature of the market, the probable needs and strategies of clients within that market, and the likelihood of repeat business. (For example, if work in your field tends toward one-time, *ad hoc* deals, then the stream of business is unpredictable.)

Lifestyle is often overlooked when settling on a specialty. I never adequately considered the fact that my own specialty, outsourcing, required not only significant travel but also lots of time at client locations. This suited me, as it turned out, but my colleagues with families seriously failed to appreciate those long periods spent away from home... Similarly, I have a friend who chose her area of expertise—trusts and estates for wealthy philanthropists—precisely because it allows her to work in a large New York City firm without putting in the long hours associated with large deals. She is now the mother of two and happy in her work, which would probably not be the case had she chosen a different area of focus.

In choosing a specialty, you should also consider the underlying subject matter, the client base most likely to need your chosen expertise, and any contacts you may already have related to that particular specialty. Let's look at these in more detail.

Love Your Subject Matter

Take a close look at the subject matter you'll be dealing with (day in, day out) in your chosen specialty. If you enjoy the underlying substance (property, financial services, entertainment, or defending heartrendingly downtrodden—if crooked—accountants in court), practice in that area will be all the more enjoyable.

As mentioned in the Preface, my first area of specialty (a long time ago!) was IT, helping small and medium-sized technology companies with the development and distribution of their products. I have to admit that it transpired by accident rather than through serious and purposeful consideration, as I'd never been interested in technology and only survived a computer programming course in college by the skin of my teeth... When I started representing technology clients, however, I was intuitive enough to realize that I needed to thoroughly understand their language and products. So I enrolled in various computer courses and routinely read IT industry journals—which, considering my addiction to fashion magazines, entailed real commitment!—and finally transformed myself into a technological sophisticate. I gradually came to understand my clients' industry almost as well as they did, and this expertise became integral to my brand. (It was especially useful at the time, because IT had yet to become a common practice area, and such a specialty was in demand.)

Now, I should have been thinking about my inner motivators, rather than forcing myself to learn about something so badly misaligned with my personal tastes. But I didn't realize that at the time! So don't make my mistake: Be sure to consider how your personal interests and areas of expertise can help you to enhance (or choose) your specialty. Remember, you're likely to be a lawyer for a very long time, so you should make sure that you enjoy it as much as possible. You'll be that much more credible—and successful—if you do.

Client Base

Similar to, yet distinct from, the actual subject matter we deal with is the client base involved. As our careers advance, we tend to spend more time developing relationships with clients one-on-one, so don't forget to consider the type of people you like to be around. If your idea of hell is an afternoon at the football pitch (that's a soccer field, for us Americans!), it is unlikely that a sports law specialty representing footballers would suit you. If your greatest dream is coming to grips with mergers and acquisitions, then make sure your idea of fun is being encased in a boardroom with hotshot bankers, consultants, and business executives.

Our ultimate objective, of course, is to build trusting relationships with clients, and that original connection is best accomplished from a starting point of commonality. If you like to talk about the latest technologies, I can tell you from personal experience that as an IT lawyer you'll spend a lot of your work-ing (and leisure!) hours with clients who are passionate about doing just that. And if your soul doesn't thrill to the latest computerized bells and whistles, then I suggest exploring a different area of expertise.

It's also important to position your brand to target your preferred clients. So as you thread your personality, passions, and history into your brand, always keep your client base in mind. Learn everything you can about your clients—what they relate to, what they're looking for, and most of all, what they *need*. Your brand should be packaged to demonstrate the value that you bring to your client, and it must meet their requirements.

Contacts

If the first criterion for choosing a specialty is genuine interest in the subject and the second is natural empathy for the people found in that business, the third factor to consider is the network of contacts you may already have in that industry. If your uncle, say, is an investment banker specializing in acquisitions within pharmaceuticals, you should definitely think about how his connections could help you.

I have an American friend who's crazy about country music, and while still in law school sought out all the country music gigs. When she graduated, she decided to combine her passion for music with her law career by moving (against advice!) to Nashville, Tennessee. Despite her limited law experience, she marketed herself as a country music lawyer, and with a bit of help from her brother—an agent—sought out the right distribution channels for her brand. Today she's "the" country music lawyer—the brand she first envisioned for herself.

FINAL THOUGHTS

Your brand should have something unique about it—something that people remember. The idea is to develop a brand that shows people who you are and allows you to compete on your own unique qualities. Make yourself into someone your clients can relate to—then suddenly you're not just a lawyer, but someone they know as an individual.

Bear in mind, however, that *less is more*. We all want to be all things to all clients, yet (oddly enough) your brand can prove still more valuable if you keep it distinct, making clear just what you *don't* do. Most clients understand

Known for his serious intellect, the "smart one" was beginning to feel insecure about whether his brand was enough.

So he tried to be all things, which made him nothing more than a dwarf.

that trying to do everything will simply lower standards and dissipate energy. Further, when clients watch us relinquish work in one area, they can be more confident that our claim of superiority in another area is genuine.

Sometimes making this clear can be stressful—it's natural to worry about driving away opportunities—but creating the strongest possible brand will always pay off in the end.

APPENDIX 10.A

TABLE OF BRAND ATTRIBUTES

Most of the attributes can be associated with one of the personality types, which are abbreviated as follows: Connecter (C), Driver (D), Perfectionist (P), and Moderate (M). Note that some traits may be associated primarily with one type but to a lesser extent with a second type.

Accepting (C/M)	Controlling (D)	Extroverted (C/D)
Accurate (P)	Cool	Facilitative (M)
Action-oriented (D)	Cooperative (M)	Flexible (C)
Adaptable (C/M)	Coordinator (P)	Focused on the bottom line (D/P)
Ambitious (D)	Creative	Formal (P/D)
Amiable (M)	Cunning (D)	Forthright (D)
Analytical (P)	Decisive (D)	Free-spirited (C)
Appreciative (M)	Deep thinker (P)	Fun (C)
Approachable (C/M)	Detailed (P)	Funny (C)
Artistic	Determined (D)	Genius (P)
Bold (C/D)	Diplomatic (M)	Goal-oriented (D)
Calm (M)	Disciplined (P/D)	Good listener (M)
Capable (D)	Down to business (D)	Great memory (P)
Cautious (P)	Emotional (C)	Handles stress well (D)
Cheerful (C)	Empathetic (M)	Hard-working (D)
Communicator (C)	Empowering (M)	Helpful (M)
Compliant (M)	Energetic (C/D)	Identifies problems (P)
Confident (D)	Enthusiastic (C)	Impartial (P/D)
Consensus builder (M)	Ethical (P)	Imposing (D)
Considerate (M)	Expeditious (C/D)	Independent (P/D)
Contented (M)	Expressive (C)	Informal (M/C)

Innovator (D)	Perfectionist (P)	Solution finder (C/D)
Intellectual (P)	Performer (C)	Spontaneous (C)
Intellectually stimulating (P)	Persuasive (C)	Stable (M)
Introverted (P/M)	Planner (D/P)	Strict (P/D)
Intuitive (D/C)	Player (C)	Strong-willed (D)
Kind (M)	Powerful (D)	Structured (P)
Lenient (M/C)	Practical (P)	Supportive (M)
Liberal (C)	Predictable (P)	Takes charge (D)
Likes to coach (M)	Principled (P)	Team player (M)
Logical (P)	Progressive (C/D)	Thorough (P)
Loyal (M)	Quick thinker (D)	Thought-provoking (P/D)
Mentor (M)	Realist (P)	Tolerant (M)
Multi-tasker (C)	Reflective (P)	Transitory (C)
Natural mentor (M)	Reliable (P/M/D)	Unemotional (P/D)
Non-judgmental (C)	Reserved (M)	Visionary (D/C)
Observer (P)	Resolves conflict (M)	Welcoming (C/M)
Optimistic (C/D)	Risk-taker (C/D)	
Organized (P)	Sees possibilities (C/D)	
Passionate (C)	Sees the big picture (C/D)	
Patient (M)	Self-contained (M)	
People-oriented (C/M)	Slow (P/M)	

Chapter Eleven

Adopting the Core Traits of a Superior Brand

Most of the previous chapter focused on developing brand authenticity and distinctiveness, but there are still core features across all good brands that must be incorporated. Google and Apple distinguish themselves through uniqueness (individual branding), but ultimately both are market leaders because of first-class products, exceptional management, and strong marketing skills. These are the behaviors and skills that we must all exhibit if we want to achieve our goals of business and leadership.

The goal of this chapter is to consider some of the core traits that should strengthen your brand and any changes you may want to make to ensure that your brand is as superior as possible. Once again, any notes you take here will be beneficial for the exercise in the next chapter.

LEADERSHIP

One of the first places to begin developing our brand is in terms of leadership. In previous chapters I've defined leadership as the ability to mobilize others toward a shared purpose (i.e., leadership as "action," or as something we perform in relation to others). But to truly succeed in this area, we must first manage *ourselves*, in two respects:

- As leaders, we have to be motivated toward a personal vision, channeling our emotions and self-belief toward achieving our goals.

- We can't inspire anyone to follow without first earning their support and respect, which means managing ourselves positively in relation to those around us.

Leaders must also be trustworthy, self-aware, people-focused, positive, and visionary. When these five traits inspire your behavior—that is, when you've fully embraced them as your ingrained way of operating—you should, by definition, be equipped to lead. (You should also have laid the foundations necessary to achieve all three goals of this book, because leadership underpins each one of them.) This will be addressed in greater depth in subsequent chapters, but meanwhile bear in mind that "acting as a leader" is critical to your success—and that leadership must "drive" your brand.

"Acting as a leader" is critical to your success—and leadership must "drive" your brand.

YOUR IMAGE

When I first started discussing this book with colleagues and friends, several suggested that I include some solid advice about grooming and attire. (One friend was dealing with a junior female in his law firm who chose inappropriately low-cut tops as her interpretation of "casual Fridays." Another colleague—still more afflicted—was worried about an associate's bad breath!) Yet despite the fact that the subject of fashion and appearance is dear to my heart, I quickly rejected the notion. After all, the need for appropriate dress and grooming is so blindingly obvious that anyone capable of cramming for a law exam must have learned it in the cradle, right?

Wrong! Once the subject had been raised, I was surprised to spot growing numbers of horribly attired, even unkempt, lawyers—people, however brilliant, who had obviously never given these matters the smallest consideration. So if you are one of these mind-over-matter types, remember that *how you look* is the very first thing people perceive about you. We cannot remake a poor first impression—and overcoming a bad one is, quite simply, a waste of effort. Get it right in the first place and you'll instantly see the difference. It's pretty rare for people to be faulted for looking too good, but many, even within my own experience, have missed out on a job or a promotion because of their appearance. (The trouble is that people generally aren't told that their appearance—which is fixable—contributed to their rejection, so they often don't recognize the need to address the problem.)

Now some employers, I admit, can be a little over-zealous. My own father, for example, has always been a stickler for polished shoes, and if someone were to come to an interview wearing less-than-shiny shoes my father simply wouldn't consider him for any job. I also know a law partner—I know it sounds bizarre—who secretly inspects people's nails. Any sign of dirt, poor trimming, or general lack of attention in that area and the would-be lawyer is automatically shoved in the "dubious" category. Yet there is some method in this madness: As one of my former clients put it, "If a lawyer lacks enough self-respect to care about his own image, why should I think he's likely to care about mine?" It saves a lot of trouble, and possible rebuffs, if you simply assume that every person you are meeting has such high standards. Try your best to live up to them!

Before leaving this topic, do this quick exercise, just to be sure that you're currently meeting exceptional standards with regard to your image:

■ Body and weight.

■ Hands and nails.

■ Hairstyle. (Is it old-fashioned or out of touch?)

■ Makeup. (Suitable or a little excessive?—or the kind that says, "I don't care what I look like and neither should you; live with it"?)

■ Teeth. (Smiles say a lot; what does yours say?)

■ Breath. (Check it, or use breath mints before meeting anyone—just in case!—especially after that amazing curry or Mexican meal.)

■ Hygiene generally.

■ Overall look/fashion sense.

■ Quality and fit of professional attire. (You don't have to spend the earth to look good—and prosperous. Think about it this way: If you were the client, would you feel good about choosing a lawyer who looks as if he has to count the pennies on suits?)

■ Color and shape. (Do your clothes flatter your figure, or are you compromising your image with clothes that are too young, too flamboyant, too dull, or too dowdy?)

■ Accessories. (What do all these things—watch, cuff links, calendar, phone, gadgets, pen, notepad—say about you? Are they consistent with your brand? Note: If you are a techie, then you'd really better have the techie gadgets!)

- Handbag/briefcase. (It doesn't have to cost hundreds or thousands—the price of designer bags can be ludicrous—but is it suitable to your position? Does it present a neat, organized, "together" message?)

- Shoes. (Check condition and style.)

- Optional accessories—especially women. (Are you using accessories such as scarves and jewelry to accentuate and individualize your outfit, or could you do with an accessory makeover?)

If you feel that you are presenting yourself and your brand positively in each of these instances, great! Dressing for success is a huge part of conveying your brand in a positive light. If you're *not* presenting a suitable, sophisticated outward image, however, you need to evaluate why not. If you think you haven't got the time to get it right, my advice is to find that time. If you find it all just too boring, I urge you to change your attitude. If you're convinced it's important but aren't sure how to go about it, I suggest you seek some expert advice. It might just be the best career investment you could make.

POSTURE

The way you stand and sit is one of the first things people notice. When your posture is straight and flexible, you communicate zeal, confidence, openness, and enthusiasm; if you allow your posture to slump, you immediately convey weariness, pessimism, irritation, or indifference.

Years ago, one associate in my group managed to maintain exemplary posture at all times. Whether in a casual meeting or just eating lunch, her stance was consistently authoritative: shoulders back, head poised, gaze straight ahead. Naturally, she tended to be perceived as more mature and more experienced than her peers—neither of which was necessarily the case! But no doubt her posture contributed to this impression. Admittedly, there were times when her posture *could* have been more relaxed, because being "authoritative" isn't always the optimal message. For example, to better communicate to her peers that she was one of them, a more casual, relaxed posture might have worked better at times. I also found it intriguing that such a good-looking person was never overwhelmed with social invitations. I frankly doubt whether most of the guys had enough nerve to ask her out!

So don't simply assume that your posture is perfect. Examine it in the mirror and work on it until you have a positive stance that reflects the stature you want to convey.

THE HANDSHAKE

A good handshake is integral to a confident brand; you say a lot about yourself in that fleeting pressure of palm on palm. A strong (but not too strong) handshake expresses assertiveness and eagerness; a lifeless handshake indicates that you're chilly, boring, or apathetic. Have you ever been introduced to someone who looks stimulating, even attractive, until that weedy, fishlike handshake (and telltale lack of eye contact) leaves you secretly doubting whether he's really worth meeting after all? Don't let your handshake convey the wrong message! Practice yours with a friend and find out what it says about you.

COMMUNICATION

Part of our brief, as lawyers, is to communicate confidently—which is probably why so many politicians first study law. Of course, some great communicators were simply born to wow juries or to bring the legislature to its collective feet, but it's surprising how rare a gift this is. Most strong communicators attain their seeming mastery by capitalizing on techniques that create long-lasting and positive impressions.

First, they understand—either consciously or subconsciously—the statistics we examined in Chapter 8 ("Positive Impact"). While it's always our goal to express ourselves through substance, in real life (sad to say), content isn't always the critical factor: Our communication skills will be judged by how we move, how we look, and how we sound.

Credibility

With this in mind, the first place to start is credibility: The better your reputation, trustworthiness, and overall experience, the more highly regarded your communication is likely to be. We've all seen those professorial experts on TV, whose lightest utterance is greeted with deference, despite a deadly delivery! Obviously, when speaking on

The secret of communicating confidently is well, ah, hmm, like, well, communicating confidently.

?!?

the law your brand and status should speak for itself, but it's still important to convey your authority. Aristotle himself said, "Persuasion is achieved by the speaker's personal character when the speech is so spoken as to make us think him credible. We believe good men more fully and more readily than others; this is true generally whatever the question is, and absolutely true where exact certainty is impossible and opinions are divided."

In essence, your audience must first believe in you as the messenger, or you run the risk that they'll reject the message. This means that you must communicate in your own style and your own words. While techniques can be polished, speaking from your own values about what matters to you is the key to credibility, followed by choosing words that accurately reflect your belief system.

> *Speaking from your own values about what matters to you is the key to credibility.*

For example, consider the motivators behind the following statements:

> *"We must win at all costs."*

> *"Great leadership is all about results."*

These messages are most likely to be produced by a Driver personality who sees business as a competitive playing field. If a Moderate personality tried to deliver these words, he (or she) might not come across as credible because the words would be inconsistent with his or her true character. In comparison, the Moderate might say, with irresistible authority:

> *"When the people in our organization feel that they are contributing and have meaning in their jobs, everybody wins—and company results fall into place."*

> *"Great leadership comes down to caring about the individual."*

Please note that none of these statements is "wrong"—or "better"—than any others. They merely demonstrate that you need to learn to communicate in a style that supports your own unique perspective and is consistent with your own brand. Don't copy someone else's style, because your credibility ultimately hinges upon your audience's subconscious acceptance of your words. It may sound unbelievably corny or simplistic, but to communicate brilliantly, you must speak from the heart.

Human Desire: Emotion and Logic

Aristotle also said that there are three means of being persuasive: "(1) to reason logically, (2) to understand human character and goodness in their various forms, and (3) to know their causes and the way in which they are excited." This is why you first need to establish your credibility—the reason why you have a right to be heard. Then you must understand the character of your audience, arouse positive emotions in them, and support your case with persuasive use of logic.

How you accomplish this depends on both your audience and your objectives. If you *tailor your message* to your audience, you will always carry more weight. Listeners have an intensely human desire to feel important and appreciated, and to view things in terms of how they are personally affected, so you should always arouse an emotion in them that engages them at the deepest possible level. Then be sure to back this up with supporting evidence.

A colleague once asked me for advice on dealing with a corporate client, a man who suspected that every lawyer was simply trying to wheedle more money out of him. I suggested that she mention that his business seemed to rise and fall depending on the portrayal of his character in the media, focusing in particular on the impact of a recent (and, of course, unfair) ad campaign from one of his competitors. She could then propose an in-depth investigation and devise appropriate remedies. It worked: The analysis of his own importance captured the client's imagination (and emotions), and the evidence that she had gathered to support her case clinched the deal.

Of course, some people are naturally more emotional, others more logical, so you may need to rely more on one tool or the other, depending on the client. However, expressing emotion *per se* is an extremely powerful tool (regardless of the temperament of your audience), because you can transfer your own sentiment to your audience through the "mirroring effect" (see Chapter 6). Remember how Hillary Clinton captured the 2008 New Hampshire primary from under Barack Obama's nose? A few (un)scripted tears, and suddenly all those female voters identified with her!

Using emotion has another advantage: People tend to remember things they feel. Have you ever noticed the wealth of detail you can retain of some emotional storm? Minor details of a meeting can be recalled with real intensity, even years later, while less "charged" meetings slip away completely, never to be recalled again! The same principle applies when we wish to communicate a message: Arousing emotion gives our content stronger impact and makes it linger longer in the memory.

> Arousing emotion gives our content stronger impact and makes it linger longer in the memory.

In his book *The Emotional Brain*, Joseph LeDoux notes that when we feel (any) emotion the brain releases adrenaline, which strengthens our memories of the event. He mentions how James McGaugh, a leading neuroscientist at the University of California, conducted a study about how emotions can be used to imprint messages into the memories of an audience. For the purposes of the trial, two separate groups read the same story, involving precisely the same sequence of events, but one narrative was written in an emotional vein, while the other was deliberately void of sentiment. Those who read the passionately told tale not only remembered the details much more precisely, but also remembered actual words more clearly.

Communication
1. Establish credibility

2. Arouse emotion by
    a. understanding your audience
    b. speaking to their issues and
       what is important to them

3. Reason logically
4. USE STORIES

Dos and Don'ts

Understand Your Audience

Another aspect to consider is how your audience receives information. Some people are visual, some are auditory, and some are kinesthetic types who rely on other senses. Try to pay attention to how your listeners communicate, taking cues from the way they speak to determine which pattern fits them best.

- *Visual*: "I can see what you mean... The time we flew to Amsterdam the sea was a brilliant blue... My view of the merger is..."

- *Auditory*: "I hear what you're saying... I'll never forget the sound of his cello... What I'm taking away from the tone of his message is..."

- *Kinesthetic*: "Wow, love the leather sofa!... While we were in Greece the breeze was fresh and clear; everything felt wonderful... My gut feeling is..."

In other words, if you can figure out how your listeners view the world, you can better harmonize your language with their outlook.

Stories are Naturally Powerful

Using stories to make points adds thrust and impact. Instructing your teen to drive safely is a yawn; telling him how his cousin spent two months in the hospital after a car crash—and lost his spot in college—just might work. Similarly, don't merely advise your client to use a contract instead of a handshake, but mention another client who got taken to the cleaners because he hadn't bothered to get a written agreement!

Remember, stories not only help to achieve your overall objectives but also demonstrate credibility by conveying actual experiences. In almost every case the strongest way to elicit emotion and provide logical support is to tell a story.

Limit Your Message

Limit your topic and organize your ideas. Winston Churchill once wrote a letter to his wife, ending with this postscript: "I am sorry I wrote such a long letter. I didn't have time to write you a short one." A master communicator, Churchill knew the importance of succinctness and self-editing. If you're considering how to accomplish a particular project, stick to it and don't meander off into another subject altogether. Also, don't be afraid to repeat the message. Advertisers are unrivaled communicators, and they depend on repetition as a core tool.

Many great communicators have a finite, core message, but they convey it in a memorable way.

Be Specific

Don't say, "I feel positive about our progress on this project." Instead, say "I feel positive about our progress on this project *because* we're going to make our budget and meet our deadline." Let everyone know *why* you feel positive. (The word "because" imposes a welcome intellectual rigor, since it must be followed up with some reason.)

Use Powerful and Positive Words

In Chapter 7 ("Thinking"), we considered how the brain computes negative—compared to positive—messages. Exactly the same principles apply when communicating with others. When we tell someone not to do something, the *negative* image is perceived the fastest. (If I ask someone not to shout, "shouting" is what his brain initially takes in. It then has to make a second leap to reach the concept that I really want: "Be quiet.") In short, a positive message is absorbed far more easily, and it also sinks in deeper and is retained longer. (As every teacher knows, "Please be quiet" is more effective than any number of negatively worded admonitions!)

Similarly, don't weaken your statements with feeble qualifiers. Compare these two statements:

"I've been thinking that maybe we should talk to Jim about working together on the project."

"I've considered the situation carefully, and I feel that working together on the project would be beneficial because..."

The second statement has no qualifiers, is naturally powerful, and follows our other rules—it's specific and it uses the "because" phraseology.

A powerful communicator avoids the word "try," as in, "This plan might work if we try to revise the scheduling." Yeah, right—but what does that *mean*, exactly? Are you going to revise the scheduling, or not? A much more positive statement would be, "With a revised schedule, this plan should work." "Try" is a limiting word, with limited value. You aren't going to "try" to make your friend's party; you either will or you won't.

Another strong communicating technique is to express an opinion as a statement rather than a question. If you put an opinion as a query it can easily be disregarded. "Don't you think it might be better if we split the tasks evenly?" will probably inspire a "No" or a shrug. The statement "I believe we'd achieve much more by splitting the tasks evenly" is likely to be considered far more seriously. It doesn't guarantee that the recipient will agree with you, but at least your opinion will have made more impact.

Evaluate Your Voice

Equally important is how words sound when we articulate them (remember Chapter 8!). Your voice is integral to your brand. Your voice conveys who you are and what you believe: It must exude enthusiasm, confidence, assurance, and authority. A timid, hesitant, or skeptical delivery will definitely not convey a strong and influential brand! The bad news is that we all judge others—and are judged ourselves—by our voices; the good news is that if our voice is inconsistent with the brand we want to project, we can actually do something about it.

I suggest that you tape-record yourself, even though (as I can testify) this can be a painful experiment. Very few people can listen to themselves on tape and claim to enjoy the experience. (Those "ums" and "ers" alone can be deeply mortifying, when we thought we were so "in command"!) Even people who speak wonderfully sometimes cringe when they hear themselves. Still, no pain, no gain!

- First, check your volume. Is it strong enough? (Perhaps even too strong?) What's your inflection like? When making a point, do you inflect up or down? (If down, you're probably conveying confidence; if up, you might be revealing nerves or inner doubts.)

- Evaluate the average pitch of your voice. Is it youthful and squeaky? Low and fake? Are you aping a more sophisticated accent than you really possess? Is the pitch appropriately varied, or do you specialize in a listless monotone? Prime Minister Margaret Thatcher was advised that a deeper vocal delivery would give her added *gravitas*: She went on to win three elections in a row.

- Note the pacing of your speech patterns. Are you using pauses effectively? An intentional pause just before making a strong point builds the moment and drives home your message; conversely, "running on" breathlessly may cause your audience to tune out. As a lawyer, you're bound to be intelligent and articulate. Just make sure that you're communicating this well and getting your message across persuasively.

Communication Methods

As lawyers we communicate in a wide range of circumstances and with any number of methods. The thing to remember is that every single communication—answering the telephone, leaving a voice mail, or sending an email—conveys your brand. At the risk of stating the obvious, let me remind you of some simple truths.

- *Email.* Never, ever treat email casually! It's the communication tool of our generation, and while it's tempting to see it as delightfully informal, in business terms you must not allow this to happen. Emails should be crafted, written, polished, and finally proofread with exactly the same care as a formal letter. Failing in this area will suggest that you are indolent and slapdash—someone who can't be bothered to get it right. Also, *always* be specific in the subject line, and never reply to a previous message that has an irrelevant subject line to the topic at hand. And last (but definitely not least), always check that you're responding to the right person!

- *Telephone.* When on the phone, of course, your voice tells the story, so keep it upbeat, relaxed, and friendly. Even if your girlfriend just walked out on you, you've smashed up a (borrowed) car, and your central heating has chosen the coldest day of the year to break down, try smiling while you talk! Remember that if you act it, you become it, even if just for the duration of the call! (*Then* you can howl, if you really need to.) Another tip worth trying is standing up; oddly enough, this can make you sound more alert and confident. And as with any communication, be sure to limit your message to essentials and avoid wandering off the topic. (It's always a good idea to assume that the person on the other end has an urgent meeting to attend, which in many situations will be the case.)

When initiating a call, always ask the recipient immediately whether or not "now" is a good time for him. Before calling, have your thoughts organized and know your objective, so you can get to the point as soon as possible after any inevitable *pourparlers.* This is still more important if your call is transferred to voice mail, and you *have* to get your immediate point across concisely. If you have to leave a message, state your phone number clearly and audibly so that the other person can retrieve it easily. Failing to do so cruelly reduces the chances of your call being returned. No one wants to replay a message five times to obtain the whole number or to distinguish "five" from "nine."

■ *Your outgoing message.* One great habit to acquire is changing your office voice mail every day. I can always count on knowing my friend Rachel's whereabouts through her voice mail. Typically, she'll say: "Hi, this is Rachel. Today is Friday, the ninth. I will be in the office all morning except for a meeting between 10:00 and 11:00. From 1:00 on, I will be out of the office and unavailable. I hope to return around 5:00 p.m. Please leave a message, and I'll be sure to get back to you as soon as possible." As a friend, I appreciate knowing when I can reach Rachel, but I suspect that her clients value this even more, as just another example of her detailed professionalism.

HANDLING YOUR EMOTIONS (ESPECIALLY ANGER!)

It's natural to feel furious at times. Show me someone who says he never gets angry and I'll show you a liar! So getting angry is not, in itself, the problem—it's the way we deal with our anger and how this, in turn, can undermine our brand.

Some people erupt with rage, taking out their feelings on the nearest person, regardless of whether or not this might be appropriate. I feel sure every lawyer will have observed scenes like these:

■ Despite daily reminders, a client has failed all week to provide his lawyer with his comments on a particular document, and instead calls the partner at 6:00 on Friday evening, still expecting the deal to be turned around by Monday. This has the potential to wreck the weekend, which the partner had planned to spend with his wife—and cancellation is not (in terms of his marriage!) a valid option. Furious, the partner slams down the phone, cursing his client and blaming his associate, who takes the full brunt of her boss's frustration. (He even claims that it's all *her* fault because she should have ensured that the client got his comments back earlier.)

■ Two new projects come in the same day, one requiring travel to Paris and the other to Leeds, England, which is not—to be brutally honest—one of the world's most thrilling places. The young associate assigned to Leeds—who'd already been there, with a very contrary client—storms into her boss's office to complain, and refuses the assignment.

■ An associate leaves a document on a partner's desk. The partner starts reading it and immediately notes that one error he had discussed at length with the associate is *still* extant. The partner marches straight into the associate's office, berating her for a lack of professionalism and informing her that her work is shoddy.

■ Two associates plan to meet at 2:00 p.m. to discuss plans for an upcoming marketing event. One associate arrives on time and waits in the meeting room for the other for over 30 minutes. As the latecomer enters the room, his infuriated colleague shouts at him for wasting her valuable time, accusing him of being unreliable and uncommitted.

Getting angry never helped anyone's reputation. Even when you have every right to be furious, choosing the rational approach will invariably bring more respect and more benefit than any display of volatility. The worst part about getting angry is that fury can blind you from dealing sensibly with the facts of the situation; when this happens, you not only lose control but you also put your credibility at risk.

The examples above actually happened—to me! And this is how the situations were resolved, after the inappropriate behavior.

- After the anger-prone partner (my boss) had finished yelling at me that his weekend was ruined, claiming it was all my fault, I was finally able to tell him that I had spoken with the client's associate earlier and that we had agreed that the document didn't need to be done until Wednesday, after all. I went on to say that I could guarantee to have it ready for his review on Monday, in good time for the client to receive it by Wednesday. I then explained that I had sent him an email that outlined the matter, leaving his vacation completely intact. My partner and I kicked off his holiday weekend then and there, with his buying me an "apology" drink in the nearest wine bar.

- OK, I admit it: It was I who didn't want to go back to Leeds, and who desperately coveted the Paris job. I felt that I'd spent enough time and effort on this particular client in Leeds, and hoped that it might be someone else's turn! What I hadn't realized is that my boss planned to put me on the Paris job as well, and was only requiring me to attend the *initial* meetings for the Leeds assignment because I had a strong background with the client and could help my younger colleague transition into the client's team. But before my boss could explain this properly, I had thrown a brilliant tantrum. Luckily, my boss was kind enough to forgive my immature reaction, and I still got to go to Paris—after much groveling!

- When my boss finished ranting and raving at me because I had "failed to excise" the clause we had agreed to omit, I was able to explain that I had put *two* documents on his desk—the original version and the revised version, showing my changes, along with a note making it all clear. We walked back to his office together, and there, underneath a pile of papers he had dropped on his desk, was the revised document—and the note from me. (It probably wasn't completely coincidental that, just before reviewing my document, my boss had been called by his wife to say that their son had been suspended from his very expensive private school for the second time. This was another case of someone venting his anger on the wrong person, without all the relevant information!)

■ When I berated my colleague for tardiness, I jumped in with both feet before giving him a chance to explain. In this case, my colleague had just been on the phone with his mother, who had broken it to him that his sister had just been diagnosed with cancer. While they were trying to sort out how to support her, our meeting had—completely understandably—slipped his mind. Imagine how awful I felt for having upbraided him! Talk about a 180-degree change in perspective...

In each of these situations, the enraged person hadn't stepped back to gather all the facts. Before barking at a colleague or fuming at a boss, make sure you understand the full situation. Ask first, get angry second—not the other way around. It saves a lot of embarrassment, and, with luck, should help to keep your credibility intact.

ASK FIRST, GET ANGRY SECOND
— not the other way around!

A tricky situation can occur because some people prefer to deal with anger in a completely different way—by *not* dealing with it! Instead of telling colleagues how they feel, they bury their frustration and suppress every corresponding emotion. For example, as the minutes tick by waiting for a colleague to hand her a brief, Suzanne is secretly raging: "Where is he? Why is he always so late? His tardiness is so disrespectful, and it makes me so mad! It's not as if I haven't got loads of important things I could be doing, but instead I'm just sitting here—yet again—just waiting for him!" Yet when her colleague finally arrives, Suzanne looks up, forces a smile, and says "No problem at all!—I was late myself!" as the colleague casually mentions that he'd been catching up with an old friend.

There are many reasons why people don't express themselves. Sometimes they're afraid people won't like them; sometimes they have a typically Moderate way of avoiding friction, meaning that they find confronting people just too difficult. The bad news is that the anger still exists and these people are still (probably) finding a way to express it, if only in an oblique way. Here are some examples of self-destructive expression:

■ After work you go out and drink too much, to let off steam and vent frustration.

■ You go home and whine to your partner, "Can you believe that jerk kept me waiting for over an hour!!??"

■ Or you go home and complain *at* your partner—sometimes for nothing! Perhaps you yell at your loved one for forgetting to vacuum, *knowing* you're dumping your frustration on the wrong person, but unable to help yourself. We've probably all transferred our anger toward an easy target, but that's no excuse—and no action for a leader to take.

■ Perhaps you *never* let your emotions out, bottling them up so tightly that you make yourself sick (literally), until you have an ulcer to show for it!

The volcanic type and the seriously repressed both need to manage their emotions better. Remember, anger is okay, as long as it's dealt with rationally. But before jumping in, try asking yourself a few questions:

■ Am I rational? Have I really calmed down? Or am I still (even slightly) in the heat of the moment?

■ Are my actions reasonable? Would I do and say the same thing tomorrow? Think of all the emails you've read that were obviously sent in anger! Having to regret an email is *not* the behavior of a superior brand.

■ Am I sure that I have all the facts?

■ Am I directing my anger toward the person I'm truly angry with?

■ Am I absolutely clear on what I am angry about—and why?

■ What is the result I want from this dispute? And is "losing it" really the best way to achieve my goal?

Choose Your Words With Care

When addressing any emotional issue, it's crucial to remain focused on the problem at hand and nothing else. Try not to bring up past offenses, and don't bring other people into the dispute. "Fred Smith said..." is probably not a helpful ploy in this situation, unless Fred Smith is already involved. Trying to rope in other people is usually a cheap tactic.

- Don't turn mistakes into personality defects. "You're so irresponsible!" is neither a fair nor an accurate argument to make to someone who has been late to a meeting exactly once. This kind of overstatement only discredits any justifiable annoyance we might have.

- In the same vein, leaders don't turn misbehavior (even repeated misbehavior) into character assassination. You can—and sometimes must—express frustration at someone's rate of productivity, quality of work, or habitual tardiness, but never by calling him (or her) lazy, stupid, or unprofessional. Don't get personal! Your comments should be limited to the action (or inaction) concerned.

- It's wise to avoid using terms like "always" and "never." ("You're *always* late." "You *never* consider anyone else's opinions, do you?") Such extreme statements are typically exaggerations and only serve to make the other person more defensive. It's also more than probable that he can come up with at least one example to rebut the "always" or the "never." ("Hang on, who saved your bacon over the Allianz deal?") Then the focus of the dispute shifts to the correctness or inaccuracy of your own extreme statement, rather than the subject that really initiated the discussion.

233

To make a point, DON'T...

- Get personal

- Use character assassination
  "You're so [lazy, unprofessional, disorganized...]"

- Use the words "always" or "never"
  "You're NEVER on time!"
  "You're ALWAYS late!"

- It's crucial to at least *listen* to the other side's viewpoint, and at least try to see it from their perspective. Remember all those people skills we examined in Chapter 6.

- Explain things objectively, and try not to make assumptions. Saying "You were so rude yesterday" is aggressive. Compare this: "When you didn't respond to me and ended the call, I assumed you were dismissing my opinion, and I just found that to be a little rude."

- Try to suggest solutions; don't focus only on the problems.

Getting angry can be the quickest and stupidest way of damaging your reputation and credibility, especially if the anger is irrational, inappropriate, or badly directed. And if it causes someone to lose faith in you, you may never regain that trust.

DEALING WITH CONFLICT

Even people routinely perceived as confrontational don't really like conflict; they only use it, as a rule. And what's even more ironic is that the people who tend to create conflict usually don't excel at it. In fact, no one seems to handle confrontation very well, and in the midst of it we typically fail to draw on those attributes that might well benefit our cause. Instead, we allow the confrontation to bring out our extremes, undermining that brand we've been working so hard to build up! This is what often happens:

- The outspoken person becomes offensive, getting more and more aggressive;

- The introvert (possibly a Perfectionist) withdraws deeper into himself and says nothing;

- The extrovert (probably a Connecter) talks and talks and talks, probably also getting louder and louder and louder;

- The stubborn fighter (usually a Driver) holds his ground grimly, conceding nothing—even when he doesn't really care much about the underlying issue! (Drivers need to feel that they're always right.)

- The people-pleaser (the Moderate) does everything conceivable to avoid conflict altogether, or to smooth over any difficulties— anything to avoid facing up to important issues.

The partners' monthly meeting

Another oddity about conflict is that different people can view conflict itself very differently. Some people use conflict as a way to work through things, a method of seeking clarity, or a way to find a resolution—a working tool, not a problem. Conversely, others see conflict as a last resort and may tend to perceive hostility whenever voices are raised.

People also recover from conflict differently. Sometimes the most volatile and explosive types—the kind who blow up in an instant—walk away from conflict almost unmoved, while those who take longer to express their positions may brood over the issue, taking far longer to get over a heated encounter. This can leave the person who is still working through the conflict with resentful feelings toward the person who has summarily moved on, leaving the former with unresolved (and, typically, unexpressed) internal tension. Sometimes this can turn into the most dangerous of all hostilities—sublimated anger that releases itself in cold, calculated detestation or icy defiance. ("It'll be a cold day in hell when I ever work with *him* again!")

So the next time you feel yourself beginning to get hot under the collar, recognize the pros and cons of your way of dealing with it and analyze how your approach works for you (or against you) in light of your opponent's personality.

For example:

> ■ If you're an extroverted arguer and so is your opponent, you can bet that you'll both continue the dispute until your last breath. So think about stepping back, calling a time-out, and scheduling another meeting after you've both had time to settle down.

- If you're an introvert and your opponent is an extrovert, specifically ask him to be silent and listen to your point of view (and make sure that you do the same for him!). Remember, as bizarre as it may seem to you, he may just be "working through" an argument, and may not be as angry as he appears.

- If you're a "people pleaser," don't give in just to avoid an argument. Conflict is sometimes necessary to reach a resolution.

- If you're a stubborn arguer, think long and hard about whether this particular "game" is really worth the candle—or whether you might actually gain more by avoiding this particular fight.

When dealing with an angry person, signal immediately that he is getting through to you, or else your (apparent) disregard may just stoke his anger. And don't argue; appearing to reject his entire position will only increase his frustration. The best thing to say when someone is angry is, "Yes, you're right—at least as far as [whatever]." This ploy can knock the wind right out of his sails—and he's probably right about *some* aspect of the issue. Then, once he's calm, you can thrash out the nitty-gritty.

Another effective way to diffuse tension is to ask questions. "Hang on. Tell me, why don't you think these marketing materials will work with this client pitch?" By asking a question, with luck you can force him to disengage from his feelings and focus on the detail. For example, an older lady I know was once the victim of a road-rage incident. She had just given a car in a parking spot a friendly honk, fearing that the young male driver was going to pull out in front of her, when he chased her at terrifying speed through some very narrow London streets, screaming abuse, leaning on his horn, and even banging his car twice into her rear bumper! At length, my friend made an executive decision. She pulled over to the side of the road, and, as the young man drew alongside, still screaming, she looked up and asked him calmly, "Why are you so angry?" Having no snappy answer, he just drove off.

Another trick is to turn the tables by asking, "What needs to happen to fix this to your satisfaction [or to change your opinion]?" Give your opponent enough time to consider his answer, and when he does come back to you, say, "And how can I help to ensure that this happens?" Hey, presto! You're no longer opponents; you're allies instead.

MEETINGS

As lawyers, when not at our desks drafting something, we are probably in (yes, you guessed it) a meeting—anything from client meetings to department meetings, from one-on-one meetings to more formal events. This is so much a part of the job that we take it for granted. Yet we really ought to try to use every meeting as an opportunity to convey a positive image and to demonstrate our brand. We do this by arriving prepared and on time, by communicating effectively, by behaving professionally, and by attempting to act interested (even when bored to the point of brain death!).

When recently discussing this topic with Hugh (a consultant with whom I've worked on various large projects), we reminisced about some of the people we had encountered, and how their behavior had affected their status within various project teams. Hugh then told me this story:

I was recently involved in a program steering committee with senior executives from across one market sector jointly attempting to satisfy an industry-wide regulatory obligation. The meeting dynamics were fascinating: everything from rampant prima donnas to a smaller minority who understood that playing a team game is the best way to achieve a shared goal. Even more interesting than the people's behavior within the room was the private reaction of individuals to that behavior once outside of the room... It reminded me of one of the best definitions of "brand" I've heard—"your brand is what people say about you when you're not around."

—*Hugh Buckley, Founder of Quortex Consultancy*

Wasted time and wasted opportunities for brand building—
unfortunately, a typical firm meeting.

Exemplary behavior is even more crucial if you're in charge. In that case, you should decide in advance the objectives and timing of the meeting, communicate that information to everyone involved, and stick to both goals as far as humanly possible. Everyone will appreciate your circulating an agenda beforehand, and this attention to detail also conveys meticulous professionalism. Ensure by the end of the meeting that every agenda item has either an action plan or a decision associated with it. If it doesn't, then your objectives—by definition—have not been met.

Close every meeting by agreeing on, and communicating, what happens next. Make sure that everyone knows his or her responsibilities and that every participant has sufficient information and incentive to complete his assigned tasks. Meetings without resolution or constructive action are perceived as a waste of time. Don't let that happen to yours!

In addition, you should maintain control of your meeting and keep it moving along, politely cutting off anyone who indulges in rambling soliloquies or veers clean off the agenda. Be remorseless with trivialities, and sidestep peripheral discussions until a more appropriate occasion. Ignore frivolous interruptions, and never allow your meetings to be hijacked by special-interest subgroups.

Of course, there will still be times when you'll have to be flexible, especially in meetings with clients. But having suffered through many dull, disorganized, dismal meetings (of every type), I feel strongly that every meeting should be regarded as a potentially pivotal event. Be prepared, organized, and in control. I have also found it useful, before every meeting, to determine (and write down, if necessary) *what and how I can best contribute, how I can get the most out of the occasion* (using my time most effectively), and *my objective for attending* (which may be information, a decision, gaining access to another participant, or influencing or meeting someone).

Once you've done this, make sure you achieve your goals. For example, if your only purpose in attending is to meet someone, then keep in mind that he (or she) is bound to form his first impression of you based almost entirely on your performance on that occasion. So if you show up late or appear disorganized or unprepared, that will be their "takeaway" view. Further, extensive business studies have shown that listening to others without ever actually contributing gives a profoundly negative and even supine impression. (What's the point of going to a meeting and acting like some kind of sponge?) Make sure you find something to say—or some question to put—even if you don't feel adequately briefed to play an instrumental part in the discussions.

Last, consider where you should sit in the meeting. If there is a particular person whom you want to influence, then try to select a position allowing you opportunities for optimal eye contact.

ETIQUETTE

Generally speaking, the generations that preceded us (especially many decades ago) were far more formal than ours, with etiquette and manners playing a much more critical role in day-to-day life. Today people can have meals standing up, sitting at desks, or even in the car. Sartorial casualness has become accepted—even expected. It's unlikely that the men we work with will ever open a door for a female colleague (and why blame them—since some women actively despise men who do?). Yet despite this comparative relaxation of standards, there are still some occasions when manners and etiquette definitely contribute to the impression we make, including business luncheons and dinners, breakfast interviews, and invitations to the boss's house. In these situations it's crucial that we exercise those "old-fashioned" manners.

One evening one of my law firm partners invited some of our young associates to a dinner. The next day he relayed to the rest of us, in disbelief, how appalled he and his wife had been at some of the behavior displayed, including arriving late, drinking too much, using table utensils improperly, and exhibiting poor—in one case, even disgusting—table manners. My partner was so stunned that he even suggested sending some associates to an etiquette class! One person, however, had arrived with chocolates for her hostess, exhibited flawless manners, and followed up with an elegant handwritten thank-you note. She was in my partner's good books forever after, and this (as you might imagine) had an extremely positive effect on her career.

CONCLUSION: PROFESSIONAL AND EXCEPTIONAL RESULTS

Whatever you're doing—especially professionally—you should exhibit your brand to best advantage. This means delivering on time and beyond expectation, and wrapping every project with extraordinary client service—whether it's for a client or not. Your services, and how they are perceived, can make or break your brand, so the shrewd move is to anticipate what others expect and then provide it—plus! This is the surest way to be confident that your value is noticed and makes the maximum impact. Remember, we want to convey a brand of superiority and distinction. These days, at least, average is not good enough!

You may have read through some of the issues in this section and thought, "But that's what makes my brand authentic and distinct. In fact, that's part of my brand promise. And now you're telling me that it must be core to everyone's brand?" We must all achieve a minimum standard of these particular skills, but truthfully, some will naturally excel at these skills, while others will have to work hard to acquire them at even the most basic level. When we have a special talent for one of the skills we've discussed, it can become our differentiator *despite* being part of all superior brands.

For example, no lawyer can succeed without being an effective communicator, but for a lucky few, communication is a special gift that gives them unique value. Similarly, we all need to dress the part of a professional lawyer, but some will choose to use fashion as a way to truly distinguish themselves, while others will elect to meet just the minimum requirement. We're all expected to deliver timely and exceptional service, but certain people are defined by their unique ability (and overriding commitment) to do so.

The key is to proactively integrate your acquired skills with your innate personality so that everything comes together to create an authentic, distinct, and superior brand.

So let's move on to the next chapter and create *your* brand.

Chapter Twelve
Brand Creation

T he goals of brand-building can sometimes seem inconsistent. When discussing them with my lawyer friend Rachel, she objected, "But aren't you first asking your readers to be completely authentic, but later suggesting that they attempt to acquire some inauthentic traits?" In the end we agreed that smart lawyers are capable of working within these potentially incompatible objectives, to achieve the right result *for them*. Rachel even came up with a good analogy (well, a good analogy for fashion lovers like us!):

As women (sorry, guys!) we may all want to be fashionable (a superior brand), but we're all endowed with different body shapes. If being fashionable means wearing a smock dress (the latest craze as I write, believe it or not), then to look good individually, we must wear it in a way that enhances our own shape. The pear shape will choose to emphasize her small waist by wearing a thick belt; the straight shape (that's me!), who has no waist but slim hips, will decide to wear her belt lower; while the apple shape will choose no belt at all, to shorten her silhouette and emphasize her trim legs.

Of course, there will always be those who break the mold altogether—people who can, and do, manage to look fashionable whatever they wear. (Kate Moss is especially effective at defying current vogue while remaining the epitome of trend-setting sophistication.) Similarly, I'm sure you've met at least one highly successful lawyer who breaks many of the superior brand "rules": someone unkempt, highly volatile, too superior to network, or otherwise seriously non-conformist. However, these people are few and far between. The rest of us don't have that luxury, and need to work within the rules: We must be our authentic self within the parameters of a superior brand.

BRAND STATEMENT

Consider your notes from the previous chapters and then put together your personal brand statement. This is not something that you necessarily have to print out in ten funky fonts and put on the wall of your office; instead, it's a private description of yourself—in essence, a mini bio. Later, we'll look at turning your brand statement into a brand promise, and, in Chapter 16, we'll consider how to take it public and work it into a verbal message. But for now, it's just for your benefit. Write it down and work through different combinations of things that you think best paint a picture of you.

Your brand statement is "your story" and should concisely combine...

- Who you are
  - Your history
  - How you behave and the attitude you project
  - Your personality, motivators, and passions
  - Your strengths, special talents, and skill set
  - Your lifestyle, hobbies, and interests
- What you do (your specialties and the clients you principally serve)
- How you add distinct value
- What distinguishes you from your competitors
- The overall experience that you promise *and* create for others
- What you most want to achieve

Here's an example.

Scott writes:

I'm a Stanford-educated corporate lawyer helping San Francisco-based businesses grow their organizations and expand their presence into the city. As a San Francisco native, I could never live anywhere else—for one thing, I have season tickets to all the 49ers' games! My dad owns a sports shop in the heart of the city (I worked there Saturdays as a kid), so I think I understand the needs of local business owners and something of the pressures they face in today's competitive markets. I feel passionate about San Francisco, and—having recently joined the Chamber of Commerce—I'm also committed to helping local businesses build strong, vibrant relationships with each other.

My goal, especially with regard to new businesses, is to be not only my clients' lawyer, but also their business partner and even their connection to San Francisco. I love providing great legal solutions, but I also want to help my clients expand their businesses. My dream would be a leading role with the Chamber of Commerce, where I'd be recognized as the "go-to guy" for organizations that need advice, or for people who just need a contact. I think this is an attainable goal for me; I'm an outgoing person who takes the initiative, and people already tend to seek me out when they need local contacts. My brand uses my business knowledge, while at the same time it speaks to new connections and brings potential business my way. I enjoy being my brand, because I love meeting people!

What makes this a strong brand statement?

First, it creates a succinct description of how Scott's attributes come together to provide benefit to his clients. Each piece of information supports the integrity of that assertion. (As far as our clients are concerned, this is the key purpose of our brand: It must demonstrate how we add value to *them*. Of course, when we do that, our brand provides us value in return.)

Next, from Scott's brand statement, we can recognize his *brand promise*: "When you retain me as your lawyer I become your business partner, because I'm interested in your success beyond the part strictly related to my legal services." Scott's brand is also compelling because it promises *unique value*: "I am significantly connected within San Francisco and I will use my contacts and resourcefulness to help your business grow." Further, Scott's brand statement evidences his *core values and attitudes*, which are completely consistent with his brand: He loves building personal connections; he is driven to achieve success for his clients; he is committed beyond merely being a lawyer; he is very sociable; and he feels passionate about having an integral role in San Francisco business.

Everything Scott wrote comes together to create a concise brand. Even his understanding of business needs (from his family background) and his aspirations with the Chamber of Commerce demonstrate his ability to deliver on his promise.

Since developing your brand statement and client promise is a critical exercise and since it's always easier to do something by example, you may want to read through the following, real-life lawyer samples, before actually working through your own.

Bill writes:

I traveled before law school, spending time in Paraguay as a volunteer engineer on development projects. This has made me passionate about the environment. I'm also very aware that our generation is responsible for much of the environmental damage, and we need to compensate for that if we want our children (two of them mine!) to live in a stable world. Not that I'm some wild-eyed environmentalist—but I like to think that I have a no-nonsense approach toward enlightening companies about their social responsibilities and obligations and showing them how to meet those demands in the least burdensome—even beneficial—ways.

As an environmental and energy specialist lawyer, I help my clients devise creative strategies to control and limit their energy consumption and costs. I've also begun to represent suppliers to the power industry, to help them provide improved processes and alternative forms of energy. My hands-on engineering experience helps me understand the technical issues and provide innovative solutions both from a practical and legal standpoint. Clients tell me that they respect me for my assertive style and relate to me as an executive, but that I can also think outside the box. That means a lot to me.

Ideally, I'd see myself as the pre-eminent authority on socially responsible energy practices. My dream is to help my clients implement programs that go beyond lip service on environmental issues and that provide businesses with tangible results from their investment (for example, by enhancing their brand). I don't merely sell my legal services—I market the business results that I deliver. I'd like to have more relationships with clients where my role transcends mere legal advice and addresses the things that get me excited, which include making the world both richer and greener!

Brand promise: "I help my clients develop creative strategies for producing and using energy in the most environmentally friendly ways."

Unique value: "I use my combined engineering and legal experience to produce innovative ideas and solutions that are both practical and regulation-compliant."

Core values and attitudes: Socially responsible; assertive; results-oriented; innovative; passionate about the environment.

Other evidence supporting his brand: Hands-on engineering experience; previous volunteer work as an engineer in a Third World country; ability to relate well to clients; talent for thinking outside the box; track record of tangible results.

Stacy writes:
I'm an Asian-born Londoner who faced serious obstacles as a female in my native country, so I've worked doubly hard since coming to the U.K. to try to succeed. (I'm also the mother of three girls.) All this has led to my caring deeply about both women's rights and diversity in the workplace. In my spare time I've also created a women's network, because I fervently believe in mentoring the younger generation of women so that they can take advantage of all their opportunities.

I like to think that I bring my own experience and spirit to my work as a human resources lawyer, which involves helping large companies with both their diversity programs and their employment practices. My personal background has made me determined to make a difference, but I hope I'm not one of those—rather scary—hard-liners! I'm not an advocate for women because of victimization—nor do I believe in pursuing my goals aggressively, which, in my experience at least, only turns people off... In cultivating diversity programs,

I try to work with my clients in such a way that everyone stays committed and on board. My goal is to convey the message that diversity makes an organization more efficient as well as more creative. And, of course, I try to make the business world more open to possibilities for girls like my daughters!

I always keep track of the results of my programs, not to create more billable work from client organizations, but simply because I care deeply about the outcomes. I think my commitment to the long term is an important part of what I offer my clients. I can show new clients a track record of success, not just a list of previous advice provided.

Brand promise: "I help my clients develop and implement diversity programs that encourage commitment and generate positive results."

Unique value: "I am dedicated to the long-term goal that your organization realizes the benefits that I promise."

Core values and attitudes: Caring; empathetic; committed; outcome-focused.

Other evidence supporting her brand: Background of her own personal struggle; stated goal of empowering other women (she even initiated a women's network); mother of three daughters; track record of benefits achieved for clients.

Casey writes:
Well, I was pretty much a disaster at law school, and only got my degree by the skin of my teeth! It all just seemed too theoretical to me. Afterwards, though, I found work in litigation, which was much more exciting than law school, since it dealt with real life and had practical impact. However, my main breakthrough occurred when I became involved in a complex civil case for one of our clients, involving intellectual property infringement, trade secrets, employment disputes, and commercial litigation. To come to grips with all these issues (all at once!), I had to immerse myself in the client's business and understand how each issue affected all the others. In effect, I became a part of the client organization.

I realized I had a talent for handling a wide range of issues at once and for project-managing the many divisions of my clients (each with its own objectives) so that the overall legal strategy achieved the optimal result. By the end of the case, my client was begging me to join the company as an executive and as general counsel. Instead, I negotiated a different arrangement, agreeing to serve as their "outside inside" litigation counsel. I offered them a very competitive rate, and in return received their highest recommendation to others. I promised to get to know their entire organization and business as well as I would if I were actually on the payroll—but at the same time retaining a wider view by continuing to work with other industries.

Today, as a result of that initial recommendation, I have the same arrangement with many clients and can enjoy the benefit of immersing myself in their businesses while still dealing with a range of industries, issues, and people. I have become to many clients what I first decided my brand should be: their "outside inside" litigation department!

I think I'm energetic, resourceful, and inquisitive (about law, facts, and people). I'm also naturally good at dealing with different types of people with different viewpoints, and this is what enables me to deliver added value to each of my clients.

Brand promise: "I will become as immersed in your business as if I were part of your organization."

Unique value: "I will be on the inside of your business but will retain the objectivity of outside viewpoints—and all at a competitive rate."

Core values and attitudes: Energetic; interested in diverse industries, issues, and people; inquisitive; resourceful; decisive.

Other evidence supporting his brand: Strong client recommendations (and track record of success); facility for simultaneously managing different views and interests; ability to integrate legal strategy into a client's business objectives.

Karen writes:

I came from the "wrong side of the tracks," with a drug-addicted mother and an absent father. But with the help of a supportive teacher and loads of free extra coaching I was accepted at Oxford, and, upon graduating, I was lucky enough to be invited to join one of London's top "magic circle" firms. Both at university and at work, I drove myself constantly—I took on a workload that was excessive by any standard, just to justify others' faith in me.

In the end, of course, my health broke down. One of the partners, who had always treated me like the daughter he'd never had, insisted on my getting counseling. That was how I finally realized that all my problems stemmed from feeling subtly inferior to colleagues who had more privileged backgrounds. I couldn't help thinking that they were more intelligent than I, as they knew about opera and had read all the classics—but they weren't (or not all of them, anyway!). Over time, I came to value my own accomplishments. I also took up yoga, and gradually learned to stop worrying myself into a constant frenzy about work. All of this made me much happier, which, oddly enough, has made me a better, less self-obsessed lawyer.

Ideally, I'd visualize myself as confident and comfortable with my career—not needing to prove anything to others, but free to just be myself. Some clients say that they like working with me because they feel at ease with me and because I'm genuinely caring and interested—which I believe is true. Also, feeling happier and more secure has enabled me to better interact with others, asserting my opinion when necessary or taking a back seat when more appropriate. I think this makes me a valuable team player. While such traits are not necessarily on everyone's list as unique talents, they can—especially in my environment—prove a distinguishable asset.

I guess my brand boils down to the fact that I'm now emotionally secure, and that I care more about working well with my clients and colleagues than about seeking external recognition.

Brand promise: "My focus is on your success, so I will listen and genuinely care about resolving your issues."

Unique value: "Your success is more important than my own ego, so you can feel at ease with me and I will make you comfortable."

Core values and attitudes: Modest; cares about the personal needs and experiences of the other person (people-focused); team player; self-assured without having to constantly take the lead; centered and emotionally secure.

Other evidence supporting her brand: Has endured hardship, which helps her focus on essentials and be at ease with herself; ego has been "burned away."

Pete writes:

During law school I was most fascinated by criminal courses, and I took summer jobs in the area of criminal prosecution. After graduating I worked as a judicial clerk, as a prosecutor, and as a public defender. My original dream was to become attorney general(!), but when my career path in government began to feel a bit stale, I decided to switch to a firm focusing on criminal defense litigation, which has proved an ideal position for me. While my private practice doesn't involve the same number of courtroom appearances or give me quite the adrenaline boost of some of my previous jobs, I've used my courtroom experience to create a niche in the profession. This niche is based on my realization that in a trial it's often human interaction and people's perceptions, rather than legal argument, that make the difference. I'd like to think that I use this awareness to optimally engage with colleagues and clients to increase the chances of a favorable judgment. I try to apply this mindset to clients, too. Being involved in criminal proceedings inevitably involves some level of trauma, so clients should be handled with awareness and sensitivity. At home I'm the only male (we have three daughters), and the females in my life have definitely bolstered my ability to understand different perspectives!

Ideally, I'd like to be seen as the lawyer who can unveil "the human face behind each case" through my ability to read people and judge situations. I also enjoy mentoring younger members of my firm, and I envision myself as a leader in my practice group, teaching others to achieve and to apply the same awareness that I do.

In essence, my brand is about people expertise just as much as legal expertise. I hope that clients and colleagues alike would sum me up as strategic, intuitive, and sensitive.

Brand promise: "I promise to understand your perspective and empathize with the emotional dynamics of your situation."

Unique value: "I have a unique insight into the human factors of any legal proceeding that maximizes the chances of a favorable judgment."

Core values and attitudes: Intuitive; empathetic; sensitive; strategic; people-focused.

Other evidence supporting his brand: Mentor; teacher; has a vision of leadership that involves empowering others.

Jenny writes:

I was born in Sweden, and love art, textiles, and clothes. I taught myself to sew and spent most of my spare time as a teenager designing clothes or crafting some sort of art project. As a young lawyer in London I kept wondering and worrying about whether my career choice was right for me, and whether pursuing fashion or art might have been more "me"! However, I'm one of those sad people who needs to have a schedule and likes to know where my next paycheck is coming from—which pretty much rules out fashion or art!

That's why I decided to see if I could combine my enthusiasms with my work. With my law firm's blessing I went around the London fashion schools and local markets and offered to help the young artists and fashionistas with any legal issues they might have—all pro bono. As it turned out, many did have contractual, copyright, trade secret, and confidentiality questions, or problems with outstanding agreements. Over time, many from this non-paying client base grew into "real" clients—including a few very profitable ones—while the others mainly became my friends. With their success I built a reputation, so I now feel a part of an industry that I love. My clients know that I share their passions and have a genuine appreciation for what they do. In return, they trust me.

Ideally, I would see myself representing the top designers in all of their issues, from design through to production and branding, while at the same time expanding my collection of designer clothes. (I must admit that this isn't perhaps the wardrobe of most lawyers, but in my area of work it's OK—and even expected—to express myself through fashion!).

I think my brand says: creative, original, and enterprising.

Brand promise: "I will help you protect your creativity."

Unique value: "I understand your concerns as an artist and share your passion for bringing your ideas to life."

Core values and attitudes: Creative; enterprising; approachable; motivated by affiliation; trustworthy.

Other evidence supporting her brand: Is an artist herself; has personal experience in fashion; understands and is involved in the art/fashion industry; is friends with her clients.

Lucy writes:

I grew up in Yorkshire, in the north of England, which means I tend to call a spade a bloody shovel! However, some people, even in law, still appreciate raw honesty, so in my previous life I was lucky enough to build a career as general counsel of an internationally recognized software company, managing a large team of lawyers. When I first moved into private practice I represented both customers and suppliers of IT products, but I've since become more interested in representing customers, because my in-house experience can really help them. I know how suppliers think, and I understand the arguments that they have (or may think they have!) for their positions. My in-house days also gave me significant experience—which most law firms frankly don't provide—in team and project management. I like to think that I use my training and motivational strengths to benefit both my firm and the deals I organize.

Also, I'm tenaciously loyal to my clients and team; I champion their causes no matter what. For example, my clients are never overcharged, and if that means that I have to take a personal hit or go to bat for them (even against my fellow partners), I'll do it. That's how much my clients mean to me. (After all, not that long ago I was in their shoes!)

Ideally, I'd like to take on more of a management role; I'd like to be offering clients tactical advice more than technical legal skill, and spending more time developing the strategy of my practice group. I've always believed that my strengths are loyalty, foresight, influence, and trustworthiness.

I believe that my brand says to my clients and colleagues, "I am your champion."

Brand promise: "I will integrate into your team and strategically help you achieve the best result when negotiating against technology companies."

Unique value: "I will use my unique knowledge as general counsel of a technology company to help you make the best arguments and position yourself optimally."

Core values and attitudes: Champion; strategist; loyalty; honesty.

Other evidence supporting her brand: Leadership experience; previous project management roles; motivational strengths.

Kelsey writes:

From an early age I knew I wanted to be a lawyer, despite a family tradition—over generations—in medicine. My father wasn't overly thrilled; in fact, when I first went to law school, he supported me financially in return for one promise—that I'd never make a career suing doctors!

Over the years I've developed a role in health-care law, initially representing physicians, hospitals, and third-party payers (such as HMOs and insurance companies). I get the most satisfaction from helping physicians and physician groups, since I can relate to them and their issues. Also, I realized early on that I could develop a unique niche by choosing to represent only physicians and medical societies, rejecting hospitals and insurance companies with their potentially clashing interests. By doing this, I've become "the physician's advocate" to such an extent that I regularly attend their conferences, giving speeches on topics of mutual interest. I've made it my goal to integrate into their world.

In terms of brand, I'd hope that mine says: "I grew up in your industry and provide a unique service because I represent only doctors. There's no conflict of interest, and that sets me apart from most other health-care lawyers." Of course, it helps that I can say to them, "I know from my father how it feels to be hauled out of bed at 3:00 a.m. to attend to a patient!" or, "I can relate to the anxiety of being a doctor in an era of lawsuits and sky-high medical malpractice insurance."

Brand promise: "I am the physician's advocate."

Unique value: "I am an authority and a genuine proponent of your causes because I have no conflict of interest."

Core values and attitudes: Empathetic; knowledgeable; focused on what she values.

Other evidence supporting her brand: Family background (understands doctors' concerns); deep industry knowledge; integrated into her clients' issues.

Stanley writes:

I am strong and authoritative, but in an understated way. As a corporate finance lawyer, I work on large-scale mergers and acquisitions, bank financings, and securities. In my spare time I train for triathlons, and I try to bring the same focus, determination, and commitment to both my athletic pursuits and my work. My wife describes me as a type-A personality, but it's my discipline and self-control that have been truly invaluable in my area of law.

For example, I regularly deal with big fish with overworked egos, resulting in an undercurrent of competition in meetings and ventures for the title of "most important" or "biggest success." This is where I like to think that my ability to temper my ego and avoid being caught in the crossfire comes in! In fact, it's a blend of strong capability and strong willpower—the ability to confidently retreat rather than compete—that's made me popular among my clients.

Ideally, I'd see myself forging deeper relationships with top Wall Street clients and contacts, who would view me as their equal but appreciate the fact that I don't feel the need to overshadow them with my brilliance. Sometimes, I admit, I visualize winning clients in the financial world just as I win triathlons—using steady, capable commitment to come up from behind and take the prize.

Brand promise: "I will assert your interests in the toughest competitive financial deals."

Unique value: "I may be brilliant, but I don't need to assert it to others."

Core values and attitudes: Competitive but understated; calmly self-confident; strategic; strongly capable; committed; disciplined; has tenacious willpower.

Other evidence supporting his brand: Strong athlete; brings this mindset to his work; driven to win, but does so in the most strategic way.

Michael writes:
I grew up playing the cello and dreamed of a future leading a major symphony orchestra cello section. Unfortunately, once I reached music college I bumped up against the hard realization that I didn't have quite enough talent to rise to the very top—and that I wouldn't be happy with anything less! My older brother James had already succeeded as a probate lawyer, and he urged me to switch to law—advice I reluctantly decided to take. Although I found law school easier than solo performing, I continued to spend most of my spare time playing string quartets with old friends and attending concerts, while dreaming of the fabulous 18th-century Italian cello I'd be able to afford when I had my own law practice.

Once I was finally practicing law, however, my free time plummeted and I found that I missed all my musical connections. One day, while having coffee with my old cello teacher, I heard that one of the city's top orchestras was in legal difficulties. I instantly wondered whether there might be a niche for a lawyer specializing in the arts (theater as well as music), sensing that this kind of work would enable me to spend time with the kind of people I feel sympathy with. My hopes were realized, and today I combine my love of the arts with being a lawyer.

My brand? I guess I am somewhat introverted, but I hope that others, especially my arts-minded clients, find me easy to work with. That said, I have an ability to perform, learned through years of "projecting" on a concert platform, that really boosts my law career. Of course, many of my clients' issues are integral to my passions, so my innate enthusiasm is easily sparked. My clients really appreciate my genuine interest, and many of the well-known arts bodies throughout the country seek me out for consultation. And the really good news—I now own a magnificent Ruggieri cello!

Brand promise: "My clients instantly perceive my genuine passion for advocating their interests."

Unique value: "As an arts enthusiast myself, being involved with the arts is as important to me as being a lawyer, so that makes my interests uniquely aligned with those of my clients."

Core values and attitudes: Easy-going; quiet, but enlivened by a passion for the arts; supportive; creative; musical.

Other evidence supporting his brand: Music and performance background; enthusiastic about relationships with people in the arts; involved in the artistic community.

As you read through each of the brand statements above, it will have become obvious just how all these individuals achieved success through their distinct personalities and their choices about what matters most to them. It's fascinating to note how they have found different ways to deliver unique value to clients *and* achieve contentment and success—the objective of these chapters in a nutshell!

Please note that while the objective of this chapter's exercise is focused on the value that you bring to your clients, it is equally important that you develop your brand promise with regard to your colleagues. It should be consistent with your client promise, as both are supported by the same brand statement (your core values, attitudes, and other evidence of who you are), but may vary slightly in the specific value delivered.

In the interests of clarity, I suggest developing separate brand promises for your clients *and* your colleagues. For example, Lucy (above) wrote in her brand statement that her brand is being a tenacious champion of other people's causes. But that will mean something different to her clients than it will to her colleagues, and the specific value she provides will be different, too.

Refining Your Brand

Maintaining one's brand requires personal development. The place to start is to ensure that we are already projecting and exhibiting the authentic, distinct, and superior brand that we've determined upon. From that solid base we can work to strategically evolve into our ideal: the best we can possibly be!

So the objective of this next section is to consider your current development and the most appropriate strategy to enhance what you already are. Remember, your brand—and, indeed, everyone's brand—is a work in progress.

Start with the exercise below to accurately determine the current credibility of your brand.

EXERCISE

Step 1. Current Brand Versus Reality

Take your brand statement and what you think you project, and then contact as many *trusted* people as you can and ask them to paint the actual picture that they receive from you.

Using the Johari window (diagrammed on the next page) can be very effective. (The Johari window was invented by Joseph Luft and Harry Ingham. See Luft, J. [1982]. *The Johari Window: A Graphic Model of Interpersonal Awareness*.)

	What you perceive in yourself	Unknown to yourself
What others perceive in you	Public Self: known to you and to everyone else	BLIND SPOTS: things you don't realise but others see
Unknown to others	Hidden Self: what you know but others don't realize	Undiscovered and unknown

A person with most characteristics in the "Public Self" quadrant is likely to be open (few characteristics will be left in the "Hidden Self" quadrant) and self-aware (a small number of blind spots will be discovered in quadrant 2). There can be both positives and negatives to openness; sharing people are typically comfortable with themselves, but if too open can make others ill at ease. On the other hand, self-awareness can bring only positive results. Three major ones that come to mind are...

- More information to work with
- Fewer unknowns to be exploited
- More control and power

So engage in the exercise with the objective of reducing your blind spots. A powerful brand depends upon it!

Accepting others' views takes courage, and it requires that you be completely open to criticism! You must agree up front that the exercise is not about "being nice" or seeking praise. (If you *get* praise, that's great, terrific, but honest criticism will be still more valuable.) What you're really after is honesty, which can be painful in the short term but extremely beneficial in the long term.

It's important not to argue with the feedback you receive—in fact, try not to react in any way, because your colleagues may notice and withdraw their honest contributions. Instead, just listen neutrally, acknowledge what's been said, and record the information you receive.

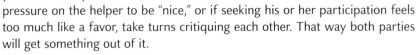

If you sense too much pressure on the helper to be "nice," or if seeking his or her participation feels too much like a favor, take turns critiquing each other. That way both parties will get something out of it.

Don't alter your entire strategy based on any single meeting, but once you've gathered sufficient feedback, you'll need to reconcile what you have been told with what you previously believed yourself to be projecting. Try filling in the following questions, once you've gathered the requisite information. You might be surprised how different things can look when put down on paper!

What I think I project/stimulate: _____

_____

_____

versus

What others see/feel/receive: _____

_____

_____

Step 2. Positive Feedback

The good news is that there are undoubtedly some behaviors consistent with your brand that you're already expressing, as confirmed in your feedback. Congratulations! To that degree, you're already being your brand. In addition, your feedback (with luck) probably uncovered some good qualities that you might not have recognized in yourself. ("I liked what was said about my being a good listener and weighing all the evidence before deciding.") Consider how you can better capitalize on these traits—perhaps including them in an expanded brand statement/promise.

Step 3. Change

Unfortunately, most of us don't yet display *every* attribute of our intended brand. Generally, we must either acquire some new skills or get rid of certain patterns of behavior—or both. Think about the feedback you received and the changes you might want to make. Also, review your notes from the previous chapter and think about any adjustments to your ways of working that might be necessary to strengthen the superiority of your brand.

Step 4. Consistent Impression

Last, reflect on how your daily behavior could better consistently demonstrate your core brand. The truth is, we're all being judged on a daily basis. People entering a train compartment instantaneously decide whether or not to sit beside us; players at a tennis club determine whether or not we're good enough to play with; and the colleague who may offer us some work will first observe our personality to determine our law skills. And these decisions are often based on very minor aspects of appearance or behavior! So you must constantly evaluate how you, even in the most trivial ways, support your desired brand.

For example:

- A brand hinging on confident assertiveness should be taking charge and leading discussions at meetings. This doesn't just mean leaping in for the sake of being noticed; it means being prepared with agendas, ideas, and structure. Background work counts!

- Someone with an extroverted, cheerful brand should consider on a daily basis how he is engaging with the people around him, communicating his energy and his ability to connect on a positive, optimistic basis. (Of course, we all have bad days, but the extroverted person should never let them affect how he is perceived.)

- If your brand is all about competence and reliability, then letting *anyone* down, however minor the issue, is a potential scratch on that shiny image (plus, you'll be angry with yourself for it!).

- A helpful "team player" offers to pitch in whenever possible, thinking proactively about how to do that in different situations. A practical example might be arranging for coffee for the group, rather than merely buying one's own.

Think about your brand and the little things you can do to reinforce it. You can even create ways to "ritualize" your actions, so that the people around you can count on the experience that your brand creates.

COMPETE ON UNIQUENESS

The whole point about having a brand is to compete for recognition and clients in a unique way. The mistake most lawyers make is to compete with other lawyers on the *same* dimension—usually technical performance—and technical skill is a difficult contest to win (as it can be almost impossible for most clients—especially non-lawyers—to judge). Thus, our energies would be more usefully harnessed by developing and projecting our uniqueness than by going head-to-head with comparable lawyers.

Client pitch, firm 1

Client pitch, firm 2

Client pitch, firm 3

Client pitch, firm 4

So ask yourself on a consistent basis...

- Am I being the authentic, distinct, and superior brand I want to be? If not, what can I change to make this the case?

- Does my brand meet an important client need? Does it meet that need uniquely?

If you can't answer these questions immediately and confidently, then you need to work toward developing your brand so that you can do so with real conviction.

Just as in the world of fashion, you should be able to deliver your superior brand in your own individual way—and when you deliver on what you promise, you build up credibility. In other words, if you consistently display the authentic, distinct, and superior experience of your brand, people will come to recognize and expect it, and clients and colleagues alike will ultimately learn to trust you.

We'll look at some additional ways to enhance our status in the next chapter.

Chapter Thirteen
Enhancing and Marketing Your Brand

The last step in the process of brand-building is enhancement and marketing. You can have the best brand in the world, but if nobody knows about it, it's useless—or, as a youthful friend of mine would put it, *mega* useless!

It's important to approach marketing in an organized, systematic, and proactive fashion, thinking about the optimal way to reach your target audience and distinguish yourself from your competitors.

EXPERTISE

In Chapter 17 we will examine how winning business involves connecting with clients on an emotional level, but before we can begin to do that we must first establish our credentials. Without the requisite expertise, we won't even be given the opportunity to compete! So the deeper our experience (focusing on a chosen specialty, not trying to be all things to all people), the more doors will open up to us.

The first step is to delegate, to the extent possible, any work that does not support this goal—in other words, *just say no*, no matter how potentially lucrative a project might turn out to be. Building a specialist brand demands sacrifice! Second, seek out clients who are strategically suited to your chosen area of expertise, partly of course because they reward you with work, but also because they provide you with valuable information about their industry; they can also act as a source of both endorsements and referrals. The latter are so critical to brand marketing that you may have to make concessions at first to engage with these clients—such as donating time, at least for a while. But eventually, as you steadfastly build your reputation, such compromise will no longer be necessary.

The bottom line is that clients buy one of two things: expertise (which is self-explanatory) or convenience (in the form of reduced fees, quick turnaround, or commoditized services). Thus, the deeper your expertise in a complex specialty, the less concerned you need be with meeting "convenience" criteria.

If you remain conscientious in developing your specialty, there *will* come a time when you can market and sell your expertise again and again—and that's when all your investment will pay off!

INEVITABLE CHANGE

We all know that over the lifetime of a career one's specialty may change, either by choice or because evolving markets require it. We need to be proactive in this change, and it's important to be fluid and flexible enough to stay ahead of the curve. For example, early in my career as a technology lawyer I began to enjoy working on outsourcing projects—an unusual specialty at that time. I set about making myself an outsourcing expert, and I even switched firms to become part of one of the best outsourcing practice groups. However, when the technology boom ended, many IT and corporate lawyers also began expanding into the outsourcing market, with the result that my chosen specialty was no longer the rarity it had once been. I realized it was time for me to find another distinguishing characteristic.

CHANGE CREATES OPPORTUNITIES

You should also keep your eyes and ears open for new legislation that could affect your clients or your target market. For example, if you're looking to acquire banks as clients, be aware of any new regulations that will affect the financial sector and become expert in dealing with those regulations. Many of today's data protection specialists developed their expertise as soon as the relevant legislation passed into law and did well by advising companies of the business implications.

NARROW YOUR NICHE

When I joined Shaw Pittman to open their London office, many other U.S. firms were also expanding into Europe, and London was their first port of call. But Shaw Pittman's strategy was different: They elected to build their office around one particular expertise—technology transactions, with an emphasis on large, complex deals and outsourcing. The senior lawyers hired by the firm all had unique competence in that narrow focus, and that's what we marketed. We were successful partly because such a practice group was unprecedented, and partly because our specificity enhanced our credibility; we could genuinely claim to be the most experienced outsourcing group in the market. Had we tried to be the best American firm in London, or the best in technology practice, our message would have been far less credible! (Ironically, after just a year we were deemed the top intellectual property/technology team in all of the U.K.—a much broader scope than we had intended to conquer.)

DIFFERENTIATE THE WAY YOU PROVIDE YOUR SERVICES

The other aspect to our message was that we brought a uniquely American approach to outsourcing into the European market. Shaw Pittman had an unparalleled reputation in the U.S. as exceptional leaders in outsourcing. These U.S. pioneers developed their initial skills in conjunction with the technical and business experts who established the U.S. outsourcing market, so they became skilled in those areas as well. They prided themselves on having not just legal expertise but an in-depth understanding of the technical, business, and commercial basis of the market. Their advice on any project encompassed technical analysis, cost implications, complicated service metrics, and even advice on structure, price, and services. In essence, they were no longer merely lawyers; they were business and technical consultants, too. They had a unique methodology and project management style that was deliverable by every lawyer in their group.

When they were ready to set up a London office, this group made sure that their new colleagues all had the requisite mastery of technology, commercial knowledge, and methodology. The message was not merely "We are the most experienced outsourcing practice in the market" but "We also boast a methodology that no other firm can offer." Our delivery of that methodology added *real* value.

Think about how you can provide your services in a different way—a way that adds value.

FIND A MENTOR

One of the most effective ways to develop an area of one's brand is to seek out a role model with that quality, and to ask advice from this person—or to emulate him or her.

As mentioned in the Preface, I had many mentors during my career, and was especially lucky in my early (and most impressionable!) years to have had various partners who took an interest in my personal development and helped to shape my career. There were...

- *Breakfast meetings with Paul.* Paul truly loved the academic side of being a technology lawyer. He delighted in exploring issues and discovering new solutions, and we spent many hours together doing just that. (Paul was not always a technology lawyer. When the property market crashed and the Internet was on the verge of taking off, Paul transformed himself from a successful real estate partner into a technology expert, merging his natural interest in "computer stuff" with a shrewd marketing instinct. He was therefore an early role model in demonstrating the value of flexibility, specialization, and authentic branding.)

- *Client development brainstorming sessions with John.* Always bursting with client development ideas, John (my early boss) loved to talk about business generation. It took me a while to appreciate his efforts to involve me, but I absorbed some of his enthusiasm and longed to emulate him.

- *Work–life balance discussions with Larry.* Another early leader in the technology area, Larry authored one of the first major treatises on Internet law, and, in common with Paul and John, taught me the importance of expertise and marketability. But Larry also encouraged me to compensate for all my hard work with a balanced lifestyle, and genuinely demonstrated how this can be done, often inviting me to dinner with his family. (I must admit that I was a fairly lousy protégé in that regard, especially in those early years, but I learned eventually!)

Back then we didn't call it "mentoring," nor did my firm have a formal mentoring program, but that's exactly what it was. And when I moved to London to work at a "magic circle" firm, I discovered new mentors. In my new environment, even my peers and juniors became sources of mentoring—helping me to navigate those subtle-but-crucial differences between the English and the American ways of doing things.

As I approached partnership—that critical stage—I was lucky enough to have a collection of mentors. The partner with whom I worked most closely, Andrew, was invaluable on various levels. With his guidance I refined my brand (although I had yet to formulate it as such) by honing my skill set and addressing my weaknesses. (It was Andrew, back in Chapter 4, who drew my attention to the fact that my driven personality was not necessarily an unadulterated plus in terms of making partner.) He also encouraged me to market myself both inside and outside the firm, and proved an authoritative sponsor of my progression to partnership.

While each of my mentors was important, from a career (and brand) strategy perspective, there was still something lacking. Ironically, I only realized this years later by observing a junior, but more instinctive, lawyer. Kerry was an alumna from my law school who moved to London and contacted me for career advice. After settling into her new job at a different firm, she asked me to be her "career mentor." Kerry's request was neither casual nor spontaneous; she arrived at our meeting having set down all her thoughts in writing. The way Kerry presented her request demonstrated that she deserved my investment of time and energy. Here's an overview of the points she presented:

Goals	Why she wanted a career mentor and what she wanted to achieve from the relationship
	Current career goals and how she felt a mentoring relationship could help her achieve them
Why you?	Why she thought I could help her
Expectations	What she would expect from a career mentor —and what she could do in return
Time commitment	Specific amount of time (number of hours) needed per _____

When I asked Kerry why she hadn't sought someone from within her own firm, she explained that she had—in fact, one of her direct superiors was also a mentor—but he was her "skill mentor." Kerry astutely realized what—as an associate—I hadn't: Having your boss as a mentor can have limitations, especially as you progress to partnership.

When you're junior, the overriding goal is to acquire skills—such as technical knowledge and the ability to deal with clients. It's in your boss's interest that you excel in these things, so your goals are aligned and there is a clear mutual benefit in your boss's guidance, transference of skills, and investment in you. However, you and your boss will probably discover at some point that an inherent conflict also crops up. (Most bosses can overcome this and will look out for your interests regardless—but by no means all!) For example, your boss might...

- Prioritize short-term demands over your development

- Feel threatened by your development

- Sabotage goals that do not benefit him or her directly

- Prefer you to remain as a subordinate (especially if you are an excellent performer who makes him look good or lessens his burden)

- Delay your advancement to avoid losing credit for your work

- View you as competition for clients and business

While these are worst-case scenarios, they *can* happen—especially if the naïve associate remains unaware that his mentor's interests have become profoundly misaligned from his own. I know of one instance where an associate's mentor guided him in developing relationships with a certain client, which benefited them both. However, when the protégé was on the verge of being made partner, the "mentor" removed him from the client's account, neatly replacing him with a more junior lawyer. Thus, by weakening the protégé's relationships within the client organization, the mentor mitigated the risk of his protégé competing with him for client credit—at least, with that particular client.

Another risk of depending on your boss is that the relationship *will* change as you advance, and you must be prepared and proactive in this transition. I have a friend whose boss was also her mentor, and once she became a partner he continued in both roles. His intention was to help her ease into her new position, but his inability to withdraw his authority both devalued her advancement and dampened her confidence. Similarly, one partner I had hugely valued as a boss, friend, and mentor changed toward me overnight after I reached partnership. Once I was no longer "part of his team" or "working for him" I was no longer a beneficial investment, and he quickly replaced me with younger, equally aspiring, associates.

Optimally, your boss *will* be your mentor, but for long-term career strategy and brand-building it's still best to avoid relying wholly on any one person. Instead, surround yourself with a variety of people, each of whom can help you in a specific area. Ask yourself "What do I need to enhance my current brand?"—and then seek out someone with the relevant expertise. The best choice, of course, is someone who has trodden your preferred path before you. (Many lawyers seek career coaches, but their value is limited because most of them have not achieved the goal you're pursuing.) A mentor is a role model of experience—the best (and sometimes only) alternative to learning through your own successes and failures.

Mentoring relationships necessarily evolve over time and even come to a natural end. With Kerry, I like to think that I contributed to her achieving partnership, but through the ending of one relationship and the beginning of another, her career goals changed, and she eventually discovered a new role in the corporate world. Our relationship is no longer that of mentor and protégé; I have little, if anything, left to teach her. Instead, we are mutual friends and reciprocal sounding boards. Ironically, lately I seem to be the one seeking counsel, rather than the other way around!

Mentors are role models of who or what we aspire to be (our ideal brand), so for women at least one of our mentors should be female—though this can prove difficult. In Chapter 15 I mention the unique challenges of women's networking, and the same issues are valid for mentoring: The pool of candidates is simply that much smaller. Further, balancing the twin demands of work and family still tends to be a female challenge, and finding a role model may require you to look outside your firm, or even the profession. There *are* successful examples (and these women have created some of the most impressive brands), but they're still far from the norm in the law-firm environment.

I was fortunate to find a mentor (and valuable friend) in one of my female bosses, Margaret, whom you may recall from Chapter 6. From the beginning she was disinterestedly involved in my personal development and career progression, and even when I became her fellow partner and (later) when she switched firms, our relationship remained constant. In my experience, that female-female mentoring relationship was invaluable.

WIN AN AWARD

Mentors are vital, but there is no better recognition for your brand than a third-party endorsement, and winning an award is the best recognition of all. When a movie or book is rated highly, interest automatically increases; if a certain product is deemed "best of its class," whether it's a gadget, a car, or a design, people generally want it. We choose colleges and law schools by their rankings. The same principle applies to lawyers—and to our services.

I mentioned earlier that only a year after setting up the London office of Shaw Pittman we won the Legal Business IT/IP Team of the Year award. We were also ranked by *Legal 500* (and other publications) in the top rank of technology practices in London. Our message was always credible ("We are different and therefore superior"), but with the award we had confirmation from a third party.

In subsequent years, I won individual awards for prominent and complex deals and received write-ups and endorsements from *Who's Who, Chambers*, and *Legal 500*, to name a few. Each one helped to enhance and solidify my personal brand.

The curious thing about many of these awards is that being in the running requires a certain amount of self-promotion. Every year lots of legal industry awards and rankings are made, but it is usually up to us lawyers to get ourselves nominated and considered. Investigate the ones relevant to you and your market, and get yourself on the list. Even if you think your chances of winning are small, I urge you to participate because you'll be getting your name in front of important people—and eventually, you might just make it! (Frankly, new candidates can have an edge.)

BE THE FIRST

The first to market always has the advantage. This doesn't mean that you have to devise a whole new legal service; you merely have to be the first in your market, however that might be defined. One lawyer I know was part of the intellectual property department in a large London firm, and was doing quite well as part of that team. However, she made the strategic decision to move to an American firm, with a much smaller office and no IP capability. She moved from being one of many data protection specialists to being the only one—first to market!—and became the exclusive expert in that specialty to her colleagues across the Atlantic, who were naturally less knowledgeable than she about European laws.

CREATE A "VALUE ADD"

My outsourcing deals were complex—some could take a full year to complete—with lots of documentation and negotiation. The resulting contracts could run to hundreds of pages, with technical schedules so detailed that one discrete paragraph could contain a key aspect of the agreement. And once the deal was signed, such contracts weren't just kept in a drawer; typically, they governed the ongoing relationship between the clients and their vendors, who provided critical services. It was imperative for my clients to understand what was covered in that great stack of papers, but the people running the contract weren't lawyers, and generally weren't equipped to grapple with the practical implications.

At the end of one deal, my client joked that the company would probably spend as much money calling me with questions about the contract as they had negotiating it! I then offered to draft him a "layman's guide" to the contract, which proved to be so valuable that on every subsequent deal this client requested such a manual up front, as part of my fees. The idea turned into an added value and extra service that I offered to all my clients—something none of my competitors were doing.

Think about ways you might create a "value add" to your services, and then test-market it with your clients. You may want to offer it for free until you determine whether or not it really does meet an untapped need. Remember, the only perspective that really matters—sorry!—is the client's.

GET PUBLISHED

How many times have you picked up the latest legal publication to see an article written by someone in your field of expertise, only to find that the author doesn't know half as much about it as you do? It can be hugely frustrating, but by simply caring sufficiently to write the article this attorney has become "the expert" in his specialty. In many cases it couldn't matter less whether or not he really is an authority; the important thing is that he's become identified as one.

For example, one young lawyer marketed herself brilliantly through writing a book about a certain, anticipated, legal event. This woman had just graduated from law school and had little, if any, experience representing clients: in fact, her only work experience was as a part-time law school intern, and at the time of her book launch she was unemployed. Yet she marketed herself by publicizing her book and speaking at various conferences—and being an effective speaker, of course, supported her purpose. A prominent firm eventually hired her, based on their perception of her experience and her book. Once hired, of course, she had to bestir herself enough to learn on the job—fast! But it was certainly a creative way of getting into a place that would otherwise not have allowed her in the door.

Assuming no pre-existing relationship (or referral), clients generally initiate the process of choosing their lawyers based on reputation and expertise. Getting published is a powerful means of showcasing your credentials and publicizing your brand.

Most of us have the same knee-jerk response to the notion of writing an article: "I don't have the time." However, it's a great idea to *make* the time!—as long as you ensure that you use the opportunity effectively.

Target Audience, Topic, and Angle

First, decide on your target audience, along with a unique topic or an angle particularly relevant to them. One of the biggest mistakes lawyers make is to write an article that is not specific enough. Almost *nobody* wants to read yet another article on the various laws, regulations, and directives associated with data privacy—I should know! However, data privacy is still a topic affecting a lot of companies, and many people are fretting about it. So if you were planning to write about data protection, you would first need to choose a specific audience, and then tailor your article to their needs. For example:

- Is your audience the human resources group, with access to personal information on a daily basis? If so, narrow your topic to the company and the type of information involved.

- IT groups are often involved in sending sensitive data to India or elsewhere, because of outsourcing. Why not concentrate on the practical transfer of such information within the confines of the law?

- Perhaps you're targeting people in a specific industry, such as nuclear technology. In this case it might be useful to focus on the right of the company to access employee information for security clearances and government licenses. (I admit that such a topic is unlikely to compete with a juicy, seaside novel, but at least the reader who requires the information for his work will be grateful!)

Whatever audience you're addressing, focus on their issues, with an angle specific to them. If you're not completely sure about their concerns, ask. Remember, everyone wants to feel important, and people love being called upon for advice. And if you connect with someone because you need advice about an article, they will probably be supportive and will help to make the article more prominent or successful.

When you seek advice ahead of time from your target audience, the discussion will often lead to their current business problems—problems, with any luck, related to your area of expertise. And even if your talks go nowhere, you'll have a reason for following up later with a copy of the article.

Winning Formulas

Forming an article in an unusual way can make it stand out. Winning formats to consider include these:

- *Case studies.* Feature a few examples, possibly with different strategies (or actions taken) with clear outcomes.

- *Interviews.* Choose a credible expert to interview. This is also a highly effective way of making a new connection or deepening a current relationship because you are making the other person feel important. (Very few people will reject the gratifying chance to appear as resident expert!)

- *Industry experts.* Directly involve someone from your target base. For example, involve experts from the industry by including their perspectives, or by inviting them to co-author the piece.

- *Trends.* When something is new, people want to know about it. What are the benefits and drawbacks? How might it alter their methods of working?

- *The competition.* Self-explanatory! Who doesn't long to know what the competition is up to? Even the smallest nugget here is gold.

- *Industry studies.* Dig up a study about something relevant to the industry. (This a great way to add authority, especially if the study is not widely known.)

In short, the key to writing an article that your audience *wants* to read is to identify an angle—and then to make it interesting! Otherwise, you risk wasting your time.

Find a Publication

Before determining the content of the article, search for a publication associated with your target audience, bearing in mind that the optimal publication for the purpose is just as likely to be a trade journal as a legal magazine. This is because industry journals allow you to showcase your skills to a broader audience—one almost certainly interested in, but unsure about, the legal implications associated with their actions. This may enable you to raise an issue and effortlessly demonstrate how it might be resolved. In the data privacy example I mentioned earlier, for instance, one possible angle might be to consider an industry practice that—although standard—remains in violation of recent regulations.

Not only do trade magazines potentially reach a grateful audience, but targeting them automatically mitigates the need for intense research and analysis. Think about it: If you hope to educate fellow lawyers (and showcase your expertise), rigorous research and analysis is required to raise a unique issue and to distinguish your competence above that of others. Writing for a trade magazine, on the other hand, provides an ideal opportunity to discuss a legal issue in layman's terms, while still providing useful information. Further, articles on legal topics are relatively rare for trade magazines, so you are automatically showcasing yourself against few, if any, other legal experts.

One practical note: When submitting your article, always send a photo, as long as it doesn't resemble Godzilla's younger sibling. Almost *any* picture makes an author more personable—and more memorable!

Getting the Most Out of Your Article

Once the article is submitted and published, a few free copies will arrive on your desk. At that point, if the only person to get a free copy is your mother, you have not adequately capitalized on your effort! You should send copies of your article to every possible client (and potential client), with a handwritten note. In some cases, sending the entire publication makes your achievement

more impressive or enhances its credibility; be sure to get sufficient copies and reprints if you choose to go that route.

Negotiate as many rights as possible, so you can reprint and reuse the article for your own marketing endeavors. (Yes, it's the old journalistic trick of regurgitating the same material with new and different packaging!) I once wrote a very long and intricate article to serve as my blueprint going forward, and it served that purpose well. I used bits and pieces of it in many subsequent articles, so although the first rendition proved a long and painful process, it paid for itself many times over.

Remember, if you're going to lose precious billable hours writing an article, you owe it to yourself to make the most of it.

PRESS RELEASES

Press coverage also builds brand credibility because newspapers, magazines, and journals represent objective third parties, and they can establish you as an authority (or at least, as someone newsworthy) by publishing your work. You should make sure that the relevant publications are notified of every major deal you complete. (Note: Sad though it seems, it's frankly only you who thinks your deal is *intrinsically* exciting, so make sure your press release has an angle.) If there is a marketing or PR department that organizes these things on your behalf, get to know those people and be proactive about providing them with information that can be pushed out to the right editors. If there is no one in the firm who deals with the press on your behalf, you'll have to do it yourself.

When sending press releases, be sure to put them in the right format. There are certain guidelines to follow for each publication, and deviating from these rules makes it less likely that your item will be picked up.

If your press releases aren't used, don't give up! After a few such attempts you may be successful, and in the meantime, simply by sending them, you're introducing yourself to the publication. The reporters there may begin to think of you as a source of information the next time they need a legal opinion. If that happens and your input is called for, respond immediately (journalists invariably want their information YESTERDAY!), doing whatever it takes to develop a relationship with the person who contacted you.

Should the publication ask for an interview, ask about the likely line of questioning. This saves both your time and the journalist's, because you'll be able to prepare short and well-thought-out answers to the anticipated questions.

Securing press attention provides priceless opportunities to advertise yourself to an audience who will (as a given) perceive you as significant. Having your name in print automatically creates respect. And remember, it's not just completed transactions that merit attention! Consider sending press releases when you're involved in anything that might be newsworthy (at least, on a really slow news day!). Also, if you are junior and doubt that you have the authority to take part in such activities, think about how you can best make it happen within the confines of your infrastructure. If your groundwork benefits people higher up in the firm, they are very likely to prove grateful for your initiative.

FEATURES

Most publications keep a list of upcoming features. You can call the journals most relevant to your specialty and obtain a list of their topics for the year, to see if any of them are pertinent to you. Then find out the name of the commissioned journalists and contact them, offering your support or point of view. Every time I did this, my approach was welcomed—because in each case the journalist had little understanding of the underlying topic, which, of course, just happened to be my area of expertise. This is also a great way to build up relationships with journalists who may, in time, come to rely upon your input.

COLUMNS

Writing a column in a trade magazine, or any other journal that reaches your target clients, can skyrocket your reputation. Figure out your subject and target audience and then research possible publications. Just the other day, while in my tailor's shop, I picked up one of his trade journals. It contained a column by a lawyer, focusing on retail business issues, that cited the author as the head of his firm's retail business group and the preeminent expert in that field. Now I'm not convinced that his firm even *has* such a group, and as a lawyer I could instantly discern that his column addressed general contractual issues that were in no way specific to retail; however, members of his target audience probably wouldn't realize that, and would almost certainly perceive him as unique to their market. So, all in all, it seemed like clever branding to me!

VISIBILITY AND THE RIGHT WAY TO SELF-PROMOTE

With regard to all your contacts, *keep your brand visible.* You can do this through a formal newsletter or a series of informal emails, providing legal updates, newsworthy tidbits, or similar information consistent with your brand. Setting up a blog, or collaborating on social networking and Web 2.0 platforms, can be enormously effective. When people discover your useful and substantive content on the Internet, their attention will be piqued—far more so than if they come across your website or résumé claiming "deep expertise."

How you use the Internet, of course, depends on your practice area and law firm constraints. I'm not suggesting that you should spend three hours a day on Facebook—or even that Facebook is necessarily a beneficial platform! Try something more business-focused, industry-focused, or even law-focused. The key is to create opportunities to keep you in the collective minds of your target audience.

Visibility is not limited to clients; it's equally critical to self-promote with regard to colleagues. By this I do not mean bragging, and I certainly wouldn't suggest attempting to bolster yourself in a "let me tell you what I've done" sort of way. (This, of course, would go against every element of people skills—aside from making you notably unpopular in the pub!) Instead, make your brand impressive by sharing your accomplishments in subtle ways—preferably in a manner that makes your story of consequence to your audience. Here's an example. Rachel Boothroyd, partner in the intellectual property department of K & L Gates, London office, writes:

I was delighted to be involved in the deal that would bring digital advertising onto the platform walls of the London Underground. I'm well aware of the need to keep one's brand visible, but I had never felt comfortable bragging about "my big deal," as it felt like showing off!

However, I was truly passionate about the technological transformation the deal would bring about. Instead of focusing on my part in the project, I described to my colleagues the sheer impact of what we were working on—something I was excited about and thought they would be as well. When traveling on the tube, instead of seeing static old-fashioned posters, they would soon be watching versatile and entertaining digital advertising. This is not only cutting-edge technology but a transformational legacy project for London. Our city was to become the leading outdoor transport advertising location in the world. As a Londoner it is great (and refreshing!) to find an area where we can share pride in our city.

When explained in this way, even some colleagues got excited about my deal! Many sent me clippings when it was written about in the media, or links to online news stories featuring the project.

Now the deal is coming to life. The digital technology is popping up in our local tube stations, and I am sure that at least a few of my colleagues think of me and our team on their (slightly less tedious) underground journeys. In this way I believe the digital sector expertise in our team is constantly reinforced to others in the firm and to those who have heard of our involvement in the project. It is a great way to remind everyone of our brand, values, and expertise.

One of the most effective ways to keep yourself visible and gain support is to obtain sponsorship from people within your firm who can influence your advancement. The first step is to add value to them and to encourage their interest in you. Although not always easy, cultivating relationships with those in authority can be enormously beneficial to your brand, and, unfortunately (or for some, fortunately!), the old cliché stands: It's not always what you know, but whom you know (or who knows you). If your boss and the people in your immediate circle of colleagues are the only ones who know your brand and how great/reliable/gifted you are, then you are severely limiting your own career progression (especially if they don't happen to have a high profile them-selves). Further, you'll notice that the people in your practice group typically come and go, but the people at the top usually stick around.

Again, women can be at a disadvantage when searching for sponsorship, for two reasons: First, there are often fewer women in powerful positions, and second, for older male partners, getting to know a young female lawyer can seem problematic. But persevere! One sponsor I had, Dave, took me under his wing in a very fatherly spirit. I'll never forget his support during one, peculiarly stressful, project. When that deal inevitably went sour (see the case study in Chapter 17), he gave me much-needed personal and professional encourage-ment. One caution: Do remember to consider how strongly your sponsor's interests are aligned to your own, just as you would with a mentor. If your sponsor is in another office or part of a different practice group, then aligning your ultimate objectives may become impossible.

YOUR RÉSUMÉ

An updated and personalized résumé also supports your brand. It should tell your story, rather than merely list (yawn) all your academic achievements and experience. For example, someone I met recently sent me some samples of his work, including his résumé. The opening paragraph gave me a synopsis of what he does, his passions, the high level of his achievement, and exactly how he has made a difference to various clients. I was immediately impressed, and curious to read on. As I did, I learned some positive and interesting things about him and even discovered leisure pursuits that we have in common. It made me warm to him as a person. How many of the résumés that have come across your desk have had that effect?! Spend time working with your own, and consider how your résumé can better reflect your brand statement and tell your story. (There's a sample provided at the end of this chapter, based on the résumé of Bill Kirkland, whom you may recall from the brand statement exercise. Some names have been changed.)

In addition, maintain a list of your client transactions and any particular projects or legal solutions you might want a new contact to know about. Update this list frequently, while the information is still fresh in your memory (unless it was one of those working experiences that you're trying to forget!). That way you have the information at your fingertips, and you don't need to dig up the details later.

NETWORKING

We will examine networking in more detail in the following chapters, but it would be remiss of me to completely neglect it here. Networking is not just schmoozing or going to events; it's a mindset of making connections with people and exposing them to you and your brand. This means that wherever you are, and whatever you are doing, you should be thinking about how to introduce your brand, and from that introduction you should demonstrate (a) commonality, (b) value (from you to them, not the other way around!), and (c) characteristics that foster trust.

If you don't think that networking can happen with almost every activity, let me tell you about Neil. Every morning Neil went to the same place for his coffee, where, as a relentless brand promoter, he consistently exemplified himself as a friendly and caring lawyer. One morning the owner of the establishment asked him for some advice in regard to a tenancy agreement, confiding his vulnerability with regard to his landlord. Although Neil was running late that morning, and his specialty was show-business contracts, he took the time to go over some of the basics with the coffee-shop owner, which relieved the latter greatly. Once back at the office Neil also made a few inquiries on the man's behalf and connected him to someone who was ultimately useful to him in his tenancy dispute. Thereafter, not only did Neil receive his morning coffee for free(!), but the coffee-shop owner also made an unexpected referral that has since played a critical role in Neil's career. The man's daughter was an up-and-coming actor and was in the process of signing her first major contract. She was feeling uncomfortable with her agent and legal advisor, and on her father's assurance that Neil was reliable (i.e., trustworthy), she called him. She has been a loyal (and lucrative) client ever since.

Neil did everything right. He consistently demonstrated his brand, even in the trivial activity of purchasing his morning coffee, and even when his consistency seemed inconvenient (or unlikely to lead to anything). As his story suggests, networking chances are limited only by your own luck and hard work. Potentially, any situation where you meet people can give you the opportunity to demonstrate who you are.

OUTSIDE INTERESTS

Cultivating outside interests can contribute immensely to your brand. At first blush, you may wonder how your career could possibly be enhanced by a totally unrelated pursuit. But diverse interests make you unique and noteworthy—even memorable—rather than just another successful lawyer (yawn). Whatever your interest—karaoke, tap dancing, surfing, urban exploration, Japanese cuisine—it provides a topic of novel conversation that people will associate you with. And if you can find others of a similar mindset you'll be creating the optimal networking platform, because these are people with whom you already have at least one connection, but who are probably not lawyers themselves. They may one day need a lawyer, or (more likely) they may someday know someone else who does. (The most improbable candidates can prove to be valuable networking partners!)

> Diverse interests make you unique and noteworthy—even memorable—rather than just another successful lawyer (yawn).

In the next chapter, I mention my taking various acting classes. Not only did I learn new skills that directly benefited me as a lawyer, but I also met new and interesting people and engaged in something creative, fun, and totally different from my work! From a "small talk" perspective, it provided me with interesting anecdotes, and a fairly unexpected answer to "What are you up to this week?" Surprisingly, I even increased my business network—fellow drama students included a McKinsey consultant, two Goldman Sachs investment bankers, and a BP executive. (All of these people were encouraged by their firms to attend the class, both as a creative outlet and as a boost to their communication skills—law firms, take note!)

But one of my favorite examples of an outside interest truly benefiting someone's career (and life) is the story of Mike O'Connor, the head of Addleshaw Goddard's Infrastructure, Projects and Energy Group:

I have always been interested in popular music and culture, and while I am not technically proficient, I played with a number of bands at university.

Some time after becoming a partner, I was asked by an acquaintance if I would like to play a few songs. Over a period of 18 months, a band was formed comprising a number of individuals whom I happened to meet either through work or through common interests.

The band has now been together for seven years and plays about ten gigs a year—mostly charitable and fundraising events, but also some paid gigs. The band provides each of its members and families a great deal of fun, and raises funds for a number of great causes.

The band has played at an internationally renowned contemporary arts festival (known for its mud!), which proved to be a fantastic experience as well as a special event for client and business contacts of band members.

While most members of the group do not work in the same spheres, business connections have been made which have proved useful to each member individually. Somewhat surprisingly, the band has also proved to be an alternative support mechanism for each member during periods of illness, job-related stress, or bereavement.

From a professional perspective, I've found chatting about the band's activities to be an effective icebreaker with new business contacts. A number of client contacts are really interested in the latest band news or want to talk about their own musical interests; they have remarked that they have felt more relaxed in talking about non-work subject matter, and that in their view I'm not "just another boring lawyer with nothing else to discuss than my work."

Through the band connections I've become a trustee director of two charities—one is an international concert theatre in Manchester, and the other is a charity that provides medical support at music concerts.

I've found the contacts I've made through the band invaluable to my practice.

ORGANIZATIONS

Getting involved in any organization, committee, charity, project, or group can provide marketing opportunities and generate rich relationships. Just as important, it can provide you with the chance to gain experience in a risk-free environment, developing skills that will translate directly back into your legal career (e.g., interpersonal, management, and leadership skills). Make sure you are choosing the right environment for your brand by researching and testing the different alternatives. (The "right" environment means one that puts you in the neighborhood of your target clients—not the haunts of your competitors!) And yet, as Neil's story demonstrates, referrals and work can come from unexpected places. Once you find the organization that works for you, stick with it, become a regular attendee, and get involved. (By implication, this means narrowing your time investment and avoiding overload.) Only by making some level of commitment do you develop strong relationships and create bonds. Just showing up occasionally will never achieve the results you are after.

VOLUNTEER—CREATE A HIGH PROFILE IN YOUR FIRM

It is just as important that you market yourself *within* your firm, cultivating a high profile by volunteering your contributions and showing an interest in all the projects and events that your firm is pursuing. It's also worth looking for things the senior management supports that might give you the opportunity to work with new people and develop and enhance your own skills.

For example, one lawyer, Zöe, was struggling in her firm and feeling uncertain about her future. Then a friend of hers, who was involved with a large charity, asked Zöe if her firm might sponsor a special event. When the firm agreed, Zöe became responsible for coordinating the sponsorship. Admittedly, it was a lot of work (all, unluckily, nonbillable!), but when the night of the event arrived, she felt very rewarded. The evening was a huge success and the firm received significant press recognition, which was attributed to Zöe. But even more important, the managing partner, who worked in a different office (and whom she did not know personally), flew in for the event. He and Zöe spent much of the evening together, giving her the opportunity to promote her brand and ignite a bond with him. His keen support was instrumental in helping Zöe turn her career around (he became her sponsor!), and she is now a successful partner. In Zöe's case, that old phrase mentioned previously was right on target: "It's not what you know, but whom you know!"

CREATE A NETWORK OR ORGANIZATION

We can build a whole community of contacts by bringing together people with similar interests. When I was starting out as a technology lawyer, my department was heavily involved in all the activities of a large technology association. This had come about because my then-boss, John (of Chapter 6's Elevator Mission fame), one of the most proficient brand marketers and networkers I have ever known, had the foresight to found the Southeastern Software Association. What began as a small group of technologists grew into one of America's premier networking and professional organizations for high-tech and software professionals, which has provided its founder (John!) with endless opportunities for networking and for promoting his brand. Here's his story...

The genesis of the Southeastern Software Association was a brainstorming session that I had with another lawyer in the firm back in 1985. I was dreaming of a nationally recognized technology law practice in the U.S., but was only a young associate with limited experience and contacts. I had a belief that software companies were growing in the community, and I needed a way to attract them to my burgeoning legal practice. I turned to my sister, a Silicon Valley executive, for guidance. She suggested that I move to California and join one of the growing technology law firms in the Valley.

After thinking about my sister's advice (and being told by my wife that she wouldn't move to California), I had an epiphany—I would start my own non-profit association addressing the needs of software companies. Unlike other organizations that were dominated by service providers (attorneys and accountants), my new association would be created by and for software company executives. The initial focus was to form an Atlanta-based organization. The plans quickly turned toward a broader geography—the southeast United States, one of the fastest-growing sections of North America. The Southeastern Software Association (SSA) was born with me hand-picking several key software executives in the community to lead the group, and having my sister as the first keynote speaker. Today, the SSA is one of the largest independent software associations in the U.S.

—John Yates, partner-in-charge of the technology group of Morris, Manning & Martin, LLP

Even if you only have a few people to bring together, think about whether forming a group could create valuable synergies among you. And if you do take the time to organize your group, do it thoroughly and thoughtfully. Find appropriate venues. Fix dates. Set agendas. Have objectives. Don't just bring people together and hope for the best!

MAKE A PLAN

This chapter is not meant to be the definitive answer on how to market yourself and your practice—there are too many different styles of law practice and far too many areas of expertise to make this practical. You know better than anyone what you have to offer and how it can best be promoted, and with luck, you'll have made notes of some ideas that should work for you. The main thing to take away from this chapter is the determination to create visibility for your brand. Develop a plan to enhance and promote yourself: Determine your target market, the methods that you want to employ, and the timing and tools you need to implement your plan. Then, in the words of one of the most successful brands of our generation, "Just do it!"

You might be amazed how things fall into place!

Bill Kirkland

For over 15 years Bill Kirkland has worked as an energy/environmental lawyer, combining his passion for engineering and his industry knowledge with his law practice, and thereby providing unique value to his clients. For many years his sole focus was in counseling and representing energy providers (including oil, gas, and electrical companies) in their transactions with regard to administrative, regulatory, and adjudicative matters. But eventually this experience, combined with a stint doing volunteer engineering work in Paraguay, inspired him with an interest in promoting alternative forms of energy, assisting developing countries with natural resource extraction agreements, and improving chemical processing for the oil and gas industries. He now actively looks for ways to integrate these enthusiasms into his client work. Most recently, he represented E-tech with the R&D and licensing of a new product to the oil and gas production industry, a product resulting in both cleaner fuel and greater refining capacity. Bill worked with E-tech to develop new markets and distribution channels, ensuring that their product helped energy companies meet new international regulations and assisting E-tech in making their new product an industry standard.

Bill makes a difference by

- Understanding first-hand the industry and subject matters of his clients

- Helping clients to deliver in the most socially responsible ways, thereby creating significant gain for them

- Contributing insights and cutting-edge ideas that improve business and invigorate relationships between his clients and their core customers

- Negotiating deals that support his clients' ongoing business objectives and supplier relationships

- Being personally involved in the oil and gas industry

- Keeping up-to-the-minute on the market as well as on regulatory matters that affect his clients' businesses

"Bill knows our industry inside out, so we never have to spend time getting him up to speed. In fact, on the technical side, his ideas can be superior to our own! His fresh perspective combined with his excellent legal skills make a powerful combination." —Ryan Peacock, Avery Power Company

"The regulatory aspects of our business demand that we be constantly ahead of the curve; Bill is proactive in helping us do that because he knows our business as well as we do." —Jeane Howard, XPower Utility

"Bill cares about our objectives and commits himself to delivering the best solutions possible—sometimes ones that we had no idea that we could achieve. We rely upon him for much more than just his legal skills." —Anton Anderson, Reed Companies

LEGAL EXPERIENCE

Zander Holt
Partner, Energy and Regulatory Practice, 1999–present
Associate, 1997–1999

- Assisted joint venture of power companies to develop innovative approaches to fuel procurement

- Successfully represented XCo Oil Company in its application for FERC approval during its acquisition of Calprise Energy, and led the team involved in implementing the transaction

- Served as counsel to international energy company in connection with its bid for (and acquisition of) PetroChemical, designed to create synergies in the production, transportation, and marketing of liquefied natural gas (LNG)

- Negotiated a power purchase agreement on behalf of a joint venture partner in one of the world's largest solar projects

- Worked closely with a distributor to the oil and gas industry to create new international distribution channels; negotiated the terms of agreement and successfully lobbied U.S. and European government entities to pass more stringent regulations (deliverable by the same client)

Bill also played a key role in building the firm's energy practice, and he takes a keen interest in the development of the junior lawyers in his group. He works hard to ensure that everyone in the practice has in-depth knowledge of the energy industry and its processes and products, an expertise that he believes is essential to best serve clients.

Bill initiated the firm's Climate Change Group, which helps energy clients and their customers deal effectively with evolving regulations and escalating social pressures.

Bill maintains his cutting-edge knowledge about industry regulations and proposals through his position on the board of the Oil, Gas & Energy Intelligence Organization, a non-profit group that he helped to found over a decade ago.

One of Bill's proudest professional moments came when he captained the firm's softball team to the league championship, hitting the final run of the deciding game!

Marshall, Leeds & Lowe
Associate, Corporate and Energy Practice, 1993–1997; Summer Associate, 1991 and 1992 (primarily representing oil and gas production and distribution companies)

ENGINEERING EXPERIENCE

IXON Chemical Company: Chemical Engineer, Hydrocarbons and Energy Department, 1986–1990. Hands-on experience in all aspects of onshore and offshore gas field research, design systems, and process engineering; ensured that processes adhered to environmental regulations. Developed an intense interest in chemically reactive systems and catalysts (used to develop predictive models for designing and improving chemical processes).

Oxydental Research Company, Research Engineer, 1984–1986

Western Gas Systems Service Corporation, Summer Engineer, 1982, 1983

PERSONAL PROFILE

Bill's father was an American diplomat, so he spent his childhood constantly on the move. Some of his schools were more inspiring than others, but it was during his high school years in Spain that he first became fascinated by chemistry. His original ambition was to be a professor of chemical engineering, but he became swept up with enthusiasm for the law while working in conjunction with the legal and regulatory department at IXON Chemical. At first Bill couldn't imagine taking three years out to complete law school, but he finally decided that his technical skills could give him an edge in his preferred scientific specialization. At law school he met his wife, Jacqueline, whom he married in 1993. Today they both practice law and thoroughly enjoy their two girls, Matilda (11) and Larissa (9). Being surrounded by women has taught Bill the art of negotiation(!) and an appreciation of the fact that—contrary to his scientific background—things are not always black and white.

Bill and his family are committed to the D.C. area, as he wants to give his daughters the stability that he missed as a child. He retains a passion for travel, however, and family holidays are a highlight of his year. Past trips have included scuba diving in the Galapagos Islands and exploring the archaeological site of Petra in Jordan. Most recently the family went to China to take in the ancient sites of Xi'an, and next year Bill hopes to resuscitate his Spanish in Granada!

RECENT PUBLICATIONS AND SPEAKING ENGAGEMENTS

"Regulatory Intervention in the Energy Market," *Policy Magazine*, January 2009

Contributing author, *Energy Reform*, chapters on "Power Exchange," 2008

"Regulations Bound to Impact Energy Resources," *34 Legal Issues and Power Journal* 425, Spring 2008

"The Mindset Shift in Energy," *Environment Energy Journal*, April 2007

Speaker, Multi-Science Conference, on "Legal Implications of Energy Production and Consumption," January 2008

Speaker, Renewable Energy Conference, "The Legal Implications of Renewable Energy," September 2007

EDUCATION

J.D., Georgetown University, 1993

M.S., Physics, University of Pennsylvania, 1986

B.S., Chemical Engineering, University of Pennsylvania, 1984, *summa cum laude*, Phi Beta Kappa

ADDITIONAL ASSOCIATIONS

District of Columbia Bar Association; Federal Energy Bar Association; Institute of Chemical Engineering; Public Utilities and Telecommunications Industry Association; District of Columbia Bar Association, Energy Division

For a full list of transactions completed, published articles, and speaking engagements (or any other information you might desire), don't hesitate to contact BillKirkland@Zanderholt.com.

Chapter Fourteen
Public Speaking

Public speaking is important for two reasons: It puts you face-to-face with potential clients, and it awards you the status of resident expert, thus greatly increasing the chance of making a powerful impression. It's a high-risk strategy, however, because the impact you make as a speaker determines precisely how competent a lawyer your audience will believe you to be. The composed, authoritative, and positive speaker will project excellence, while a hesitant, unclear, or diffident one invites doubt about his or her abilities.

But, as with so many risks, public speaking is a risk worth taking. There is no more effective tool to market your expertise and brand than public speaking—when done well.

"WHAT'S THE WORST THAT CAN HAPPEN?"

I don't know how many times people have said to me about public speaking, "So what's the big deal? I mean, frankly, what's the worst that can happen?" Well, I'll tell you. Failure. Judgment. Humiliation. I've risked my entire career on the success or failure of one speaking engagement (which is a pretty *unhinged* thing to do, if you think about it!). Remember the toxic thinking we examined in Chapter 7? Well, public speaking is one of the ways I've expended a lot of toxicity—and, although the worst never happened, I have to admit that I sometimes messed up. However, I can now look back on those imperfect performances with a smile, conscious that my career has survived—even thrived!—and that I learned some important things from the experience.

Once, at a major conference, I was asked to stand up, introduce myself, and answer a simple question from a large audience. A straightforward task, and one I was accustomed to doing—yet as I watched the moderator heading inexorably toward me, I realized that she was bringing with her a very large microphone. Now I had done lots of public speaking by this point, and I had learned which setups work for me and which ones don't. I had learned how to control a trembling voice, how to project with (seeming) confidence, and how to correct rushed pacing. Unluckily, one thing I'd never conquered was the tendency for my hands to shake, especially when holding something. I made a point of never holding anything in my hands—no papers, no cue cards, and definitely no microphones.

With each second the horrible microphone came closer, and I was convinced that I would drop it, igniting hilarity and ridicule. I was caught in a downward spiral of toxic thinking. As it happened, I didn't lose my grip, but I was so consumed with hanging onto the microphone that I felt more nervous than I'd ever felt in front of an audience. I could hardly remember anything about my practice, which under normal circumstances I'd have discussed passionately and at length.

YOU'RE NOT ALONE IN YOUR FEAR

When this happened, I thought I was completely alone in my struggles with nerves. But afterwards, as I tried to laugh it off with my partners (while I was still quietly dying inside), several told me of similar experiences. One partner, a veteran trial lawyer who had made his presentation that very day with consummate ease, told me that he'd known most of the people in the room for years but had still felt a bundle of nerves as the microphone headed his way.

I've told this story to other lawyers, too, and heard some in return. One lawyer, Lance, told me that he had recently attended a banquet to celebrate a completed deal. During the pre-dinner cocktails, the CEO of the company had asked Lance if he would care to address the attendees during dessert about a certain aspect of the transaction. Now Lance had lived and breathed this transaction from soup to nuts; he had made presentation after presentation, and had relished being center stage on each occasion. But the very thought of having to get behind a podium, on a formal occasion, and address many of the same people as before worried him to the point that he felt he just couldn't cope. Instead, he told the CEO that he was unable to stay for dessert because he had a sick child at home. (Lance didn't have a sick child—in fact, he had no children at all!)

I've heard many similar stories, with different solutions and varying results. A few have handled their nerves in the worst way of all by having one drink too many beforehand, with predictable (and even painful) results. It's a bad idea to count on a stimulant or similar substance to boost your confidence; instead, develop your skills and confidence gradually and naturally.

YOU CAN OVERCOME THE FEAR

I've sometimes wondered what it is about a podium or a microphone that makes so many people so nervous—especially lawyers, who, after all, spend a significant portion of their lives making arguments, giving advice, and presenting cases. True, it's a different environment and (usually) a larger audience, but the root of the worry still puzzles me. However, it's important to realize that you're not alone in your fear, and that the problem of nervousness *can* be overcome. Just as you learned to be a lawyer, you can develop the skills of public speaking—and even grow to enjoy it as well. (Though not to the point that you become one of those tedious lawyers who, once they get up, become so enraptured with the sound of their own voices that they never seem to sit down again!)

START NOW

It's fairly easy to avoid public speaking in the early stages of a law career; as we all know, the emphasis for juniors is to contribute to billable work. However, it's during this stage that you should really be building up your public speaking skills. First, by starting early you can develop a delivery that best suits you; second, as with any new skill, it's best to approach public speaking in an incremental way. By taking small steps, you can build up your confidence and put yourself in a strong position that is likely to achieve a more powerful result.

The worst-case scenario, and unfortunately a very common one, is to be thrust into a public-speaking obligation without being fully prepared. Remember learning to drive? Your parents didn't just toss you the car keys on the requisite birthday, did they? No, you had lots of lessons, took plenty of practice drives, and finally obtained your learner's permit. Only after moving successfully through those stages did you feel ready to undergo the final test. The same principle applies to public speaking.

Another incentive for beginning early is that doing so benefits every aspect of your career. Effective public speaking boils down to confident and potent communication, which not only pervades everything we do as lawyers but is also, crucially, part of our brand. For example, as our presentation skills improve we should find ourselves becoming increasingly articulate and persuasive when speaking to clients, or when called upon in a meeting. Gradually, a quiet confidence in our ability to communicate should overflow into every area of our public and private lives.

It's fairly easy to avoid public speaking in the early stages of a law career; as we all know, the emphasis for juniors is to contribute to billable work. However, it's during this stage that you should really be building up your public speaking skills.

AVOID REGRET

I'm extremely envious of people who can just get up in any forum, whatever the circumstances, without notes, and impart their knowledge—whatever the subject... But these people are few and far between. However, if we acknowledge our fears and mitigate them, then with practice and dedication any lawyer can become a polished presenter. It simply takes a bit more effort for the rest of us than for the lucky few!

If you have no fear, make sure your confidence doesn't arise out of ignorance. The worst speakers are those who rashly assume that they will "rise to the occasion," "feel the mood of the audience and extemporize," and so on. Usually

they don't, and they only realize their mistake (to their audience's regret!) too late. The situation is much like that of the fit swimmer who fails to train for his first marathon, and only realizes what he's up against after his brand-new running shoes produce his first blister.

START SMALL, WITH MINIMAL RISK

When embarking on the journey of public speaking, start small and look for opportunities to practice in places where your anxiety should be manageable. It's probably wise to focus on home base: your own firm. In Chapter 7, we examined facing fear with FEAR (Face Everything And Recover) and mitigating anxiety through manageable risk and small, repetitive, successes. This approach builds a broad base on which to develop your skills as a speaker.

When I was still a junior lawyer my department held weekly meetings, and I routinely volunteered to report on new cases or on topics relevant to our practice—opportunities I treated as mini-presentations. The risk was minimal, as my audience consisted mainly of members of my department lounging over their early-morning coffees, yet it provided an opportunity for me to develop confidence. I still had that butterflies-in-the-tummy sensation in the beginning, but I prepared carefully—I probably over-prepared—and this helped me through those first few attempts. As time went on, my confidence and speaking skills improved until one day, to my amazement, I noticed that all my nerves were gone.

If you lack opportunities to cultivate your skills, I'd urge you to look outside your firm—even outside the legal world. Get involved in local politics (if you can stand it), or your local Rotary Club. Take a presentation course, or join Toastmasters, a debating society, or an acting class. I can personally recommend this last idea as a fun and risk-free method of improving communication skills. I only wish I'd started earlier in my career! Improvisation classes in particular were terrific confidence-boosters, boasting the following "rules": (1) It's impossible to fail (anything goes!); (2) no judging or second-guessing is allowed (don't analyze whether it's good or not, just say/do it!); (3) there are no constraints—in fact, going against the voice of reason is positively encouraged (in improvisation, bizarrely enough, it's quite acceptable to "eat a hat" or "wear a banana"); and (4) the objective is to support the scene, rather than contend for the spotlight. For me, these "rules" removed my inner nerves and pressures, enhancing my confidence and willingness to learn. (Too bad the work environment doesn't share the same educational foundation!)

Exceptional public speakers convey a confident brand, communicate assertively, and make a positive impression on everyone they meet. Why not become one?

PRACTICE, PRACTICE, PRACTICE (SIGH)

If there's one factor that's integral to effective public speaking, it's this: Practice your presentation over and over again. Skilled presenters may *look* as though they are speaking naturally, even off-the-cuff, but rest assured that they've rehearsed carefully.

A good contact of mine was a marvelous public speaker. His talks generally covered roughly the same ground, but he astutely tailored each speech to his audience, with the result that his words came across as extemporized and he himself as very engaging. Once, while we were on our way to one of our joint speaking engagements, I asked him whether he felt nervous. "No," he replied, "what's to be nervous about?" ("Lots of things!" I thought, as I tried to control my turbulent stomach.) "Do you practice your speech beforehand?" I wondered out loud. He shrugged. "Normally I just sort of wing it, but it usually works out all right."

And yet, at a purely social occasion years later, this man's wife told me that her husband actually practiced each speech meticulously, like an oil painter finessing a work of art. In fact, he even videotaped himself to better scrutinize both his voice and his delivery! She joked that she herself could probably deliver most of his speeches, because she's had to sit through them so many times. I laughed right along with her, but I also kicked myself for having been so naïve as to believe him in the first place. I should have known better than to imagine that anyone could be *that* good with so little effort!

Even Sir Peter Ustinov practiced his speeches *ad nauseam*. In fact, when Laurence Olivier was nominated for an award and couldn't attend, Ustinov agreed to deliver Olivier's acceptance speech on his behalf. Ironically, it was Ustinov who won an award that night (to his great surprise). So with a bit of stuttering and stammering, and changing a word or two, Ustinov accepted the award using the speech he'd prepared and practiced for Olivier. (Isn't it fascinating that delivering a speech not particularly applicable to himself was preferable to making up something on the spot, even for someone of Ustinov's communicative gifts?)

If you research the habits of most prominent speakers, you will find that preparation and practice are the overriding common elements. (Improvisation may play a part, but it is nowhere near as important.) Mark Twain, one of the best speakers of his day, said that it took him three weeks to prepare a "spontaneous" talk, while Winston Churchill spent the best years of his life preparing "impromptu" speeches. So why would we imagine that we can trump genius? My advice is, be like them and leave nothing to chance. Practice every word of your speech until you reach that wonderful moment when the words and the message override your nerves and take you from mere speech to true communication.

If there's one factor that's integral to effective public speaking, it's this: Practice your presentation over and over again. Nothing trumps practice!

PRACTICE LIKE AN ACTOR

Having played a difficult shot to perfection, an international golfer heard a member of the crowd comment "That was lucky!" "Yes," the golfer replied, "I find that the more I practice the luckier I get."

Rarely do we consider exactly what has gone into making something work. With a background in theater I am aware that whatever we see on stage, it has taken the combined efforts of numerous highly skilled, highly trained professionals to create each moment we experience. And of course it doesn't all just mysteriously come together on the night. Everyone spends a lot of time practicing. Even comedians practice. They may appear spontaneous but they practice. To be spontaneous to effect, one must know one's material inside out, which is one of the reasons entrepreneurs often make such good speakers.

Jennifer is right when she says nothing trumps practice. Nothing does.

When it comes to presentations and public speaking, the same applies. Yes, there are "naturals" but for the majority of people standing up to speak does not come naturally. No matter, help is at hand! The techniques an actor learns to create presence on stage, to bring authenticity to a text using voice and body, and to make a vision of the world come to life are available to everyone. And when you boil it down, the purpose of all these techniques, no matter where they are applied, is to communicate effectively. By learning acting skills and techniques and by practicing, anyone can greatly improve his or her presentation and public speaking.

Time and time again I have watched speakers grow in confidence the more they practice. As they become more and more familiar with their words and their delivery, as they practice using time, space, and movement to best effect, as they go over defining what it is exactly that they want to say and to what purpose, and as they rehearse getting up on their feet and delivering it again and again, a transformation occurs. Practice really does make perfect.

—Christine Kimberley, a director and acting coach who trained originally as an actress. She uses these transferable skills to train people in presentation and public-speaking skills.

CHOOSING YOUR AUDIENCE

Writing and preparing a talk takes a significant amount of time—one of the commodities lawyers generally don't have much of. So select an audience that not only wants to hear what you have to say but might also receive real benefit from your message. If you're a property lawyer, consider whether it's really worth your while preparing and speaking to a group of other private-practice property attorneys—that is, your competition! Unless you're hoping to increase your reputation, such an audience might not be optimal. First, as property lawyers, they already know your subject matter, and will automatically possess high standards for new knowledge; second, they aren't likely to be looking for your services. A group of property developers might well be a better bet: They may actually need an expert property lawyer, and you should also possess some knowledge that will be genuinely useful to them.

PREPARING FOR YOUR AUDIENCE

Be sure to think about your audience and adjust your message to their wants and attitudes. As an outsourcing lawyer, I could give any presentation from three separate perspectives—the customer buying the services, the vendor supplying the services, or both—and my talk was very different depending on which perspective I chose. For example, if speaking from the customer's viewpoint, I would warn the audience about the dangers of dealing with service providers who take advantage of their customers, and I would explain how customers could protect themselves. Now, obviously, for an audience of vendors this would be entirely the wrong message, so it was imperative that I did my homework and chose the appropriate angle of approach.

Make sure that you evaluate your audience so that the essence of your talk meets their needs. If you aren't providing your audience with valuable insights, then you've either got the wrong audience, or (for your purpose, at any rate) the wrong information.

> *Be sure to think about your audience and adjust your message to their wants and attitudes.*

CAPITALIZING ON THE ENGAGEMENT

Once your talk is finished, *don't charge off*, even if you feel relieved to the point of delirium. Instead, hang around. Be approachable. Have you ever tried to engage the speaker at a conference and been rebuffed? Your opinion of the speaker instantly deteriorates. Keep in mind that even though your talk may be over, your audience's judgment of you is still malleable. Smile. Answer questions. This is, after all, the moment when you should be able to capitalize on all the work that went into your preparation. It's certainly the easiest time for you to network, because simply by virtue of being the speaker, you qualify as a VIP.

Also, if you can, try to work something into your talk that might encourage a listener to follow up with you afterwards. For example, mention a detailed article about your subject, or dangle the prospect of being included on your monthly newsletter, or of receiving something else of value.

TIPS FOR PREPARING YOUR TALK

For most lawyers, the process of public speaking goes something like this: You're asked by a boss, colleague, or outside person to give a talk, and, succumbing to either flattery or optimism, you accept. Through procrastination, a heavy workload, or a lack of sufficient notice, you fall behind in your preparations, and you discover that you have a topic but precious little else prepared when the conference organizers send you—sometimes ridiculously early—a request for slides. At this stage, you either throw something together or—still worse—borrow or adapt something presented previously, either by you or by a colleague. Then, once you finally sit down to figure out what you want to say, you're obliged to wrap it around some hastily thrown-together slides, which make the talk itself peripheral to what you really want to discuss.

There are lots of problems with this scenario (starting with why you agreed in the first place?!), but the worst one is that the process itself is backwards. The talk should be developed first, well before the slides, which should feature—if at all—only as a supplementary visual. In short, you must organize and clarify your material first, and then design your visuals or other supporting tools.

Some things you might like to consider when preparing your talk:

Know Your Own Message

Tragically, research has proved that, at best, your listeners are only going to remember *10 percent* of what you tell them, so first decide what you want them to take away. What's your real message? Articulate this in one simple statement; if it takes two, you already have too much material. Then develop your speech so that it communicates this theme AND NO OTHER. If you manage this, three benefits should result: (a) Your presentation will have continuity and focus, (b) that continuity (in turn) will give you the clarity of mind to present your speech with poise, and (c) your audience will have a fighting chance of retaining at least a modest proportion of your message.

And don't try to be all things to your audience. I remember reading a commentary on one of President Clinton's speeches which said something like, "It was a speech about everything, and therefore about nothing." Don't go there.

Structure Your Presentation

There are various ways to do this. You could posit a problem and offer a solution, or it might be appropriate to organize your subject chronologically by a series of events (e.g., if you are describing case law). Or you may want to shape your talk around a case study. Whatever structure you choose, your presentation should have a succinct beginning, a fact-filled middle, and a blistering end.

The Beginning. The beginning should introduce your topic and outline the points that you'll be making. If, for the sake of argument, your chosen topic is the law of contract, then your introduction might be as follows:

> *"Today I'm talking about the formation of contracts. Contract formation criteria were first developed in the nineteenth century, yet they still apply today. According to this formula, four elements must exist for a contract to be formed: (1) an offer; (2) an acceptance; (3) consideration; and (4) contractual intention. If we have all four, then we conclude, legally speaking, that a contract exists, assuming that the parties are of one mind. Now I'll examine each of these elements, with examples."*

This opening—unarguably—serves the purpose, but it's still unspeakably, irredeemably, and unutterably dull. You must keep in mind that your audience will form an opinion about your talk, and about *you*, during the first five to ten seconds of your address, at most. In the next 30 to 45 seconds that opinion is likely to be either reinforced or qualified, but it will typically not be reversed. So the first words out of your mouth must instantly hook your audience. If you fail at this point it won't matter how brilliant the rest of your talk might be, because your audience is not going to be paying attention. Instead, they'll be regretting having had that dessert, wondering what the taxi situation will be like at the conclusion of the evening, or planning for that crucial meeting the next morning.

A less relentlessly boring introduction for a talk about contract formation might start like this:

> *"Any company doing business on the Internet is aware of the myriad laws now governing this domain, including electronic commerce regulations, data protection acts, and rules about cookies, spam, security, and privacy. Yet despite all these complex new regulations, one of the most critical laws for Internet retailers remains the rule of contract formation. Although first developed in the 19th century, its criteria remain valid today—just ask Kodak, Argos—even Amazon! Each of these supposedly e-commerce-savvy companies has made the expensive mistake of pricing articles wrongly on their websites. And it was the rule of contract*

formation that ultimately determined whether they had then legally entered into a contract with their Internet consumers. In the case of Argos, this meant whether their customers were actually entitled to Sony televisions at—get this—exactly £3 each.

"So in the next 20 minutes I'm going to talk about the rule of contract formation, examining each of its four elements, which are offer, acceptance, consideration, and intent. As we discuss these we'll look at different examples, until, by the end of my talk, you'll be able to apply the law, and thus determine whether in fact those Argos customers received their £3 TV sets—and why."

Yet even this: clear, concise, informative—could still be pithier. How about starting with this:

"How many of you recall the Argos £3 TV fiasco? Imagine the sweat on the brows of those Argos representatives when they first realized that they had willfully opened themselves to the prospect of parting with brand new Sony TVs for almost nothing."

In other words, with every presentation, think first about how your introduction might interest, or even entertain, your audience. Here are a few ways you might begin:

- *Humor.* Notice that I failed to entitle this section "jokes." This is due to the sad fact that very few people can kick off a presentation with a joke and be really funny—and that most of these people can make a reasonable living doing stand-up comedy. It's especially difficult to pull this off when you are at your most nervous, before you have found your feet and gauged your audience. This is why I urgently propose that you avoid such hurdles by choosing *not* to commence your speech with a joke. This doesn't mean that you have to avoid humor or irony entirely; in fact, an amusing anecdote, preferably one with a personal angle, is one of the best ways to give your topic life.

- *Quotation.* A relevant quotation can certainly enrich your message. But be careful not to charge right out of the blocks with an overused or outdated quote, resulting in feigned smiles, disguised yawns, and vague mutterings of, "Want to head out for a quick smoke?"

- *Question.* A question can prove a dynamic opener, immediately involving your audience—or at least, the part of it that is listening.

But you first need to imagine every possible response and how these may adversely affect your message. (The fail-safe way to avoid an awkward—or even nonexistent—response is to ask your question rhetorically.)

- *Fact or statistic.* Opening with a fact or statistic can really catch the attention of your audience, especially if you can find an unusual or surprising one, or one that debunks a common myth.

- *Personal story.* Telling a personal story works extremely well. It engages your audience's emotions and gives them something to relate to.

The importance of a strong opening *cannot* be overemphasized. If you can capture your audience and provide a clear roadmap, then they will be yours: willing participants in the journey of your speech.

The Middle. The middle contains the bulk of your talk, and it's where you make your most serious points—by analysis, example, or elaboration. When I rough out my message, I've found that it's best to begin with the middle (the content) and connect each point logically to the next. (The easiest way to do this is to organize your talk around a number of points and then, in your introduction, list what those points will be.)

For example, in the talk about contract formation I introduced four elements, which simplifies transitions. "Let's start with the first element of forming a contract: an offer. An offer is...[define term]... The second element of a contract is acceptance, which represents..." And so it goes, until the finish line beckons.

Transitions are the glue that holds an effective presentation together, reminding your audience where they've been and elucidating where they're going. Further, with each transition you are (with luck!) concisely summarizing your main point. This not only helps your audience to remember your subject matter, but also helps you maintain direction.

It is easy to dismiss transitions. Don't—even if, in those "I need to look intelligent during this talk" moments, they might feel simplistic and repetitive to you. Remember that your audience has never heard your talk before, making incremental summaries essential.

The End. Your conclusion should succinctly summarize the points you've made, closing with your most powerful example. Remember that your conclusion is the audience's final and lasting impression of you, so work to make your finish memorable. Try these:

- Tell your audience what to do (direction/inspiration).

- Push your main point one last time.

- Wrap up with a funny story or quotation (as long as it's relevant!).

- Return to your opening, with added zest. (In the example about contract formation, go back to the original question and tell the audience whether the Argos customers actually got new TVs for £3...and if not, why not.)

Forget What You Learned in Law School

More points and more supporting arguments are *not* always better. Instead, stick to three major points. I know this is difficult, but—and I recommend you write this on your cuff—the three-point system is tried and tested, and the most successful public speakers apply it consistently. If your topic necessitates going beyond three points, tread carefully to avoid information overload and make sure that each point is absolutely crucial to support your overriding theme.

Examples and Stories

Especially with topics related to the law, audiences hunger for real-life stories, whether funny or informative or both. Being able to tell "your client's story" is a huge plus; it makes topics more emotional and thus, as we examined in Chapter 11, much more memorable. If you can't use your own clients, use hypothetical cases, or swipe real-life stories from your colleagues. It's so simple and useful to integrate stories, yet many lawyers just ramble turgidly from one legal point to the next.

Especially with topics related to the law, audiences hunger for real-life stories, whether funny or informative or both.

Stories also lend credibility—even without your having a direct connection to the participants. One of my former colleagues recently spoke about the integral role of IT in business operations—and particularly about its impact on mergers. To make her point she discussed the well-known acquisition of Safeway by the supermarket chain Morrisons, and the problems encountered in that merger due to incompatible IT systems. She also referred to the expensive termination of the Bank of Scotland's outsourcing contract when purchased by the Halifax Bank. Both examples were completely in the public domain, and (as it happened) none of the companies involved were her clients. Yet by using well-known examples she immediately gripped and convinced her audience.

Final Preparation Tips

One of the most common mistakes lawyers make is to fail to distinguish between how they write and how they present. Write your presentations to be heard, not read. Keep it conversational, use simple language, and make your sentences memorable—and preferably short! Other pointers...

- ■ *Watch for legalese.* Give your spiel in layman's terms, especially if speaking to non-lawyers or persons outside your specialty. If you want to use legal terminology, then explain your terms. Don't refer to a *force majeure* clause; instead, connect it to something your audience understands.

- ■ *Keep it simple.* The simpler and more concise your message, the more valuable your talk is likely to be. Once again, this is something that we lawyers tend to mess up, big time. We often meander around in extraneous legal details, sublimely unaware that not only have we lost our audience, but that some in attendance may have lost the will to live...

- ■ *Use visuals.* Highly recommended—especially for those areas of your talk that you really want the audience to retain. Most people learn from what they see, and visuals, if done well, can also add impact to your talk. Try graphics, charts, or cartoons instead of lots of words—and instead of poorly designed PowerPoint slides. (See following paragraph!)

- ■ *PowerPoint.* When was the last time you heard a talk that was *not* supported by PowerPoint slides? (No, I can't remember, either.)

And did the slides actually add to the presentation, or not? In many cases the graphics are too cluttered to be effective, or worse, the presenter will read the slides, almost verbatim, to an audience desperately wondering where its next glass of wine is coming from. When preparing your PowerPoint, always apply the "less is more" rule. It's a supporting tool, not a summary. If your slides attempt to be the presentation itself instead of a visual aid, you're not using them appropriately.

TIPS FOR PRESENTING YOUR TALK

Preparation and practice are the keys to success.

Logistics

Try to find out the logistics of the room and the setup for your talk, so that you can prepare and practice in a way best suited to those arrangements. If there is a podium, then you will know that there is a place to set your notes (if you use them); if a hand-held microphone is planned, you will be able to practice ahead of time with a hairbrush. *Always* test the technology beforehand to make sure it works.

Check Out the Room

If at all possible, get an idea of the room where you will be presenting. Where will you be standing? Where will the audience be? I recommend that you do this as early as possible, so that you'll have time to adapt to any surprises. Also, by getting comfortable with the environment, you'll mitigate the anxiety factor. Once, before giving a talk to an extremely large audience at a European conference, I set my alarm hours early and sneaked into the auditorium when everyone else was still sleeping. I even went to the stage and practiced projecting to the empty rows of seats! As a result, I felt much more at ease that afternoon, when the seats were filled.

Knowing your surroundings is a crucial component of the visualization techniques we examined in Chapter 7 ("Thinking"). This is a fantastic tool, which is why professional musicians, athletes, and actors all espouse it. Just imagine going confidently into the auditorium, giving a flawless presentation, and dealing effortlessly with the questions that follow. If you go through this process often enough while in a state of relaxation (remember that alpha-theta!), your subconscious mind—and the activated neural network we learned about in Chapter 7—can help to program reality into following your visualizations, enhancing your performances beyond all recognition.

Stage Fright

Stage fright can be combated through practice, but certain techniques can be helpful as well. Deep breathing is employed by many professionals to defeat excessive adrenaline surges. Self-talk can also be tremendously beneficial: Before you're on, give yourself a pep talk, telling yourself that you're prepared and ready. Don't let nerves trap you in the vicious circle of toxic thinking ("I feel so nervous that I'm bound to fail... I'm bound to fail because I feel so horribly nervous..."). As examined in Chapter 7 ("Thinking"), this is not only self-defeating, but it can even be self-fulfilling! Instead, tell yourself that nerves are just adrenaline, and that adrenaline is critical to create the energy needed to fuel success.

RECAP AND SUMMARY

To recap, we can all become competent—perhaps even brilliant—public speakers if we follow this simple formula:

- Develop our skills incrementally;
- Invest enough time in writing and preparing; and
- Practice, practice, and (yep) practice.

If you follow this formula, over time you will notice that you look forward to public speaking instead of dreading it, and that your general communication skills and confidence have improved. That's because—in the context of being a lawyer—how we present has an impact upon everything we do.

PUBLIC SPEAKING

STATISTICS AND POINTERS

- Chapter 8 refresher course:
  - Verbal content accounts for only 7 percent of first impressions
  - Type/style of voice accounts for 38 percent
  - Body language/physical image (non-verbal qualities) account for 55 percent

- Listeners will only remember 10 percent of what you tell them—so articulate one message!

- Audiences form an opinion about your talk (and you) in the first 5 to 10 seconds

- In the subsequent 30 to 45 seconds, that opinion is either reinforced or qualified, but rarely reversed (so your opening is critical!)

- Regardless of structure, the presentation should have a well-defined beginning, middle, and end

- The three-point system is tried and tested; don't get into information overload

- Use transitions to hold the presentation together

- Close powerfully

- The single most critical factor affecting our success is PRACTICE!

With this chapter we conclude the section on our first "ball"—brand. By now, you should have an idea about your own authentic, distinct, and superior brand and how to best demonstrate and market it to others. But unfortunately, that might still not be enough. Many lawyers make the mistake of thinking that marketing is the pivotal and final step in the process, and that once their marketing is working, all they have to do is sit back and wait for the desired results (getting business). But winning business is a wholly different "ball," requiring the separate (and critical) step of developing relationships.

So let's move into the next section to examine exactly how to go about it.

Chapter 15: **Networking: The Reality**

Chapter 16: **Expanding Your Network**

Chapter 17: **Winning and Developing Business**

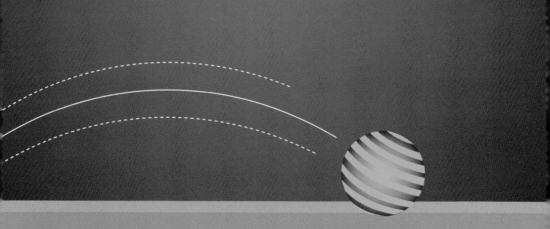

Business

Chapter Fifteen
Networking: The Reality

Having mastered the importance of a personal brand, we can now move into the second area of career building: business. Business development, like becoming your brand, doesn't happen overnight; it requires a long-term strategy and consistent investment. There is no scientific formula, and genius-level IQ is not required. Instead, it's about building relationships with the tools you have at hand—understanding personalities, using people skills, working with the right motivation, maintaining confidence through a positive attitude, and projecting the right image.

Networking is a big part of business development, but for some this overused term has negative connotations. It *does* mean more than attending events, enjoying buffet food (not!), and joining organizations! We will examine its pivotal role and illustrate how networking eases the process of business development, making it more satisfying as well as likelier to succeed.

THOSE TUESDAY MORNING MEETINGS

When I first joined one new firm, I discovered that my department met every Tuesday (at, would you believe, 7:30 a.m.) for a "networking roundup." Since I spent most evenings working late in the office, such a schedule was extremely unappealing. Still worse was the meeting format: Each person was given the spotlight (that is, put on the spot!) to talk about his or her networking successes from the previous week.

Most of our department partners were insanely well-connected, so they always had a lot to report—events they had attended, who had been there, who'd said what—and, ultimately, what new project they were working on as a result of these gatherings. For me, each meeting was the same: As my turn grew nearer and nearer, I felt more and more uncomfortable. At the very least I would be expected to describe my attendance at some appropriate networking event, mention people I'd met, and describe our conversations. My reports always seemed somewhat inferior. I began to dread Tuesdays, and although normally sociable, I started to cringe at the mention of anything remotely associated with networking.

I now know that the partners' overriding purpose was really to involve and train their juniors in the value of networking, but, ironically, their chosen method ultimately defeated their purpose. To achieve the short-term goal of having something—anything!—to say on Tuesday morning, we juniors focused on—well, just that. Each week we sought out an event (usually an after-work drinks event) for the sole purpose of being able to report a "networking success" the next Tuesday—with "success" of course being loosely defined as engaging the perfect client, which was a wildly unrealistic goal. Of course, young lawyers get used to sink-or-swim scenarios, and each of us duly kicked off our shoes and headed out into the networking waters. For me, walking into a room full of strangers was difficult in itself. As I approached the door my confidence level would sink lower and lower... After all, I was just a young lawyer, still figuring out the ropes. How was someone like me ever going to meet and impress the perfect client?

My technique was always the same: First, I would scan the room (usually in vain!) for someone who looked vaguely approachable. Then I'd head to the drinks bar instead (that well-known procrastinating trick). Finally, after gathering my remaining courage, I would introduce myself to someone, usually a male intent on sharing with me the delights of his latest stock car race. (I knew exactly zilch about stock car racing, yet I was so grateful to be talking to someone—anyone!—that I didn't care.) With each successive conversation, I would feel increasingly worried that I wasn't being engaging or entertaining enough—or, worse still, that I had nothing to say. (At this point I had yet to figure out the "be interested, not interesting"

technique covered in Chapter 6.) Sometimes a battle would rage inside my head the whole evening: My anxiety urged me to leave (or at least take a break in the ladies' room, where I could "correct" my makeup for about ten minutes), while my natural persistence told me to stay. After all, failure at the Tuesday morning meeting wasn't exactly a palatable option either.

As I left each event, I would decide yet again that I just wasn't gifted at networking. I had evidence: I was leaving without business from—or for that matter, ever coming within a country mile of meeting—my elusive prey: the perfect client.

WHAT I NOW KNOW

I now know that my conclusion was wrong; it's just that I'd come equipped with the wrong agenda. Networking is *not* about walking into a room full of unknowns and nailing the perfect client, nor is it about securing business or making a sale. Instead, it's the necessary *precursor* to these happy outcomes. I learned that I *could* network—and so, for that matter, can anyone.

Unfortunately, I lacked the tools or experience at that time to understand the errors in my thinking. Our Tuesday morning meetings had led me—credulous as I was—to believe that my colleagues were turning total strangers into keen new clients in a single evening, solely through their exceptional ability to mingle and impress on the spot. To me, networking was like cold calling. (And if, like me, you've ever had a summer job doing just that, you'll probably agree that that is not a positive correlation!)

Our partners were doing us juniors a signal disservice by not painting a full picture. They were emphasizing (or perhaps we were only concentrating on?) the desired result, rather than the process by which we might hope to reach it. Trust me, *very* rarely does anyone walk into a room full of complete strangers and leave with the phone number of the perfect client, and on the rare occasions when this does happen, there's usually a strong connection behind it—a common contact, a referral, or a shared interest or organization. Further, any networking success story of necessity involves the mundane (but absolutely critical) things never mentioned during our Tuesday coffee mornings: connecting with people. Listening. Demonstrating interest. Understanding needs. Responding appropriately. Making phone calls. Sending correspondence.

Looking to meet a lawyer—you!

Perfect Client

Giving referrals. Providing information. Offering help. Being generous. Following up. (And so on!)

Now, of course, there are exceptions. You may one day have the extraordinary good fortune to bump into someone who came to the event just to look for someone like you—in my case, it was the CEO of a technology company on the verge of embarking on an initial public offering and keen to land outside counsel. The serendipity client! Well, yes—it *can* happen. But my advice is, don't sit around and wait for lightning to strike. If, instead, you can build up a network, that network will generate clients effortlessly, over and over again.

So let's focus on what those Tuesday morning meetings failed to address.

WHAT IS NETWORKING (REALLY)?

I've met many people who are great networkers—yes, some even lawyers! —but my father, a doctor, is to me the clearest and best example of a natural networker.

My father would never think of himself as a networker; he'd just protest that he honestly cares about his patients, colleagues, friends, and the other people that he meets. Generous by nature, he's always sincerely enjoyed helping people, without the smallest consideration as to what might be in it for him. He never hesitates to pick up the phone on someone else's behalf, and he goes far beyond what anyone could possibly expect of a doctor.

It's also natural for him to nurture relationships. If someone comes to mind for some reason, he never thinks, "Wonder what he's up to? I ought to call him sometime." Instead, Dad calls the person *at that time* (or at the earliest possible convenient moment), because he's genuinely interested in that person's welfare. This is how my father has maintained friendships with people from as long ago as his schooldays—because he cares, and he shows that he cares.

My father's list of friends and acquaintances is formidable because almost all the people he's helped want to do the same for him. Rather than using his network for his own purposes, however, my father uses it for the benefit of others. He routinely brings friends together for no other reason than their mutual short-term needs or interests. Dad's network grows, much like one of those (revolting) pyramid schemes, but for a genuinely altruistic reason: He just has a natural focus on helping people, both as a person and as a doctor. Yet through the law that those who give will almost inevitably receive, his natural bent (friendliness) has also provided him with great personal and professional benefit.

Definition of Networking

▪ Networking is *taking an interest in people* and *helping others* (in short, being generous).

▪ It ultimately generates the same in return, but as a beneficial by-product rather than an end in itself.

TAKE AN INTEREST

So the first "prong" of networking is simply *taking an interest* in others. Now, most people feel some interest in others, but the breadth and depth of that interest varies: Some are very curious, while others reserve their full attention for a few select people. Yet regardless of our natural tendencies, we can all improve our skills in this area.

Good Intentions are not Enough

The difficulty for most people is taking their interest to the next level and going out of their way to do more. Take the simple and obvious example of wishing someone a happy birthday.

Sure, it's easy to remember the birthday of your friend Bob, who works just down the hall. You might not have the date hardwired in your calendar, but in all the years you've worked together you've always remembered to wish him a happy birthday. (The fact that he tends to parade around with a pin saying BIRTHDAY BOY may assist you in this enterprise!) But what happens if Bob leaves the firm? Will you remember his birthday? Maybe—maybe not. However, let's say (for the sake of argument) that, despite not having it on your calendar, you do recall that March 5th is good old Bob's birthday. Will you pick up the phone or send him an email? Certainly you'd *intend* to...but even dashing off an email admittedly takes more effort than just saying hello in the hallway. Throw in your busy schedule and a rabid client or two, and Bob's chances of receiving his annual birthday congratulations from you are greatly diminished.

The Proactive Networker

The proactive networker would have put the date in his calendar long before Bob left the firm. Further, the perfect networker would probably (God knows how, busy as we all are) find the time to post a handwritten card. This takes a little more effort than a phone call or email, but it has a far greater impact—as does anything personal—and it can, of course, be written in advance, so a manic day at the office wouldn't affect whether Bob receives his birthday card or not. (And yes, I know that most of my male readers would rather be slowly roasted over an open flame than send a colleague a birthday card. Instead, try taking your old buddy Bob out for a beer. How often do you go out for a quick drink with your colleague down the hall instead of planning a drink in advance with an ex-colleague, who is across town at a different firm?)

As a side note, remember that in Chapter 6 I mentioned a consultant I know who figures out the birthday of each of his contacts and sends every one of them cards. (A hugely proactive networker!) Those who think this consultant probably "needs to get out more" should note that at least one mere acquaintance was transformed into a lucrative client and good friend on the basis of his annual birthday card. It turned out that this acquaintance had been feeling a bit low, and the card—the only one he received—meant a lot to him. He called up my consultant friend to convey his appreciation, and that call sparked a deeper working relationship.

So don't discount even something as simple as a birthday greeting!

HELP OTHERS

The second prong to our definition of networking is *helping others*. Most of us enjoy helping other people out. (If you really don't, then I can think of a few other books you should be reading!) No doubt you've helped close friends on various occasions, as a natural consequence of friendship. But the same should hold true for your networking circle.

Set Aside that Agenda

So what about the unspoken agenda (getting work)? Should your motivation for networking be contingent on what you expect in return? Absolutely not!

In its purest form, networking should occur *without an agenda*, with zero expectation of return. Remember the rules of people skills? Be generous without expectations and one of two things will happen: (a) you'll get nothing back but you won't notice, because that wasn't your agenda in the first place; or (b) because of the law of the universe, your generosity will be repaid, sometimes many times over!

Having said that, this chapter aims at improving your professional network. We all live in the real world, so to optimally achieve your work-related goals you should not only network, but network (follow me closely here) with a *purposeful focus*.

"So," you're thinking, "what exactly is the difference between having an agenda and having a blinking purposeful focus?" The answer is, the person with an agenda is focused only on getting business, and is using networking as a means to an end; in other words, without the possibility of pecuniary benefit, he wouldn't bother. By contrast, the person with a purposeful focus prioritizes (and enjoys) networking *even while he is cognizant* of using it for a personal benefit (such as finding new clients). I admit that it's a fine distinction, but the point is still worth making. Over the course of a career, the person motivated solely by an agenda is bound to be the less successful networker. Many people in our profession are quick to detect insincerity—you can fool someone for a while, but sooner or later you'll be fingered as a fake.

> *In its purest form, networking should occur without an agenda, with zero expectation of return.*

Genuine People Skills Trump Charm—Every Time

I worked for many years for a company who also retained one of my colleagues. This colleague was an ebullient fellow with a huge ego, used to getting what he wanted, but he could also be extremely winning, especially where his own interests were concerned. He never hesitated to call on people within the client organization to schedule dinner or face-to-face meetings, or even just "to see how things were going." At first clients were enthralled by such overt charisma, and they eagerly gave him work as a result.

However, my colleague was not genuinely interested in the clients he used so adeptly. Afterwards, he never said "What a great meeting!"—unless, of course, he was referring to his own sublime rhetoric, or to some lucrative work he had won. Instead, he invariably had something derogatory to say: The general counsel was dullsville, the chief financial officer anally retentive, and the CEO a waste of space. Yet, despite these sentiments, he was always more than willing to take on their work...

I, on the other hand, really enjoyed working with the people in this client organization, yet I never initiated meetings with the right people, and I never set up opportunities to prompt my contacts for work. (Perhaps I should have, but I was naïve enough to think that doing a great job should be sufficient!) However, I did make sure that I treated everyone in the organization with respect.

Eventually, the stunned admiration these people felt for my colleague began to dwindle, and they saw through his self-satisfaction and insincerity. In the end, the person without an agenda (me!), who had demonstrated sincere interest (again, me!), won more work from the client, rather than the superior operator who focused only on himself.

A LONG-TERM EFFORT

Networking is, by its very nature, unpredictable. There are no set rules or predetermined avenues for success. You never know when certain people in your network might individually make a difference, and sometimes all the socializing is bound to feel like a waste of your (precious few) spare hours. At such times, stay the course! Remember that networking is a long-term effort, and that you can't have a successful law career in today's market without it.

USE YOUR PEOPLE SKILLS

The first place to start in cultivating your network is to concentrate on the number-one rule of human desire that we examined in Chapter 6 ("People Skills"): *Make others feel important and appreciated.*

Second, be generous with your time and your efforts; think about how you can help the people in your network. This is not about keeping score ("Gosh, how they'll owe me for *this* one!")—instead, it's a mindset you should apply to every person in your network—not just people you think might one day prove useful, but *everyone.* This is partly because business isn't the be-all and end-all of a happy life, and partly because you want your networking skills to become instinctive, which will not happen if you choose to be selective about whom you treat well.

Notice that effective networking is not about fakery, charms, and wiles. Even an introverted person can learn to network, because it's all about how we treat others. Every personality type is capable of going the extra mile! Admittedly, Connecters have an edge in the overall process, because their personality type is naturally social, but networking is about much more than going to parties. It involves genuine care for, and interest in, the people we meet when we get there.

So let's take a look at some of the specific ways to develop your network, building on the newly honed people skills learned in Chapter 6.

Congratulate and Compliment

Most of us mean well when it comes to praise and encouragement, but we often don't follow through. Are you shy about such things, or afraid of coming across as a flatterer? Grit your teeth and do it anyway! When you hear something positive about someone, make a real effort to congratulate the person, no matter how long ago you may have had contact or how tenuous a relationship you might have had in the past. ("I don't know whether I mentioned it or not, but Harriet just raved about your presentation at the European conference. We all got fed up with hearing about it!") Congratulating or complimenting someone makes that person feel special, and represents the single easiest way to establish—or improve—rapport. (How would you feel, if it were you?)

As an example, while I was still practicing law, I was mentioned one day in the cover story of a legal journal. A consultant I'd worked with a decade before sent me a copy with a congratulatory note. I felt so pleased that he'd remembered *me* and taken the time and trouble to acknowledge my accomplishment! Thanks to this friendly gesture, we reconnected, and I've since gone out of my way to provide him with beneficial contacts.

Passing on compliments is even more effective than giving them directly. It can also provide the opportunity to get in touch with someone. Think about it: How would it make you feel if your colleague said, "I was having lunch with Andrew on Wednesday and he was telling me what a great job you did on [whatever it was] and how superb you were to work with." Somehow this makes you feel even better than Andrew's telling you himself! Now Andrew and your colleague, the messenger, have both gone up in your book. So don't hold back: If you hear something good about someone, pass it on!

Know (and Remember) Things About People

Personalizing and remembering things about people inevitably creates positive connections, especially in our selfish, unconnected, use-'em-and-lose-'em society. A recent encounter of mine illustrates this point. Some months ago I met Jeff very briefly at a social event. During the ensuing conversation, I casually mentioned that I was doing a charity run the next day. When I bumped into him subsequently, he immediately asked me what the charity run was like. Impressed, I was flattered and thought, "Imagine his remembering that!" I instantly concluded that Jeff was a great guy and decided to help him out, if I ever had the opportunity.

Gather information about your contacts: their partners and children, hobbies and interests, likes and dislikes. Then develop a way to keep this information at hand. If you have a photographic memory then of course you don't need to worry, but if you're a normal lawyer with a hectic professional schedule, jot down some notes. Once you're back in the office, put the information into your contact database: "J.B. = pain in ass, but always unbends if you ask after his torpid genealogical research; great-great-great-great-great-great-great-great uncle (twice removed) was Charlemagne." Or, "C.B. = insanely proud of pianist son (n.b., but don't volunteer to attend another recital!)."

One morning, in a crowded underground station, I ran (literally!) into someone with whom I'd lost touch when he had temporarily moved abroad. In the past he'd been a good source of referral work, and I'd always enjoyed working with him. As he handed me his new card and rushed to his train, I promised to give him a call. I did—but before doing so, I refreshed my memory with the names of his wife and children, and a few other details I'd collected in my database. From that call we re-established our relationship, and he began referring work to me again. Much later, he told me what a difference it had made that I'd asked, by name, about his family and what they had all been up to since I'd last met them.

Although some of the information you collect may seem insignificant, it's far from trivial to the people concerned. Why on earth collect enough information to write a short biography without *using* it? Send John tickets when his favorite band comes to town. Email Frank when you see that his idolized football team has just won some boring championship or other. If Joe goes on a holiday to Aruba for two weeks, make a note to ask him about it. Not just, "So, how was your holiday?" but, "Hey Joe, how was the golf in Aruba?" or "I bet Sharon picked up some new ideas for the house!" (Your secret notes on J. and S. might well read: "Joe: lives for golf; Sharon: noted victim of *Better Homes and Gardens* blight.")

Small Things Matter

No matter how small a single gesture may seem, it will always be valued. No form of generosity is ever "too small to bother with," especially if it sets you apart from all the ruthless types who are only in it for themselves.

COMMIT TO THE SUCCESS OF OTHERS

An effective network is contingent on the success of each person within the group. As other individuals in your circle become more successful, they not only extend their power and influence, but also their chances of being able to help *you*... In short, by boosting the careers of others, you probably increase the likelihood of gaining your own rewards. (Remember the Elevator Mission: Lift people up emotionally, and they will, in return, appreciate you. Well, it's also important to lift people up professionally—they will probably lift you up in return.)

Second, through the act of helping, you reinforce relationships. When you are generous with referrals, contacts, or support, a mutual bond is created. Through recommendations, you're not only telling the other person that he is worthy (subliminal message: "I trust you"), but you're also cultivating *his* trust by providing something of value without asking for a return. So even when you think helping someone else might prove detrimental to your interests, you should still consider extending that support. Giving something is always better and healthier than any short-term reward that you might receive from hoarding it.

Share Your Knowledge

Every lawyer possesses information that would be valuable to others in his immediate network. Never underestimate the value of your knowledge, and go out of your way to share it willingly. The worst mistake you can make is to treat any of your research, documents, or templates as proprietary: There will be far more benefit—both to yourself and to others—if you circulate them among clients, colleagues, and contacts.

Connect People with People

One of the keys to helping others within your network is to bring people together for their mutual benefit. This is what networking is all about, and the results typically achieve more than any other act of generosity. As a credible source making an introduction, you automatically generate trust between the people you bring together, and they're able to commence a beneficial relationship with confidence—feeling gratitude toward you as well.

Give Referrals

Similarly, we should always be on the *qui vive* for ways to refer business. Doing this is the most profound way of telling someone that we have confidence in his (or her) ability, and (in business at least) there is no greater compliment. Further, when you give someone a referral he is automatically over 80 percent down the line of the sales continuum; a referral from a credible source instantly creates the requisite trust.

One of the best examples of someone who does all of these things is my old boss John—yes, one of the well-intentioned mentors who arranged those Tuesday morning meetings. I can only describe John as a networking guru—using networking in line with *our* definition, because generosity and a genuine interest in people underpin everything John does. But let me tell you what one of his clients had to say about him in a 2004 *Harvard Business Review* case study ("Ockham Technologies: Living on the Razor's Edge," by Noam Wasserman):

When we decided that we were going to start the company I remembered my chat with John [six months earlier] *and knew that he was involved in the technology community in Atlanta* [since he had been introduced as a big rainmaker for the technology practice of Morris, Manning & Martin, an Atlanta law firm]*...so I called him out of the blue and set up a meeting... I walked through what we wanted to do, and John gave me a list of about eight people to call. Call this guy for your office space, call this guy who's looking to be a VP of sales, call this guy for your accountant, boom boom boom. After that, we would affectionately refer to the people we met by how many degrees of separation they were from John Yates, because everyone seems to tie back to him. John's a* *people connecter. We would joke that John's at the center of our company, and we're all around John.*

And it's not just with his clients (or potential clients) that John networks. When I moved from Atlanta to London, he gave me a list of contacts—people who might be able to help me in both my personal and professional life. Since that time (almost 15 years ago!), John has stayed in touch with me, and whenever he visits London—even in the midst of a tight schedule—he always manages to fit me in and somehow make me feel important. The last time I saw him, he introduced me to a colleague as "his brightest star ever"...certainly a huge exaggeration, but it still made me feel great! (It's obvious that John knows how to make other people feel good, because it was he who imparted to me the Elevator Mission in Chapter 6.)

When John was my boss, I was naïve enough to truly lack appreciation for the depth and artistry of his networking skill; I just thought that everyone operated that way. Being older and wiser, I've come to realize most people don't—but they should!

FIND COMMON INTERESTS

We are all constantly looking for connections and common interests. When we do find them, we create associations, camaraderie, and friendships—and, of course, we expand our personal network.

Create a Bond

Finding things in common can be so simple! Sometimes even one shared experience will do. ("Hang on. Weren't *you* at that appalling conference in Toronto where...?") In fact, sometimes a single incident can create a lasting bond. I have a former client, Owen, with whom I negotiated a deal in meetings that went on until dawn. When I run into him today, he always teasingly introduces me as the "the lady lawyer with whom he once spent the night." By telling that story, Owen makes me feel more like a friend with a shared past than a legal advisor!

Use Your Family

I was single through a good part of my legal career, and I always felt excluded when my colleagues turned business development activities into family occasions. Perhaps what I really felt was envy, as I watched my partners cultivate relationships with their clients through common family interests. I truly believe that merging personal lives with business relationships forges deeper connections.

Use Your Interests

While my male colleagues were using their families (and sporting events) to generate camaraderie with clients, I looked for and found my own angle—fashion. For years I had taunted my partners by saying that if they could take their clients to rugby and football matches, I might just take mine to London Fashion Week...and then one day I thought, "Well, why not?"—so I did! Over time this became a unique networking event that conveniently meshed with my personal interest in fashion. And while football and beer-minded clients naturally outnumber fashionistas, I did find plenty of like-minded people. Membership in *my* network was that much more exclusive—and tightly knit!

MAKE OPPORTUNITIES

I must show everyone how fantastic I am.

You may think that you currently lack the resources for effective networking: "Referrals? You've got to be kidding. I'm in no position to help other people!"

Never underestimate your capabilities, nor the contributions you can make toward others simply as a lawyer. Think of yourself as a robust resource and then strategize about how to use your skills. Find excuses to contact people. Suppose you spot an outstanding review of a new ballet production, and you know that your client Fiona has a talented daughter at the Royal Ballet School. Why not send Fiona the review? Even if she's seen the review (or the production), she'll be tremendously grateful. She can't help but be flattered by your interest in her, which has that natural boomerang effect.

Sometimes we worry too much about how other people will take our actions. ("Won't they be put off, or annoyed, or bored?... Won't I just be bugging them?... What if they think I'm simply desperate for work and reject me?") No, Fiona will be pleased that you remembered, and she would never, ever be bored or irritated by anything to do with ballet. And since when did showing a thoughtful interest in someone signify desperation?

Remember, too, that if your actions are in alignment with our definition of networking, then you're focusing not on yourself but on the needs or interests of

the other person concerned. By virtue of this approach you not only portray yourself in the best possible light, but you also instantly eliminate any risk of rejection.

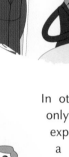

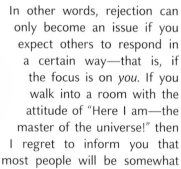

In other words, rejection can only become an issue if you expect others to respond in a certain way—that is, if the focus is on *you*. If you walk into a room with the attitude of "Here I am—the master of the universe!" then I regret to inform you that most people will be somewhat underwhelmed. But if your concern is for others, your impact (or lack of same) doesn't figure in the equation. Entering the room with "Great! There you are!" is all you need to do to make yourself look terrific in their eyes—every time.

The same principle holds true for most networking issues. If you contact someone with his or her interests in mind, then the reaction will probably be positive and supportive. So don't be afraid to make the first move, and try to use every situation as an opportunity to network.

Rejection can only become an issue if you expect others to respond in a certain way—that is, if the focus is on you.

LEVERAGE OPPORTUNITIES: FOLLOW UP

Good intentions aside, we normally fail in networking at the follow-through stage. Suppose you have lunch with someone and discuss some ideas of mutual interest. On the way back to the office you have some inspired thoughts on how to follow up on said conversation. Yet once back in the office, reality socks you in the stomach. Everything seems behindhand and chaotic, and all that focused enthusiasm dissipates quickly. Still worse, you may even fail to follow up with an email, warmly thanking the person for lunch. (And if you're still wondering: "What email? Thanking him for what? Who's got time for lunch?" then you're really in trouble!) You don't want to send the email without expounding on some of your most brilliant follow-up thoughts—so you put it off until the fires of enthusiasm are quenched and muddied by routine. *Then* you're too embarrassed by your failure to say thanks that you don't write at all, much less call. Time goes by, your powerful ideas are forgotten, and the opportunity is irretrievably lost.

It's vital that you put just as much emphasis on pursuing and following up networking possibilities as you do on (seemingly more urgent) client-based work. Believe me, disappointing potential networking partners could prove just as detrimental to your career as missing a deadline, if not more so.

The benefits of networking are derived *primarily* from follow-up commitments, so it's important to network systematically and logically, scheduling time for nurturing contacts. During this time you should try several approaches.

- Send notes and thank-you letters (preferably hand-written).

- Return messages (always within 24 hours, unless provided with a doctor's note of excuse).

- Call people you haven't spoken to in two months or more to revive and reactivate dormant relationships. Of course, don't begin by saying, "Clive! Gosh, I've missed hearing your voice! How's your ninth marriage coming along?" No, you have to legitimize your call and justify taking up the other professional's time by providing some value. On the basis of our evolved "people skills," we have a useful tool kit for doing just that. Look at the following examples.

Reason for call	Value provided
Requesting advice *("Clive, I'm thinking about getting married again...")*	Making him feel important
Asking for information *("Clive, do you recall the name of your last divorce lawyer bar three?")*	Making him feel helpful
Extending congratulations *("Clive! Congrats on being named the divorce lawyer's client of the year!")*	Allowing him to feel recognized
Providing information *("Clive, I happen to know that your next-to-last wife, to whom you pay the most alimony, just won the lottery.")*	Getting information
Providing referrals *("Listen, Clive, hope this is OK, I gave your name last night to a guy writing a book who needs an expert in relationship problems...")*	Receiving introductions/business

■ Invite people to lunch and to other events of interest ("Clive, thanks to your advice, my book *Surviving Serial Divorces Without Losing Your Shirt* has been accepted for publication. Do come to the launch, won't you? And bring the, uh, wife?").

■ Schedule meetings with a date and a time (*don't* just say, "Let's do lunch again sometime," which really means "low priority" and, in the end, "forgotten").

One of the most people-connected partners I've ever met arrives at the office about an hour early every morning to spend that time methodically completing the things on his networking "to do" list. He reckons this hour one of the most important of his entire day, and he considers his (related) networking database his most valuable asset. I think his rainmaking achievements reinforce the credibility of those statements.

NETWORKING IS NOT SELLING

As you cultivate your network, remember that you're building relationships, *not* selling. I accept that this can seem a very fine distinction, but it's still one you must never cross until the relationship is strong enough. Trying to sell to a contact too soon is a sure-fire way to destroy a connection, along with all that hard-won trust.

I like to compare networking and winning business this way: You are standing on the edge of a canyon with the goal of getting the other person, stuck on the opposite side, to leap across the divide.

Now she is a bit wary and unlikely to jump on her own initiative, so you must first cross over yourself (probably more than once), until at some point she decides to try the leap over to your side.

This choice may happen swiftly, or possibly tortuously slowly, but it eventually takes place for two reasons: First, you've cultivated trust (by making enough of an effort), and second, you've built an invisible bridge (by reaching out to her again and again). In other words, her confidence must be such that entrusting work to you doesn't feel like a leap, but more like a casual stroll across a bridge.

Trying to sell before that bridge is firm can be compared to throwing the potential client a rope and telling her blithely, "Trust me!" She *might* grab hold of it, but it's not very likely. The exception, of course, is when your legal services are actually requested or when it's abundantly clear that by offering your services you're not soliciting, but assisting—which is your networking obligation in any case.

A FEW TIPS FOR THE JOURNEY

We must build our networks one person and one day at a time. If you proactively exercise the principles of this chapter, networking should become a habit ingrained into the texture of your everyday activities. As you work toward the ultimate goal of cultivating a valuable circle of connections, enjoy the journey, and keep the following points in mind.

Enjoy Your Network

Although we are technically talking about business, the reality is that networking is about relationships, and is based upon exactly the same principles as friendship. Thus, each networking relationship will be subtly different from every other, and each person in your network will possess his own individual attributes, strengths, influence, and aura. However, each one should be someone you respect, trust, and *enjoy*, and the relationship, not the potential benefit, should be the driver.

Remember That Positions Change and Grow

Suppose you look at your network and think that nobody there is of real value. Perhaps the people in your inner circle have no current relationship to your area of law, or perhaps—at least at this point—they are still too junior. Yet someone who might not appear helpful today can become helpful in the future. When talking to lawyers about their clients, I hear hundreds of stories about work that resulted from unanticipated circumstances or unexpected people, and it's quite common for someone in a network to move unexpectedly into a position requiring legal services.

Likewise, remember that people who may currently be valuable to you might not necessarily remain so. People can lose their jobs, or they can move to a company where you have a conflict of interest. Don't rely too heavily on any one person in your network, because things so often shift and change. Preparing the groundwork (just in case!) is part of a mature approach to building your career.

If you do find yourself in a situation where a previously valued contact can offer you little or nothing, I do hope that you will not commit one of the worst of all networking sins: displacing this person from your network. Never ditch someone who has been loyal to  you simply because of a change in circumstances. You might as well wear a T-shirt proclaiming, "Once someone's no longer beneficial to me, I no longer give a s**t!"

I've watched this happen many times. Frequently it occurs not because the lawyer is actively unkind but because he feels that he must, in such a case, prioritize replacing the financial value of the connection, even though this means completely neglecting the once-important contact. However, this is a mistake on many levels. First, do you really want to be known for treating people like machines, to be chucked away after they've outlasted their usefulness? (Not exactly a positive notch on the "belt" of your brand!) Second, if a person has been valuable to you in the past, then clearly you have established rapport with him or her, and to create that level of trust with someone new will take considerable effort for a far less certain result. And third, fickle fate may choose eventually to reward your former contact with a new or better position, and you really won't want to be a "former friend" at that time!

A colleague and I some years ago together built up a relationship with "Kevin," who over many years advanced in the client organization to a level where he was able to engage legal services for the projects he ran. Kevin continued to give both my colleague and me lots of work, and I believe he considered us friends as well as business associates.

Eventually, though, Kevin was made redundant as the result of an international restructuring. He took this as an opportunity to change career direction, which meant that he was no longer involved in engaging legal counsel. I stayed in touch with him, however, and was able to help Kevin in his new venture by providing some contacts. Years later, when he moved into another position where he was once again in need of legal advice, he immediately contacted me. As I was then in the process of leaving active practice, I suggested to Kevin that he instead contact my previous colleague—his friend, or so I thought. Kevin's response was an emphatic, "I will *never* give him work again!" It turned out that this had nothing to do with my former colleague's law skills: It was simply that, once Kevin was out of work, my colleague no longer gave him priority. According to Kevin, my colleague, who had previously been extremely courteous and attentive, didn't even bother to return his phone calls!

What If Your Position Changes?

Just as others' positions can change, so can your own. During my years as a technology lawyer, my ideal network was made up of senior management in technology divisions or companies—which is where I focused my efforts. But things have changed for me: My clients today are not technology people, but fellow lawyers. That doesn't mean that my technology contacts are no longer worth my time! It's just that I need to reevaluate how I network with them. Some relationships will become more like friendships than business contacts; others may provide new and different benefits in my own new and different situation.

As things change for you, people you discounted previously can become a networking gold mine. That's why it's critical to treat everyone appropriately. Every person you meet must be regarded as someone potentially worthy of becoming part of your network.

Adversaries Can Be Contacts, Too

As lawyers, we are trained to be aggressive on behalf of our clients. However, this does not mean we should be disrespectful, arrogant, or obstructive to the other side. If your reaction to this is, "Well, of course not!" then congratulations; you get to skip this section. Go get yourself a coffee, or feed the cat! However, I've come across plenty of lawyers—even really smart ones—who definitely do need to read this section (in some cases, more than once). To be honest, at one time I would have benefited from a few reminders myself.

This is the point: We can be extremely good and effective at our jobs without ever being disrespectful or difficult. If you question that, or feel the need to exhibit any of those (more disagreeable) traits, then ponder this: Your adversaries of today may one day prove critical to your network—or your ability to attract a new client, or land an important job.

A few years ago, lawyers on the other side of a transaction asked my opinion of a former colleague, a relatively junior lawyer. I said that I thought he was an excellent lawyer who had great skill and great passion for his work. "Yes," they admitted, "but when we dealt with him he was also so incredibly arrogant that it was almost impossible to come to any agreement with him. In the end, his attitude so hindered the deal that people were unable to stand either him or his client." I had to admit that this story did sound plausible, as the lawyer in question has a tendency to give way to his ego and his emotions. Nor was this an isolated incident: Subsequent to that discussion I heard a similar story about the same person, making me think long and hard about how his naïve egotism could create real problems for him in the future.

That same week, ironically enough, I encountered two past adversaries of mine—people who, during our earlier encounters, I'd never imagined might ever influence my future career. The first came in the form of a job interview. I was meeting with a firm about possibly joining them—and I felt nervous, knowing that someone I had negotiated against many years before was currently one of their partners. The deal, which I remembered perfectly, involved issues in which I had had particular experience. I'd secretly felt quite smug about it, and had even occasionally felt frustrated due to the other lawyer's comparative lack of knowledge. Naturally, I felt some trepidation about how he might remember those events.

I was relieved to find that he recalled them positively. He even laughed, saying, "You were very patient with me. I was certainly well outside my comfort zone!" Like most lawyers, I have an ego—so I was grateful that I had controlled it on that occasion!

The second encounter was the wedding of a client whom I had originally encountered as an adversary in an extremely antagonistic transaction. The hostility was not between us (it was the fault of his company's lawyer), and I had been careful to avoid retaliation, thereby earning goodwill and respect from all around the table. So when the opposing client switched companies he contacted me, and since that time he has been both a good client and a good friend. Hence the wedding invitation: another reminder that to treat the opposition disrespectfully is not only shortsighted but possibly detrimental to your career.

I have a friend with a thriving practice in New York City whose habit after every deal is to call the lawyer on the other side to say that he enjoyed working with him or her. Sometimes his adversaries seem a bit taken aback—especially if the negotiations in question were long, traumatic, or difficult—but by the end of the conversation they always seem to appreciate the call. My friend reasons, "Think about it. Who else but your immediate adversaries really know how good a lawyer you are? If they perceive you as technically skilled and you then cultivate a relationship with them, they become a highly probable source of referral work... And even if they don't, they'll find it hard to be rude about you!"

Never Burn Bridges

It seems an obvious point, but almost all of us have done it: We send off an email or say something that we later wish we hadn't. That "something" then lodges forever in the other person's mind, and we know, no matter how hard we try, that it will never be forgotten. This is why every piece of correspondence, every departing note, and every good-bye gesture must be thought through and its implications considered.

For example, take the chain of emails on the next page:

From: Bateman, Larry
Sent: Wednesday, December 12, 2008 9:29 AM
To: ODonnell, Trevor; Project Alexander Working Group
Subject: Power Point Presentation
    1 Attachment, 180 KB

Dear Trevor,

I thought that you would like to see the presentation that will be given to the Steering Committee at tomorrow's meeting.

Thanks,

Larry

------Original Message------
From: ODonnell, Trevor
Sent: Wednesday, December 12, 2008 10:01 AM
To: Friedman, Caroline
Subject: FW: Power Point Presentation
    1 Attachment, 180 KB

Caroline:

Can you please review the presentation (the one I mentioned to you the other day) and let me know if there are any over-arching legal considerations that we need to build into it? I'm not sure whether our legal department has been involved, but I'd like to have your opinion.

Thanks,

Trevor

------Original Message------
From: Friedman, Caroline
Sent: Wednesday, December 12, 2008 10:23 AM
To: ODonnell, Trevor
Subject: Re: Power Point Presentation

Dear Trevor,

I can't imagine that anyone from the legal department has reviewed it because there are some major issues here, while the positions in the presentation just don't stand up, and are significantly deficient, not to say unsound. To avoid looking imprudent, I advise that the presentation be heavily reworked, and without loss of time.

I would be glad to help you.

Caroline

You can guess what happened next! Trevor forwarded the chain of messages directly to his legal department (including Caroline's forthright opinion, which implied that if they *had* reviewed the presentation, they must be notably incompetent). As it turned out, the legal department had indeed been involved, and they—not unnaturally—perceived her words as a direct insult. To make matters worse, Trevor happened to be a long-term acquaintance of Caroline's and someone with whom she had been developing a networking relationship, hoping it could eventually lead to projects with his company. In fact, by requesting her opinion, Trevor had been trying to help her achieve that goal. Yet with one hasty email, Caroline made it impossible!

Throughout my career, I have seen many similar situations (and many worse emails) from people who probably never considered that their words could come back to haunt them. I remember one departing associate's "Good-bye To All" email (at some point received by the greater legal population), in which the author referred to his colleagues as gossips and backstabbers, said that the decision to leave the firm to become a "trophy husband" was a quick and easy one, and indicated that he would rather be dressed up like a piñata and beaten to death than remain among such colleagues. His words, as you would expect, became the subject of many journal articles, blogs, and after-work discussions. I only hope for the sake of that young author that his position of trophy husband worked out successfully. If not, his email might prove a life-long lesson in regret!

I must admit that I have burned a few bridges in my time—with jobs I didn't really like and law partners I didn't really respect. But people have a way of popping back up unexpectedly, both in our lives and in our careers, and often at peculiarly inconvenient times. The truth is, we usually burn bridges when our own egos are out of control—we imagine that we don't need that person any more, or that we are moving on to a better place. But where?—and for how long?

Network Now, When You Think You Need It Least

Now is the perfect time to create a reservoir of goodwill that you can use later. The most successful and strategic networkers reach out when they need it least!

The most successful and strategic networkers reach out when they need it least!

I recently had lunch with Roger (not a lawyer), whose networking ability is legendary. Since I was thinking about this book, I couldn't help asking him when and how he started networking. I assumed he would say that he had always been a "people person" and that networking came naturally to him, but his answer surprised me.

Roger was one of London's corporate elite, having been the IT Director and CTO of some large British and international companies. Some years ago one of his friends had unexpectedly sustained a job loss due to a merger, and since the friend had never built up a network, he struggled in his search for a new position. Roger himself felt a *frisson* of nerves, realizing that if he were ever to be in a similar position, he'd feel just as helpless. From that moment Roger made the decision to cultivate his connections, developing (over time) such a wide, deep network that when his company was taken over and he was let go, he was able to move forward with confidence and start up a company of his own. His company's success, in fact, has been founded on the network of friends, colleagues, and acquaintances that he had the foresight to create.

So start networking now! Don't leave it until you're out of a job—or until you become a partner and suddenly realize that you lack enough clients of your own—or until your biggest source of business gets taken over, and (overnight) no longer requires your services! Business, by its very nature, is uncertain. Prepare for the worst, to make sure that the worst never happens to you.

Network Within Your Firm

Roger's story is not intended to imply that your current co-workers aren't part of your network. They are—and on three separate levels.

1. You should network with your co-workers to distinguish and promote yourself within your firm (brand marketing). For example, if you are in the firm's tax department you should be networking routinely with the lawyers in the corporate department, because they require your services. You should be making yourself known to them, and assisting them whenever possible. Invite them to lunch. Treat them just as you would someone in your network. Being well-connected within the firm gives you a huge advantage.

2. You can only obtain your goal of leadership through good working relationships with your colleagues—something that networking automatically helps to achieve.

3. When circumstances change and colleagues move into situations where they can engage legal services, you will have already put yourself on their radar screens. And—I promise you—that time will come sooner than you might expect.

Network Within Your Contact Organizations

With each major contact, consider how you could further your connection within their organization. Set up on-site visits, or request introductions to other key people. Widen your contacts and depth within the company, or use projects as a way to get in more deeply. In any large transaction, I always offered my time to the client for two key purposes: First, if the contract required support from different departments, I would help the project sponsors present the benefits of the contract to other parts of the organization. This helped them garner the support they needed and also introduced me to new and important people. Similarly, once the contract was signed I helped the client implement its provisions, which again brought me into contact with people I might not otherwise have met.

Network at All Levels

Always remember that it's worthwhile to network *at all levels*. No one is ever too junior! Those below you will appreciate your interest in them and will be all the more likely to remember you when they're in a position to steer work your way. Many of my former peers as a young lawyer—and even quite a few who were not long ago my juniors—are today general counsels or members of executive boards. Some of them got there unexpectedly, while others climbed up the corporate ladder with amazing determination. Regardless of how they made it, however, they all remember who helped them—and who ignored them—when they were "mere" junior associates.

Look around at your peers, and even those junior to you. Soon some of these people will have the power to give work to you—or take it away. Sometimes the people you least expect end up in positions of clout!

Here's the story of "one of those people"—a good friend, once junior to me. Years ago, as an associate, I worked for the same partner he describes.

When I started out my law career I was lucky to have a boss, Chuck, a senior partner with my firm, who was an incredible mentor and good fun to work with. Although I was just a young associate, Chuck treated me with respect and took a special interest in my development as a lawyer and in me as a person. But still more unusual, when I decided to leave the law to pursue something completely unrelated, his relationship toward me remained the same. He had cared about me while I was an associate who worked hard for him and his clients, but he also showed me the same interest later without that personal benefit (or any other hope of "getting something out of it").

Years later, when I unexpectedly returned to the law, and then found myself in a position to retain outside counsel, Chuck was the first lawyer I called.

—Chris, General Counsel of a technology company in Atlanta, Georgia

Develop Your Current Network

When considering your preferred strategy, keep in mind that it takes much less time and effort to develop your current network than to start anew. All too often we fail to focus on the network we have, instead trying too hard to search for new and "better" connections.

Re-evaluate Periodically

As situations change, re-evaluate your network. Everyone in your network is a valuable person, but that doesn't mean that they will all remain beneficial to your practice. After a while, you may need to move some of them from your business network to your social network. Likewise, use your imagination to determine how people you now consider friends could become business connections.

Then there are the people who have had their day—not through loss of position but through disloyalty, lack of generosity, or change of character. You know who they are—the ones who keep taking and taking without giving anything back, or who even repay generosity with unkindness. The higher goal is to be gracious, but there are still times when escape is indicated.

A SPECIAL NOTE TO WOMEN

Whatever your viewpoint or experience, the legal career path can be different for women. I never felt at a disadvantage as a woman. (In fact, I believe that some of my clients, both male and female, gave me preference because of my sex and because of my having a different approach from some of my male colleagues.) However, I know women lawyers whose experiences were very different from mine. I well remember my friend Jane's excitement when she was assigned to lead a high-profile project in which she would be overseeing two of her male colleagues. She worked all weekend to prepare for the kick-off meeting on Monday morning. When she arrived, however, she discovered that her male colleagues had not only bonded during a Friday night out together, but had taken the opportunity to agree upon an approach for the project. Through their collusion, they proceeded to undermine her role as the leader.

When I asked another, extremely successful, friend whether she thought female lawyers experience isolation from their male colleagues, I was surprised to hear her say, "Absolutely!" She mentioned that every time she enters the equity partners' meeting, her male colleagues are inevitably discussing sports. They often treat the meeting as an extension of their exclusive male club, where her presence—as someone who frankly considers football irrelevant—is, at best, merely tolerated.

My positive experience may have derived from my insanely driven personality, which was similar to the mindset of most of the men I worked with and enabled me to compete on their level. (I'm not advocating behaving like a man. I believe that women bring a different mindset, perspective, and experience to their work, and this adds more value than merely "being one of the boys"— and ultimately contributes to their success.) The key, regardless of gender, is to work with your strengths, and not compromise who you are.

Undoubtedly, another factor contributing to my lack of isolation was that I wasn't trying to balance my career with motherhood. (Jane's unlucky experience was exacerbated by the fact that, as the mother of a young child, she rushed home on Friday nights while her male counterparts headed out for a beer.)

Despite my experience, the reality is that women are different from men, and these distinctions can be most apparent with regard to networking. While some women can really enjoy football (soccer), golf, or rugby, those networking events were never of interest to me (except for the fact that some of the athletes tended to be more than usually good-looking!). I actually only went on the annual golfing trips to use the spa and attend the evening dinner, which didn't make for much bonding with golf-crazy clients. And I must admit that I too have been excluded from evenings out for the simple—and undeniable—reason that I was born female.

Personally, I found these impediments only minor irritants—and certainly no barrier to my career goals. However, as I became more senior I did encounter a problem: My network of female supporters inevitably dwindled, as many of my female clients and colleagues left the work force. One remedy for this, which I believe could be extremely beneficial, would be to become involved in formal women-focused networks, where the individuals may change but the numbers remain fairly constant. Why should men get most of the networking chances?—Networking matters!

Each woman's experience will be unique, and every woman in the business of law should seek many views and figure out the best approach for her, in light of her own personality, environment, and goals. We're back to the same principle examined in Chapter 4 ("Personalities")—that all of us must leverage our own unique strengths. As a broad generalization, some strengths tend to be dominant among men, while others are dominant among women, but that doesn't change the principle that one strength is no better or worse than another, and that, to succeed, each of us must be authentic to our own. When we work with our strengths, we achieve the best possible outcome—whether male or female, and whether working with a male- or female-dominant strength. And when we synergistically combine our different strengths, we can achieve even more, whatever the mix (I believe the key is in the different personalities and experiences, not necessarily the gender).

NETWORKING AS A WAY OF LIFE

The bottom line is that most people want to interact with and support others, so try to see each person you encounter as an opportunity for relationship-building. As you do this, it will start to feel more and more natural to you, and your activities will generate their own momentum until, one day, you'll suddenly realize that you've fostered opportunities, created deeper relationships, and pulled off networking successes. Let's recap exactly how:

1. Take an active interest in other people and help them.
   This is the definition of networking!

2. Support your networking activities with the people skills we examined in Chapter 6, which can be summarized as *helping others to feel important and appreciated*.

   a. Congratulate and compliment.

   b. Remember personal things about others and use that information to make them feel significant.

3. Maintain a generous mindset in terms of your actions, efforts, use of time, and values.

   a. Commit to the success of the people within your network by sharing your knowledge, giving referrals, and connecting people.

   b. Cultivate relationships through common interests and use everything, no matter how insignificant it may seem, as an opportunity to network.

c. Consider everyone you meet as worthy of your network, including juniors, adversaries, and people you just don't like. Resist the impulse to burn bridges, as someone you may be tempted to disregard today could tomorrow be the one to decide whether you have work—or even a job.

d. Network within your firm and your client organization.

e. Be systematic about your networking follow-up, because it's through these pursuits that networking yields the most beneficial results.

   i. Reactivate dormant relationships by calling people to whom you haven't spoken in two months.

   ii. Send notes and thank-you letters (preferably handwritten).

   iii. Return messages (always within 24 hours).

   iv. Invite people to lunch and to events in which you might be participating.

   v. Schedule meetings for a definite day and time (rather than the all-purpose, "Let's get together again sometime").

f. Be purposeful, but also enjoy your network and the process. Yes, you benefit—but the benefit to you is *not* the sole motivation for your networking efforts.

g. Network, starting *today*, with patient commitment, recognizing it as a long-term endeavor and knowing that your goal can only be reached through incremental steps.

Chapter Sixteen

Expanding Your Network

(Meeting, greeting—and connecting)

Between 50 and 80 percent of people, depending upon which survey you prefer, would describe themselves as timid to uncomfortable in any given social situation. Further, going to an event full of strangers has been described as most people's number-one social fear, and it is believed that one in ten suffers from acute social anxiety at some point in life.

If you are reading these statistics and thinking, "Bizarre! I like meeting new people. A room full of strangers is a room full of possibilities!" then you deserve that smug little smile. The only question for you is whether you're capitalizing on your natural sociability. If, however, you're at the other extreme, thinking, "Frankly, I'd rather be hit over the head with stinging nettles than be imprisoned making meaningless small talk with strangers," then persevere with this chapter. Like it or not, making small talk (and making it well) is essential to your career. At some point we all need to make our networks grow, and the only way to do that is to reach out and make new connections.

Most of us fall somewhere between the two extremes described above— sometimes apprehensive with introductions, sometimes at ease. It probably depends on the situation, the people we happen to meet early on, and the level of control we feel over our circumstances. It may even boil down to something as simple as our mood on one particular day.

No matter where you currently stand on working a room, by practicing a few skills you can enjoy an occasion full of strangers, and even transform the evening into new connections or new networking relationships. Working a room in this way involves many things we've already considered throughout the book. So let's just recap a few of them, and examine their implications with regard to meeting and greeting.

FIRST IMPRESSIONS

Working a room well depends on making a positive first impression. You convey your brand the moment you enter a room, so remind yourself in advance of what you're trying to project and make any necessary adjustments to mood or appearance. As you know, body language and voice make up a big part of first impressions, so on entering a room concentrate first on maintaining good posture, exhibiting relaxed alertness, and communicating a warm and friendly tone. Remember that in Chapter 6 ("People Skills") we examined those

feel-good factors: positivity, smiles, energy, and enthusiasm. Invoking those things will create the right chemistry for a high-impact impression.

Also, you should think about being your brand at all times, not just when engaged in conversation. You never know who may be observing or listening! At a conference, I once met a suave, elegant, and impressive man, with whom I had a lengthy discussion. Yet later on, while trying to find the ladies' room (that well-known parlor game), I turned a corner and encountered him shouting abusively into his mobile phone. This inevitably altered my perception of the authenticity of his wonderful brand!

Have the Right Attitude

The first step to working a room is *attitude*: You should either feel happy to be there or be able to convey a decent impression of the same. So get into that mindset, or you might as well go home (indeed, I would urge you to do so)!

We've all been introduced to people who would frankly rather be somewhere else. Their eyes are glazed over, and as you talk they look over your shoulder; their eye contact is nonexistent, and they seem to begrudge every syllable that escapes them. They seem distracted, bored, or annoyed. It's just human nature to boomerang such negativity right back at them! Their behavior is probably the result of their own discomfort, but regardless of the reason, the result is the same: No connection is generated, and the only impression created or cemented is likely to be negative.

So, no matter what, make sure that *you* aren't the person appearing detached or fed up. And if surrounded by these unfortunates, just keep moving until you find a more comfortable position.

Be Enthusiastic

Treat every introduction as a thrill. Do this quick exercise: Pretend that your best friend—whom you haven't seen for ages—is about to walk through the door. How do you feel? Excited? Happy? Lit up? Now try evoking that same emotion before you meet someone new. Admittedly, you're not going to actually feel toward that person as you do with your best friend—that would be a strong symptom of insanity—but you should still try to exude the same energy. An enthusiastic greeting creates instant rapport and makes a powerful first impact.

Be Positive

The more positive you are when you begin a conversation, the more favorable a first impression you make. I recently attended a luncheon at which the person placed next to me arrived midway through the meal. As he took his seat he commented, "Sorry I'm so late. The City just gets worse and worse! First my tube train broke down, and then I had to get a cab. But, of course, there were no cabs, thanks to the foul weather. And when I finally got one, would you believe that the stupid driver couldn't find the street!?" After that introduction I had a difficult time warming to my luncheon partner, despite the fact that he subsequently became much more engaging. If he had started with, "Wow! Murderous getting here, but I'm so glad I made it!" how different my first impression might have been!

The more positive you are when you begin a conversation, the more favorable a first impression you make.

THINK LIKE A HOST

Rather than entering the room with the attitude of "Here I am!" you should maintain the networking mindset of taking an interest in others ("There you are!"). My former colleague, Chris, takes concentrating on others a step further. He has a knack of treating everyone as though they are important guests and he's the host—even when he's technically a visitor, too. Chris is always the first to ask if anyone needs a drink or a bite to eat. He looks after everyone's comfort and makes sure that each person is properly introduced. If there aren't enough seats, Chris always tries to find another, or goes without one himself. Whatever the situation, he takes responsibility for making other people feel at ease. Not surprisingly, people respond to Chris's warmth just as guests respond to a great host—and Chris's attitude always makes him the most popular person in any crowd.

So glad you could make it. Can I get you a drink? Have a seat.

So whenever you meet someone you should focus on his needs, on supporting and empowering him, and on putting him at ease. This does two things: First, it actually makes you more relaxed by switching your attention away from your own discomfort (if any). Second, it subtly alters the dynamics of the encounter, subliminally elevating you into a host, or even into a leader. (Real leadership is all about empowering others—but we'll get to that in later chapters.)

CONVERSATION SKILLS

Be Interested

As discussed at length in Chapter 6, the key to being a good conversationalist is focusing on others. The bottom line is that most people love to talk about—themselves! So the more you ask and listen, the better a conversationalist you'll be deemed to be.

Be focused: Give the person you're speaking with your full attention. If he's boring beyond belief, you should tactfully excuse yourself (the ladies' room can be enormously useful!). This is far more polite than feigning interest, which almost never works.

Listen

There are two purposes to being a good listener. First, it's an opportunity to pick up nuggets of information about people and their circumstances, their businesses, or their needs. But it's also an opportunity to be empathetic and appealing—and even to come across as a great conversationalist! (Remember my friend Margaret from Chapter 6, who was labeled "highly entertaining," even though she merely listened.)

Listening can be your most important contribution to the discussion, so be sure that your body language shows that you're attentive. Above all else, maintain eye contact—this is not the time to people-watch, or to lustfully scan the buffet table!

It sounds straightforward, but the next time you're at a dinner, notice whether you are fully focused on the conversation. Most people glance around the room, more from habit (as experienced multi-taskers) than from actual boredom. Now, good friends probably wouldn't even register your subtle glance across the room, but a person you're meeting for the first time very likely will. He is subconsciously testing your reactions, and when you fail to give him your full attention, he (or she) will tend to decide that you're either bored or arrogant. The result is a complete absence of rapport—all because you fell for some trivial distraction!

Obviously, there may be times when you really *do* have to multi-task. Perhaps your new boss is meeting you, and it's necessary to look out for her arrival. This is not a problem; just let the person you're talking to know what is going on. "Listen, Zack, Penny will be here any second and I promised to introduce her around, as she's only just crossed the big duck pond—so if I keep checking over your shoulder, it's not because your conversation has failed to grip..."

Show Expression

Have you ever had a conversation with someone whose eyes are so locked on yours that you begin to wonder if he's psychotic? Don't concentrate so hard on maintaining eye contact that you lose your natural animation! Nod your head when appropriate. Show expression, smile occasionally, or knit your brow to signify deep (ha!) thought. Let your body language tell the speaker that you are positively engaged.

Verbalize Your Listening

When really interested and engaged, you should follow up on the speaker's statements. This shows that you are listening with intent. Note that such comments are not interruptions! If well chosen, they should have a number of beneficial effects:

- They encourage the speaker to continue: "I can't believe that you coped when [insert unbelievable situation] happened. Tell me more!"

- They subtly flatter: "That's so impressive. Personally, I could never jump out of an airplane at 12,000 feet. Sometimes I need a glass of wine just to get *into* one!"

- They suggest that you empathize: "Gosh, that's awful—the first and only time I was rushed to the hospital with an injury, I fainted before I got there."

- They provide openings for questions: "How on earth did you manage that without any support?"

And if none of these are appropriate, you can at least acknowledge that you're taking it all in with the occasional comment, "Gosh...amazing... Tell me more!"

Ask Questions

Remember that hoary old cliché that there *are* no stupid questions? In fact, the question that feels most cringingly stupid at the time probably, in retrospect, convincingly demonstrated both your humility and—ironically—your confidence. And, of course, it showed that you were interested—your main conversational objective!

When I started out as an outsourcing lawyer, people often asked me, "What exactly is that?" While the answer was of course quite obvious to me, I never thought anyone inferior for not knowing about it, and I always answered the question fully and enthusiastically. As far as I was concerned, people who never asked, but whose ignorance later became clear, made a far worse impression; I could only assume that they never inquired because of either indifference or insecurity. Think about it: When has someone ever asked you a question about yourself or your work, hobbies, or interests that you weren't glad to answer?

When you're in a group of people and some question begins to tantalize you, it's a better-than-even bet that others in the group are wondering the same thing. The person with the confidence to ask the question actually reaps the reward, because the speaker focuses on him (or her) while providing his answer. I can't tell you how many times I've finally ventured a question, only to have a colleague admit later that he wished *he'd* been the one to ask.

The best questions for fueling conversations are open-ended. Listen for clues about when and what to ask, and try to ask about things that might allow a speaker to address his (or her) special interests or particular passions—the things that induce the most positive emotion. Even when a line of conversation appears to have shut down, be alert to opportunities to reignite it with a question.

The best questions for fueling conversations are open-ended.

Make It Part of Your Brand

My friend Margaret does all these things with genuine feeling, which is what causes her to delight almost everyone she encounters (I've seen it happen again and again; she can charm almost anyone!). In Chapter 17, we will learn why our ultimate goal with clients is to establish long-term trusting relationships—akin to, if not based on, friendship—so it's interesting to note that many (if not most!) of Margaret's past and current clients are her friends. (No, not the type of friendship where the client gets a free meal and the lawyer is combining business with a bit of pleasure, but the "real thing"—the friendship that transcends work contacts altogether.) I'm convinced that this is a direct result of her conversational skills. After all, isn't friendship based on good conversation, and knowing that the other person is in fact interested in you? Granted, for men, a bit of beer and sports might well factor in, but I've seen Margaret find something to interest her in the most tediously male-oriented sporting event as well.

Whenever Margaret's name comes up in conversation, at least one person immediately mentions what a warm and likeable person she is. In the terms of this book, it's part of her brand. (Margaret would never say such a thing about herself, but after all, a brand is only as good as others perceive it to be.) So if this is how you'd like your clients (or anyone!) to speak about you, then cultivate these conversational skills until they become as natural to you as they have always been to Margaret.

Remember the Answers

It's great to make a terrific impression in a short time—but what a pity to blow it afterwards by failing to remember what you learned! A while back I met both Samantha and Greg for the first time. Both struck me as genuine, intelligent, and interesting, and both seemed to fully grasp the art of listening, asking questions, and empathizing. At the time, my husband and I were in the process of moving, and the subject seemed to pervade my every encounter. (And yes, I know that I need to get out more!) However, both Greg and Samantha seemed alert and interested as I expounded on my moving mishaps. We all seemed to have suffered similar experiences, and we laughed about them together.

Recently, however, I bumped into Samantha and Greg at another meeting. Samantha immediately followed up on our previous discussions. She asked me about our new house and neighborhood; she also asked if my husband and I had found some local restaurants, obviously remembering that we've developed the (fattening!) habit of eating out. Greg, on the other hand, vaguely asked me where I lived! In other words, Samantha expertly used our previous conversation as a "placeholder" bid for building further rapport, and by recalling it she let me know that she'd given me her full attention and consideration.

Unfortunately, Greg negated his good initial impression by not remembering even the most basic outline of our discussion.

DON'T BE SHY—COMPLIMENT!

Everyone is subconsciously seeking personal acknowledgment, which is why paying compliments creates instant affinity. In addition, compliments can be a great way to start a conversation and can provide an excuse to seek someone out at a social or professional occasion. There are several ways to do this, depending on the situation.

Use His Reputation

If you know someone by reputation, tell him so—assuming, of course, that you're not being introduced to someone only known for his illicit affairs and gambling habit! There is no faster way to establish rapport than to validate another person's general standing. Don't make the mistake, however, of competing for eminence, thinking that boosting his or her ego somehow makes you inferior. The goal is not (I repeat, *not*) to impress the other person, but to make him feel comfortable with you. Try something like this:

> *"I've so looked forward to meeting you! Rob mentioned that you'd probably be here and that you're the London expert on..."*

> *"I saw you were attending and hoped we'd have the chance to meet. I read your article/ heard about your recent promotion/ attended the function where you won the award for..."*

> *"Actually, we're in the same area of work. I've come across your name so many times, especially with regard to corporate financing. I couldn't be more thrilled to finally have the chance to meet you in person!"*

Use the Firm

It's quite possible that you may know nothing about someone as an individual but that you might still know something about his firm. In this case, find something intelligent to say about the organization; after all, its reputation reflects on him. Something as simple as, "I've heard great things from my colleagues about Stoat, Mender and Big's work in the corporate sector," can immediately bolster a strong first impression.

Use a Positive Story

Whenever I first meet someone through a mutual acquaintance, I try to remember a positive story I've heard about him or her. "Matthew told me that you plan to have a go at the 65-and-over triathlon this year!" The reaction is always the same: sheer, unadulterated gratification. When you tell someone that he has been discussed in a positive light, he can only feel pleased and, as the messenger, you've set yourself up to receive some of the glow.

Use Something Special

If there's anything special about the way the person looks or what he or she is wearing, don't be afraid to say so. "That red is stunning and a great color on you."

REVEAL YOURSELF

So far we've focused on keeping the spotlight on the other person. To make a real connection, however, the conversation can't be wholly one-sided; the other person needs information about you to relate to, or to help him form an impression of you. Furthermore, if you share nothing of yourself then you are automatically limiting your means of connection. You want the other person to identify with you, perceive commonality, and (ideally) experience an emotional affinity. This will require that you reveal things about yourself. ("I know that I may look like a pretty ordinary sort of guy. However, once I move into a telephone booth, some pretty strange things happen...")

What you choose to disclose, and how you do it, are key to achieving your objectives. There are some factors that can clue you in as to what is appropriate. If you follow the lead of your conversation partner and do your best to match his or her preferred level of disclosure, you're probably in the right ballpark. Suppose the other person indicates that he just went through a messy divorce, and your response is a feeble "Oh." You've probably made him feel vulnerable, or even stupid, because *you* have chosen to reveal (follow me closely here) exactly nothing. On the other hand, revealing too much can be even more threatening. Replying with a self-indulgent tale about your own recent break-up, complete with sordid details about how he ran over your iPod with his Porsche, could be overkill. The optimal response might be, "My parents got divorced, so I realize something of how tough it can be." In this reply you have revealed something about yourself *and* displayed empathy, but without making your acquaintance start checking out the exits.

The optimal way to share things is *in response to questions or in relation to the topic at hand.* Ideally, the other person should feel as though he is discovering *you.* For example, if you ask someone about his preferences or interests (such as his musical tastes), he's more or less honor-bound to ask about yours in return, so consider this when you are soliciting information. The brilliantly prepared conversationalist has usually already figured out how to respond to the inquiry just asked of someone else.

When you self-disclose it's natural to want to show off your very best attributes, but there's a fine line between impressing others in a professional way versus coming across as irritating and vain. So keep in mind all the things we considered previously in relation to people skills, and, in particular, your objective: making the other person feel important. Being humble about your own accomplishments—perhaps sharing a deficiency in yourself, or a mistake that you've made—can put the other person wonderfully at ease.

> When you self-disclose it's natural to want to show off your very best attributes, but there's a fine line between impressing others in a professional way versus coming across as irritating and vain.

I recently met a successful and distinguished man who was previously a practicing lawyer but who now runs his own company. I was admittedly a bit intimidated by his aura and his reputation until I asked him how he'd started up his company. He admitted, with a smile, that he'd been rather pushed into his decision because his law firm had fired him! As you might expect, he suddenly seemed much more human and approachable to me. My unease quickly dissipated, and we soon felt like friends.

The optimal topics to bring up about yourself are the things that you feel positive and passionate about, because talking about them naturally makes you exude feel-good (and, as we learned in Chapter 6, "mirrored") energy. But, of course, don't hog the spotlight. The best conversations are much like a good tennis match—back and forth.

BE CAREFUL ABOUT THE "ME TOO" STORY

Whenever someone mentions a point of common interest, or a similar story to your own, it is vital not to jump in with a "me too" tale. First, allow the other person to tell his or her story—"and then the Burmese government hoods threw me into jail for defending my client's interests!"—and then, if the time is right (and if you aren't "capping" his story), tell yours. Do not say, "Actually, I was once thrown into jail in Zimbabwe, to be gnawed by rats, and only thrown moldy chunks of bread twice a week." It's better to just mention your experience briefly, to show the similarity of interest, without giving your story equal billing. Never try to make yours sound more exciting/incredible/horrific than his.

I have an acquaintance, Sharon, who is a very successful businesswoman, but is unhappily prone to boasting and will habitually "top" any story. Last year I invited her and a friend of mine, Gundula, to a social event. Gundula is general counsel and an executive of one of the top automotive companies. At one point in the evening I found both women engaged in conversation with the same group. One man, having known Gundula by reputation, was asking her about the obstacles she had faced as a woman in her male-dominated industry. In response, Gundula recounted her early days as a "lone female," but she also downplayed her achievements by emphasizing that those days were over and by highlighting the more recent successes of other women in her industry. Then, predictably, Sharon had to break in with her "topper." She told everyone that she was the golden girl of *her* business, as well as being a rare female entity in *her* male-dominated environment. Everything she said was true, but her interjection posed two problems: First, no one had asked for it, and second, by *having* to tell it, she discredited herself, and no one really seemed very impressed.

I watched the impact these women had on the guests that evening. Although they were equally successful in their careers, Gundula, by being humble, had made the better impression. There is a place and a time for self-promotion, but a first encounter is not it!

PRACTICE, PRACTICE, PRACTICE

Be sure to practice your conversation skills throughout day-to-day activities. My mother was the first person who told me that making conversation is easy. "Just ask questions!" she would say. "Don't be afraid of showing interest in others." While my mother is not herself a businesswoman, her advice was right on target, and she invariably practiced what she preached. My mother knew the names (and the circumstances) of the dry cleaner, the mailman, the gardener, the repairman, her hairdressers, and everyone else she saw on a regular basis, simply because she took an interest in them. At every encounter she would engage them in conversation by asking questions—and then she would take the trouble to remember the answers. "What was the conference like?" "How was your trip to San Diego?" "How's your house expansion coming along?" Each question built on the previous answers, and she quickly established relationships that went beyond the initial associations.

Make a conscious decision to initiate conversation with the people you come across in daily life. Before you approach them, plan how you could conceivably generate a conversation and establish a connection. When this works for you, make a mental note about which statements and questions appear to be most effective. If you practice your skills every day, they will benefit you when you're in a more formal situation—in other words, when you need it most!

BEFORE YOU GET THERE: MAKING THE MOST OF ANY MEET-AND-GREET

Determine Your Objectives and Do Your Homework

Our schedules as lawyers are normally busy enough with client work, so fitting in networking time is not always easy. Sometimes getting to an event is a last-minute, haphazard rush. Perhaps this situation sounds familiar: You are heading out the door (late!) while making final edits to an important document. On the way, you are dictating (OK, shouting) last-minute instructions to your secretary. You're not even sure of the location of the meeting as you charge to your uncertain destination (Wembley or Waterloo? WC1 or W1?), simultaneously fumbling for the crumpled invitation in your bag.

If you recognize this scenario, then you, like me, should make some adjustments to ensure that you get the most from the time you spend networking—*before* you rush out the door.

1. Understand your objective for attending. Is it...
   - Meeting people with something in common?
   - Hoping to encounter a specific person (or type of person?)
   - Exposure?
   - General networking?
   - Learning something?

2. Then, with your objective powerfully in mind, make sure that you do your homework. Think about how you can best achieve your purpose and what preparation may be necessary. For example...

- If attending an event with known speakers or attendees, read their bios and research their companies. You might just find something of interest, or a link steering you toward an intelligent question.

- If you hope to meet someone specific, contact him or her in advance. Recently, I wanted to meet a certain speaker at an event. I knew that his time would be limited and that access on the day was certain to be difficult. So a week before the event I sent him a brief email, introducing myself and mentioning that I hoped to make contact with him. This enabled me to walk directly through the crowd after his talk and introduce myself much more easily than if we had not previously corresponded.

- Call the organizers of the event a week ahead of time and obtain a list of attendees. Study it and consider whom you might want to meet, if possible.

What Your Objective Isn't

Regardless of your primary reason for attending any event, your objective should always include relationship cultivation, and you should always go with the right mindset to make connections. You're there to meet people and, with luck, develop enough rapport with them to establish the right to take the next step: the beginning of a networking relationship. But your ambitions must be limited to that alone—you are not (repeat, NOT!) there to sell your services (your brand, yes; your services, no). Allow me to repeat what I emphasized in the previous chapter: Trying to sell too soon risks destroying the connection you have worked hard to generate. (Remember the "bridge" from Chapter 15.)

Prepare Your Introduction

The introduction of who you are and what you do usually comes within moments of any first meeting, and thus critically influences that all-important first impression. The way you choose to introduce yourself can either attract people or turn them off—all in less than ten seconds! Think about how often you introduce yourself on a daily basis. When asked, "What do you do?" what's your typical answer? Do you reply with an enthusiastic response that provokes curiosity, or do you merely say, "Oh, I'm a lawyer." If the latter, take the time to develop an introduction that conveys your brand and might well generate interest in *you*.

> *The way you choose to introduce yourself can either attract people or turn them off—all in less than ten seconds!*

Here are a few guidelines:

- ■ Your introduction should follow the same principles as your brand statement (Chapter 12) and should emanate from that message. Delineate who you are and what you do, showcasing your uniqueness (best done by telling what you're passionate about, how you approach things, or what special value you bring to your client-based work).

- ■ Use phrases that people can relate to and that arouse emotion. Keep it short, snappy, and simple. If they want to know more, they can always ask!

- ■ Practice it out loud until it sounds natural and warm. Remember that an introduction should take no more than 30 seconds— ideally less.

You may want to create different versions of your introduction for use in various situations. For example, when I attended a social function with my husband's colleagues I introduced myself as Marcus's wife, rather than as the head of my firm's global outsourcing practice. Tell your audience what they really want to know. Here are some examples:

"Hi, I'm Ann Jones. I know that there is no more boring name, but I'm passionate about helping people turn their ideas about new corporate start-ups into real businesses."

"Great to meet you! I'm Angus McManus. I work to avert strikes in the public sector, which is probably why I'm prematurely gray..."

"Glad to be here. I'm Scott Sanders. Growing up I desperately wanted to be a singer—until one day I actually recorded my own voice. Not good! However, now I'm lucky enough to represent people who really can sing."

"I'm George. Admittedly, I am a bit technology-obsessed, but it's helped me win infringement cases for my technology clients because I understand how the technology works."

What about the lawyers showcased in Chapter 12 ("Brand Creation")? Here's how a few of them might introduce themselves:

> "Hi, I'm Steve. I like to think of myself as a businessman even more than a lawyer, because I use my legal expertise to get business results. My favorite part of the job is connecting clients to create more business for everyone."

> "I'm Casey—the outside/inside general counsel. I immerse myself in my clients to the point that they think of me as being on the payroll."

> "I'm Bill. My passion is changing corporate responsibility from a burden to a bonus by showing my clients what business benefits they can achieve by making an environmental difference."

> "Lucy Simpson. I'm now a private practice lawyer, but I started out on the other side of the street as general counsel of a software company. I like to use my past experience to help my clients level the playing field against the technology giants."

> "Good to meet you. I'm Kelsey—the physicians' advocate. My father only agreed to pay for law school if I promised not to sue any doctors. So I figured I'd represent them instead!"

Prepare Your Introduction Follow-Up

You should have some idea where your introduction might lead (with some forethought), and you should prepare related anecdotes to follow up your initial impression. Depending on the crowd, I soon figured out what might happen following my introduction as an outsourcing lawyer. ("What exactly does an outsourcing lawyer do?" was the obvious question.) So I conjured up a few "impromptu" (not!) anecdotes that described what I spent my life doing, trying to ensure that the one I selected on the spot was something to which my audience could relate and which might even stir up some emotion. One favorite revolved around a major bank outsourcing its call center to India—something almost everyone understood and felt strongly about.

Involve the Other Person

As a speaker, you should be eager to involve your listeners. So in telling your story, try to use it to turn the spotlight on the other person. In my "outsourcing to India" explanation, I used to ask my listeners whether they had ever been frustrated by being put through to someone in a faraway country who was equipped with neither the information nor the English to help them with their problem. In most cases I received a resounding response, sometimes so much so that the conversation became focused on my listeners' experiences and frustrations—which, of course, was the point!

Conversation Openers

Just as you prepare your introduction, you should also both compose and practice some opening lines, which provide the opportunity to engage in conversation. They can be about anything, but questions that lead somewhere yield the optimal result.

- "What do you think about the event/the speaker/the venue?"

- "Have you tried the lobster/spinach mousse?"

- "I suppose you probably already know lots of people here."

- "How did you first get involved in X?"

- "Great to meet you! Now look, I have a question about the conference organization that you can probably help me with."

The best opening lines relate to something that you have in common with your new acquaintance—even though such commonalities may actually be limited to being in the same place on the same evening. Before attending any event, think about some intriguing statements or questions that you might be able to approach people with in that particular situation.

Of course, you can practice opening lines in all sorts of circumstances. In the shopping mall elevator, an opening line might be, "I never thought there'd be such a crowd here today." In such situations it doesn't matter if the conversation actually goes anywhere; who cares if you get rebuffed as long as you can practice without risk? And as you practice in different environments, your opening lines begin to feel less staged, and you will discover that by being willing and able to initiate conversations you're much more likely to make others feel at ease. (Remember, most people feel relieved when they don't have to make the first move.)

If you are attending an event with speakers, then pay attention to their presentation, however outstandingly dull they might be. Make mental notes, jot down queries, and then when the mingling begins you'll be armed with opening lines. To one of the commentators you might say, "Hi. I'm Ann Smith. I have to say that I really identified with the remarks you made with regard to advertising in China." You've both initiated the conversation *and* proved that you listened—so regardless of where the discussion goes, you'll still have made a good connection.

Prepare Small Talk

When you meet someone for the first time, your discussions will often be held together by small talk. If you find this aspect of socializing difficult, there's good news: Just as with other conversational skills, you can prepare yourself to make it easier.

When I first moved to London I was thrilled to be invited to a dinner party by Rachel, one of my colleagues. I arrived to find other colleagues as well as some of Rachel's friends from her Cambridge days. Over dinner the conversation flowed easily through various topics, but I found myself listening rather than contributing; everyone else seemed knowledgeable about subjects that seemed obscure to me. As dessert was served, I could hold back no longer.

"Sorry, but I'm confused," I said. "Is it because I'm American, or just because I'm stupid? I really just don't know much about the subjects you're all so clued in to. I read the newspaper, of course, but obviously I am not reading the same newspaper you are!" Rachel looked at me in astonishment, asking, "But don't you listen to the radio in the morning?" "No," I admitted. I then learned that every single person there (along with most of the U.K.'s movers and shakers) listen to Radio 4 in the morning and that every topic discussed that evening—in one way or another—had sprung from that morning's program. And although I've never quite caught on to the exact appeal of this very British institution, I've still learned to listen to it before attending any gathering hosted by Rachel!

Similarly, before attending networking events you can easily prepare some lines of light discussion. These can be about anything except politics and religion—and (come to think of it) death, serious illnesses, personal issues, or attempts to lose weight. After all, the point of small talk is to fill up the time—pleasantly—before moving into business talk. If done right, it can amuse and intrigue; if done badly, it can embarrass and obstruct.

Small talk can come from anywhere. Rachel (who happens to be very good at it) has told me that she gets most of hers from offbeat newspapers and magazines. She says they always have great tidbits, and they tend to avoid the no-go topics of politics and religion. However, as a defensive move she always arms herself with mainstream news as well. Here are some more examples of small-talk topics:

- Vacations or favorite sports
- Hobbies or particular interests
- New restaurants, exhibits, openings

■ A new book, a recent play, an unusual movie

■ Current projects—preferably rewarding or unusual

■ Something funny or meaningful that recently happened to you or to someone you know

■ Local activities, issues, causes

In addition to topical subjects, it can't be beyond the wit of any lawyer to prepare small talk relating to any event, including information related to the host, the other guests, or the subject of the night. (I mean, what's Google FOR?!) I recently went to a luncheon in one of the historic Guildhalls in the City of London. There I bumped into an old client, Owen. (Yes, the same one who always mentions the night we "spent" together!) As we walked through the long, glorious hallway into the dining room, he told me all about the history of the building. When I asked him how he knew so much about it, Owen admitted that he had read up on the venue on the Internet. No wonder Owen always has something relevant and interesting to say. He prepares!

WORKING A ROOM

Most networking opportunities involve a room that you must maneuver through before ever reaching the small-talk stage. This has to be the least comfortable aspect of the venture, but it, too, can be made easier through preparation.

Business Cards

I have learned the hard way to never, ever go anywhere without business cards. Picture the indignity of being caught without one, and scribbling your details on someone else's card (or—still worse—on a cocktail napkin). How unprofessional does that look?! (A better way of coping, should this catastrophe ever happen to you, is to take the other person's card and email him the next day with your contact details. But you should be doing that anyway, of course; to capitalize on introductions, always follow up within 24 hours by confirming your pleasure in the conversation—and, ideally, by referring to something discussed at the time.)

Easy access to your business cards and the ability to retrieve them without loss of poise are essential. Similarly, find a place to neatly store the cards received. Fumbling around looks amateurish, while dredging out a crumpled heap of cards from the bottom of a bag is just plain embarrassing.

When you receive a business card, use it to write down the details of your discussion (alternatively, pull out your favorite gadget and take notes). It's even OK to do so in front of the other person if it directly relates to something you're planning to follow up on, or if there's an agreed-upon action to take. If that's not the case, make your notes afterwards—and as soon as possible. All great connecters return from networking events with notes on mutual interests and other pertinent information. And then, of course, they systematically record it and follow up on it.

The Name Badge

The power of a cheap plastic badge, oddly enough, should not be underestimated. Every boring seminar, kids' event, and PTA meeting has its badge, not for the benefit of the wearer, but to increase the chance that someone might remember you thereafter. I usually bring my own back-up badge, in case mine isn't on the table that greets me when I arrive, and I also try to use badges as an opportunity to provide the information that I really want others to have (depending on the event, that would be my title, my job, or my connection in terms of the function). This can also make it easier for people to start chatting to you.

It's important to put your badge on your *right* shoulder (as we shake hands we automatically glance into each other's right lapel), first ensuring that it's not obscured by your divinely long tresses or your collar. The idea is that when you shake hands with someone, his eyes will focus on your name. I always follow this rule. One final note: If you're female, *don't* put the badge on your cleavage—you want your name to be the memorable part of the encounter!

Size Up the Room and Choose a Target

Before walking into a room, first have a quick look around. Which position are you going to take? If there's no seating plan, choose a seat deliberately, not haphazardly. If there is someone you know you want to talk to, try to locate him or her, deciding in advance how and when you will approach.

If you find that you know no one, you should still choose a target, rather than waiting to be chosen. No one is ever offended (and many are actively relieved) upon being approached. If all else fails, head to the drinks or the buffet table to find someone in whom you have genuine interest. Most people at some point during the evening make their way to such spots—and they usually do so alone.

No Food, Thanks

We've all made the mistake of eating at a social/professional function simply because of nerves, because it provides something to do. Don't! Holding food can lead to a variety of awkward moments, as when you fumble a handshake or struggle to extract a business card... Further, holding a plate of food between yourself and the other person puts a barrier (subconscious, but powerful) between the two of you. So when you're at a venue on business, remind yourself that you're not there to eat! Eat before you leave home. (The food at these occasions almost invariably looks better than it tastes, anyway...)

Hover—To Break In

If you look around the room and everyone else seems engaged (unlikely, but possible), then choose a group that looks vaguely congenial, and hover. Nonverbal indications that you're interested are usually enough for someone within the group to make space for you; making eye contact with one individual will help. If they don't invite you to join in, you can still break in, but speak only at an appropriate moment (and at no great length, at first). If you've listened long enough to gauge the level of the conversation, you won't be intruding, and this should also prevent you from accidentally interrupting a deep or personal conversation. If you do accidentally intrude, excuse yourself ("So sorry; I didn't realize you were discussing private matters," not, "...your recent redundancy/love affair/takeover bid").

If you are able to ease yourself into the conversation, then address the speaker; otherwise you will be interrupting, and "stealing" his or her audience. Wait until the appropriate moment to introduce yourself. Once in the conversation, be careful not to take the spotlight; respond and contribute without taking over.

If there is someone you specifically want to meet who appears constantly engaged, try the hovering technique. If you aren't invited in, it's OK to ask permission to intrude from the other person (your non-target). Once this person says "yes," you can ease into conversation with the person you want to meet. You will be accepted because you have asked permission, but be careful not to exclude the person who allowed you to enter his or her discussion in the first place.

Making an Exit

People expect to be approached, but they also expect you to eventually end the encounter and buzz off—so don't feel obligated to continue the conversation beyond its natural length, and don't attach yourself like a limpet to any one person, either. A useful and elegant exit line is, "I've so enjoyed speaking with you, but I promised to look out for Elaine and I really must see if she made it." This allows you to affirm that you enjoyed the encounter and makes it clear that you are only moving on to fulfill a prior commitment. The perfect moment to exit is when someone else enters your group: You can introduce the person you've been speaking with and then pass the baton to the person next in line.

Remembering Names—and Other Information

We all forget things—especially people's names and information. To get around this, I've trained myself in a few memory tricks. I'm a visual person and always remember things best if I see them, so I always try to get the other person's card early in the conversation and study it. When I first practiced this technique I used to feel awkward during the pause, but it now feels natural and comfortable.

As I peruse the card, I will typically make a comment that permits me to read at least some of the information out loud. "Oh, that's an interesting spelling of "Alice"—A-L-Y-S-S-E. Is that a family tradition?" Asking a question provides me with that much more time to commit it to memory, while simultaneously pursuing small talk. "I see you have offices in San Francisco—such a great place! Have you ever been based there?"

Sometimes it's impossible for me to get the card, so I always repeat the name at least once when introduced. "Great to meet you, *George.*" If the name is unusual, I might also ask something about it, or how it is spelled. "Gundula. One of my best friends—she's German—is also named Gundula." If you are able to make the name itself a topic, this can also help you to recollect it. A very famous baseball player in the U.S., Don Mattingly, shares my maiden name, and in the States I was routinely asked whether he was a relation! He wasn't, and the people who inquired probably guessed that he wasn't, but I am certain that they asked the question to enhance their memory of my name, and maybe even to connect me (a lot of people do this) with baseball. Maybe they were picturing me at that moment in a baseball uniform!

There are loads of memory tricks, and many books available on the subject, so I won't waste time detailing the various methods. The key is to figure out the method that works best for you, and then apply it until it becomes habitual.

If you are lousy at remembering names, the next time you go to a function, pause before you enter and select a single memory technique—and throughout the event, remind yourself to use it. If you do this often enough, your chosen method will become so ingrained that you will eventually no longer have to think about it (much!).

Forgetting Names

If you do forget someone's name, take comfort—you're certainly not the first! It's generally wisest to own up to your slip and ask for the name again—unless your forgetfulness would somehow be perceived as insulting to the other person. Generally, it's far better to ask than to find yourself in the embarrassing position of not being able to make an introduction to a third party.

Sometimes you can sidestep the problem by nimbly reintroducing yourself. "Hi, I'm Jennifer Overhaus. We met last year at the Women In Technology luncheon." With luck, the other person will then respond by restating her name as well. If not, ask. If she doesn't remember you, then by all means provide information that might conceivably jog her memory. "Susan James introduced us, and you spoke about..."

If the person fails to remember you, this is *not* a rejection but an opportunity, especially if you can track down something from your previous conversation. "I seem to remember feeling very envious that you were just off on vacation to Mauritius. How did it go?" By using this technique you have not only set the conversational ball rolling, but also made the other person feel flattered and important.

Introduce Others

The most successful networkers are focused on bringing other people together. By introducing others you become their connection to each other, and they are grateful. You also become their host, and (by implication) the leader of the group—all from making a simple introduction.

Always be on the lookout for people to welcome into your conversations. When you do, introduce yourself and others. "Hi. I'm Susan, and this is Bill." (Note: You have just impressed Bill, your conversation partner, because you have remembered his name—maybe by using a newly learned memory trick!) "We were just talking about the great turnout they've attracted tonight."

The most successful networkers are focused on bringing other people together.

Tell It Again

Even better than making an introduction is giving someone the opportunity to tell a story. Let's say Bill was just telling you about the closing of his last deal. As you welcome someone else into the conversation, ask Bill (enthusiastically) to repeat his story. "Bill was just telling me about the deal he closed yesterday with Legal and General. It's absolutely fascinating." Just as a performer appreciates an encore, a storyteller will appreciate being asked to recount his tale. Especially if it's a story in which he shines!

This is an especially beneficial technique if the conversation is beginning to lag and you're not entirely sure how to move it forward again. At this point, you can make a graceful exit—assuming, of course, that the person you've just welcomed isn't someone you had hoped to meet yourself.

Maintain an Open Mind

The last thing to remember about making connections and working a room is this: Don't make up your mind too quickly about people. You never know where a conversation may lead! Thinking, "He can't help me... Talking with her is a waste of my time... He doesn't seem like someone who..." is likely to cause you to miss potential opportunities.

Give people a chance! Also, unless you're unusually brilliant at acting, your negative feelings will probably express themselves through body language and demeanor, and you don't want to come across that way.

Conversation Sequence

■ Open the conversation (the best openers are leading questions and relate to something in common—even if limited to the event itself).

■ Introduce yourself (on the basis of a prepared *and practiced* introduction).

   ■ Know where your introduction might lead, and have relevant anecdotes at hand.

   ■ Use anecdotes that can involve the other person—preferably turning the spotlight on him or her.

■ Inquire about the other person (ask questions!).

■ "Verbalize your listening": Follow up on what the other person says.

■ Reveal something about yourself to arouse interest; create the possibility of commonality, but avoid taking the spotlight (and definitely don't trump *his or her* story).

- Fill any pauses with small talk (the best topics are ones with the potential to generate commonality).

- Discover common interests. Create a placeholder for deepening rapport and cultivating a bond.

- Exchange cards. Offer something to follow up with ("I'll send you the details of that restaurant...").

- Make an exit (pass the baton, or use a prerehearsed exit line).

- Make notes of relevant information and action plans (on the back of the person's card or in your diary).

- Follow up within 24 hours.

Work the entire room with the same sequence. Try to avoid getting stuck with any one person longer than 10 minutes (unless he or she is a particularly top prospect).

THE KEY TO SUCCESS IS PREPARATION AND PRACTICE.

ON-LINE SOCIAL NETWORKING

This chapter would not be complete without addressing on-line social networking sites like Facebook, LinkedIn, or Twitter. Do they help us increase our business network? What about on-line forums that allow lawyers to provide advice? Or sites dedicated solely to lawyers, such as Legal OnRamp?

Obviously, joining these sites is a low-cost investment that allows us to simultaneously connect with a wide range of people. And if your clients are using these tools themselves, then you can employ the sites to get to know your clients better, and even give you insight into their needs and opportunities to fill those needs. Further, using such sites can be the quickest way—if not, perhaps, the most effective way—to interact with clients and to alert potential or current clients to information of value to them.

Using these sites effectively requires the right balance of self-promotion, information provision, and responding swiftly to what others in your business community might need from you. It certainly does take time and investment, but if you make the effort, you can potentially build relationships and increase your network—without even leaving your desk! But remember that your time should ideally be focused toward your target audience, not those who happen to be your best mates on Facebook...

YOUR ROOM IS UNLIMITED

While much of this chapter revolves around meeting people at formal occasions, application of these principles is not limited to such events. You can "work a room" anywhere, and your ability to do so is only restrained by your initiative and imagination.

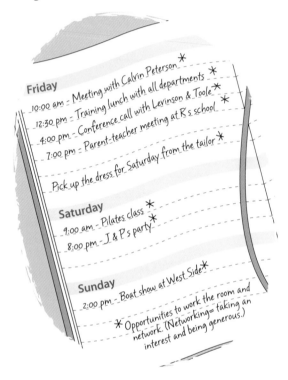

Friday
10:00 am - Meeting with Calvin Peterson ✻
12:30 pm - Training lunch with all departments ✻
4:00 pm - Conference call with Levinson & Toole ✻
7:00 pm - Parent-teacher meeting at R's school ✻

Pick up the dress for Saturday from the tailor ✻

Saturday
9:00 am - Pilates class ✻
8:00 pm - J & P's party ✻

Sunday
2:00 pm - Boat show at West Side ✻

✻ Opportunities to work the room and network. (Networking= taking an interest and being generous.)

Obviously you have to use good judgment, but places like trains, waiting rooms, airport lounges, and a local gym can be just as good as any official event. If you keep your eyes open for opportunities to make connections, you may end up in the right place at the right time—through resourcefulness, not serendipity. If so, remember these tips:

1. Think about all the things we examined in Chapter 8 ("Positive Impact") and make sure you are communicating with your posture, body language, and voice a confident and friendly image—along with the brand you want to convey.

2. Your communications should be supported by these feel-good factors: a positive approach, enthusiasm, and occasional smiles (Chapter 6).

3. Maintain a host mentality and focus on the other person's needs, to empower him or her.

4. Be interested, not interesting: Focus on the other person, and choose to listen. Prove this by following up on the speaker's statements and asking pertinent questions. If you can also acknowledge or compliment, you'll make the other person feel important and appreciated.

5. Self-disclose enough to create commonality and to deepen your connection with the person you're speaking to. However, don't disclose too deeply at first, and don't swipe the spotlight for more than a moment.

6. Before you attend any formal networking event, understand your objective(s) and prepare.

   a. Research attendees you may want to meet (and, if appropriate, contact them).

   b. Prepare and practice your introduction, as well as related follow-up anecdotes and ways you can involve other people.

   c. Compose and practice conversational openers, small-talk topics, and anecdotes.

   d. Plan several intelligent-sounding exit lines.

7. When working a room, make sure of the following:

   a. Have easy access to your business cards and a safe place to store cards received.

   b. Have a badge that achieves its sole purpose and objective: giving others the best possible chance of remembering you.

   c. Choose your targets, and hover if necessary. You must expect to approach complete strangers, remembering that they're usually happy for you to do so (you must also graciously accept introductions to complete strangers who introduce themselves to you).

   d. Whenever possible, make introductions, which elevate your status and make you the connecter.

8. Always focus on remembering names and any information people volunteer. (If this requires you to take notes, then take notes!) Remember, the information you're given is your placeholder for connecting further, and this is your real goal: to make a connection and move forward, ultimately, into a networking relationship.

9. Practice all these things in your day-to-day activities. Wherever you are, and whomever you meet ("Hi, good-buddy-whose-name-I've-temporarily-forgotten-but-who's-selling-me-my-first-cappuc-cino-of-the-day!"), you can find opportunities to practice your conversational skills.

By polishing these until they become natural, you should find that you're better able to leverage your skills in more formal settings—something absolutely essential to any successful legal career.

Chapter Seventeen

Winning and Developing Business

As we examined briefly in Chapter 9, the most crucial goal with regard to networking relationships (especially client relationships) is to cultivate trust. We do this through the sequence of steps represented in this diagram.

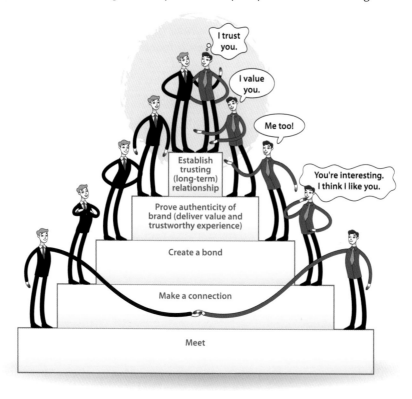

Most of our previous examination of relationship-building has focused on the first two steps of the process: connecting, and creating a bond. When you achieve the third step—proving the authenticity of your brand—the client will trust you to deliver, and you'll find (what a relief!) that you no longer have to sell your capability. However, this is only the *penultimate* step in the sequence, because your true goal is to realize a long-term relationship that enables both sides to count on the deepest level of trust and loyalty.

By "long-term relationship" I mean a situation in which your concern for your client is based on the relationship and your actions further his or her interests as well as those of the partnership. Of course, this level of commitment goes far beyond merely securing work or billable hours, and the client recognizes this to be the case. It's possible that such a relationship would include every-thing from baby- or dog-sitting to furthering the other person's career—con-ceivably, at the expense of your own.

In previous chapters I compared networking relationships to friendships, because in both cases we meet, connect, and (ideally) bond through commonal-ity. Friendships are sustained by consistent and reliable proofs of trustworthi-ness, and for a friendship to grow both parties must be open and honest. They must also feel secure enough to express differing opinions and desires. (OK, you love *cordon bleu*, she's into takeaway Chinese. You can live with that.) However, despite potentially opposing agendas, each friend is rooted in the knowledge that the other has his or her best interests at heart and—still more crucially—that the relationship itself is far more important than any short-term pursuit or advantage. There is compromise, collaboration, give-and-take—and trust.

When you achieve this level of trust with your clients, you reap considerable benefits. Here are just a few:

Client	Lawyer
Thinks of you first when information or potential work arises	Can ask for information or a favor—can even ask for work directly
Is willing to sole-source work to you (because he or she no longer questions your capability or your fees, and believes you to be transparent and honest)	Doesn't have to compete on, or sell, capability or billable rates/price
Seeks and relies upon your advice	Can afford to be open with advice, even when well aware that it may not be what the client wants to hear
Listens amenably	Can make recommendations and have real influence
Is open about his or her issues and requirements	Can optimally meet the client's needs because the client feels that he can trust you with *all* the information

My client base has always been made up of a small number of organizations who give me repeat business; even when I was an associate it was generally acknowledged inside my firm that if I worked with a client I could usually bring in more work from the same source. For a long time I assumed that this was the result of my superior performance and the client's view of me as an exceptional lawyer(!). It was only when I became a partner and began to examine client relationships and my own business that I realized that my technical skills were a very minor part of the equation. The real reason clients were retaining me was that they believed I cared about them and that I was motivated by obtaining the best deal for them. That was precisely what I did care about; taking people for granted is luckily not part of my character.

Many of my previous clients are now friends, and it's both surprising and gratifying to hear their original impressions of me. Apparently, in the first project meetings I became a part of their team straight away, by using "we" rather than "you" and by convincing them of my passion to support and further their interests. By doing so I gained their trust and admiration, convincing them early on that their deal (whatever it was) would be vitally enhanced by my participation. Theodore Roosevelt wrote, "Nobody cares how much you know, until they know how much you care"—which I think puts it brilliantly.

Nobody cares how much you know, until they know how much you care. —Theodore Roosevelt

None of my actions were calculated, but—fortunately for me—they were right on target. Caring (and *showing* how much you care) automatically builds trust and elevates your position in the eyes of your clients. So let's take a look at some of the ways to do this.

- **Deliver.** Pivotal to demonstrating your dedication is delivering on promises and providing exceptional service. (For able lawyers this almost goes without saying.)

- **Communicate.** Taking on an assignment and disappearing until it's delivered may well be satisfactory service, but it can't be considered exceptional. Telling the client how and when you will deliver and keeping him up to date on your progress is a simple courtesy that can take your work to the next level of client satisfaction. Even if you haven't been able to do anything on the project at all, an email admitting that your child's home sick from school or your washing machine is on life support is always appreciated, and even helps to make you more of a real person to the client—as long as your excuse isn't stupid (as in, "we had to put down one of the goldfish") and as long as it does not convey to the client "you are not a priority."

- **Return phone calls promptly.** Not responding to client messages ASAP subliminally suggests "I'm too busy with other clients/projects to worry about you" or (still worse) "You're not all that important to me." Both these messages break the number-one rule of people skills and client development. If you're genuinely too crushingly busy to even return a call, then at least send an explanatory email or have a secretary send word of your next window of availability.

- **Think "outside the box" of direct client instructions.** I once did significant due diligence for a client, looking at their internal IT systems with the view to outsourcing. In the end the corporation curtailed its outsourcing plans, but only after my team had run up quite a bill. On my own initiative, we took the information we had acquired and turned it into a report on how the client could make its own systems more efficient and cost-effective—all with no charge to the client, and with relatively little trouble to my team. That report told the corporation that we were looking out for its interests, not merely our own. Ironically, the report generated more work when the client requested additional study and several formal presentations—which *were* chargeable. In the end the client decided to outsource after all, and we were perfectly situated to help, having demonstrated our unique value, keenness, authority, and client-consciousness.

■ **Get feedback.** Making assumptions can lead to misunderstandings, and arrogantly considering your work to be innately satisfactory is simply naïve. It may *feel* risky to ask recent clients about their perception of your work, but failing to do so is actually far riskier. Furthermore, asking your clients for feedback gives you the chance to correct any misapprehensions and to convey that you value their opinions as well as their custom. Again, we're back to people skills: nurturing people's need to feel important. Here are two simple questions to ask your clients, directly or indirectly:

- ■ What do you like/not like about the way I've delivered so far?

- ■ How can I make things easier for you? (Note that this question cuts to the chase, because our job is to facilitate our clients' roles by streamlining their reviews, analysis, decisions, and workloads.)

Client feedback is critical, but it will be useless if you ask for it but fail to put it into practice! If the client says, "Your work is fantastic, but I thought it would arrive more quickly," it's your job to make sure that the next stage of the project arrives at crack of dawn. This is because (within reason, of course) the client is always right. (On the other hand, if the objection is, "I expected it to arrive at noon and it showed up two minutes and 39 seconds late," you are entitled to decide that this particular client has serious issues!)

If you are hesitant to ask for feedback, keep in mind these things, which are statistically proven: Most clients who perceive poor service will walk away without giving *you* the reason, but they will very likely express their dissatisfaction to someone else—who just might be a target client of yours. Even satisfied clients are not necessarily loyal clients; a high percentage of satisfied clients will use a different lawyer the next time they require legal services. This means you should also be determining whether your clients are really loyal by asking them, "What is your level of satisfaction?" "Do you plan to use my services again?"—or, still more tellingly, "Would you recommend my services to someone else?"

■ **Understand their business.** You must "speak their language" and see your client's problems and opportunities from the standpoint of their particular business objectives. If you don't already know what those are, then ask questions or do research until you do. It is not—repeat, not—nosy to adopt an attitude of inquiring about your client's business. As an absolute minimum, with every client, you should be aware of:

- The structure of the organization, and where your contacts and their divisions fit into that framework.

- The products and services of your client, including those sections that you may not be dealing with personally.

- The client's main suppliers and customers.

- The client's main competitors(!).

- The client's market share.

- The client's current state of profitability.

- The makeup, strengths, weaknesses, current trends, and likely future of the industry.

- How your projects fit into the client's overall organizational objectives.

Understanding your client's business enables you to provide far better legal services and (still more critically) to position yourself as a business partner rather than a mere legal advisor. It also effectively demonstrates that you are client-focused and willing to invest time and effort on the client's issues. Further, when you know something about your client's business you can use it long-term to add value to your service—and short-term, to help you make intelligent small talk. For example, if you learn that the client's stock price just soared, you might casually mention it. This is nothing special in and of itself, but think of

the potential impact when you weave your knowledge into your proposed solution: "In light of the firm's stock market surge late yesterday, it could be beneficial to..."

Reading legal journals and keeping up your continuing education is obviously essential to your expertise, but knowing your clients' businesses and taking the time to read their industry journals can provide added value. I mentioned in the context of building a brand that as a technology lawyer I spent considerable time learning the products and business of my IT clients (and even taking computer courses—which, believe me, are *not* really my thing!). Yet without my doing so, my brand as a technology lawyer would have felt dishonest to me, or at least incomplete; and I could never have negotiated so strongly on behalf of my clients, or helped them to the degree required in the pursuit of their business objectives, without the technical and industry knowledge I'd acquired. (Although one of my partners did point out to me that leaving *Distributed Infrastructure for Dummies* sitting on my shelf for all to see might present a mixed message!)

But I digress. How else can you show clients that you really care?

■ **Learn your clients' personal interests.** As discussed in previous chapters, the starting point for making connections and creating bonds with clients (or, in fact, with anybody) is to become interested in their issues and to listen and learn about the things most important *to them.* With this in mind, you need to understand your clients' personal objectives and how your services might fit within that purpose. There is a critical distinction between the needs of the organization and the needs of the client, and attending to both is important for developing the relationship (although not to the extent of breaching a fiduciary duty toward your "true" client). You should be able to answer the following questions:

■ Who is your contact's direct boss, and what is your contact's reporting line?

■ Who are the contact's supporters and adversaries?

■ When, and from what position, was your contact last promoted?

■ What career path does your contact probably envision?

■ How do any of the projects you're working on further your contact's career path and/or personal objectives?

■ What can you do to help your contact on a personal level? (And no, advising him to quit smoking or dump his wife is NOT what we're after here...) For example, your contact might well be concerned with increasing company revenues and the stock price (organizational needs), but he's likely to care about that price much more in relation to his own shares in the company, or with regard to a possible promotion based on its strength (personal needs). Appreciating the distinction gives you the insight to better meet all of the client's expectations.

■ **Know and promote the right objectives.** When you thoroughly understand your clients' business and objectives, then you can absorb their issues quickly and advocate with their perspective in mind. This is the starting point for building a completely trusting relationship. You can only build a relationship when you are working from your client's perspective—not from your own, and not from what you think the client's *should* be. (Naturally, once trust has been established, you could conceivably influence him toward a different perspective, if necessary.)

■ **Become part of the team.** Rather than casting yourself as an external advisor, make it your goal to become part of the client's team, working with your contacts as co-workers and with a collaborative mindset. Whenever possible, work on-site as a recognized part of the organization—even if being on-site means creating reasons for being there, and even if you do so without charge. (It's amazing how much more likely you are to be rehired if an unspoken perception exists that you're already part of the scenery!)

■ **Take the initiative to provide value.** In Chapter 15 ("Networking") I emphasized the importance of sharing information. This is absolutely critical, and the key is to do it on an ongoing basis, not just during current projects or during periods when the client is giving you work. Your mindset, initiative, and willingness to provide value cannot be based on a "you-scratch-my-back, I'll-scratch-yours" mentality. Remember, client relationships are about the long term, and the investments we make *must* be made on that basis. (And, as mentioned above, bear in mind that you're actually on the same team!)

■ **Transparency.** Be open with your clients and transparent about the way you provide your services. Work with them to come up with the most favorable approach, and be honest enough to admit it when you may *not* be the best person for a particular job. It surprises me how many high-level lawyers lack the confidence to do this! I once suggested that my client use a different firm because mine couldn't provide the particular employment expertise required for a certain transaction. My client so appreciated my honesty and disinterestedness that he requested that I remain involved to provide high-level advice and to manage the firm who did deal with those employment issues. (In fact, you should relish any situation that allows you to clarify exactly what you don't do, because it reinforces what you *can* do, thereby strengthening your brand.)

■ **Giving advice.** This is a very tricky one. The way you give advice can either cultivate or kill off your client's trust—regardless of whether or not your advice is sound. When you give advice, first consider the personalities, emotions, politics, and business/personal agendas of the client, and then tweak your advice to suit. It's no good telling Mr. Know-It-All that his project lacks vision, even if it's positively astigmatic; you have to present it as, "This is fantastic and even inspiring, but have you thought of trying...?"

The way you give advice can either cultivate or kill off your client's trust—regardless of whether or not your advice is sound.

Here are a few other examples:

■ Sean was a bank's newly appointed project manager, with a strong background in IT. He knew his technical stuff inside out but had never led a large project before. He was feeling seriously insecure, although he didn't want to admit as much. He needed me to provide him with a project management roadmap and to demonstrate how to lead a deal—all without undermining his position in the eyes of his new colleagues. It was my job to make him look in control, and in doing just that, I gained his confidence and trust.

■ Ian hired me to negotiate a single systems integration contract for his large retailing company. However, once involved I discovered that the company had significant inconsistencies in the terms of its major software contracts; in fact, they were in breach of the agreements, which was bound to cause critical problems with the impending deal. I had to demonstrate that resolving these (past) issues was far better than ignoring them, and I had to do this without being perceived as (a) creating problems or (b) being irritating or (c) blowing the issue out of all proportion. Clients want lawyers to fix their problems rather than add to them!

To resolve the issue for this client, I had to work closely with the head of purchasing and the COO—Ian's colleagues—and the people who had been involved in negotiating those original contracts that were proving to be the source of the problem. Now this was a very nervy situation, since my uncovering the problem implied that they'd done something wrong. So I had to give my advice in a way that demonstrated that I was acting as their ally—and that I wasn't some young hotshot lawyer on a faultfinding mission.

Rob was the project manager of a large outsourcing project whose boss had promised him a large bonus (and a promotion) if a certain deal was completed by the end of the year. So Rob didn't much care whether the contractual terms stood up in the long run—he just wanted it sewn up by the date designated. So he never relayed accurate news to the board, but instead only gave them the sugar-coated (mis)information: "This deal is right on target to complete by year's end."

Rob was the original nightmare client, because (above all else) I want the deals I advise on to be *right*, yet I knew that arguing with Rob would get us absolutely nowhere. Instead I gently demonstrated how meeting the original timetable would result in a disastrous deal and the—eventual—destruction of his just-launched career. In the end, we worked together to take the difficult news to the board, and we gained the support of his boss and those at the top of the organization. Rob received his promotion and bonus on the basis of a solid deal rather than on meeting an artificial deadline. Simultaneously, I achieved my objective (a deal done right!), but in a way that made me Rob's ally.

Aside from giving advice in the right way, the other thing to remember is to guard against (a) acting more important than the client or (b) obliquely criticizing the client—especially if something has gone wrong previously. (Remember Chapter 6, "People Skills"!) With that said, however, there are some clients who expect and even prefer to receive advice directly and without sugar-coating, even if it might be immensely critical. My client Colin always wants the bottom-line answer—although, as a fierce Driver, he then mulls it over and decides for himself whether he wants to take it or not. Silvi, a very different client, also wants a direct answer, but for a different reason: She wants me to make the decision for her!

A word of warning: After advising clients on *ad hoc*, discrete matters, lawyers tend to put the matter on the back burner and move on to the next client.

Instead, *check to see* whether your advice has been implemented or not, and—if so—whether it's been successful. Following up has two benefits: It shows your clients that you care (in an easy and effective way), and it helps you to improve your advice in the future. It's also a good way to stay in touch with the client and keep the relationship from becoming dormant.

> ## Pause for thought:
> When you deliver brilliant advice, are you focused on the experience you are giving the client? What emotions do you evoke? How does the client feel when he or she walks away from you? Do you *really* understand what is at stake for the client—personally, professionally, and on an organizational level? Are you effectively dealing with the politics, emotions, and personalities of the individuals involved? What are your client's *real* needs (not the ones *you desire* for him or her)? And how do the answers to these questions factor into your advice?
>
> These are the questions you should be asking yourself—that is, if you want to go beyond mere client satisfaction toward long-term, trusting, loyal relationships.

SELLING

At times, you will have to sell yourself or your services to new connections or to people in your network with whom you have yet to develop long-term, trusting relationships. In these situations you will have to undergo the typical selling process, which may involve formal RFPs and competitive selection methods. Although the exercise is more constricted, the goal is precisely the same as it is with networking and established relationships. When you pitch for work, your goal is to make a connection; create a bond; prove the authenticity of your brand (i.e., your value and trustworthiness); and convey that your goal is to establish a long-term relationship based on trust.

We're often so focused on impressing people that we forget what clients really want: a trusted advisor who meets their needs. And, of course, different clients will have distinct needs, which your brand should ideally (and authentically!) address.

Often we fail to support client needs because we confuse what our clients want with what we want for them (or for ourselves), or even with what we would prefer to deliver. One firm I know, with the genuine intention of meeting a large client's needs, chose someone from within the firm to be the client's relationship partner without involving the client in the decision. Predictably, the client was unhappy with the choice and insulted by the firm's dictatorial attitude. So if you *really* think about your clients' needs as your priority, you can stand out from the pack!

Regardless of what specific value clients are looking for, they want a trusting relationship because they need to feel an innate certainty about the value being delivered. So how can we go about reassuring them?

There are three stages to the selling process. The first two are filters: the rational filter and the emotional filter. We have to make it through these two stages to enter the final phase of competing for work.

1st filter:
Rational selection

2nd filter:
Emotional selection

FINAL STAGE:
Winning business
Proving the value and
trustworthiness of your brand

The first filter, rational selection, involves a fairly bald and academic assessment of whether your professional credentials meet the perceived requirements of the project. If your academic qualifications, the reputation of your firm, and your individual expertise are reckoned adequate, you obtain the right to move to the next stage.

If you *do* advance to the next stage, credentials generally no longer play such a significant role. In fact, highlighting them as you move into the second stage can actually backfire, because to progress through the next filter you must first make a personal connection with the potential client. Academic supremacy will never supersede the need for emotional connection. So (yes, you guessed it!) we're back to people skills: You must connect by being interested, *not* interesting. Don't expound on your unique qualifications—focus on the client, ask pertinent questions, and solicit in-depth information to explore what his or her situation, concerns, and problems might be.

Academic supremacy will never supersede the need for emotional connection.

As part of this "connecting" stage, you must listen carefully and absorb the information provided. You have to convince the clients that you're dedicated to solving their problems and to helping them perform more strongly. Mere professional expertise is not enough! Later, if you move on to the proposal stage, you have to further prove beyond a doubt that you deserve your clients' trust.

If you're yet to be persuaded that expertise is not the definitive differentiator, consider this recent comment from one general counsel—a man who hires lawyers from top-tier international firms: "For the most part, the difference between any single lawyer or firm that I hire is inconsequential because they are all similar firms, providing the same services, in the same way. Which cleaning firm we use has more impact, because their differential is more visible." Further discussion with this general counsel revealed his frustration that one law firm after another has paraded their similar (if not equal) credentials without showing how they are different from all the others. This goes back to the principle that should drive your brand: *Compete on what makes you uniquely valuable*—and usually that will *not* be your credentials, firm history, practice group structure, office locations, or international presence!

"...similar firms, providing the same services, in the same way."

In common with networking activities, the proposal process requires that you demonstrate genuine concern, and I reiterate that this *cannot be faked*. If you are not genuinely interested in the client's objectives and in forging a long-term relationship, your insincerity will become apparent sooner or later, after which point even the most adept salesmanship in the world will fall flatter than a sunken pancake.

The stages of the pitching process overlap the networking trust sequence, as follows:

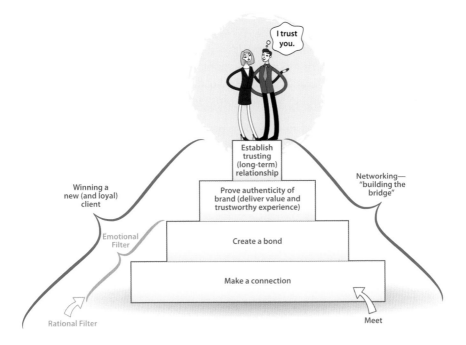

About the time I first qualified at law, my best friend from high school went into real estate. At the time I didn't really understand the true process of selling; I still associated it with a dire telemarketing job I'd held briefly over the holidays—in other words, with intruding on people when they preferred not to be disturbed, endeavoring to sell them something they had no interest in receiving. With this mindset, I decided that Debbie's choice of profession was my worst nightmare, but I still had to concede that she was suited to it. Debbie is the original Connecter: the most bubbly, extroverted, and enthusiastic person I know. Not having that personality type myself, I felt comforted by the belief that my own chosen career involved intellectual challenge rather than selling.

How wrong I was! In the end, my success hinged on exactly the same criterion as Debbie's: the ability to sell! And that ability boils down to one starting point, which is identical in almost *any* modern career: to our belief in our "unique product"—in the case of lawyers, ourselves—and to our ability to persuade clients that, without our product at their disposal, they'd be worse off.

During my career, my team was generally recognized as unique because we provided advice in a way our competition did not. (They focused on traditional legal analysis, but we could advise on the whole of a commercial deal—including business strategy, pricing structure, and technology decisions.) In essence, in addition to our deep legal experience we could act as business consultants, and by doing that we delivered real bottom-line business results that other firms could not promise. I therefore felt extremely frustrated if any client failed to understand this. I even suspected that clients who did not retain us were risking the success of their deals. You may be thinking, "Wow, this woman's ego was seriously out of control!"—and you might even be right—but my self-belief still won me lots of work. In fact, that self-belief did most of my selling for me—because when I convinced my clients, I proved not only the authenticity of my brand but also my commitment to their interests.

In fact, a passionate belief in your own brand is your greatest sales tool and does more to win over any client than methodology, closing techniques, or any other psychological strategy. You can only truly convince the client of the authenticity of your brand if you passionately believe in it yourself. With that said, you must also recognize (however upsetting you might find it!) that your clients only care about their own perspective and any possible benefit that accrues to them. So you must determine precisely what they value and which benefit(s) they're looking for, and sell your brand *from that viewpoint*—otherwise you're wasting both time and energy. Remember, the only opinion that *really* counts is the client's.

Persuading From an Innate Understanding of Personality

Just as we have to deliver to our clients from a strong understanding of personalities, we must also sell to our prospects in light of their particular temperaments: the way in which they make decisions and prefer to buy. When we do this, we communicate and persuade in alignment with their personal decision-making concerns.

Obviously, to tailor your proposals most persuasively you must first determine as quickly as possible your target client's personality type—preferably prior to your first meeting. Some clues to consider in personality evaluations include the client's manner; style of dress; favored communication methods; word choice; and overall attitude.

Let's look at how some of these things reveal the four personality types that we looked at in Chapter 4: Connecter, Driver, Perfectionist, and Moderate.

CONNECTER	
Manner:	Most casual. Sits relaxed in a chair—even with feet up on the desk. Conversation is light and relaxed, interlaced with anecdotes and small talk. Talks quickly and speaks before thinking or while thinking. Office is casual, personal, and probably on the messy side.
Dress:	Casual; bright colors; likes to stand out (vibrant ties!)
Preferred Method of Communication:	In person or by telephone
Words Used:	"I feel..." "My team..." "I'm excited by the opportunity..."
Attitude:	Optimistic, can-do, certain
Buying Mindset:	Wants immediate action and results Wants to feel good Quick and easy Wants whatever is sleek and aesthetically satisfying Cutting edge Impressive client list can help to persuade (seeks being in the "in crowd")
Decision-Making:	Spontaneous and emotional
Best Pitch:	High level; not persuaded by detail. Ask questions and keep him involved and entertained, with pictures, charts, and a fast-paced presentation.

DRIVER	
Manner:	Businesslike; office displays awards and achievements
Dress:	Formal; dressed for success
Preferred Method of Communication:	When possible, through the secretary
Words Used:	"I need to push this through…"
	"We need to win…"
	"Our competition involves…"
	"The solution must be…"
	"I see what you are saying."
	"Show me!"
Attitude:	Assertive, positive, authoritative
Buying Mindset:	Prefers clear benefits and results
	Wants to achieve the best solution, as recognized *externally*
	Most persuadable with examples of other successes
Decision-Making:	Quick, rational
Best Pitch:	Fast-paced; keep it moving. Bottom-line results speak volumes.
	Will look at details—but only briefly.

PERFECTIONIST	
Manner:	Most formal. Sits straight in chair with erect posture. Office is neat and tidy, revealing little. Speaks thoughtfully; considers each angle before offering an opinion or a comment.
Dress:	Formal, meticulous
Preferred Method of Communication:	Written
Words Used:	"I think…" "What do the numbers/details prove?" "There are several possible steps." "The analysis suggests…"
Attitude:	Pessimistic (the sky is falling!)
Buying Mindset:	Wants the best process, with optimal long-term results; values astute analysis Most likely to value credentials
Decision-Making:	Logical
Best Pitch:	Thorough and detailed analysis. Values written follow-up (this personality type is the most likely to actually read what you write!).

MODERATE	
Manner:	Relaxed
Dress:	On the casual side; rather unostentatious
Preferred Method of Communication:	One-on-one (or written, if strongly introverted)
Words Used:	"Our team...with support...I'm seeking advice about..."
Attitude:	Unassuming, even submissive
Buying Mindset:	Looking for natural and mutual collaboration; solution should be easy and nonconfrontational
Decision-Making:	Least decisive; naturally cautious
Best Pitch:	Lead him (or her) to conclusions, but never get pushy; allow him the time he needs. Remember, Moderates may seem passive but can be excessively stubborn once their minds are made up. Make it abundantly clear that you're there to help, not to sell. This type of manager is particularly wary of being taken advantage of.
	(Consider inviting one of his more decisive colleagues to encourage him toward a decision? Or consider a hunger strike?!)

Everyone Wants a Personal Benefit

When pitching to a prospect, your principal objective must be to demonstrate the value you add to the project, but if you can show a prospect a *personal* benefit you will exponentially increase your chances of success. (Remember, everyone is always thinking, at least subconsciously, "What's in this for me?") For example, if you're dealing with genuine Connecters, you know that they want to have fun and be admired as the born performers they are, so you need to suggest to them that working with you will deliver just that. Similarly, if your client is a Driver you know that he prefers to lead, and if you can improve his status you'll be pressing all the right buttons.

This goes back to the distinction between organizational and personal needs: While clients should (and probably intend) to hire you strictly on the basis of organizational goals, they will still be influenced by personal motivations.

Be Curious

You may not always be able to instantly pinpoint a target client's personality or the benefit he's seeking, but it's still your immediate goal to smoke it out. So pay close attention until you're pretty confident about his or her individual perspective, particular concerns, and "to-do" list. It's a good idea to avoid giving your own opinions until you've ascertained the client's viewpoint. Ask questions and keep your antennae out, watching especially for what is left *unsaid*. If you ramble on about your credentials or about benefits irrelevant to the prospect, you may hinder—or even abort—your ultimate objective.

We've already considered various ways of eliciting answers (see the chapters on networking), and the same principles apply in a selling situation. Open-ended questions work best and provide you with the most information. Some strong, if obvious, candidates include...

- "Why?"
  - "Why is that important to you?"
  - "Why is that a problem for you?"
  - "Why do you want to achieve that?"
- "What's the reason for that?"
- "Can you fill me in on the background here?"
- "How have you approached this issue previously?"
- "What do *you* perceive as the ideal solution?"

Ideally, let the client answer in full before interjecting (this is tough if you are a Connecter or a Driver), and only speak when a follow-up question is necessary. Avoid making snap assumptions; asking for confirmation is a far better approach. ("Fine, now let me be sure I have this straight: You want me to investigate the jurisdictional implications of offshore bank embezzlement? As I see it, that would involve these steps...")

The Purpose: Discover Their Problem

The purpose of your curiosity is to discover the problem (read, opportunity!) from the client's perspective, and then to demonstrate not only an understanding of the situation but a genuine sympathy for the client's objectives. Only by first agreeing on a common problem can you begin to offer creative solutions. If you've listened well enough to perceive the case exactly as the prospective client does, it should be relatively simple to suggest a compelling solution.

Offer Solutions

Once you've identified the problem, avoid jumping to a conclusion or aggressively pushing your preferred solution. Instead, you should collaborate to structure the optimal result, allowing the client to "co-own" the strategy, whatever it is. For example:

> *Agree on the issue.* "So, it seems to me that your core problem
> is that you have two service providers working independently,
> with neither taking full responsibility for the deficiencies on
> the ground. Is that how you see it?"
>
> [Probably "Yes!"]
>
> *Establish the optimal result.* "All right, good. On that basis, what is
> your preferred outcome? Keeping both providers, or retaining one
> to provide all the services?"
>
> [Probable answer: "One would be organizationally optimal,
> but impractical; since one provider is so specialized, we might
> still need both."]
>
> *Confirm.* "Fine. Now, as I see it, the result you're looking for
> involves keeping both providers but appointing one as guarantor
> for the whole?"
>
> [Probable answer: "Yes."]

Propose the Right Action

Only after the desired result is confirmed should you propose action. Too often lawyers charge in before they've even bothered to ascertain the client's desired objective ("Right, in that case there's no question that we should immediately..." or, "Listen, in the case of MNO International we did..."). Believe me, there's no faster way for the client to decide you're incompetent than to go this route. (Actually, competence is not even the issue; you've just run afoul of the principle that the way you give advice is just as critical as the advice itself.) Only by first agreeing on the objective should you follow up with your suggested approach. This allows you to do two things simultaneously: propose a plan—and close the deal.

Transparency

I once followed all these steps only to have my potential client determine that he had three separate problems, each with a separate desired result. At that point I said, "Look, I have to be honest here. I can help with your third problem, but I'm *not* the ideal person to help you sort out the first two." In that single moment, he put his total faith in my brand and trusted that I could help him with all his worries. Remember, you do more for your brand by making it clear what you *don't* do than by trying to be a "super-lawyer" who pleases everyone.

Listening

The critical component involved in getting to this stage is listening, because everything needs to be aligned with what the client really wants to achieve. Only once you've dug deep enough can you begin to tailor your proposed solution to his or her requirements. This may seem like strange advice to fellow lawyers: "Isn't it our job to tell the client what he can, or should try to, achieve?" Well, possibly. Sometimes. But often merely listening sells our expertise best. In fact, sales training literature and statistics show that the most successful sellers spend 70 percent of a pitch listening and only 30 percent talking.

The term "listen" isn't entirely accurate, because by listening I really mean "data gathering." For example, before even thinking about an action plan, you should be able to answer the following questions:

- How does the prospective client currently meet his legal needs in relation to your proposal?

- Does this appear satisfactory to him?

- If yes, what makes you different? In other words, why should he (or she) switch to you?

- If the current arrangement doesn't appear satisfactory to the client, where does it fall short? What would the optimal legal advisor/ arrangement be for this particular prospective client?

- Is there a way you can meet the perceived need?

  - In such an event, what would your biggest obstacle be? Can you mitigate that obstacle? If so, how?

- What is your unique proposition?

  - Is this something of direct relevance to the prospective client? Does it entirely address his concerns and achieve the result he wants?

  - If it is relevant, how does that factor into your solution—for example, does it outweigh, or merely balance out, any obstacle cited above?

- How can you best demonstrate what you hope to deliver?

- How can your client measure your delivery? (That is, how can you ultimately prove that you *have* delivered on your promise?) This is a difficult, but absolutely critical, question for us as lawyers because often clients can't evaluate whether we have delivered on the technical side. (*We* know that we sweated over every clause in the contract and that it's watertight, but does the client know this?) So sometimes we have to come up with a different benchmark for measuring our performance.

A Common Mistake: Overemphasizing Your Credentials

One of the biggest (and most common) mistakes in a proposal is to waste time emphasizing your personal experience or your firm's credentials. Remind yourself that credentials are useful only for the first filter, that of rational selection; it's not the basis on which most clients select their lawyers.

Remind yourself that credentials are useful only for the first filter, that of rational selection; it's not the basis on which most clients select their lawyers.

Sales jargon speaks in terms of features and benefits. Successful marketers don't sell features, they sell benefits. Credentials are a feature, yet the value you provide—solving a problem, increasing revenues or business, or mitigating the consequences of a lawsuit—is a benefit, and that's what you should focus on in your allotted talk-time.

Having said that, there are three exceptions to this rule:

- When the client still needs to be convinced of your credentials.

- When a specific experience can be used as evidence of a precise benefit you offer ("Last year we solved a very similar problem for our clients XYZ, which resulted in..."). Avoid sweeping generalizations ("No worries, we've done this type of work for loads of clients!"); remember that generalizations are normally unhelpful—especially when dealing with Perfectionists or Drivers.

- If your credentials really and truly are unique. But don't lay claim to this one dishonestly, or you risk relying on a potentially detrimental strategy.

Objections

People will typically do anything to (a) gain a tangible benefit or (b) avoid a potentially nerve-racking situation. Clients are no exception. If you've followed the steps outlined above, then your proposal should provide them with a clear benefit, and any remaining objections will be anxiety-based—anxiety that your price isn't guaranteed, that you won't deliver as promised, or that you're not as brilliant as you appear to be. Therefore, your first job is to mitigate these concerns.

If you're honest with yourself, you can probably predict your prospect's doubts—and if you're *really* truthful, you may even have similar anxieties roosting somewhere in the back of your mind. How *will* you deliver? Are you certain that your colleagues will be available when you need their help? Can you *really* meet the schedule, within the promised fee parameters? This is when your goal of transparency kicks in—which, in practice, means frankly acknowledging your doubts to the client. By acknowledging your concerns and reassuringly discussing the solutions, you can alleviate the client's anxiety and at the same time convey your own honesty and trustworthiness.

Fees

Most clients are concerned about fees—and they have every right to be! Issues about fees should always be addressed honestly, up front, to avoid problems down the road. The four biggest lessons I have learned are...

a. Clients will sometimes forget the final price paid, but they will *never* forget or forgive poor work.

b. Avoid financial surprises. It may be distinctly painful to contact your client to say, "Sorry, but I feel you ought to know that our bill is now roughly five times the national debt of Guatemala," but this can still be one of the most astute phone calls you will ever make. The short-term discomfort of making the call will be negligible in comparison to the long-term consequences of not doing so.

c. Be aware that clients who are *not* looking for a long-term, trusting relationship will

- Nickel-and-dime every transaction and document;

- Require excessive services for free (you know the type: They call all the time, demanding service "immediately," only to later complain about the bill);

- Continuously shop each project and give out only bits and pieces (the "crumbs").

Attempting to build a trusting relationship with these clients is nearly impossible, and trying to do so can be a frustrating waste of valuable time.

d. The best price scenario is not one that is "won" by either you or your client, but one that furthers your joint objective of a long-term, trusting relationship. There's nothing worse than leaving a client feeling ripped off—except having the same hard-done-by feeling oneself. Fair trade is not just for developing countries!

A final point: Many lawyers and law firms are feeling the pressure because clients are treating legal services as commodities (e.g., using online procurement tools), so fees are being squeezed. But this takes us right back to our number-one rule of marketing: Pricing only becomes the determining factor when everyone is competing on the same thing. When you provide something that is important to your clients, and do it uniquely, your pricing will not be the compelling issue.

> *Pricing only becomes the determining factor when everyone is competing on the same thing. When you provide something that is important to your clients, and do it uniquely, your pricing will not be the compelling issue.*

While on the topic of fees, I must comment on invoicing. My old boss John, previously mentioned in Chapter 6 for teaching me the Elevator Mission and in

Chapters 13 and 15 for his networking prowess, is also adept at seeing every situation through the lens of the client. Thus, he is emphatic about giving the client a clear and readable invoice that states *exactly* what the fees encompass. *Before* I joined the firm, John sent me his standard memo about client care, detailing the way he expects his team members to treat his clients. This memo even included protocols on how to record time, so that when bills were generated all the entries were consistent regardless of which lawyers were working on the project. For example:

■ References to names should include the first initial and surname. In the case of Henry Smith, everyone's time entry for activities involving him must read "H. Smith"—thus avoiding the disarray of "H. Smith," "Henry Smith," "Mr. Smith," "Henry," or even "the client."

■ An entry should not merely read, "Drafting purchase agreement." It should be specific: "Amending purchase agreement on the basis of negotiations held the previous day, with specific consideration to the licensing rights granted back to XCo in the core technology used in the retained business." Likewise, a telephone call entry should state what was discussed. Any follow-up activity should then refer back to that telephone conversation: "Draft letter to J. Reed about [_____] pursuant to discussion by telephone with H. Smith."

■ If two lawyers work simultaneously on something, or if one lawyer reviews another lawyer's work, exactly how that adds value needs to be clarified with consistency by both lawyers. (If the second lawyer's involvement doesn't add value, John doesn't bill it.) John avoids putting anything on the invoice that a client could perceive as over- or double-billing, even if that means writing time off— something John was famous for!

John's objective is to provide clients with an invoice they can understand and which, in essence, chronologically "tells the story" about how the project is progressing. Each person's involvement and specific contributions are detailed day by day, so John's invoices substantiate and justify the fees, and clients can find no basis to question the validity of any aspect of the bill.

"John's rules" (as I call them) have stuck with me, and I have practiced them throughout my career. Many of my clients have personally thanked me for the professional nature and clarity of the bills I have given them. (How many of your clients have thanked you for a bill?!) I was shocked when I moved to London and discovered that some firms on this side of the pond deliver their bills (in some cases involving mammoth fees!) with the simple phrase "in regard to [fill in the blank]." When I reported this to John, his response was dismayed silence! The goal is *to stand in the shoes of the client*. So ask yourself, "If I were the client, which type of bill would I prefer?"

An additional benefit of following John's rules is that it forces you to record your time every day. This good habit (also learned in the U.S. working for John) earned me the shocked admiration of many of my London colleagues, who were accustomed to scrambling around at the end of every month, trying to remember just what they had been doing during that billing period.

Handling Rejection

The risk of getting a "no" is inherent in client development. However, rejection can still be viewed positively. First, it's a learning tool, as our failures are typically far more instructive than our successes. Did you bid too high, pitch too wildly, research your client's needs insufficiently? If not—or even if you haven't actually been as astute as you might have been—it's still important to remember that a "no" now isn't necessarily a "no" for all time, and that any contact you've brought to that stage is likely to remain within your network. In fact, after a rejection, the pressure to persuade can be removed and the relationship can benefit.

I was once rejected on a pitch but made a strong connection with the prospect on the basis that we had both recently returned from Tuscany and could compare our preferred Italian wines. Despite not winning the work, I later sent her a bottle of my favorite vintage—which set the stage for our subsequent friendship. About a year later, I received a substantial project through this client...this time, a project without competition!

DISCOVERING NEW OPPORTUNITIES

Winning new clients requires searching for new opportunities, and the best place to discover these is through your network. This sounds simple enough, yet it requires determination, activity, and organization. As a starting point, I suggest that you write down and categorize everyone in your current (or potential) network. For the purposes of this exercise, please distinguish each person by how well you know him or her. Each person will fall roughly into one of three categories:

■ **Established relationships.** These are the people you know well or have access to on a regular basis.

■ **Possible access.** These are people you've met (or would like to meet)— or people to whom you have a connection, but no regular access.

■ **Stale contacts.** These are people who fell into one of the above
categories at one time but are now inactive. (Note: If you contact
your connections on a regular basis—at least once every two
months, as proposed in Chapter 15—then you won't have anyone
to put into this category... But hey, who's perfect?)

In addition to these categories, you should also differentiate the people in
your network by *how* you know them (work colleagues, clients, friends, family,
organizations, etc.). Your networking chart might wind up looking something
like this.

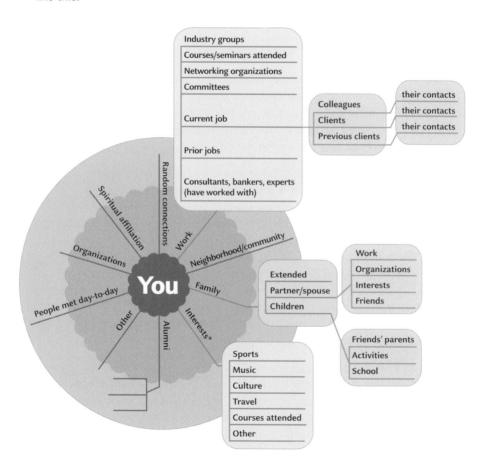

*The more diverse your interests, the more diverse and valuable your network is likely to be.
  The best contacts can come from the most improbable places.

Start with your established relationships. For each person in this category, ask yourself:

1.	A. Can this person help me? AND	B. Is this person willing to help me? If so, have I done something recently to help this person, or to make him feel appreciated?
	OR	
2.	A. Can this person help me? AND	B. Have I developed a trusting relationship with this person? (Note that this is a step *beyond* the relationship encompassed by question 1.B.)

Those people about whom you can answer "Yes" unequivocally on questions 1 (A and B) or 2 (A and B) are the ones you should be asking for help (the "ask" category). But before you do, there are a few other points to keep in mind: Know what you want to achieve from the transaction, and be sure to show a benefit—not only to you, but also to the other party.

First, be clear in your own mind what you want from him, and how you can help to ensure that he provides it. For example, if your friend is on good terms with the general counsel of his company and you want an introduction, don't just casually say to him, "Fascinating. I'd really like to meet your general counsel one of these days!" Instead, be specific. Offer to take them both to lunch, suggesting definite venues—even dates. Further, make sure your friend understands your objective for the introduction, and that he is willing to convey this purpose to his general counsel. Is your friend introducing you on a general basis (two lawyers who might have something in common)? Or is it more specific? Perhaps you happen to specialize in environmental issues, and their company has recently encountered legal problems in this area?

Then let's consider the situation when your friend barely knows the general counsel, but does have access: A friendly lunch in this case may not be incentive enough, or even entirely appropriate. You may need to be much more resourceful and offer the GC something else instead. Ask your friend about his (or her) hobbies or interests, or invite the GC to a presentation/discussion on some relevant topic. You'll probably have to do some research, and maybe even make substantial investment or preparations (such as possibly hosting the presentation yourself), but nothing worth having in business development comes without some effort.

Remember Chapter 6: Influencing someone involves benefiting him in some way. You just have to discover what that benefit might be, and it's usually something that goes beyond legal services.

Never Bury Your Own Benefit

Be up front about what you're asking for, and make sure each party involved has a clear understanding of the other person's probable expectations. I once asked my friend David for an introduction to his senior colleague. Out of the blue I received an invitation for the meeting, and I enthusiastically rearranged my schedule to accommodate it. When I arrived, I was surprised to find David and his colleagues sitting in the boardroom, eager to extract some free advice from me! It was only after giving numerous recommendations that I was introduced (very briefly!) to the colleague whom I'd thought I'd come to meet.

I wasn't annoyed about being asked for advice, charge or no charge—I even felt rather flattered—but David should have been honest with me about the real reason behind the invitation. Had he been forthright, my advice would have been more pertinent and I would have arrived with realistic expectations about the transaction on offer.

Transition from Personal to Business

Like it or not, meetings typically begin on a personal or small-talk level— such as kids' achievements, spouses' traumas, or the wine the company chair imbided the previous night at some famous restaurant. However, at some point, the conversation must shift from a personal to a business discussion. This can feel awkward, but one of the simplest (and subtlest) ways to make the transition is—you guessed it!—by asking a question. For example, if the contact's company has recently changed management, you might ask, "Tell me, Joe, and shelving just for a moment your daughter's fantastic showing at the horse trials, how has Z's recent restructuring affected you?"

The key is *preparation*. You can construct, well before your arrival, questions and potential avenues for steering the conversation where you really want it to go. If you leave everything to chance, you risk going nowhere.

Don't be *that* Casual

Asking a favor is tough to do; that's why it can be tempting to be overly casual in your approach. If you've been dying to ask your tennis friend Cameron for a favor for about a month and a half, then saying during your weekly tennis game, "Hey Cameron, old buddy old pal, why don't you take me to one of your company events one of these days?" is probably not the best approach! If you're too elliptical, the recipient tends to respond casually as well.

"Sadie" asked me recently for some names of appropriate conference speakers. I thought about it for about two seconds, passed a few names across to her, and thought nothing more of it. A few weeks later I received a frantic email from her, desperate to land a really prominent speaker. If she'd only told me in the first place how important it was to her, I'd have put much more thought and effort into her original request!

Don't Push a Favor

It's extremely tempting to circumvent the appropriate steps when asking for a favor, but if you do this you run the risk of not being taken seriously—or even offending people. Further, once you've dared to ask, reiterating such a request can make you look pushy.

A few months ago my friend Andrea introduced me to Robert, an acquaintance of hers. When Robert later suggested that we get together for lunch, I agreed—although I didn't quite understand what he was after. We had a delightful lunch and discovered a number of common interests. However, Robert's real motivation became evident about a week later, when I finally grasped that he wanted a favor from my husband, whom he'd never even met.

Feeling somewhat duped, I did indeed pass along his request to my spouse. (I could have done it more positively, but still, I did it.) After my husband elected to pass up the opportunity offered him, however, Robert continued to call me and email me, constantly trying to persuade me to change my husband's mind. His ill-judged fervor only dampened my enthusiasm for helping him.

His final error was to pursue his request unilaterally, without leveling with Andrea (our mutual friend), who was frankly embarrassed by his tactics. Robert should have asked Andrea, as the introducer, whether or not she thought it was appropriate to contact me. By not doing so, he abused his networking relationship, and Andrea is now reluctant to make further introductions for him.

Referrals

Statistics show that a referral generates 80 percent more success than meeting a potential client without that attempt at goodwill. So when evaluating your network and determining who might fall within your "ask" category, don't merely examine whether he (or his organization) retains legal services; think about others he may *know* who might be likely to require legal expertise. Think of every contact in the light of potential referrals.

As with any favor, the most effective way of asking for a referral is to be specific about what you want—that is, to give your contact a profile of what you're looking for. An IT lawyer might ask a friend, "Do you know some CTOs whose companies have recently gone through an acquisition or who are otherwise struggling to integrate different systems?" (You may get the response, "No, and did you see 'American Idol' last night?" but hey, you never know!)

If you do receive the desired answer, be sure to get the specific name and details, and ask your contact for permission to use his or her name. Then follow up the very next day.

Remember, Help Others First

If you're like most of us, many people in your potential network will fall outside what I call the "ask" category. Don't be discouraged by this—instead, remember that one of your goals is to move casual contacts up into the "ask" area.

Now, of course, you may have a few people on your chart who might well be willing to help you, but you can't yet answer Questions 1.B or 2.B affirmatively with respect to them—either you haven't helped/supported them recently, or you have yet to find an opportunity to win their trust. I would suggest that you follow the general rule of not requesting anything of these people until you've found a way to support them first.

There are two reasons for this. First, people are bound to be more willing to help you if you've done something for them—and asking them under these circumstances is much easier on your nerves; second, it helps you get to the networking starting point of generosity. However, there are no set rules here because the appropriate approach for you is bound to be dependent on the dynamics of your individual network.

By definition, the people falling into your "possible access" and "stale contact" groups will require extra effort and extra imagination compared to those you can already count on. However, by following the principles discussed in previous chapters and always keeping the *other* person's interest as the highest priority, you should still be able to maintain integrity in the process.

ORGANIZATION

It's not enough to gather busloads of business cards and maintain a somewhat up-to-date address book. Making the most of networking opportunities requires serious organization—even for happy-go-lucky Connecters, or easygoing Moderates!

Contacts Database

Critical to your business development is having a system to maintain and update relevant information about your contacts. This could be as old-fashioned as a Rolodex or as cutting-edge as a software management system. Whatever your choice, make sure that it works for you and is both accessible and useful—and, most crucially, be sure to keep it relentlessly up to date!

This is because it's imperative to constantly record and refresh your database with relevant information and then *use it*. If you lack such a system, you need to establish it *now*. Giving business cards to your secretary and having her put them into your address book doesn't count (if it did, we'd all be heroes)!

Yet even the right database is useless without the right data. The place to start is with your intelligence-gathering practices and daily agendas. We've already established that a substantial part of making connections and furthering bonds requires you to gather information about people, remember it, and follow up on that information. Phone calls, conversations, emails, letters, and invitations all contain information that can be used to develop contacts. I suggest having a notebook (or a fancier gadget if technologically inclined) that you don't (repeat: *don't!*) go anywhere without. Be attached to it by an invisible umbilical cord; sleep with it under your pillow. Whenever any action, thought, potential opportunity, or piece of information comes your way, be sure to record it.

Also, make sure that you keep a folder with your notebook/gadget so that you can store papers and notes. And *never* trust anyone else (not even your secretary) to do the follow-up for you. There are three reasons for this: By doing it yourself, you ensure that it happens; it makes you look professional and reliable; and it gets you in the habit of being proactive (which is unspeakably valuable!). Actually, there is a fourth reason, getting back to that personal touch I keep going on about: No matter how accomplished your assistant might be, there's simply no substitute for the personal touch.

THE CLIENT EXPERIENCE: The Personal Hospitality Mentality

My husband and I eat out frequently, and enjoy traveling the world doing just that, so we have eaten in a lot of restaurants. Yet our favorites invariably have something in common: a unique personal warmth that goes far beyond great food.

One place we visit often to enjoy the wonderful food (and the shopping, of course!) is Paris—and, when there, we never fail to visit our favorite restaurant (usually more than once!)—Guy Savoy—which is owned and run by the eponymous three-Michelin-star chef.

All three-Michelin-star restaurants deliver amazing food, exceptional service, and first-class ambiance—but Guy Savoy goes far beyond that. He creates a uniquely personal experience. Upon arriving at the George V, our hotel, we always discover a personal message from the restaurant, welcoming us to Paris and confirming our arrival time for dinner. In the evening we are warmly greeted at the door, by name, as if we are their most important and most welcome guests. (And if we haven't been there for a while, we feel we've genuinely been missed.)

Huber, the restaurant manager, takes great care to make every aspect of our evening personal. He always refers to our previous conversations, as though we had just spoken yesterday, and as if he is genuinely interested in following up. Our discussions feel like those of long-time friends, rather than patron and guest.

At the table, our favorite water is promptly poured and two glasses of rosé champagne quickly follow (our preferred apéritif). My husband's favorite Chateau Margeaux is waiting to be decanted, in anticipation of his usual request. Huber always suggests a special menu for me, one tailored to my known preference (fish!). And when he makes his suggestion, he inevitably refers to my previous visit, however long ago it occurred. ("Last time you had the poached sea bass, so I thought we

---

would do something a bit different for you tonight and try salmon.")
And then every one of our favorites appear, like magic, made to our
particular wishes (without our even having to specify).

Now, I'm not so naïve as to believe that Huber effortlessly remembers
every detail of our likes and dislikes, or that his thoughts revolve
around the details of his last conversations with us. I suspect that he
has an amazing database about all his guests, which he uses to make
every experience astonishing. And it works! When I'm at Guy Savoy,
I feel elevated and cherished, as though I'm the guest of honor at a
party, surrounded by people devoted to me and my every interest.
(Even Guy Savoy himself always takes time out of his kitchen to
look after us.)

Now the people at Guy Savoy could rely on the restaurant's superior
technical delivery (exquisite food, impeccable service, and delightful
surroundings, as substantiated by the restaurant's long-standing rating
of three Michelin stars), but they choose to make it into a unique
and personal experience. For us, that is their brand, and this is what
distinguishes Guy Savoy's restaurant from other three-Michelin-star
establishments and secures our loyalty. (It is interesting to note that
Guy Savoy's own words on his website articulate this same brand:
He calls his restaurant "my corner of the world where I entertain
my guests," not just a showplace for his amazing food.)

With each visit to Guy Savoy, I make the same comment to my
husband: "If only lawyers took such care to give their clients the
same personal touch!" Especially as there's absolutely no reason
why we can't.

In the chapters on brand, I emphasized the Elevator Mission and
the importance of creating a positive experience. With regard to our
clients, we must always be focused on the experience they receive—
because the only brand we really have is the experience we give to
our clients. And the more personal, the better!

I have a friend who works (very passionately!) in the hotel business;
in fact, we met when she worked in a hotel that I frequented. Because
she, as a manager, worked very hard to convey a personal touch, our
relationship grew beyond mere business. Since becoming friends,
she has given me many tips from her industry about the way hotels
gather data on their guests and how they use the information (as I
presume Huber at Guy Savoy does) to create a personal touch. One

example: On my birthday I received a gift from the hotel where she then worked—some wonderful green teas, wrapped in blue paper. It turns out that the hotel had not only noted my birthday and observed that I liked green tea (it's what I regularly order at breakfast), but had remembered that I liked the color blue. Because the staff valued (seemingly irrelevant) pieces of information, the hotel was able to make me feel special.

Similarly, pay attention to the tastes of your clients, and use those details to bolster them and distinguish yourself.

Make sure that you manage the information you receive by spending a certain (allotted) time period each day putting it into your diary and database. In addition to that diary time, consistently schedule a particular time slot for networking activities: reactivating dormant relationships, sending handwritten notes, returning friendly messages, and scheduling meetings and social events (as examined in Chapter 15). Finally, time should be set aside weekly to consider your personal vision and the activities that are going to support it (which will be discussed further in the next chapter).

MY SCHEDULE OF IMPORTANT ACTIVITIES		
WHEN	TIME ALLOTTED	ACTIVITY
Daily—first thing	15 minutes	Diary time! PUTTING INFORMATION GATHERED INTO DIARY, DATABASE
Monday morning—first thing	30 minutes	Networking activities—writing notes, scheduling events
Wednesday morning—get in to the office extra early	20 minutes	Making phone calls, reconnecting, following up on networking activities (primarily through voice mails, before contacts are in the office)
Sunday evening	20 minutes	Alone time, strategizing about goals, self-development, etc.

Remember, if your daily agenda is consumed by firefighting (quadrant 1 activities), how can you ever expect to achieve your greater goals? They can't be accomplished overnight; they'll require a systematic, incremental, purposeful daily agenda.

Long-term success, in essence, comes down to your daily agenda, so make sure to manage yours proactively!

DO YOUR HOMEWORK

Before meeting with anyone in your contact base, make a plan. Ask yourself...

- When did I last talk with this person?

- What's my objective for meeting him (or her) this time?

- What do I want to ask this person? (**WRITE DOWN** your questions —even if it feels fatuous!)

- What do I want from him (information, support, an introduction)? Whatever it is, **WRITE IT DOWN**. This will help to articulate it in your mind.

- Is it something he can do? (If not, is he really the right person to approach?)

- Does he have the power or influence I need? (If not, does he know someone who does?)

- Have I already done everything I can to enable this person to help me?

- Was I helpful the last time he or she contacted me?

- Is there anything I can currently do to help this person?

- Does my request require any follow-up? (If so, rough out some suggestions for making it happen.)

CREATE A PLAN

About once a week, make sure that you pick a business development project to achieve. It can be as easy as making a phone call or as time-consuming as attending a useful organizational meeting (even if it's about something that might not interest you!). In general, however, investing your time in things of genuine interest has the greatest likelihood of paying off, because authenticity will bring out your positive self and your genuine passions, which will inevitably attract others.

Choose your objective in advance and make its achievement one of your personal priorities. This is especially important if selling arouses some level of anxiety in you. In that case, try to use the technique learned in Chapter 7 and face down fear with FEAR (Face Everything And Recover). By taking incremental steps in your weekly business development activities, you'll soon realize that selling, at its most basic level, is just about creating relationships—and there's nothing scary about that!

CASE STUDY

Throughout this chapter I've often described my various client relationships as examples of success. However, I wouldn't be completely honest if I didn't also mention the most frustrating experience of my career.

This began when the client's general counsel, in relation to a large IT project, chose my firm as its legal advisor through a competitive bidding process. We were selected for two reasons: my partner's long-standing relationship with the company (he had developed a trusting relationship) and my applicable expertise (which made getting through "filter one" possible).

Yet before legal counsel was even considered, consultants were working with the IT group within the client company (the project's primary stakeholder) on initial analysis and strategy development. Now these consultants had hoped the client would use lawyers of their choice and had not only advocated these lawyers for the project—which is common—but had actively disparaged us! I only discovered much later that they were particularly antagonistic toward me (though we had never met) because they had had a dispute with some of the partners I had previously worked with.

The general counsel selected us anyway, over the consultants' protests, but the project manager was still subliminally influenced by their antagonism. The situation not only undermined the integrity of our involvement but—still worse—created a rift between the IT stakeholder (who had hired the consultants, and thus supported them) and the legal department (who had strongly backed us).

During the first stage of the project, the client's senior counsel and I espoused a different approach to that of the consultants, making the atmosphere even more tense. The consultants' resentment boiled over when the client selected our strategy, reinforcing the "us" and "them" mentality.

There were many other contributing factors and events, all far too complicated to relate here, but the bottom line is that the situation deteriorated to the point that new lawyers had to be retained (though not the consultants' first firm of choice).

In short, although the approach I advocated was probably the best from a legal standpoint, my proposing it created conflict. Understandably enough, the consultants thought I was co-opting *their* project and criticizing their work— not exactly the path to undying friendship! Of course, it was only later that I discovered the underlying reason for their animosity, but there's no question that I was insufficiently sensitive to the political and personal dynamics of the situation. My efforts should have been bent on fostering an alliance with the consultants, who had power in their relationship with the IT stakeholder (the ultimate decision-maker on the project).

Another mistake I made was not doing enough "hand-holding" and relationship-building with the IT stakeholder (to mitigate the consultants' malignant influence), as opposed to just driving the deal with my legal team to get all the documents in place. The sad truth is that a successful deal can be far more dependent on building the right relationships than on delivering the best product. In this case, I undoubtedly lost my focus—and dropped the ball.

Interestingly, despite my failure, my partner, Ed, never faltered in his own trust-based relationship with the client, and when it was decided that fresh lawyers would be brought in, he made sure that we did everything we could to help with the transition, including sharing our documents and working with them behind the scenes. Our removal as the primary legal advisors may have been unfair, but my partner still refused to let it affect his relationship with his client.

Although this story is about a "client failure" and the most frustratingly disappointing moment in my legal career, I also learned a lot from it. Don't we usually learn the greatest lessons from our mistakes? But I also absorbed a lot from Ed, who demonstrated what client relationships *should* involve, and in the process also taught me about authentic leadership (which we will examine in the next chapters).

RECAP AND SUMMARY

It really doesn't require a charismatic personality or magical selling technique to make a business grow; the simplest insight into the minds of your clients is all that is necessary. Some conclusions will be unique to the individual, but most are universal, and so obvious that they run the risk of being overlooked.

Allow me to recap:

1. The goal of any client relationship is a long-term trusting relationship (similar to friendship), meaning that the motivations are based upon the relationship rather than on short-term gain. You can achieve this through a familiar sequence of events: connecting, creating a bond, proving the authenticity of your brand (by delivering value and a trustworthy experience), and (ultimately) achieving a trusting relationship.

2. Everybody wants to know that the other person cares—and clients are no exception! They want to know that you care about them and are there to obtain the best deal for them. Always work toward the best deal for the organization as well as toward a personal "best" for your individual contact.

3. You cannot authenticate your brand unless you deliver. To deliver optimally, you must...

    a. Communicate with your clients about progress and delivery, rather than disappearing "to get the work done." Silence makes them feel unimportant and unappreciated.

    b. Return phone calls ASAP. Again, not doing so tells your clients that you are too busy for them (not a good message!).

    c. With every instruction, think outside the box. How can you add extra value? (This does *not* mean, "How can I bill more hours?"—a disastrous mindset!)

    d. Ask for feedback—then act on it.

    e. You cannot provide exceptional service without understanding your client's business...and I mean *really* understanding it. If you don't truly understand, then ask, recognizing that asking questions demonstrates your interest, makes others feel important, and shows that you are confident enough in what you know to expose what you don't yet know. By asking, you should learn critical information that enables you to deliver value.

    f. Make sure that you also understand your personal contact's agenda. Armed with both sets of information, you should be able to work from the standpoint of your client's objectives, rather than your own.

g. Become part of the client's team by being transparent in everything you do, even if that means admitting you *can't* do something (such as meeting their budget, timetable, or experience requirements).

h. The way in which advice is given can be just as important as the advice itself. Always consider the personalities, emotions, politics, and business/personal agendas of every client situation, keeping in mind that advice given clumsily can be perceived as criticism or self-promotion and could be at odds with the client's wish to look good.

i. Always follow up on advice!

4. There are three phases to the bidding process, the first two being merely filters:

   a. Rational selection, the first filter, occurs when the client evaluates your résumé and the credentials of your firm. In most cases, once through this threshold, credentials no longer play a significant role, and emphasizing them might even backfire.

   b. The second filter is emotional selection, in which the client must connect with you on a personal level. At this stage you must call on all of your well-honed people skills to connect and create an emotional bond. If you don't, you may progress no further.

   c. The third phase, in which you authenticate your brand and prove that you deserve trust, is the time when you really win the client. You can best authenticate your brand in a time-constricted selling period by truly believing in yourself and by exhibiting a natural passion for the unique value your brand brings to the deal. The challenge is to transfer your belief to the client by selling to his concerns and persuading from his perspective.

      i. To every extent possible, pitch your deal to suit the buying mindset of the client by first evaluating his or her personality. If you're clued in, you can demonstrate that you're able to provide him a unique benefit.

      ii. Ask questions (preferably open-ended ones) to discover the client's situation and then collaborate to structure the optimal result. By using this approach, you allow the client to co-own the solution. Only then do you offer advice and an action plan.

iii. Your biggest job is to ask questions and listen. The more data you gather, the more likely you are to meet the client's needs.

5. If you've done your job, any remaining objections to your firm must be based upon fear (e.g., that you won't deliver). Dispel fears by addressing them in a transparent and open way.

6. Rejection can still leave the door open for other opportunities. "No" is not necessarily "no" forever, and the smart lawyer looks on every contact as yet another member of his or her network.

7. The best place to discover new opportunities is in your existing networks, so continually monitor them, strategizing about how your established relationships might help you and how you can move your other contacts into the "ask" category. Remember, it's not just work that you're looking for, but also new contacts or referrals.

8. When you ask a favor, you must...

   a. Know exactly what you want and make it clear to your contact how he can provide it. In the process, you must show him (or her) a clear benefit.

   b. Never bury your own benefit. Be up front about what you want from the other person and the benefit you're seeking.

   c. Prepare a natural transition into business discussions.

   d. Try not to be overly casual about your requests.

   e. Never push for a favor.

   You should always be cognizant of helping others first, working within your networking mindset (that is, being concerned about the interests of the other person, not just your own gain). This gives integrity to the process.

9. Organization is key! All successful business generators are organized and systematic. Their information database is their crown jewel. With this in mind...

   a. Keep your notebook/gadget always with you, as you never know when and where some helpful information might be disclosed.

   b. Use a designated time to refresh and record information into your database. This is *in addition* to your "networking time," during which you reactivate dormant relations, send notes, return messages, and schedule meetings with contacts.

c. Before any meeting, do your homework and devise a plan. Always be able to answer the following:

- What is my objective for meeting/talking with this person?

- Is it something he (or she) can do directly? If not, is he really the right person to ask?

- Is there anything I can do to help this person?

- Does my request require any follow-up? (If so, prepare suggestions for making it happen.)

d. Since we always have the bigger picture in mind, each week you should pick a business development project to achieve—then do it!

A final word: While I've chosen to focus on the business facets of your career *before* taking on the question of leadership, there's no question that business development is contingent upon your being a leader. Leadership is typically thought of as an internal achievement within a firm, but to be a genuine leader you must be people-focused, positive, and honest. These are also essential attributes for business development, without which you can't hope to foster sustained and trusting relationships with your clients—or to become the lawyer you've always wanted to be.

Chapter 18: **The Three Dimensions of Leadership**

Chapter 19: **Self-Leading**

Chapter 20: **Leading Within Relationships**

Chapter 21: **Leading a Team**

Leadership

; /

Chapter Eighteen

The Three Dimensions of Leadership

B y now you should be familiar with our three-step incremental levels of leadership: self-leading, leading within relationships, and leading a team.

Self-leading involves developing a personal vision and working toward its accomplishment by consistently managing yourself. This involves maintaining self-belief, especially when things are difficult or when unexpected obstacles crop up... In essence, by self-leading you treat yourself just as you would prefer your leaders to treat you: by bolstering (rather than undermining) your sense of confidence.

Leading within relationships involves methodically constructing a network of support that will reinforce and sustain your ultimate goal of leading. This means maintaining good relationships with colleagues at all levels and working with them in a way that both achieves your personal objectives and recognizes and reinforces their support. Successfully managing these levels of leadership makes it possible to achieve the third step, *leading a team*, by mobilizing others toward your personal vision and by inspiring them with a shared purpose.

This third level of leadership can sound rather daunting, especially if you're currently junior, but most lawyers actually attempt it fairly early in their careers. For example, as associates, we're often given the significant responsibility of running deals with little or no partner involvement. This requires communicating the "shared purpose," managing other people, understanding how to motivate and influence team members, setting realistic expectations, cultivating relationships to get results, and leveraging the talents of others. (OK, maybe nobody manages *all* of these *all* the time, but hey, it's still a goal!)

Once you achieve senior level, you'll probably be expected to coordinate the vision (perhaps for a practice group or client team) and to marshal every resource necessary to achieve it. This also requires that you empower team members to develop and attain their own goals within the framework of the group vision.

Now by "leadership" I'm not referring to any attempt to become head of the firm or to oversee monumentally strategic transformations inside it (although both could certainly be the case). I'm referring to becoming a leader *within* your firm, by working through the incremental steps of leadership.

Business jargon routinely distinguishes between the terms "leading" and "managing," although the two can—and often do—overlap. In general, managers work with processes (typically the status quo), while leaders work with transformation; but since it's people who perform, both managers and leaders—by definition—must be able to inspire others. However, though good leadership is contingent on (and built upon) good management skills, it requires still more than that. To be a leader you must not only manage yourself and others but do so within the context of a *vision*—ultimately, a shared purpose.

I've chosen to break leadership down into the three levels given above for two reasons:

■ No one can lead—not even a reasonably sized dachshund—until he can first lead himself. Further, as discussed earlier, lawyers tend to begin their careers with near-tunnel vision for the technical aspects of law, leaving any dreams of leadership for later in life. However, leading yourself *can, should,* and *must* begin on Day One. The plaintive whine of "Me?—but I'm too junior" or "I have no one to lead" is no excuse at all.

■ Second, I hope you have realized by now the importance of relationships—and that means *all* relationships. Sometimes lawyers choose to prioritize client relationships over those with their colleagues. (Hands up, those who ruefully recognize this behavior from lawyers in your firm...) This may even be the preferred method of some supposedly "model" partners. However, in today's changing business environment the ancient tradition of tolerating self-centered, egotistical, and abusive colleagues is coming to an end, and fast! (It may not *look* that way in your firm—law firms are notoriously

behind the times in organizational behavior—but believe me, it's happening.) So if you aspire to become a leader within your firm, you must first concentrate on relationship-building.

And note this: Just as the steps of rising to leadership are cumulative, leadership skills usually develop over time. Don't wait until you achieve some critical rank to begin acting as a leader! Leadership is founded on core characteristics that we can all implement, regardless of where we are in the pecking order. In short, leadership is an attitude of mind.

CHARACTERISTICS OF A LEADER

So what characteristics are required of a leader? Well, if you have been reading the chapters in sequence you'll already be familiar with a few. But let's remind ourselves of their resonance within the context of leadership. In my view, there are five: trustworthiness, self-awareness, people-focus, positivity, and vision.

Characteristics of a Leader

1. **Trustworthiness:** Demonstrates loyalty, honesty, and reliability

2. **Self-awareness:** Knows the truth about his own personality, emotions, thinking, strengths/weaknesses, and personal motivators

3. **People-focus:** Concerned with other people's needs; knows how to motivate

4. **Positivity:** Views circumstances, himself, and others positively, even in adversity

5. **Vision:** Knows his goals, which are supported by his underlying values and personal needs

Trustworthiness

As lawyers we have taken an oath to be trustworthy, and as leaders we should apply these same principles toward every single person around us, taking care never to lie, cheat, exaggerate, take advantage, cut corners, let someone down, gossip, fail to follow through on a commitment, or stab others in the back. This is naturally important for the reputation of anyone's brand, but for a leader, integrity becomes still more essential. No one—not even the dimmest person in the firm—is likely to follow someone he doesn't trust, end of story. In fact, in just about every leadership study honesty ranks as the top trait people look for in their leaders. (See *The Leadership Challenge* by Kouzes and Posner.) Also, in the aftermath of recent financial scandals generated by amoral leadership (of which Madoff is only the most notorious), the need to trust the people at the helm is at an all-time high. Regardless of every other quality you may possess—quicksilver intellect, risk-taking genius, or whatever—in today's environment, if you aren't trustworthy, you will never be accepted as an effective and sustainable leader.

Self-Awareness

Today's leaders are more self-aware than ever, meaning that they try to understand themselves and how their actions affect others. Leadership requires a positive impact on other people, and failure in this area requires immediate action. The sad truth is that if you choose not to do this self-analysis you may never know how your behavior could be holding you back. Thousands of able and ambitious lawyers have been overlooked for partnership simply because of their inability to constructively influence others.

I once worked with a brilliant colleague who was widely respected except for one thing: Everything that came out of her mouth contained the subtext, "See how clever I am!" She desperately needed applause and admiration, and if it wasn't forthcoming she generously took it upon herself to remedy the omission. On every subject she was the self-appointed instant expert, and if a colleague so much as touched on a legal problem, she immediately stuffed a solution down his throat. She was (and remains) a remarkable technical lawyer, but she could never grasp the negative impact she had on people—despite being repeatedly warned by her superiors. She has lost promotions and business because she has refused to accept the fact that her attitude is impeding her career.

Deciding *not* to change is always possible, of course, as long as you've stepped back and acknowledged what it might cost you. But if you aspire to be a leader, you need to do self-analysis on a serious basis, making changes when and where appropriate.

So, what do we need to be self-aware about?

■ *Personality.* Leaders understand their own behavior patterns and personality traits. Without thoroughly understanding yourself, you have very little chance of analyzing and improving your interactions with others.

- *Emotions.* Similarly, leaders make their emotions work for them. As a leader you must maintain control over your feelings and impulses, ensuring that they support, rather than undermine, your objectives.

- *Strengths and weaknesses.* (This one's obvious!) Leaders use and take advantage of their strengths while working on their weaknesses.

- *Motivators.* Leaders know what really matters to them and use that understanding to drive their behavior. Working in alignment with your inner motivators (your core needs and values) conveys consistency, commitment, and passion, which are key in influencing others toward your vision.

- *Thinking.* Leaders realize that their attitudes can make the difference between success and failure, so they monitor their thoughts and their self-talk to support their goals.

To be a leader you must have sufficient humility to ask yourself on a consistent basis how you are doing. Still better, ask others—trusted friends, colleagues, and family. (If you haven't already done this exercise within the context of developing your brand [Chapter 12], then now is a good time to set it up for *both* objectives: brand and leadership.) Use the feedback you receive to identify problems that you need to address and occasions when you may be sending out wrong signals to clients and colleagues. Remember, everyone has blind spots... The difference is that leaders discover and address them, never letting their weaknesses impede their progress.

People-Focus

Leaders focus on other people, creating enthusiasm and motivating those around them. Some of history's greatest business leaders have asserted that they achieved their success and power through their ability to encourage and inspire others. Andrew Carnegie, the founder of the U.S. iron and steel industry and one of the greatest entrepreneurs and philanthropists of all time, wrote his own epitaph: "Here lies a man who was able to surround himself with men far cleverer than himself."

Leadership within a law firm is no different. As you advance, your success becomes increasingly dependent upon the performance of others and, by implication, upon your ability to delegate to them and to motivate them—and you can only do either if you deal with people effectively.

Positivity

Survey after survey confirms that successful leaders share a quality of great optimism. This "glass half-full" attitude affects every aspect of being a leader, from perseverance to building a team. It's a cliché—yet, like most clichés, true—that where most people see problems, true leaders see opportunities.

You probably won't be surprised to learn that my college roommate Becky, described in Chapter 6 ("People Skills") as incredibly positive, is today an executive of a large organization, and is regularly rated as a top businesswoman and an exemplary leader. Mark Buckingham (author of *The One Thing You Need To Know*) has studied leaders for almost 20 years in his position with the Gallup Organization. In a recent *USA Today* cover story he said, "The opposite of a leader isn't a follower. The opposite of a leader is a pessimist." His research suggests that the common thread among leaders is that they view themselves and their world as a lucky place, and that this perspective enables them to uncover positives even while experiencing great adversity.

Now even the *notion* of seeing things optimistically can make lawyers' pulses flutter, because we've been trained to think realistically, anticipate problems, and identify risk, none of which tend to produce deeply positive patterns of thought. But when dealing with career advancement and leadership skills you must remain alert to the opportunities in every circumstance, even while you concentrate on finding solutions to pressing difficulties. Your self-awareness and mental program (negative in/negative out versus positive in/positive out) will be critically important.

A pessimist sees the difficulty in every opportunity; an optimist sees the opportunity. —Winston Churchill

Leaders are not just positive about situations but about themselves and where they are going, and they are equally upbeat about the people around them. Leaders believe (in themselves and in others), and by virtue of this, they also believe in their organization. Furthermore, leaders manage through optimism and enthusiasm, rather than through anxiety and fear, thus creating environments that allow others to shine. In fact, the natural consequence of adopting a leader's positive attitude is that it intensifies the people-focus we've already discussed; there's a strong natural link between the two.

Vision ("Dream from the heart")

All leaders have a vision of the future, a vision propelled by the leader's underlying values and motivators. If you don't know your motivators, you can't effectively work toward your goals *or* create a shared purpose for others. Leadership requires that you imagine possibilities (leadership is all about

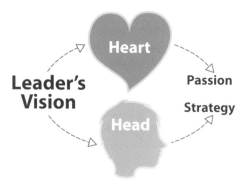

change for the better!) and then take action, through planning and strategy. In short, the concentration of the head must be combined with the passion and commitment of the heart.

■   ■   ■

Charisma is a characteristic often associated with leadership, but I think charisma comes to anyone (admittedly, in very different manifestations) when dreaming from the heart and spurring others to imagine the same possibilities. In essence, charisma only radiates from most people when they are leading with these five traits: trustworthiness, self-awareness, people-focus, positivity, and vision.

You may have realized as you read through the leadership characteristics that much of what they involve directly corresponds to the content of the initial chapters of this book (the "awareness building block" section). The work done there should lay the foundation for effective leadership, just as the preparation done in the earliest years in the profession should lay the foundation for progression and partnership.

Five Characteristics of a Leader
(Foundations for Leadership)

To some degree, the five leadership characteristics are interwoven.

TYING IT ALL TOGETHER

It should be easy, at this point, to see how the three dimensions, or levels, of leadership rely on the five leadership traits. Consider self-leading: Doesn't maintaining integrity toward your personal vision depend on being trustworthy and honest with yourself? Isn't awareness of your strengths and weaknesses a key component of achieving as much as you can? How about being visionary—isn't doing your work from the heart, and pursuing the right goals, the first step in the process of self-leading (see Chapter 5, "Motivators")? And isn't your persistence in achieving your goals dependent on a positive attitude about your abilities and situation?

The same principles apply to leading within relationships, or to leading a team. To be a team leader you must be perceived as trustworthy, and success in professional relationships dictates that you be aware of your own personality and behavior patterns. No one will follow your lead if you don't genuinely exhibit your own devotion to a compelling vision—likewise, maintaining a loyal and motivated following requires you to be tuned in to your followers (people-focused). And we all have stories to tell about how a lack of positive leadership led to team breakdown! Toxic emotions create toxic environments, but both can be avoided by the exercise of positive leadership.

Shared Purpose (ultimate act of leadership)

Lead a team (enthuse, motivate, inspire loyalty)

Lead within relationships

Self-lead

Positive Visionary

Trustworthy Self-aware People-focused

TRANSFORMATIONAL LEADERSHIP

As you move through the three dimensions of leadership and embark on the process of leading others, your focus must necessarily be about transforming people and situations. This means that you have to inspire others to will that transformation and to take action to make it happen—even if it seems, in the short term at least, to be detrimental to them. For example, to achieve a goal one person may have to move outside of his comfort zone, while another may have to sacrifice an immediate benefit—security, a promotion, a coveted role, or even personal billables. Transformational leaders inspire others to rise to such challenges because they can demonstrate the long-term gain involved and because their colleagues trust them to achieve it.

Transformational leadership first emerged as an important leadership style in James MacGregor Burns's classic book, *Leadership,* and has since been refined and elucidated by other experts—notably Bernard M. Bass and Bruce Avolio. The theory of transformational leadership maintains that the most effective leaders use four types of influence (which are not, of course, mutually exclusive):

Idealized influence. We employ this type of influence by capitalizing on our confidence and competence, by exhibiting a strong sense of commitment, by acting in a way that is consistent with our values, and by working toward our vision. In short, we inspire trust and admiration. We motivate because others feel pride in being associated with us, and—possibly—even hope to model their careers on ours. Haven't you ever admired someone so much that, in an effort to be more like him or her, you worked harder or better? We will refer to this as "leadership (influence) through EXAMPLE."

Inspirational motivation. By being enthusiastic and by passionately communicating a clear and compelling vision, we inspire others to commit. Colleagues and clients are influenced because they get emotionally carried away and long to follow, and because they are energized by our purpose and meaning. In essence, people get caught up in the excitement! I call this "leadership (influence) through ENTHUSIASM."

Intellectual stimulation. When we encourage others to think innovatively, they become inspired to develop new ideas. We can motivate people to new breakthroughs and original thinking by allowing them to benefit from our experience. We'll refer to this as "leadership (influence) through CHALLENGE."

Individualized consideration. Everyone wants to be appreciated, and recognition inspires people to work even harder and do even better. Appreciation, and spurring others to progress and succeed, ultimately brings out their best and achieves the most! This is "leadership (influence) through EMPOWERMENT."

Just as each dimension of leadership (self-leading, leading within relationships, and leading a team) draws upon our five characteristics, so too do the transformational methods of influence. Let's examine how this plays out in practice. If we look at leadership through example, it's clear that you can hardly achieve your goal of being a role model unless you possess integrity (trustworthiness), and you will not convey confidence unless you maintain an upbeat and optimistic outlook (positivity). Leadership through enthusiasm or challenge cannot occur without ideas and passion (vision), and leadership through empowerment (which naturally involves mentoring) will never work unless you're tuned in to the needs and talents of others (people-focused). Finally, self-awareness about your own strengths and personal goals provides the necessary insight to choose the most effective style of leadership in any given situation.

Review the table below to see how this works in more detail.

FIVE LEADERSHIP CHARACTERISTICS

LEADERSHIP (INFLUENCE) STYLE	BEING TRUSTWORTHY	BEING SELF-AWARE
Example: behaving as an exemplary role model; demonstrating clear goals, confidence, and commitment	A prerequisite for being a role model	Exemplary behavior is contingent on being true to one's values, which requires self-awareness and the ability to work optimally with one's strengths and weaknesses
Enthusiasm: demonstrating enthusiasm, passion, and vision; inspiring with energy and fervor	The enthusiasm must be genuine to be trusted	Maintaining enthusiasm requires the monitoring of one's emotions, thinking, and mindset; one can only convey passion and a compelling vision if first supported by an awareness of internal values
Challenge: educating, facilitating, and stimulating intellectual challenge and achievement	To educate, the leader must first be respected	Equips the leader to facilitate, as self-awareness gives the insight to discover the right intellectual challenges to motivate others
Empowerment: coaching, facilitating, and nurturing (of others' talents and one's own); inspiring vision in others	To effectively coach, the leader must first be trusted	Provides the insight to facilitate and nurture other people's self-discovery

BEING PEOPLE-FOCUSED	BEING POSITIVE	BEING VISIONARY
Prevents self-absorption (in the goal), which can exclude and demotivate	Supports confidence and competence	Demonstrating a goal is dependent on first having the vision
Supports and generates enthusiasm in others	A positive attitude is integral to being both enthusiastic and inspiring	Leading from the heart underlies enthusiasm, as well as a passionate and compelling vision
An understanding of others generates the appropriate stimuli and the ability to create challenges	Positive conditions and reinforcement create the optimal environment to achieve	Intellectual challenges must be aligned with a valuable goal (the vision)
Drives the ability to empower others	Positive reinforcement and belief in others is the best way to facilitate and nurture	The leader's vision helps others to discover their own—optimally within the context of the leader's own vision

REALITY CHECK: HOW ARE YOU DOING?

The four styles of influence have traditionally been advocated in relation to influencing others, but I think they apply equally to self-leading. Self-leading is surprisingly similar to leading others, so you can generate your own motivation by using these techniques. Ask yourself...

■ Am I leading through example? Do I act in alignment with my values? Am I proud of my actions? Am I confident of my abilities and clear about my destination?

■ Do I lead through enthusiasm? Are my goals interwoven with my passions? Do I support myself with positive reinforcement? Am I able to override any negative thinking? Can I perceive opportunities even when confronted with adverse situations?

■ What do I really find most intellectually stimulating? Have I discovered the right challenges to inspire me? Have I integrated them sufficiently into my work to fuel my motivation?

■ Am I leading by self-empowerment? Do I encourage myself? As I succeed, do I praise and reward myself (as opposed to concentrating on any negatives)? Am I stimulating myself sufficiently?

If you can't answer these questions affirmatively, then you still have work to do—perhaps by better accessing your strongest leadership characteristics. Or maybe it's not your internal self, but your external environment that is holding you back—which may mean that it's time to make a change. Whatever the obstacle (if any), you must first enable yourself if you want to lead—or achieve a specific goal, whatever it might be.

Shared
Purpose
(ultimate act
of leadership)

Influence
a TEAM
through example,
enthusiasm,
challenge
& empowerment

Lead
a team
(enthuse, motivate,
inspire loyalty)

Lead within
relationships

Influence
OTHERS
through example,
enthusiasm,
challenge
& empowerment

Influence
SELF
through example,
enthusiasm,
challenge
& empowerment

Self-lead

Positive
Visionary

Trustworthy
Self-aware
People-focused

To succeed through each dimension, we must think and behave in accordance with each leadership characteristic and then access them all to influence ourselves and other people. (Without influence we cannot lead!)

It's self-evident that leadership excellence is dependent on the five leadership characteristics. As you work through the next chapters, continually ask yourself, "How can they help me lead better and achieve more?"

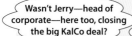

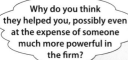

Chapter Nineteen
Self-Leading

If we want to achieve leadership, or even success, we must begin by leading ourselves. By managing our thoughts, controlling our emotions, and maintaining our focus on our personal vision, we behave as leaders and encourage others to follow us.

THE POWER OF VISION

Leaders are focused on where they are going and how they intend to get there; they are cognizant of their personal vision, and they act consistently in the kinds of ways required to achieve their goals.

Our objective is now to ascertain (or, more probably by this stage, to refine) your vision. So, as you work through this section, make notes that will be helpful to you and that will support you in developing your strategy.

At this point, I would expect that you have developed a personal vision that is both motivational and achievable. For example, you've worked through the "awareness building block" chapters, designed to provide you with a key understanding of your own character and how it can be used to develop inspiring goals, for you and for those around you. One of the purposes of working through Chapter 4 ("Personalities") was to identify your strengths, because your talents are naturally aligned with them. (It's been established that trying to achieve goals poorly aligned with one's temperament or talents not only makes tasks less fulfilling but also, inevitably, makes one much less likely to succeed.)

Avoiding the Wrong Goals

Similarly, with an understanding of your strongest motivators (Chapter 5), you should be able to avoid chasing the wrong vision. You are, of course, unique—so your goals should be suited to you. Don't fall into the trap of trying to be a carbon copy of a colleague, no matter how successful he or she might be. Just because his goal is to manage the entire department doesn't mean that administering a practice group is the right goal for you. (Administration, like any professional role, requires a unique skill set!) You might be far better suited to working with one particular client or to developing personal relationships with various other people in that organization. Also, don't allow others to steer you toward the wrong goals: Your boss may prefer for you to develop skills in a specific area, or the firm may propose a particular role for you (probably to fill some gap of its own), but before taking on any such "imposed" vision, you must evaluate whether or not it's really compatible with your own plans for your future.

Setting the right goals helps you to feel contented, not only when you eventually attain those goals, but—crucially—during the process of getting there. Think honestly about your motivators and whether your vision is likely to satisfy them. For example, if your goal is partnership, do you truly understand the parameters of reaching that goal? What activities will you have to engage in to get there? Are these the kinds of things that you *really* enjoy doing? Is your paragliding/novel-writing/chess championship going to have to be sacrificed? Just as important, once you achieve your goal, will the role actually fulfill your ambitions? Think long and hard about all the things we examined in Chapter 5.

Your Desired Client Base

Think for a moment about your brand, and how it aligns with the client base you want to address. Even though I chose to emphasize brand first (instead of business or leadership), the actual starting point is to understand one's client base, because you can't possibly build any brand without that knowledge. Your brand must communicate the value you bring to your clients, just as it shapes your behavior to deliver on that promise. So you must begin the business of brand-building with a vision of your personal client base.

Since the "ideal" brand is (or should be!) the personification of your personal vision, your brand and your goals must be complementary by definition. The only reason you can pursue them simultaneously is because each works to support the other.

My goal is to be on the Board of Woodbridge Healthcare.

So, I must enhance my reputation in the healthcare industry as part of my brand, making sure I deliver a consistent message that supports my goal.

Finding Your Own Vision

If you still feel a little uncertain about your own vision, one of the simplest things to do is to interview a few people who have already attained the goal you're considering. Check out the reality, the bad as well as the good. Believe me, a lot of positions in our profession look glamorous and appealing from the outside, and rather less so from the inside... There may also be sacrifices that you're not prepared to make, for the sake of your family—or you may find that achieving your ambition will routinely require your working more hours than you can cope with! Remember, there are many different ways of being a successful lawyer. Don't be one of those people who take the line of least resistance and wind up regretting it.

The bottom line is that your personal vision must be something that gives you purpose, and this purpose matters far more than those extrinsic motivators (like wealth or status) associated with a more traditional definition of success. Without this sense of purpose you're almost certain to lack enough inner fire to fuel you. Further, there is probably someone among your peers or competitors carrying that same flame, making him (or her) far more likely than you are to achieve and sustain that same goal...

Writing about leadership during the 2008 U.S. presidential campaign is fascinating, as I can't help but analyze the potential candidates in the light of my research. At one point early on, polls showed unparalleled support for Al Gore as the Democratic nominee, even though he wasn't even running!

No one could deny that Gore had plenty of backing in 2000 (in fact, some would argue that he *did* in fact win the 2000 presidential election), yet he certainly lacked the passionate following and the wide-ranging clout that he carries today. So what made the difference? My theory is that Al Gore ran his 2000 campaign without a compelling vision. His relentless speechifying about payroll taxes and Social Security benefits just didn't cut it—either for him or for the voters.

However, the Al Gore of today is miles more impressive, inspiring a significant following as a campaigner against global warming. Many commentators have already noted that if Gore had run for president in 2008 he could have commanded a level of support far superior to that of 2000. The difference? His political *raison d'être* is now propelled by a compelling and authentic personal vision, which creates both passion for his cause and trust in him as a leader. (This also explains why Gore is probably more effective in his current role as an environmental activist than he would be as president—it allows him to focus on what matters most to him.)

The importance of discovering the "right" personal vision is no different for us. When we find the goal that really motivates us, we're fired with enthusiasm, and this inspires others not only to support us but also to share our dream.

SOME PRACTICAL ADVICE

Write It Down

Take a step back and think about your vision, and once you've found one sufficiently compelling, write it down. Then write down all of your goals as they relate to this vision.

If you find that you feel a bit hesitant about this ("Why should I make a list? Life is short!"), then try to remember when you last made a list. Maybe yesterday, recalling which exes to avoid inviting to the same party? Perhaps last Tuesday, about what to pick up from the supermarket, on pain of excommunication by your eight-year-old? We're all constantly making lists, and the reason is simple: lists work. They prevent us from forgetting something, and they maintain our focus on the task at hand. However, very few people (fewer than five percent!) ever take the trouble to make a list encompassing the biggest aspects of their lives: their goals. And because people fail to do this, they lose focus amid hectic daily schedules and a range of small, distracting, niggling problems.

Research proves that the simple step of writing down your goals dramatically increases your chance of achieving them. Writing your goals down makes you focus much more powerfully—especially when you write in a positive vein, in the present tense. (In other words, don't write "I no longer choose to slave for other people's clients," but "I have"—present tense—"my own clients"—a positive statement!) This is because, as discussed earlier, the subconscious possesses the means to manifest what you believe. If you write your goals down in the form in which you want to achieve them, then your mind instantly begins to figure out independently how to accomplish their fulfillment.

Of course, listing goals is only the first step; the second step is to include the detail. Don't just put, "I have attracted a new client." Instead, write "I have an initial project from a new client in the financial industry bringing in around $100,000 in fees, which should form the foundation for an ongoing relationship. My client and I work well together and I am further developing this client relationship by doing (a), (b), and (c)."

Once you've added the detail, you need to think about what your goal looks like; then you can visualize yourself having achieved it. How do you see yourself in that picture? Where are you? What are you doing? Whom are you with? How do you look? What does that satisfaction feel like? Give yourself a clear picture of the situation. Be specific on your worksheet: "I am wearing Jimmy Choo shoes and a cream suit. I feel the way I did in high school the day I heard I'd made valedictorian!"

"Why all the detail?" I hear you ask. Well, for two reasons. First, if you make yourself visualize your goal, it forces you to focus on what you really want. You might want a nice house (OK, right, who doesn't?), but what sort of house? Where is it? What does it look like? Doing this exercise can be eye-opening. One young lawyer I mentored was feeling uncertain, so I asked her what her goal was. "To make partner, of course," she replied. However, when I asked her to do this exercise, she realized that she had never really thought about the details of her goals—or (worse still) about what achieving them would really mean to her. The exercise made her recognize that she did indeed want to achieve partnership—but at a very different type of firm.

Don't Forget to Picture Your Success

Second, as you recall from Chapter 7, visualizing a goal as though it were already reality gives your mind a powerful blueprint (read: weapon!) for what you want to achieve. When you do this, your subconscious inevitably responds, "Fine, if that's how things look, then what can I do to make the reality match that picture?" And by visualizing yourself acting out your goals, you can create or strengthen the neural network in your brain to support their implementation. Visualizing causes the same neurons in the brain to "fire" as if you were in fact doing whatever you're imagining, whether it's showing the prime minister around your law chambers or winning the Masters golf tournament in Augusta! When you then attempt to achieve your goal, the brain is pre-patterned for success and instantly envisages a foundation to support your endeavors. (See Chapters 6 and 7.)

Another great technique is to draw a picture of your success, or to cut a photo from a magazine that represents its achievement. This makes your vision clear, vivid, and personal, and if you look at the same photo over and over again, it "centers" the subconscious. I mentioned earlier that tennis champion Chris Evert is known for espousing visualization techniques. While commentating during a Wimbledon championship, she told a story about Venus Williams that struck me as significant. When Venus was still a young and relatively unknown player, she and her father visited Ms. Evert. During the visit, Mr. Williams asked permission to take a picture of Venus holding Evert's Wimbledon trophy. Evert agreed. In these photos, Venus held the trophy up as if it were her own—and by implication, I assume that she studied these photos again and again. How prophetic, as the picture was finally played out (so far, five times) in reality!

One of my (very successful) friends routinely inspires himself by imagining himself with every image and every trait that he aspires to. His daydream always ends the same way, as his biggest rival comes up and grudgingly congratulates him on winning some "unwinnable" case!

> When you create a goal in the positive and present tense
> and put that into a visual picture (your "ideal brand"), your
> subconscious says, "If that is how things look, then what do I
> have to do to make reality match the picture?"

In his best-selling book (*The 7 Habits of Highly Effective People*), Stephen Covey suggests that we should all begin with the end in mind (Habit #2), a theory based on the principle that every accomplishment is in fact created twice, first mentally, and then in physical reality. Whether it is building a law practice or a house, the idea has to come first. Sometimes the mental creation is unconscious (perhaps an outcome of other people's agendas or of things we once heard), and thus the result is unintentional—that is, the consequence of the faulty subconscious, which was examined in Chapter 7 ("Thinking"). Nonetheless, the principle of mental creation *first* is still at play.

So I strongly advocate your taking control of that first, crucial, step: Generate a purposeful mental picture manifesting the goal *you* want to achieve, and then use the visualization techniques examined in Chapter 7. All the great achievers today do this, from top businessmen to professional athletes. Lee Iacocca wrote, "The discipline of writing something down is the first step toward making it happen" (*Iacocca: An Autobiography*), and he also acknowledged how the mind works in conjunction with such a step. The pioneering American psychologist William James said, "The greatest discovery of my generation is that human beings can alter their lives by altering their attitudes of mind." So use it! Here is an example from Rachel Boothroyd, partner, K & L Gates (a truly remarkable story!):

Writing down goals and then using the mind to support their achievement can achieve powerful results. I could give many examples of how this has worked for me, including one time when its effects were both positive and negative, which—bizarrely—was exactly the result I had requested. My goal was to land a new client and [a] big project from them, "whether it killed me," which were the exact words I remember using to myself repeatedly in an attempt to focus my determination on this much-wanted goal.

I subsequently succeeded in my goal, winning a significant job for the firm from a new client. I loved working on the job, and the demonstration of my skills at winning new business and new clients helped me to achieve equity status as a partner.

Simultaneously, though, and consistent with the message I had given myself, I was diagnosed with a serious heart condition—which very nearly did kill me. That old phrase "be careful what you wish for" is so very true.

The best example I can give of how powerful our minds can be relates to my sister Carrie, who has learning disabilities. Many years ago when she was a resident in Mencap sheltered housing, she had a lengthy session involving several counselors, who worked with her to refine and write down her goals:

1. *Working with horses;*
2. *Owning a dog;*
3. *Living independently in her own house; and*
4. *Spending time by the sea.*

Carrie then embodied her goals in a picture, which she put up on her bedroom wall. My parents, who had also attended the goal-setting session, confided in me how angry they felt at the creation of what they believed to be wholly unrealistic dreams for Carrie. They felt furious that the counselors were filling her head with "false hopes."

Carrie kept the picture on her wall and explained to everyone what her dreams for the future were. In this way I believe she continually focused her thoughts on the pictures of her new life.

Despite lacking the capability to really pursue her goals in the same way that most other people can, somehow the world turned to manifest her vision. Today, Carrie works at a stable with horses, owns a dog, lives independently in her own home, and spends time in a recently acquired family home by the sea. There is no logical rationale for Carrie's success—she just had unwavering belief in her personal goals.

TAKE ACTION!

At this point you should have already done two things with regard to your personal vision:

1. Developed the right one for you on the basis of your unique strengths and motivators, and

2. Created a mental blueprint.

Obviously, the last step is to put the vision into action. We can't just scribble our goals down and blissfully expect our brains to turn them into reality!

Instead, first identify a strategy and then analyze what needs to happen to turn the goal into reality. And, then, of course, make steady progress toward that plan.

Just as I can't determine the appropriate goal for you, I can't map out the right plan to enable you to achieve it. However, I *can* tell you that most successful people are propelled more by their vision (what matters to them) than by their plan itself. That said, we all need some sort of a map, and yours has to work for you, in light of your motivators, personality strengths, and—obviously—personal goals.

One thing that your strategy must include is how you will achieve your client-related goals, and—as discussed in the context of winning business—this encompasses not merely marketing but also delivering a unique value to your target clients. Doing this requires constant development and improvement of whatever that value might be because, by its very nature, selling unique value requires staying ahead of any competitors who might seek to provide similar value; in fact, one of your goals must be to discourage them from even trying. (Not competing with others on precisely the same dimension is what "unique value" is all about!) So go back to Chapter 13 and consider your "uniqueness strategy": what you are doing to promote—and maintain—the individuality of your own product.

As so many people have emphasized before me, it's important to keep your thinking positive; otherwise you risk getting sidelined or undermining your best chances for success. For example, if your goal is to become a partner but you find yourself constantly undercutting the senior people in your firm, you *must* be giving your mind conflicting information! At other times, everything objective may seem to be against you, yet your subconscious remains sublimely unaware of every obstacle between you and your dreams (sometimes dreams really *can* come true!). So use all the tools we discussed in Chapter 7, and let them work their magic. You don't have to analyze every step that will take you to your goals; you only have to be completely sure of where you really want to be.

Naturally, the more specific the goal, the easier it is to measure your progress toward it. But it is most important that you monitor your goals regularly, maintain your focus, test your commitment, and feel confident that your goal continues to be the right one.

I'm reminded of the story about the frog and the pot of boiling water. If you put a live frog into a pot of boiling water, he will immediately jump out. However, if you put the same frog in the same pot with room-temperature water, he may notice that he's no longer in optimal conditions ("Hey, what happened to my lovely pond?"), yet he tends to adjust. If you then gradually turn the heat up, the frog does nothing, and before he knows it, he's actually in boiling water again—and *voilà*! Frog soup! In the same way, if you don't keep your focus, life can creep up on you and subtly lower your powers of resistance.

Here's a real-life example of this syndrome. Justin joined the litigation group of his firm, though he felt less than enthusiastic about it until he became involved in a case dealing with complex intellectual property (IP) rights. It wasn't the litigation that enthralled him, but the fascination inherent in intellectual property issues. After the dispute was settled, Justin began working with his firm's corporate department to create "standard practice" IP guidelines, which he then began marketing to clients. He realized that he truly enjoyed explaining how to organize and protect clients' rights and helping clients implement their preferred strategies. He transitioned into the firm's corporate department and built up a very satisfying practice specializing in these matters.

One day a client firm asked Justin to help reorganize its corporate intellectual property worldwide—in effect, his dream job. Gradually the size and importance of the engagement increased until Justin found himself working almost exclusively with this client, traveling around to their many locations, giving presentations, and implementing programs. He couldn't have been happier!—or more trusted. However, when the client firm became involved in several contentious disputes, its board immediately engaged Justin to lead their defense, putting him back in the throes of a litigation practice. Despite this vote of confidence, Justin found himself inexplicably unhappy. He puzzled over it. After all, he was still working with the same client, and he was still immersed in subject matter he found profoundly interesting. What was wrong?

Only by stepping back and being honest did Justin realize that his new role neither played to his true strengths nor allowed him to do what he enjoyed, and that it was up to him to have the discipline to "just say no!" When his firm tried to persuade Justin to continue with the litigation and, in fact, even suggested that he use the experience gained to develop and market a (related) specialty practice, Justin steadfastly refused. He transferred the main duties of litigation to one of his colleagues and returned to doing what he loved: corporate IP strategy and development.

Had Justin not been focused on his personal vision, he might have found himself heading a litigation practice, which was not the right place for him (in spite of the fact that it was likely to prove extremely profitable). Instead Justin remained vigilant, and thrived.

YOUR BRAND

The last thing to consider with regard to your personal vision is that it must be pursued in tandem with your brand. So if you haven't thought about your brand for several chapters, I urge you to reflect on it again.

■ Does your brand support your personal vision (and meet the expectations of the clients pictured within it)?

■ Does your "ideal brand" coincide with the mental picture you have of the future, which shows you achieving your vision?

Vision-Building

1. What is the **vision**? What are my long-term aspirations?

2. What are my **goals** toward achieving that vision? (Include both client ambitions and brand-development ambitions.)

3. What's my **strategy** to achieve those goals?

   a. Does my strategy include delivering a unique value, as opposed to simply competing on the same dimension as other lawyers? What is my unique value, anyway?

   b. Does my brand help me achieve my strategy and deliver on the value I promise?

   c. How do I plan to enhance my brand so that my experience and superiority deepen and evolve?

   d. What is my plan for marketing and promoting myself?

- Pursuing my vision, goals, and strategy should
  - leverage my strengths
  - spark my inner motivators, and thus generate both inspiration and the inner fire needed to succeed and find satisfaction
- Along the way, I will
  - monitor my progress
  - test my commitment
  - imprint the vision and associated goals into my mind by seeing them in the present, as though they have already happened

POSITIVE PERSEVERANCE

Because leaders generally zero in on the "right" personal vision for them, they tend to be hugely optimistic about their ability to deliver. In Chapter 7, in the context of developing confidence, we discovered that a person's belief about his ability to achieve something (whether that optimism is actually justified or not!) is one of the greatest determinants of whether or not it happens—as proved by internationally recognized psychologist Albert Bandura (a theory called *self-efficacy.*) It will therefore come as no surprise to hear that leaders have this self-confidence: barrel-loads of it! This is in large part because leaders tend to gravitate toward the "right" personal vision for themselves, thereby ensuring that it leverages their strengths. We all feel more confident when working with our strengths because we succeed more easily, and because each such success only serves to compound our self-belief.

For the same reason, the leader's vision naturally tends to satisfy his core needs and draw upon his most fervent passions. This relates to what another prominent psychologist, Mihaly Csikszentmihalyi, calls *flow*—defined as the zone of satisfaction (even elation) that we feel when immersed in a challenge that plays to our strengths. The flow, an optimal state of *intrinsic motivation*, is characterized by an ideal mix of great freedom, enjoyment, fulfillment, and skill—which, not surprisingly, tends to lift the person involved into a mood of confident optimism.

When we're in a state of "flow," we are involved in an activity for its own sake while our skills are being used optimally. *In short, our focus, motivation, and goals are perfectly aligned for peak performance and ideal job satisfaction.* This is the leader's state while pursuing his personal vision—as well as the state of top performers in every discipline at the peak of their form. Just watch an entrepreneur "working" his skeptics—or a soprano wowing her critics!

The real secret is setting the right personal vision, and that must be preceded by self-awareness. When you align what you do with who you are, you succeed by capitalizing on your own unique makeup.

MANAGING EMOTIONS

As discussed earlier, managing your emotions is not only essential to people skills but is equally crucial to supporting your brand. It's also a clear sign of mature leadership development. When discussing the challenges of career advancement with those at the top of the legal profession, I repeatedly heard things like this:

> *"One of the hardest things for me to learn on the partnership track was that I not only had to <u>feel</u> like a leader but also had to <u>project</u> myself as a leader—which means that if I felt angry or upset, I had to find a way to manage those emotions intelligently."*

> *"That was when I learned that I had a choice—quite a simple choice, really! I could either get mad and make myself look stupid, or else deal with the situation and make myself look good."*

> *"I was never taught to manage people in a team framework: This was just thrust upon me. One of the most difficult things to learn was how to deal with frustration when people let me down, so that my annoyance didn't isolate or antagonize them completely."*

In common with these three lawyers, you have a choice about how you deal with your emotions. You probably can't change the things that make you angry, but you can change how you respond! This not only affects others' perceptions of you, but it is fundamental to your capacity as a leader because, as we examined in Chapter 6 ("People Skills"), it's been scientifically proven that emotions are contagious. If you emit toxic emotions, you create an aura of toxicity around you as well, leading to misery and a lack of productivity.

You have a choice in how you deal with your emotions: You can't change the things that make you angry, but you can change the way you respond.

MANAGING STRESS

Stress is as unavoidable in law as it is in all professions—but it can be managed. First, understand what creates stress for you. This is usually an intensely personal issue. I know when I start feeling stressed because things that

446

wouldn't normally irritate me suddenly start to bother me immensely. For example, standing in line waiting to pay for my lunchtime sandwich feels like an affront, and instead of being personable and friendly with the cashier, I can barely muster a professional smile. Maybe you get irritable too, or perhaps you do something different: shout at people, eat too much, smoke or drink excessively, lose sleep—or even become ill. Whatever it is, you know the signs as well as I do.

So what's the answer? When you see (or, more likely, *feel*) the warning signs, force yourself to take a step back and think about what you can do to alleviate the pressure. Failure to do this just prolongs the stress, which will ultimately result in greater harm to your overall health and your psychological well-being.

I realize as lawyers, that we're supposed to be machines—especially Drivers like me, who revel in their ability to work and work and work. Big projects, tough deadlines, and grinding through the night were always my *forte*. I even got a "buzz" from overwork! I truly believed that I worked my best under such conditions, when my adrenaline was at its peak. But I was wrong. I wasn't working better: I was just working harder and harder and faster and faster, like a hamster on its wheel, going nowhere fast!

I now know that to manage stress and achieve *more*, I have to find a way to relax my mind every day—even if it's only for five minutes. By this I don't mean watching TV or having a drink with a friend after work; I'm talking about letting the mind calm itself—optimally in the alpha-theta state we examined in Chapter 7 ("Thinking").

If you already meditate, you'll know what I'm talking about. But if you, like me, find it hard to relax, sit still, or even temporarily shut your brain down, then you're probably already protesting, "I don't feel comfortable with that New Age stuff. It's the fact that my brain's always rushing around that gives me an edge!" Believe me, I've felt that way too, but I was wrong—and you might just be wrong too!

Consider the "fight-or-flight" response, originally discovered by Harvard physiologist Walter Cannon. This is our body's innate emergency reaction to danger, physically preparing us, like all animals, to react fast when threatened. It is triggered by the brain's hypothalamus, which releases a surge of adrenaline and related hormones, which in turn increase heart rate, respiratory rate, and blood pressure.

While most of us no longer require the fight-or-flight response for its original purpose (saber-tooth tigers not being *too* much of a threat these days, even in our profession!), we actually activate it more than ever—through stress. Most lawyers get tense on a daily basis: sitting in rush-hour traffic, fretting about missing a deadline, rehashing what was said in an argument... And each one of these moments—not exactly useful—can trigger the fight-or-flight response. Over time, frequent activation builds up stress hormones, which can result in health disorders.

Renowned Harvard cardiologist Herbert Benson, M.D., believes that the more anyone activates the fight-or-flight response, the more likely he or she is to develop high blood pressure. To counter-act these repercussions, Dr. Benson has introduced the "relaxation response." As the name implies, this is a state of relaxation in which the practitioner quiets the mind, causing a different part of the hypothalamus to release neutralizing chemicals. These chemicals trigger a decrease in heart rate, respiratory rate, and blood pressure, while boosting beneficial "alpha" brain waves.

In his book *The Relaxation Response,* Dr. Benson mentions many techniques for relaxing (including meditation and yoga), suggesting that, whatever method we choose, we do it for at least ten or fifteen minutes, once or twice a day. Although he refrains from recommending one method over the others, he does prescribe two essential steps: repeating a word, sound, phrase, or muscle activity—such as deep breathing—and disregarding everyday thoughts as they come to mind.

Initiating the relaxation response doesn't have to be complicated: just taking a walk or lying in a warm bath can work. Meditating can even be done in the midst of commotion—for example, on the underground while traveling to work—though this takes more practice.

Calming the mind is not merely beneficial in terms of the fight-or-flight response. Groundbreaking research is proving that meditation can alter the structure of the brain, just as thoughts and actions have been found to change the brain's neural networks (see Chapters 6 and 7). Evidence shows that meditation can modify the neural connections between the thinking and emotional parts of the brain, promoting greater empathy and resilience (both necessary for strong leading!). Meditation can also be used as "brain training." In a recent study,

Harvard neurobiologist Dr. Sara Lazar showed that brain regions associated with attention and sensory processing were stronger in people who meditated.

Another thing I'm sure you know—but which bears repeating—is that exercise is proven to reduce stress and increase energy levels. I can hear all the excuses already: "Exercise? I'd love to, but I don't have the time." Well, I don't buy it; the problem is not lack of time but misplaced priorities. What if a doctor told you that unless you exercised three times per week, revamped your diet, and lost 50 pounds, you'd be dead within a year? (This actually happened to a friend of mine.) I bet you'd somehow *find* the time, just as my friend did. For most of us it's not about schedules; it's about motivation.

Exercise can also metabolize harmful stress hormones. Personally, I find that running quiets my mind (for me, it's like meditation) and restores my body to a calm, relaxed, and energized state, but I'm not wild-eyed and evangelical about it, like some runners... Whatever exercise works for you is great.

GAINING STRENGTH FROM A CRISIS

Almost everyone faces a serious professional setback at some stage, and most of us face at least one genuine career crisis. If neither has happened to you, count yourself lucky, but not immune; who knows what might be around the corner? And when a crisis comes—redundancy, recession, whatever—you must dig deep and find resilience, persistence, and a whole lot of other things to get you through it, and (with luck) out the other side. The process is likely to be one of the hardest educational experiences of your career, but everyone learns the most when times are toughest, and the person who steps up to the plate without self-pity is certain to develop an enviable inner strength.

Just as someone who is overstressed (or who smokes or drinks too much) will avoid changing his habits until he must, a lawyer in career trouble may ignore the warning signs. Often there are hints that a problem may be hovering over the horizon, but most people do nothing and hope for the best until disaster strikes. A leader, however, notices the signs of trouble and takes action. This is what distinguishes a leader from the rest.

- The rest ignore all warning signs. The leader analyzes the situation.

- The rest blame the circumstances, their bosses, or the people around them: "Poor me!" The leader looks inward: "The situation is not good. What can I do to make it better?"

For example, "Quentin" was recently made partner. For the first few months he found very little work and he was beginning to feel frustrated and uncomfortable without his usual high billable hours (the Valley of Death!). Luckily, Quentin's partner had some overflow work and handed a project to Quentin, which enabled him to supplement his chargeable hours. When that project came to an end, however, Quentin again felt nervous and restless.

If Quentin is typical, he will

- Ignore the situation and hope more work will come his way

- Secretly blame his firm for not having a better client base

- Resent his partners for not being more cooperative in sharing their work

- Consider changing firms because he's certain it's really his environment that is causing his problems

However, if Quentin is a leader, he will

- Analyze the situation and acknowledge his problem, which is (you guessed it): HE HAS NO CLIENTS!

- Take responsibility for the situation and think, "What do I have to change about myself to improve my position?"

- Dig deep and ask himself, "How are my personality, thinking patterns, brand, and people skills affecting my performance? How can I be more resourceful?"

The leader does not blame the conditions around him (or her) but looks **inward**, for three reasons:

First and foremost, he understands that the only thing he can control is himself, so he first looks at how he must change his own actions to improve the situation. If he doesn't get along with his boss, for example, he cannot control his boss's behavior, but he can at least control his own. He can either do things that might improve the situation, or he can simply take control of how he responds to his boss.

Second, the leader does not place false blame—on life, on other people, or on circumstances. He honestly acknowledges that *he* plays the biggest role in what happens to him.

Third, a leader knows that he can't solve his problems with the same actions and thinking that got him there. Something has to change, and the leader knows that the change must come from within.

CHANGE IS INEVITABLE

It's normal not to like change. When change happens, however, we can choose either to crawl back into bed and bury our heads under the covers, or to face it head on. And if we're strong enough to face it, we can even go one step further and try to turn it into an opportunity. For example, I'll bet some of the biggest improvements in your life were the result of unexpected change, sometimes even of what—at the time—you considered to be a complete disaster! Here are a few.

■ Your boyfriend dumps you. *Big* change. You haven't been single for ages. You feel devastated for weeks, and think your world has come to an end. How can you operate as a single? How can you cope, especially with your workload? But slowly you do, and you start to make new friends, and you begin to discover yourself again. Eventually, as a more mature and a more impressive person, you meet a much nicer boyfriend than that jerk you were stuck with before...

■ Upon graduating from law school, you lose the job of your dreams —to your best friend. Disaster! You finally accept a position at a much smaller and less prestigious firm, which feels like an appalling letdown. However, while there you discover talents you'd never even thought about exploring; you feel excited and alive and full of possibilities. Meanwhile, your best friend is slogging away in his posh job for 14 hours a day, in a windowless office, in a department he hates.

■ You're fired, and feel devastated because your whole identity was wrapped up in your job. Unable to find a position similar to the one you had, you step back and think long and hard about what you really want to do. And then you find it! What a break it was, in retrospect, having been made redundant!

When change—even bad change—happens, we're often forced to contemplate our next step and change ourselves. Leaders instinctively accept this as just part of the process of growth. Rather than fighting change, they attempt to view each surprise or setback as an opportunity to uncover something even better. This positive mindset is a key aspect of what sets leaders apart. Note, too, that *motivating others toward a shared purpose* (our third and final phase of leadership) is all about leading change and becoming adept at managing it, for which the ability to spot opportunities (and to inspire others) is essential.

I can't tell you anything about dealing with change that hasn't already been captured in a brilliant little book entitled *Who Moved My Cheese?* by Dr. Spencer Johnson. If you haven't read it already, I urge you to do so. It's very short, but its message is both wise and entertaining.

> A leader knows that he cannot always change a situation, but he can change himself within it.

MISTAKES ARE THE BEST LEARNING TOOL AVAILABLE!

Leaders acknowledge, and learn from, their mistakes. Most successful people have failed at some point or other, often quite miserably. In all likelihood not only your firm's best rainmaker but even its managing partner have made massive professional mistakes, though they probably don't go around trumpeting it on their résumés (the secret of writing a strong résumé is knowing what to leave out!).

Nobody actually sets out to fail, but *there is no better education*. Through our mistakes we frequently learn the most valuable lessons in our lives—the things that no Ivy League or Oxbridge education can begin to teach. But, of course, this is *only* the case if we admit our mistakes and take intelligent steps to prevent them from recurring. This doesn't mean beating ourselves up for our faults—it just means learning, accepting, and growing.

Sometimes it's tempting to lose heart and give up after a major error. However, any leader will tell you that this is the most crucial time to focus on one's goals, to maintain one's self-belief, and to fix what went wrong. By embracing both problems and failures, we join the same club as some of the world's most successful businesspeople. Steve Jobs, the "man of the moment" with his iPod and his iPhone, was once fired by Apple, the very company he helped to found—which he now leads. Bill Gates, Richard Branson, Donald Trump, and almost any other markedly successful business name that springs to mind all suffered major setbacks, including bankruptcy (Trump) and jail (Branson). What makes these men different from so many other error-prone hopefuls is their ability to grow from—and grow out of—their mistakes.

When you don't learn from your mistakes you are doomed to repeat them, over and over again. You may switch departments or change jobs, but if you take your negligent behavior or arrogant thinking with you, you have resolved nothing.

If right now you've been knocked back, or even knocked down, think long and honestly about how your own actions might have contributed. Failure to do so simply means that you're setting yourself up for another disappointment.

LEADERS THRIVE!

Leaders don't just survive adversity—they thrive on it! One example is Lance Armstrong, who is not only an exceptional athlete but also an inspiring leader. When faced with a cancer so invasive that he was given survival odds of less than 50 percent, he chose to endure a brutally aggressive treatment. In the end, his choice (along with his positive attitude) saved his life. Armstrong's battle with cancer would be extraordinary by itself, but what makes his story still more remarkable is that he used the experience to become an even better athlete, a still more positive person, and a still more impressive leader. Cancer taught Armstrong that he had an incredible (but previously untapped) physical and mental strength, which he credits for his subsequent seven Tour de France titles. Because Armstrong acted as a leader, he empowered himself with self-belief and optimism. (In his book *It's Not About the Bike: My Journey Back to Life*, Armstrong writes: "I didn't fully see, until the cancer, how we fight every day against the creeping negatives of the world.") Within months of his diagnosis, Armstrong set up the Lance Armstrong Foundation, which remains dedicated to spreading his message that cancer, like any other challenge, may only be an obstacle in the mind. In essence, through surviving the ultimate challenge (by acting like a leader), he grew into an even more impressive person!

While I hope that you will never have to face anything quite as traumatic, I can guarantee that you will still have challenges, which is when Armstrong's example can help and inspire. Don't let adversity defeat you; instead, use it to empower yourself. Call upon (and ultimately test) your leadership qualities, viewing your challenges merely as opportunities to develop or transform yourself. This is the mindset that distinguishes real leaders.

ALWAYS LEARNING

Leaders see beyond the day's workload—they are always planning, learning new skills, and trying to develop themselves. They are focused on the things that are *important* but not necessarily *immediate*—that is, the quadrant 2 activities that we examined in Chapter 2. Leaders know that the only way to attain their vision (or to visualize what that future could hold in the first place) is to seek greater knowledge and to master new skills.

If, once we've reached our immediate goal, we decide that we no longer need to learn and grow, we're sadly mistaken. Such an attitude immediately puts our hard-won position of leadership in jeopardy, because leaders—by definition—prioritize personal growth. In fact, study after study has shown that one of the biggest differentiators in high-performing leaders is that they are constantly seeking out and identifying areas in which they still need to grow.

RECAP AND SUMMARY

To move into our next stage of leadership, we must start by managing our own behavior, emotions, and mindset. We do this by drawing on the five characteristics of a leader discussed in the previous chapter: by being trustworthy, self-aware, people-focused, positive, and visionary. This in turn sets off a powerful chain reaction: We develop confidence in our vision and enthusiastically influence ourselves toward achieving it—even in the face of unexpected or unwelcome challenges. Our optimism favorably affects others and helps us to influence them (the subject of the next chapter!), while it simultaneously improves the behavior and moods of everyone around us.

Such an environment promotes the goals of every leader and every law firm: trust, motivation, and accomplishment.

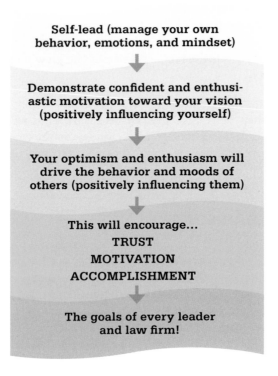

Self-lead (manage your own behavior, emotions, and mindset)

↓

Demonstrate confident and enthusiastic motivation toward your vision (positively influencing yourself)

↓

Your optimism and enthusiasm will drive the behavior and moods of others (positively influencing them)

↓

This will encourage...
TRUST
MOTIVATION
ACCOMPLISHMENT

↓

The goals of every leader and law firm!

So, before moving on to the next step, allow me to recap how we manage ourselves as leaders:

1. We develop and maintain the right personal vision, and work toward it daily;

2. We sustain positive perseverance toward our vision through self-belief and internal motivation;

3. Rather than allowing natural emotions to undermine us, we manage them intelligently, keeping in mind that our behaviors and moods—however foul—are likely to be mirrored by those around us;

4. We acknowledge that we perform best when in good physical health and in command of stress, so we act to make these benefits more likely;

5. When a problem arises, we face it head on and look inward to identify causes and locate solutions, rather than assigning blame elsewhere;

6. We view change, first and foremost, as an opportunity;

7. We turn our inevitable mistakes to our advantage by learning how to avoid their repetition;

8. We commit ourselves to life-long learning because only in this way can we expect to become high-performing leaders in the long term.

SUMMARY: If you want to be a leader you have to manage yourself as one and play the part of one. You have to feel it, think it, and be it, even (and especially) in the face of emotional struggles and difficult challenges. And if you do, the people around you will perceive it and respond positively to you.

Chapter Twenty
Leading Within Relationships

In Chapter 18 we first examined the characteristics of a leader. However, genuine leadership cannot be demonstrated by the display of any single trait, however admirable. Instead, leadership exists through the perceptions of those we hope to influence; it's something that happens between people.

Leaders know this and build up a network of power through their relationships. They do this in three ways:

1. By generating trust;

2. By knowing how to influence; and

3. By synergizing their talents with those of others.

Relationships cultivated out of such soil facilitate the leader's personal vision and set the foundation for mobilizing others toward a shared purpose. This happens because people within the leader's network tend to be alert to the leader's best interests, to support his (or her) goals, to willingly work for the leader (occasionally even against their own best interests!), to provide complementary strengths and talents to those of the leader, to reproduce the leader's leadership—or even to choose to become one of his clients.

Leaders cultivate a network of power through creating trusting relationships, knowing how to influence, and synergizing their talents with those of others.

CONNECT AND COLLABORATE

We subconsciously consider our colleagues mainly in terms of their relation to us—peer, boss, teammate, or competitor. Yet, when used in isolation, this becomes a self-limiting strategy. We should build relationships with these people in exactly the same way as with our clients: by working to generate their trust. You may not consider all your colleagues to be friends (though at least some should qualify—with luck!), but doing so is critical for leadership. Friendship is the most positive of all relationships and puts you in the strongest possible position to influence others. As Abraham Lincoln said, "If you would win a man to your cause, first convince him that you are his sincere friend." This may seem blindingly obvious, but amid all the stress of day-to-day commitments it's easy to forget the most obvious things.

Admittedly, you'll probably also have a few colleagues who frankly could never be perceived as friendship material, and it's then that your ability to build relationships comes powerfully into play. Leaders identify value in all their colleagues and leverage everyone's abilities to achieve the best possible results. Allowing your emotions to affect your judgment is at best self-indulgent and at worst self-defeating, even if one or more of your colleagues had a charisma bypass at birth!

I once had a colleague who, despite having *no, nil, zero,* and *zilch* experience in my area of expertise, coolly required me to relinquish all my previous deal materials so that he could bag all the credit. In short, he not only marketed my expertise in his name, he even managed to exclude me from the process! Furious, I decided to retaliate by refusing to share more of my knowledge with this colleague, a decision that I now recognize as foolishly impulsive. I would have achieved far more by acknowledging his strengths (for example, he had no qualms about knocking on people's doors and advertising his credentials—even if they were actually mine!). A combination of his marketing dexterity with my deal experience would almost certainly have been mutually beneficial. Instead, I withheld my proprietary knowledge and withdrew from all interaction with him, turning him into a rival. I was the real loser, however, because he continued to market brilliantly (and win business) in spite of my actions, in some cases even using *my* track record of deals and experience to gain new clients.

In a similar situation, my friend Rachel reacted differently. She was offered an opportunity to pitch for a deal, but first had two difficulties to resolve. First, her firm's rules required an equity partner to head any pitch, and Rachel was then only a junior partner. Second, by far the most suitable equity partner for the job (in terms of credentials) was someone she particularly disliked—and with good reason. It was galling to think that she had done all the work to develop the opportunity, yet this partner would certainly take all the credit if they won the deal! However, she weighed her options and finally invited him into the project. In the end, he did indeed receive benefit as the named equity partner, but as the person with the real client relationship it was Rachel who gained most over the long term, because winning that deal created more work for *her*. Had she chosen not to team up with her rival, she would almost certainly have lost out.

Sharing opportunities and knowledge with colleagues is essential to your success, whether you like it or not—and, to be honest, most people don't. I admit that this often feels like relinquishing a personal advantage, but the sacrifice is often returned many times over. Imagine giving opportunities to ten different colleagues: If only four or five give something back, that's still a high rate of return!

Turning Obnoxious Colleagues into Allies

When you have obnoxious colleagues the best thing to do is turn them into allies, using all your diplomacy and finesse. The first step is to make sure that you don't allow personal antagonism (on either side) to cause you to overlook their strong points; the second is to understand their point of view. The values and needs that appear to be driving these colleagues may, on the face of it, appear illogical or even contemptible, but it's your job to dig deeper.

One example of this scenario occurred between two partners, Karen and Alan (not their real names!). Alan was a senior partner who boasted a handful of strong client relationships along with a less enviable reputation for (a) never sharing billable credits and (b) never bringing other lawyers within hailing distance of "his" clients—unless absolutely necessary. As the junior partner, Karen put in significant time and effort to help Alan on a certain client pitch; in fact, it was mainly due to her special expertise that they won the deal. Subsequently, however, Karen realized that Alan had taken full origination credit. Not unreasonably, she stormed into his office, where the following scene ensued:

Karen: (annoyed)	"I can't *believe* you took full credit! At the very least, I should get half of the origination!"
Alan: (amused)	"Listen, I was the one who built up the long-term relationship in the first place, and you'll still get billables

out of the project." (Although, as we know, billables are worth much less than an origination credit.)

Karen:
(fuming) "But without my expertise, you'd never have landed the deal in the first place!"

Alan:
(coolly) "OK, and without my client relationship, you wouldn't have landed anything, end of story! You should feel lucky to get the billables you'll get out of it."

At this point it was clear to Karen that the conversation was going nowhere, so she left Alan's office. Thinking about it more rationally later, she realized that she had three choices:

1. She could settle for far less credit than she deserved and vow never to help Alan again.

2. She could go higher up in the firm and complain about Alan's behavior (which would only create further antagonism).

3. She could attempt a new tactic.

Karen chose option 3. First, she thought long and hard about Alan's perspective. He was an older partner with limited sources of revenue, primarily centered on this one, supremely loyal, client. She also knew that during the pitching process she had appeared to impress the clients and connect with them, possibly in a way that Alan himself couldn't have done if he were meeting the same clients for the first time. She was even mature enough to admit to herself that in Alan's position she would also feel vulnerable. In the end, she selected her strategy and returned to Alan's office.

Karen: "Hi, Alan. I've been thinking, and I agree that I was fortunate that you've developed such a good relationship with this client—and that you gave me the opportunity to be a part of this project" (making Alan feel important and appreciated).

Alan: "I'm glad you're seeing it my way, Karen."

Karen: "I also think we worked really well together on that pitch and that possibly we could do more for this client together."

<table>
<tr><td>**Alan:**</td><td>"Look, let's just get through this deal first and then we'll see" (still clearly feeling nervous that Karen might be encroaching on his connection with his client).</td></tr>
<tr><td>**Karen:**</td><td>"Of course, and that's why I'm going to settle for billable credits in this instance. But I still think that we might get some more opportunities in the future, so—if I'm right—I'm going to come to you with my ideas. I'd just like you to agree now that when I do, we'll approach the client together as a team and that you'll give me my fair share of the client originations."</td></tr>
</table>

Obviously, Alan could only agree, because Karen had approached him with a true understanding of his perspective, and because she was offering a benefit rather than depriving him of something. (Of course, she was also smart enough to follow up with an email confirming their agreement!)

Nurturing Positive Relationships

Another drawback of failing to nurture positive relationships with colleagues is that their antagonism is likely to come back to haunt you, and not just in terms of relationships with your fellow lawyers. For example, after someone in the marketing department resigned from my firm—partly due to negligent treatment from someone else in the firm—she contacted me about a lucrative project that her cousin's company had to offer. It ended up being a significant piece of work for me, yet from our very first discussion she made it crystal clear that she would not permit that other person to be involved in any capacity. (Little did he know that his casual mistreatment of someone "merely" in the marketing department ended up costing him significant revenue!)

A similar situation happened recently, when I was recommending a particular firm as rare specialists (and, incidentally, great people) for a large project being undertaken by a friend's corporation. After engaging them, my friend Jake discussed the project team with me, whereupon I learned that an ex-colleague of mine had moved to that firm and was eligible to work on the project. I was in no position to comment on his competence, but I *could* testify that, as his colleague, I had found him to be impossibly arrogant, self-satisfied, and difficult. When I described my personal encounters with this person (which I felt sure were very different from the impression he created with his clients), Jake decided that he would prefer not to employ him. So he went back to the firm, making it clear that he would not accept any billable hours invoiced by my ex-colleague. Again, this person is likely oblivious to the fact that his treatment of a one-time colleague could so negatively affect him years—and several career moves—after the event. Never forget: It's a small world—especially in the law.

In the unlikely event that you are still unconvinced about the importance of good colleague relationships, let me just mention Robin, who was shocked when passed over for partnership. A superb lawyer, Robin had also proven her relationship-building abilities by charming one client who had proved impossible for any other associate to handle. She was therefore bewildered when her firm told her that she wouldn't even be given another chance at a leadership position until she had further developed her "people skills."

Following my advice, she resolutely went about gathering feedback from her colleagues and found that her support among them ranged from nil to negligible. Further, although she performed exceptionally well on a technical level, their opinions of her work were biased by their lack of connection to her. Thus, ironically, she was universally viewed as an inferior performer, despite being one of the most accomplished lawyers in the firm. In the end, Robin became convinced that her firm had been right to withhold partnership, because, had she been given the position, she wouldn't have commanded sufficient support to maintain it. (Remember, strong leadership is wholly contingent upon the support of willing followers!)

Since that time Robin has learned to use her people skills as adeptly with her colleagues as she had always done with her clients, having learned the hard way that building the right connections within her firm is just as critical to one's career path as bringing in business. Eventually, Robin did succeed in her efforts and was made partner.

INFLUENCE

Since leadership so often involves the ability to persuade others to accept change, it naturally starts with influence. The most straightforward form of influencing others is known as "transactional" leadership. In this scenario, leader and follower generally agree on a performance level, with the leader doling out rewards for exceptional performance and taking corrective action if the required level is not met. (In other words, meeting the agreed-upon performance levels is simply the norm.) Transactional leadership works—and it *does* work—only because it is clearly in the subordinate's immediate interest to meet performance expectations (to receive a bonus, higher salary, better title, or desirable client project). It has serious shortcomings with regard to creative or long-term challenges, but it remains a common leadership style for many lawyers, who are either unable or unwilling to adopt a superior method.

Contrast this with the transformational leadership we first examined in Chapter 18 (leading through *example, enthusiasm, challenge,* and *empowerment*), and it will be clear that transformational leadership motivates far more powerfully. It doesn't "trump" transactional leadership (which will always have its uses), but instead expands and improves upon it.

By this point in the book you should be acutely aware of personality types, and therefore will have already recognized that each style of influence uses particular character strengths. *Influencing through example* (being a role model of confidence and competence) draws on the Driver's naturally assured and capable personality. *Influencing through enthusiasm* is the Connecter's best card, as he or she has no difficulty communicating a vision and creating passion for any particular goal. As the most sophisticated seeker of quality, the Perfectionist has an understandable bias toward intellectual stimulation and *influencing through challenge*, while the empathetic Moderate is focused on the individual concerns of those around him and generally prefers to *influence through empowerment.*

Consider this diagram of personality strengths as they relate to the four transformational ways of influencing as a leader.

Inspires with optimistic enthusiasm ("influences through **enthusiasm**")

Empathizes, coaches, and advises individually ("influences through **empowerment**")

CONNECTER

EXTROVERTED:
people-driven

Enthusiastic
Optimistic
Expressive
Spontaneous
Energetic
Playful

MODERATE

INTROVERTED:
but one-on-one relationship-focused

Even-tempered
Tolerant
Empathetic
Diplomatic
Facilitative
Process-oriented

EXTROVERTED:
activity-driven

Goal-oriented
Powerful
Takes charge
Capable
Visionary/intuitive
Forthright/direct

INTROVERTED:
very introspective

Task-oriented
Perfectionistic
Analytical
Logical
Structured
Principled

DRIVER

Maintains vision, confidence, and commitment ("influences through **example**")

PERFECTIONIST

Provides intellectual stimulation ("influences through **challenge**")

While each personality type naturally employs one form of leadership more readily than the others, bear in mind that we are all *capable* of implementing any form of leadership. You may simply need to consciously develop some of the styles that come less naturally to you.

One of the biggest stumbling blocks is that your natural method of communication may not be the best way to influence a person whose character differs from yours. I once read a book called *The Five Love Languages* by Gary Chapman. The premise of the book is that people want to feel loved in one or more of five ways:

- Quality time
- Words of affirmation
- Gifts
- Acts of service
- Physical touch

The cleverest part of Chapman's thesis is that you tend to express love in the way that you most long to receive it—which, of course, might (or might not) be consistent with your partner's preference. And when you're out of synch with your partner, the two of you are effectively speaking two different languages. For example, if your wife craves quality time but you're stuck working long hours in the office, then you're not communicating love in the language she needs, regardless of how much money you're bringing in. And when you bring her flowers (mainly because *you* happen to enjoy receiving gifts), she's unlikely to appreciate them as you expect her to, because you're still not communicating in her desired "love language." (Try canceling your weekend golf game and taking her out instead!)

Similarly, to motivate your colleagues, you must first learn how they prefer to be inspired. Everyone responds to each tool of influence to some degree, but one method will typically prove more persuasive than all the others. Again, this takes us back to personality types. As a typical Connecter, Nick uses enthusiasm to motivate, but Cynthia (a deep Perfectionist with Driver undertones—she has strong analytical skills and desires resolution) is best motivated when presented with an intellectual challenge that she can solve. So if Nick wants to influence Cynthia, he should supplement his impetuous enthusiasm (which Cynthia might secretly view as just hot air) with a challenge that Cynthia can sink her teeth into.

Conversely, if Cynthia hopes to influence Nick, then rather than presenting her issue as just another challenge requiring resolution (which Nick will probably view as somewhat depressing), she should summon all her enthusiasm to breathe life into her project, endowing it with purpose and meaning.

By speaking to Nick's heart, Cynthia will enlist his natural passion and fire him with support for her idea.

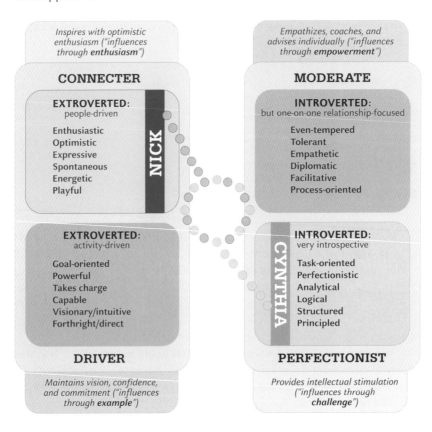

Regardless of personality type, we all respond to being influenced through empowerment, since everyone wants to feel encouraged and appreciated. But one of our biggest challenges with regard to motivating others through appreciation is realizing that different people react to different *types* of appreciation.

■ The hardest workers (probably Drivers) are most strongly motivated by *getting things done*. So they seek acknowledgment of their effort, especially because they tend to think that they are carrying a disproportionate share of the workload. Acclaiming their achievements and recognizing them as the *best* will help them to feel that their efforts are appreciated.

■ Extroverts (probably Connecters) are most strongly motivated by *public approval,* which is the source of their energy. Entertainers at heart, they crave an audience—and applause. Give them praise, especially in front of others, and they will be inspired to new heights. (Also, remember that Connecters are easily bored, so they need *ongoing* encouragement, not merely on project completion.)

- Perfectionists are motivated by *getting things right,* and they feel most recognized when their need for—and even occasional delivery of—perfection is acknowledged. It's also worth bearing in mind that disregarding or downgrading an idea from a Perfectionist is by definition demotivating because he or she will certainly have put significant effort and logical analysis into the concept; even putting it on the table will probably represent something significant for the Perfectionist. (This level of preparation is utterly foreign to the typical Connecter, who will often toss out an idea—take it or leave it—without having thought it through!)

- Moderates usually prefer to get on with the job. As the least extreme of all the personalities, they are accustomed to being overlooked. The Connecter has cornered center stage; the Driver is out there winning awards; and the Perfectionist is often intellectually superior. The Moderate doesn't stand out in the same, rather obvious, "look at me!" style, but he still needs to feel special and appreciated. When leading a Moderate, it's your job to make sure that he knows he's a valued and integral component of the team.

To recap, if you want to spur your colleagues into action, you can certainly use transactional leadership, especially for short-term projects with clear-cut deliverables for which some extrinsic reward (such as money or a title) is appropriate. But if you hope to work with deeper levels of influence (intrinsic motivators) toward more visionary goals, you have a better chance of achieving your desired result with transformational leadership. Influencing through *example, enthusiasm, challenge,* or *empowerment* connects colleagues on a shared level of motivation so that the leader's purpose becomes inseparable from that of his or her followers.

Each factor of transformational influence can be effective, though one may still have greater impact than another, depending on the personality you are trying to influence. But every lawyer is usually influenced by all of them, at least to some degree. And when you are able to employ them all, the result should be what you're seeking: performance beyond all expectation.

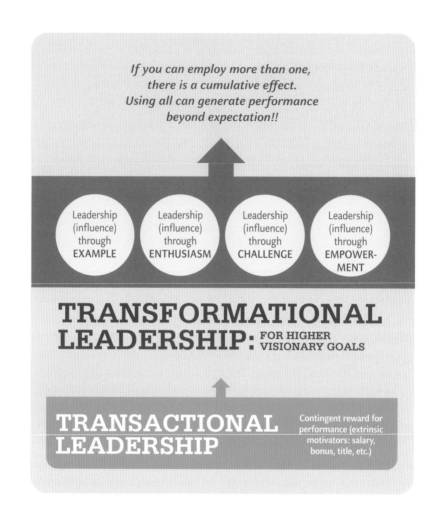

If you can employ more than one, there is a cumulative effect. Using all can generate performance beyond expectation!!

Leadership (influence) through EXAMPLE

Leadership (influence) through ENTHUSIASM

Leadership (influence) through CHALLENGE

Leadership (influence) through EMPOWER-MENT

TRANSFORMATIONAL LEADERSHIP: FOR HIGHER VISIONARY GOALS

TRANSACTIONAL LEADERSHIP

Contingent reward for performance (extrinsic motivators: salary, bonus, title, etc.)

THE DRIVER AS A LEADER

Most lawyers with leadership ambitions (most lawyers?) will have at least a smidgeon of the Driver personality. The Driver's motivation to achieve is the source of his or her strength, but any such advantage (as you know) can prove a double-edged sword: Too intense a focus can damage relationships, and a blinkered determination that leads to shortcuts or a lack of communication can fatally undermine trust.

Nicola exemplified this problem. A superb lawyer and a partner in a large international firm, she had achieved her enviable position through gut-rock determination and a driven personality—in short, to some degree on an outdated model. Once she became a partner, she continued to display those behaviors, demanding blistering performances not only from herself but also from everyone around her. She saw no point in tolerating colleagues who lacked her drive, and routinely abused her junior associates. (She once called one of them on a Saturday, ordering him into the office within the hour, despite the fact that he was hosting his daughter's sixth birthday party!) She regularly reorganized her associates' work, and rather than help them develop would berate them for their "incompetence." Unfortunately, the best three words to describe Nicola's brand were *arrogant, unsympathetic,* and *demanding.* On the flip (positive) side, however, she channeled her impressive drive into obsessive business development, consistently delivered beyond client expectations, and won massive amounts of work. (Obviously, Nicola viewed client development as crucial and colleague relationships as immaterial.)

David McClelland, a Harvard-based psychologist, spent his career studying motivations (particularly ambition and drive) and their effects on leadership. McClelland identified four types of motivations that stimulate leaders:

- *Achievement.* People with a high need for achievement long to excel and are driven to meet or even exceed a certain (usually self-imposed) standard. They have little patience for those who can't keep up and generally prefer to work either alone or with people like themselves. (Achievement is always the main motivation for Drivers, but in a less single-minded manifestation than Nicola's this can still have positive outcomes.) High-achieving lawyers will naturally influence others, either through their confidence and competence (*influencing through example*); through conveying a clear and compelling vision (*influencing through enthusiasm*); or through spurring innovative thinking (*influencing through challenge*), all of which are important tools for effective leadership.

- *Affiliation.* People with a high need for affiliation desire harmonious relationships with other people and want to feel accepted. This type of motivation epitomizes the Moderate personality. While this can appear a relatively weak or casual motivation, its consequence is to foster aligned goals and to cultivate a shared purpose, so within the context of leadership it has a significant role to play.

- *Personal power.* People who seek personal power want to direct, control, and influence others, which at first glance might appear to be reasonable motivations for a leader. However, those who are dominated by these considerations will tend toward coercion and manipulation, which will fatally undermine their cause. (This can also happen if the Driver's power-oriented personality becomes obsessive and if he dismisses others' feelings as being inferior to his own goals.)

■ *Socialized power.* People motivated by socialized power influence others by helping them develop their skills and grow in confidence, effectively resulting in *leadership through empowerment.* When driven by socialized power, people achieve far more than they could when fueled by their own personal aspirations, because (as we know) championing, encouraging, and uplifting others is a powerful motivator. In fact, the person driven by socialized power is so concerned with the collective good that his or her purpose becomes inseparable from the interests of any followers. Not surprisingly, this is by far the most effective and authentic form of leadership.

Unfortunately, in relation to her colleagues, Nicola, an extreme Driver, was accessing merely the typical Driver motivators of achievement and personal power, which—especially in such a highly concentrated form—combined to create the worst possible scenario. Further, because she didn't consider colleague relationships to be important, let alone beneficial, she never tried to adjust her behavior to achieve better results.

Eventually, Nicola's personality critically undermined her ability to build relationships, and as her workload increased, the consequences became more and more damaging. Since no one could perform to her entire satisfaction, and since those she considered tolerable gradually became less willing to support her, she became still more overworked and stressed, which only worsened her already negative behavior. Nicola's work suffered, and her problems began to seep into her client relationships, resulting in loss of business. The firm had previously turned a blind eye to her obstreperousness due to her ability to bring in clients, but once she started to lose clients she was left with neither business nor support. Exhausted and failing, Nicola was forced to recognize that something had to change.

Nicola started by exercising the leadership characteristic underpinning all the others: self-awareness. She acknowledged that her natural ambition had been compounded and even warped by the fact that throughout her life she had (consciously and subconsciously) been driven to please an absent and overly critical father. Armed with this self-knowledge, Nicola realized that she could use different behaviors to achieve better results. (In her case, those "hard-to-access" behaviors included patience, empathy, and self-control!) Since her breakdown, Nicola has consciously and consistently worked on those skills. At first it was awkward and, especially in moments of stress, she longed to revert to her brusque style of working. She also had trouble believing that some gentler behaviors (including empathy) actually compounded her strength, rather than making her look feeble. But by dint of perseverance Nicola gradually learned new ways of dealing with her colleagues, and she has succeeded in building relationships that have rekindled both her business development and her leadership ambitions.

As a by-product, Nicola realized that she did have wider motivations beyond those of pure achievement and that she enjoyed encouraging and enabling others. This naturally opened up broader means of influence. Recently, as part of a feedback report, Nicola was even praised for creating an environment in which people *wanted* to perform well. At the same time it's important to note that Nicola's goal-oriented personality will never alter, and that as long as she tempers it, it will continue to be her greatest strength. In fact, since Nicola has discovered better ways of influencing her colleagues, one associate announced that her goal was to be "as competent and successful as Nicola"!

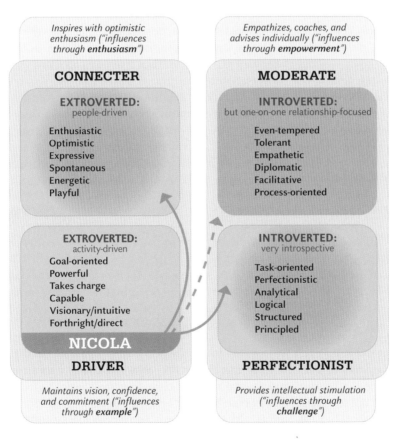

As examined in Chapter 4 ("Personalities"), the lines of development (the behaviors) most foreign to you (and therefore the ones you probably need to focus on) are usually those in your opposite personality type. As an extreme Driver, Nicola was least open to Moderate ways of influencing others, but in the end these methods were to give her surprising and satisfying rewards.

THE OFTEN-FORGOTTEN INFLUENCE

One important (yet often overlooked) factor in getting along with colleagues is that *everyone wants to feel needed and useful*...so when you ask a favor of a colleague, you may actually be gratifying him (or her). I always feel honored when someone thinks enough of me to request my advice or assistance. I've been made to feel appreciated—sometimes the greatest benefit of all!

> *Everyone wants to feel needed and useful...sometimes the greatest benefit (and motivator!) of all.*

When I first moved to London, I had no local friends and knew no one in my new office. I found it very difficult to meet new people, and making friends seemed even harder. But then, by accident, I discovered a little ruse. I asked one of my colleagues, Clare, about finding a local dentist. She was very help-ful, told me the best place to go, and even offered to walk me there at lunch-time—going well out of her way to assist me. That afternoon, as Clare walked me to the dentist, our conversation opened up on matters far more interest-ing than the extraction of wisdom teeth, and the excursion initiated a strong friendship. I realized that although the English may be slightly more reserved than Americans, they still enjoy feeling helpful. Emboldened, I began to ask each of my new colleagues for some information valuable to a newly arrived expatriate—everything from the best local gym to where, as an American, I could hunt down plain peanut butter (back then, a nearly impossible task!).

For me, asking for help proved a far more effective way to initiate friendships than trying to offer something. I often found that someone who was "too busy" to stop for a coffee had all the time in the world if it was a matter of helping me out. When you make others feel needed, they become your allies! You can use this response in all sorts of situations. For example, you can obtain a buy-in on work: By asking people to help you, you give them a personal stake in your project. (And beware—if you deliberately exclude your colleagues, they just might turn into your in-house opposition!)

While still at college I was chosen to represent my class in a political debate in Washington, D.C. Some of my classmates were extremely disappointed at being passed over, and several made it clear that they were disgruntled enough not to support me. I would have felt immense pressure to perform no matter what, but the attitudes of my peers made me feel doubly stressed! I needed help, however, and as I began preparing for the debate, I sought (very hesitantly) the advice of my classmates. With each request, I felt their antago-nism soften. As I incorporated their ideas and input, hostility was suddenly transformed into a willingness to help. What had started out as "my" debate became "ours," and by the big day I really sensed the encouragement of my classmates. I genuinely couldn't have prepared without their help, and because I made them feel needed, I was able to win them over.

UNDERSTANDING OTHERS' MOTIVATIONS

Influencing others will be heavily dependent on understanding the result they most want to achieve, and (as you have probably guessed!), this is usually defined by what drives them.

- Connecters want *things to be fun.*

- Drivers want to *get things accomplished.*

- Perfectionists want *things done right—or not at all.*

- Moderates want *everyone to get along.*

Pam's experience as a partner in one of the smaller offices of a large international firm demonstrates this point perfectly. The other partners in Pam's office were concerned because their associates were unwilling to perform non-billable activities, yet marketing was needed to bring in the level of business that the largest offices were already attracting. However, the firm's global policy actively discouraged marketing by associates, because the top management viewed client work as a more important use of time. In fact, associates who focused on marketing at the expense of client work were (in effect) penalized, as bonuses were only rewarded on billable hours.

One day Pam's partner Charles told her that he had decided to demand a threshold level of marketing hours from each associate in the office. As a Moderate, Pam empathized with the associates' impossible position and knew that forcing them to participate (especially if they were, effectively, penalized for doing so) would only cause conflict and dissension. But when Pam tried to convince Charles of these potential negatives, she got nowhere. So instead, she put herself in Charles's position. As a Driver, Charles clearly wanted bottom-line performance results for the office, meaning more work and more clients. Charles wasn't overly concerned with the associates' feelings or their level of job satisfaction. Pam realized that she was wasting her breath on arguments about unhappy associates or unfair expectations from management. Instead, she simply told Charles that his demands would inevitably end in a mass exodus of associates, with all the resultant damage to the firm—lost resources, training costs, recruitment investment, and extra strain on those who remained. When it was put in this context (a logical framework that Charles could relate to), he was persuaded, and he was willing to consider a different tactic that might satisfy the associates' requirements while still meeting the office's marketing needs.

ANGER FAILS THE "INFLUENCE TEST"

Like criticism, anger cannot motivate. It may encourage someone to do some-thing short-term—primarily to avoid being targeted again—but it is never a long-term solution. Anger might win the battle, but it can never win the war. I know of a partner who was extremely short-tempered with everyone—his secretary, the paralegals, his associates, and even his partners. To avoid his wrath, people generally did whatever he was currently ranting about, but no one respected his actions, and (to the extent possible) people avoided working with him.

If you're raised to a position of power, you can usually influence by using anger and fear, but what happens the moment you no longer hold that position? Your influence will evaporate, because it wasn't anger but self-preservation that was the real motivator. What do you think happened when the testy partner I mentioned lost his biggest client, and, with it, his major source of revenue? Suddenly top management informed him that his tantrums were no longer acceptable. When he lost the root of his authority, his power slipped away.

Think about it. Don't those with extrinsic authority, money, or status get away with behavior that the rest of us wouldn't dream of using? Don't they lose their tempers when they don't get what they want, and throw a mega-wobbly when they receive bad service? Yet despite all this, people fall all over themselves to "fix" the situation ("So sorry, sir; please forgive us, madam! What can we possibly do to make it up to you?"). Well, if those same angry people lost their positions, who do you think would be falling all over them? Right: nobody. Without their authority, people who use anger to influence find that they have no influence left.

NOBODY'S PERFECT

Real leaders accept that nobody's perfect, and they know how to capitalize on this reality. The story I gave you previously about my shameless partner (the one who promoted my credentials as if they were his own) is the perfect example. Rather than view my partner as a liability, I should have capitalized on the strengths that he did possess to generate a better result for us both. Ironically, this is what true partnership is all about (and partnership is the goal, right?). Mother Teresa put it best: "You can do what I cannot do. I can do what you cannot do. Together we can do great things."

It's unfortunate that law firms *and* individual lawyers so often forget this simple truth. We need to work with our colleagues to create the strongest synergies and produce the best results. Law firms should encourage their top people to lead the way, resulting in the greatest benefit to each individual and to the firm as a whole—but sadly, they usually don't.

LEADING UPWARD

Let's face it—the people above you are much more important to your career than you can possibly be to theirs, and they typically aren't focused on your interests. However, it's possible that you can lead your leaders, especially if you find ways to add value to their agendas.

It's possible that you can lead your leaders, especially if you find ways to add value to their agendas.

The Boss

The focus of this book is not about how to be a good lawyer (I'm simply assuming that you are one!). But if it *were*, there would have to be at least one chapter on how to manage your boss. Your boss is normally the single most crucial outside influence on your success, yet most of us spend far more time managing relationships with subordinates (to ensure the delivery of our work product) than promoting ourselves to those above us.

Put bluntly, counting on your boss—or any other senior person—to further your interests is a risky proposition. First, your boss may not even be aware of having this responsibility toward you—or he may not care. Second, even if your interests do constitute a faint blip on your boss's radar screen, it's unrealistic (in the average law firm) to assume that he will always provide you with the right information and correctly identify the support you need. Your bosses are generally far too stressed, self-focused, involved in their own agendas, and fallible. It's up to you to cultivate a productive and beneficial relationship.

Obviously, you are dependent upon your bosses (to provide you with knowledge and resources and to connect you to the higher levels of the firm), but they are also dependent on you (to cooperate, provide information, maintain loyalty, and deliver to *their* expectations). And the more you increase their dependence on you, the more you can improve your relationships. You should never assume that your boss doesn't need information—about your gallant failures as well as your resounding successes. Furthermore, nothing is more damaging to your boss than a lack of exceptional delivery, so you must be consistently reliable and proactive.

Throughout this book I have constantly emphasized that to build relationships and influence others you must first understand *the other person's* perspective. Most people would instantly acknowledge the truth of this, yet it's strange how few of us consider this when it comes to bosses. You expect them to consider your point of view; shouldn't you stop to think about theirs? Understanding the personality, motivators, and objectives of your boss can be enormously beneficial.

For one thing (as examined in Chapter 4), everyone has his own preferred working style, and it's generally up to the junior to adjust his or her behavior to complement the boss's approach. When you are able to provide the missing ingredient in his personality, balancing your strengths against his weaknesses, you add value—which is the best thing you can do in terms of building relationships.

Contrary to popular belief, bosses actually are "just like the rest of us," and they, too, need to feel motivated by their work and their environment. If you can figure out what motivates and satisfies your boss, you can often provide what he (or she) needs; conversely, if you know what stresses your boss, you can avoid contributing to the problem. Make it your goal to understand your boss's goals, both organizational and personal, just as you do your clients'. For example, if you know that your boss has long been a champion of the firm's recent merger, he will naturally want it to succeed on an organizational level, but it probably goes deeper than that: His personal credibility will also be on the line. Similarly, if your boss was always publicly skeptical about some major deal, it's pointless to rush to him for help and consolation when it falls apart.

The last thing you can do is to try to appreciate the pressures your boss faces by understanding what he may be trying to achieve. Without this you cannot adequately relate to your boss, and you may even create unintended friction.

While still an associate I had a boss who used to casually drop work on my desk and then disappear without a word, leaving me to get it all done. Over time I developed a deep resentment for being the one doing "all the work." Only years later, when I became a partner and headed a practice group with the mandate of expansion (a position analogous to that of my previous boss), did I suddenly gain a better understanding of her pressures and concerns. My boss *needed* to be out of the office to promote the department and cultivate the relationships that would ensure our growth. In fact, had the boss been focused only on immediate client work, she would effectively have failed the rest of us!

Making a good impression tonight is really important. I'd rather be home, or even in the office, but this is my responsibility to the group.

Had I ever tried to see things from my boss's perspective, I could have provided value by supporting and appreciating her activities. (Remember, even a boss needs appreciation!) Ironically, just doing something that simple might well have generated significant support in return.

You may blame your bosses for expecting too much, demanding unreasonable turnaround, or failing to understand your life, but much of the time you may share at least some of the responsibility. It's up to you to set the ground rules and educate your boss on how you expect to be treated. How? By delivering on reasonable expectations and by behaving as a leader yourself.

Assuming you're meeting expectations, you've earned the right to set some of the rules of engagement. I once had a young associate who always delivered and consistently did extremely competent work. This allowed him to assert his ground rules—which he did. One day he flew with a colleague from the U.S. to London to work on one of my projects—a task naturally involving grueling hours. The two associates arrived in the office from their flight, and I put them straight to work. Now this associate had done his preparation and therefore finished his day's assignment in record time. As he handed it to me, he mentioned that he was tired and would see me the next day—because he had finished his assignment and was not willing to take on more work that day. I accepted this *because* he had first delivered. Meanwhile, his colleague slogged on, probably bitterly complaining about that overbearing partner—me!—who made him slave away in spite of his jet lag. In the end, ironically, it was the associate who left early who gained my respect.

There are times in *every* job when life feels tough, when we sit at our desks in the middle of the night, matchsticks propping up our eyelids, wondering what on earth made us choose this career in the first place... Yet, bizarrely enough, this is the time to display leadership behavior (especially to your boss).

RECAP AND SUMMARY

Leadership only happens in the context of relationships. With this in mind, develop relationships with your colleagues by following exactly the same steps as with clients: making connections, building bonds, authenticating your brand, and cultivating trust.

Leadership only happens in the context of relationships.

A common mistake in leadership development is to focus only on those immediately below you, but effective leadership requires support from all sorts of people—even those over whom you have no direct authority. For that reason alone, if you hope to lead, you must invest in relationships with *all* of your colleagues. You never know whom, down the road, you might need to influence.

As a leader you must be able to influence by drawing on a wide range of effective motivators. Always start by understanding the other person's perspective and by providing him with a benefit that takes into account not only his personality but also the result he's looking for.

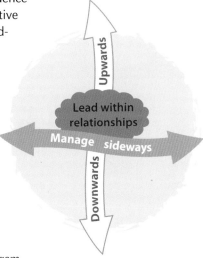

The most basic path to influence is through *reward for performance* (transactional leadership), though it has inherent limitations for long-term or highly creative projects. For these loftier goals, seek to influence as a transformational leader, using *example, enthusiasm, challenge,* and *empowerment.*

When employing all of these influences, the result can be performance beyond expectations. Furthermore, when your motivation is to encourage and help others (regardless of your own needs), then you possess the most effective possible influence. This is when your goals become entwined with those of others, resulting in the most authentic type of motivation: socialized power.

And because leadership is about influence rather than position, we can at times even "lead" our leaders. We do this by looking at things from their perspective and proactively providing value to their agendas. Never forget that everyone—amazingly enough, even bosses—wants to feel needed and appreciated!

Finally, as a leader you must learn to capitalize not only on your own strengths but also on those of your colleagues. When you collaborate synergistically, you achieve the best possible results—for you and for your firm.

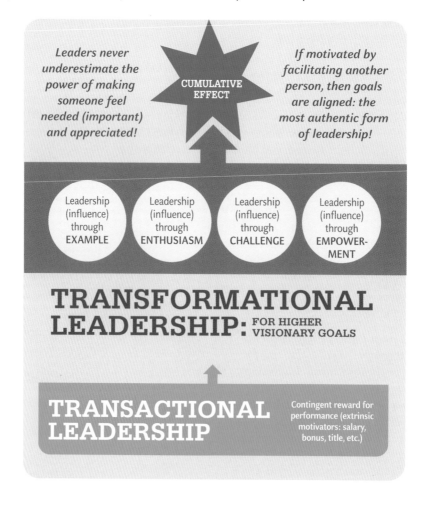

Chapter Twenty-One
Leading a Team

To maximize our influence we must leverage the skills of others, which requires—of course—effective leadership. Leadership is not about seniority, but rather about behavior and the ability to influence others. The exact skills required can vary, however, because team leadership is situational by its very nature. It may be required unexpectedly or in the middle of some strategic plan, and in everything from small projects to whole-scale, cathartic transformations.

One can be unexpectedly thrust into a situation of leadership for many reasons, but the starting point of leading is always the same: assembling the right team and communicating a vision that motivates each member toward a shared purpose. This is probably the leader's foremost responsibility, and in one swoop it generates authentic leadership, socialized power, and a disciplined, committed team.

CREATING A SPIRITED TEAM

I have worked for team leaders—and so, I suspect, have you—whose attitude could best be summarized as, "Listen, you don't have to like your assignments; you don't have to like each other! Just get the *&^*&# job done!" This can work, of course, and there will be times when the leader *has* to bang heads together in this way. But a team that values everyone's contributions will accomplish so much more—*and* feel rewarded in the process!

So, what can you do to make it happen?

It's obvious that you, as a leader, must have a good relationship with each team member, but it's also your responsibility to foster strong relationships *between* team members, as well as to further the impression that each individual is making a valuable contribution and is being rewarded appropriately. In addition, you must exemplify the team's values: A leader whose behavior is consistent with the values he espouses (who "walks the talk") will automatically inspire commitment and emulation (*leading through example*). This starts with your own vision, because we tend to lead by example when pursuing what really matters to us. It also inspires us with self-confidence—which is a sure-fire determinant of team performance, as the leader's confidence (or lack thereof) inevitably affects the entire group.

By this point, you will already be aware that you can only inspire your team's real engagement through your own positive emotions (*leading through enthusiasm*), as it's been proven that others will mirror your emotions—positive and otherwise—right back at you. Further, positive emotions generate positive action and influence long-term attitudes, creating a more imaginative, innovative, risk-taking team.

Obviously, there are times when optimism is simply inappropriate. Nobody is impressed when the leader of a failed business blusters and brags, especially when he also pockets a personal payoff! Effective leadership requires a judicious mix of both positives and negatives, because while positive moods promote confidence and creativity, more sober attitudes can inspire a sharper focus and better results.

This goes back to your ability to fit the most appropriate behavior to the situation or personality you're dealing with (see Chapter 4). In fact, as you transition into leadership within your firm, your capacity to access the full spectrum of personality behaviors becomes increasingly important. As they progress in the profession, many lawyers find that they need to decrease their reliance on tactics that succeeded at a more junior level and embrace new and different ways of behaving.

Technical Brilliance

Take Claudia, a senior associate whose intelligence, attention to detail, and superior expertise had won her one client who routinely engaged her to deal with a certain product line. When this client launched a new device involving a range of expertise beyond Claudia's, the client still appointed Claudia the project coordinator for a team drawn from various legal disciplines, as well as from separate marketing, research, and development divisions.

Straightaway Claudia found herself in deep water. Accustomed to working solo for this client and being relied on as *the* definitive expert, she suddenly found herself in an entirely different situation: She needed to extract the right information from her team and rely on it. Unfortunately, Claudia routinely rejected advice, and at one critical juncture she refused to rely on one expert's opinion and was subsequently proven wrong by the client (something completely new in her experience!). This caused Claudia to withdraw entirely into her comfort zone: micromanagement. She not only failed to lead, but also subtly demoralized her team members by intruding on their tasks and negating their more imaginative contributions.

As a leader, Claudia dropped the ball because she was unable to transition from being a brilliant technical performer into an astute project manager. Her favored work methods, which had previously brought her easy success, were no longer enough, and—in addition to refusing to develop skill sets that came less naturally to her—she also rejected any suggestion that she cultivate trusting relationships that might have filled in the gaps in her knowledge.

The bottom line is that Claudia failed where this book begins: with self-awareness. Only by assessing our behaviors honestly and rigorously can we choose the best means to facilitate the success of our team.

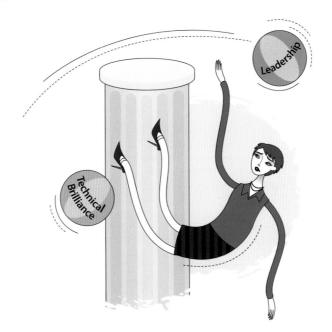

ALIGNING THE TEAM

Nowhere do personalities become more important than within a team. To get the most from each member and to achieve the team's goals most effectively, the leader must understand how each of the members' temperaments relate—not only to the team's overall objective, but also to each other. In an ideal world, the team will have some measure of all four of the temperaments examined in Chapter 4:

- The Connecters will maintain a lively working environment, and will enjoy, and excel at, things involving personal interaction. Connecters do well at "thinking on their feet" and will happily multi-task.

- Drivers are the best choice to oversee projects, form vision-oriented goals, and develop overall design and objectives. They also ensure that deadlines are met and goals accomplished.

- Perfectionists will contentedly labor over documentation and ensure that the solution is the right one by intellectually challenging the team. They provide strong structure and loyal support.

- The Moderates will facilitate every process, guarding each team member's emotional interests and providing smooth diplomacy, while never complaining about any burdens of the job.

However, it's rarely this simple! Unfortunately, as leaders we generally have to deal with unbalanced teams—teams crammed with inveterate Connecters, intense Drivers, or unyielding Perfectionists, sometimes without the ameliorating presence of even one genuine Moderate. Despite this, you still have to devise a way to achieve your goals.

In-depth knowledge of team members helps. As team leader you must put individual "players" into their right positions, just as a top soccer coach places his players in the role where they best belong—the strikers toward the front, the enablers in the middle, and the defensively skillful at the back. Remember Tony from Chapter 4 (Appendix 4.D), who failed his team members by delegating assignments wildly out of line with their personalities, and only turned his business around when he reconfigured the tasks?

When hiring team members, the most effective leaders focus on individual members' strengths, which indicate their greatest potential value to the project. Great teams are composed of individuals capitalizing on their potential, and creating synergies through collaboration—which suggests that their leaders not over-focus on credentials and experience but also consider the candidates' particular personality traits and how their natural assets can best be used. Most people can acquire the requisite technical ability or experience, but they can't cultivate an innate talent without the core personality to support it. With this in mind, leaders should focus more on personal traits than on credentials.

My personal experience is that most lawyers fail to invest sufficient psychological energy in the initial hiring process. I often fail here myself: On more than one occasion I've rushed to an interview without reading the candidate's résumé, or without thinking through the real needs of my team. Yet I've also observed "best practice" from colleagues, and have come to realize that getting the right person on board from the start can save a huge amount of difficulty and worry.

Recently, I met a practice-group head who has put together an immensely successful team single-handedly. When she began building her group she targeted her opposites, meaning that the first associate she hired possessed diametrically opposite strengths from her own. They worked well together, creating synergies with their differing styles and strengths, until it seemed only natural to invite him to become her partner. She continued to apply this mentality as the business flourished, choosing each new lawyer to fill an existing gap in the team.

I once had a boss who openly confided his excitement at having finally found a replica of himself: a hard-working, capable, and ambitious Driver (me!). However, our experience together demonstrated the drawbacks of precisely replicating one's own strengths. In the early years my boss and I were a good fit, but once I grew in seniority, our team had *two* assertive, ultra-intense Drivers—and became severely lopsided. We often overwhelmed our clients, since we both had a tendency to take control of meetings! Our team—and our clients—would have benefited from the addition of someone with a more flexible, easygoing style.

SHOWING YOU CARE

Team spirit requires that each individual member remains motivated, loyal, and results-driven. However, you're mistaken if you think you can command such attributes by virtue of your brilliance, or even of your seniority. You have to be the kind of person others *want* to follow, and this is best accomplished by employing the core elements of leadership influence we examined in the last chapter: leading through *example, enthusiasm, challenge,* and *empowerment.*

But embedded within those leadership tools is another, sometimes undervalued, concept: empathy. Without this, even the most brilliant vision or plan will lose meaning. *People only want to follow someone who understands and values them personally.*

Here's a question: Who's your favorite teacher/boss/coach/mentor of all time—and why? Isn't it because you knew he (or she) was committed to you and your success? Didn't his (or her) attitude toward you *inspire* you to succeed?

Anyone who has studied leadership will be familiar with the concept of "emotional intelligence," which deals with many of the leadership qualities discussed here: self-awareness, self-management, social awareness, and social skills. The author of *Emotional Intelligence,* Daniel Goleman, has done extensive research on what makes the best leader. While his sources have been wide-ranging, from famous professors to top executives, the answer to his question remains near-unanimous: The most successful leaders are those who are connected to their teams and *personally committed* to helping each individual member succeed.

Here's a question: Who's your favorite teacher/boss/coach/ mentor of all time—and why? Isn't it because you knew he (or she) was committed to you and your success? Didn't his or her attitude toward you inspire you to succeed?

Look Out for Them

A good leader always takes the concerns of his (or her) team members seriously. As an associate, I once worked extremely hard on a particular deal for nine endless months, including many late nights and most weekends, only to have the client eventually stall completion. The deal, originally supposed to have been signed before Christmas, was delayed until after the New Year. At the same time, the client announced that he intended to work throughout the upcoming holidays. I had already missed Thanksgiving because of his project, and listened with horror as my partner on the project volunteered my services yet again. Without even asking about my holiday plans, this partner immediately said, "Jennifer here will be at your disposal." I felt like crying, and my family back in America was appalled to hear that yet again I would be missing a family gathering due to work.

I met with the big-shot client over the holidays, in a dark and isolated building, because everyone else was away enjoying Christmas—including, naturally, the partner who had volunteered my availability. To add insult to (considerable) injury, what we achieved in no way justified my canceled trip—in fact, we were just there because the client happened to have nothing better to do, and because my partner had not valued my personal time.

The point of this story is that I never again went out of my way to oblige that particular partner. In fact, since he had not considered my interests, I felt that his abuse of my loyalty had pretty much absolved me from any need to consider *his* interests.

Compare this to my other partner's attitude! On a similar occasion, this man actually turned to a client and said, "Sorry, but I believe Jennifer has plans that week. I would strongly recommend that you delay your project long enough to get the best associate for your project." I felt touched that my partner was looking out for me, and the client was delighted that my partner insisted that he have the best associate for the job. All of a sudden I became more important in the client's eyes—someone worth waiting for, not just the 24/7 commodity my other partner had made me out to be.

Show Appreciation

Everyone wants the leader to acknowledge and celebrate his or her contributions, and by doing this you can make an impact out of all proportion to the effort involved.

> *Everyone wants the leader to acknowledge and celebrate his or her contributions.*

Simon's practice group was falling apart at the seams, and he and his partners were barely speaking to each other; resentment and criticism were the order of the day. One afternoon Simon called a team meeting and everyone grudgingly arrived, expecting Simon to carp as usual about the lack of team spirit. But instead, announcing that he was going to do something "really radical," he proceeded to acknowledge something positive about each colleague, praising his or her contributions to the team. Suddenly the entire tone of the meeting changed! In Simon's words, "In a matter of minutes, the faces of my team changed from gray and grim to illuminated and focused, and the energy in the room was transformed!" Thereafter, everyone did the same exercise: one-on-one, celebrating each other's strengths. By supporting each other, the members of the team felt encouraged and inspired, and when from that foundation Simon finally addressed their limitations, everyone felt motivated to work to overcome them.

By knowing your colleagues intimately, you should be able to personalize such recognition, which makes a much greater impact. Believe me, it's a terrific mistake to rely on law-firm recognition systems, which are typically very impersonal, and which seldom properly acknowledge your team's moments of glory. Suppose one lawyer brings in a new client, while another pitches in to help his colleague at midnight *despite* the fact that he has been working around the clock on his own deal. At the end of the year both get a bonus, but without any differentiation between them, and without any correlation to their moments of extra effort or sacrifice. While salary, promotions, and bonuses will always be important, most people need more personal and more immediate appreciation. On-the-spot recognition makes the greatest impact because it is unexpected, specific, and—above all—personal.

Further, when you celebrate the accomplishments of a team member, the praise should reinforce the values of the group. If teamwork is a strongly espoused value, then rewarding someone for single-handedly bringing in a new client (however profitable!) sends the wrong message—especially if the process excludes teammates who could, and perhaps should, have been involved.

EXPECTATIONS AND FEEDBACK

Giving feedback is crucial, but it cannot be effective (or fair) unless you have first made clear what you expect. By making your expectations clear and concise, you create something to measure performance against.

But what if someone's performance is actively bad? (Ugh!) In this situation, no one shines. Typically people deal with this problem by one of three methods, each as inefficient as the next:

- *Erupt in anger.* We've discussed before why anger doesn't work. Managing your emotions always achieves a better result.

- *Skirt the issue.* Dishing out criticism is difficult, so on this occasion people may not be as straightforward as they ought to be. Don't meander around with euphemistic comments about learning curves, time management, or performance goals, and don't be dishonest. Have you ever given someone an above-average score in a review when you secretly think he didn't really make the grade? ("Well, he's a lawyer so he has to have above-average intelligence—right? And besides, I don't want to offend anybody.") It is not a kindness to allow a lawyer to advance inappropriately beyond his or her comfort zone, which could well happen if you sidestep the issue.

- *Ignore the problem.* The worst-case scenario is to simply fix the problem(s) caused by the lawyer in question without addressing issues of competence. This allows the legal "disaster zone" to become someone else's headache, but for obvious reasons, this "solution" has to be the worst option.

A true leader knows that giving productive (read: honest) feedback, however hard it may be, is essential to his team as well as to his own ambitions. The team is a reflection of the leader's values, and the leader knows that team members can only adapt and improve through honest feedback.

There are loads of articles and books on how to give appropriate feedback and criticism. If you are managing people, I suggest that you take the time to read at least one of them. In the meantime, here are a few approaches that I've found effective.

- *Start with a positive.* If at all possible, I start out with some measure of praise or appreciation. This does two things: First, it tells the other person that I retain some confidence in him, and second, it softens the blow of the negative comments that are soon to follow. ("Richard, I really appreciated your enthusiasm in the meeting, and I think you had some really good ideas that the client found helpful. For our follow-up meeting, however, I'd prefer it if we talked through them together first and then prepared a joint strategy for the client. Are we on the same page?")

EXAMPLE OF BAD PRACTICE: "Richard, you really got on my nerves today by interrupting both me and—much worse—our client. What makes you think anyone wants to listen to your half-baked notions, anyway? Why don't you just zip it?!"

If there really is no positive with which to commence the discussion, an alternative (and even stronger) approach is to begin with, "Look, Richard, I'm going to be honest with you, because I do really care about your development." (Knowing that one's leader cares can be the most positive praise of all.)

■ *Make the point with questions.* By using questions, I can sometimes get the person I am criticizing to make my point for me—and avoid antagonism. EXAMPLE:

Me:	"Richard, do you think that leaving an unreviewed document on my chair and buzzing off home was a sensible thing to do?"
Richard:	"Well, probably not."
Me:	"And who did you think was going to get the document finalized and out to the client?"
Richard:	"I thought it was good enough to go out, and that you would send it. I guess I didn't think it through."
Me:	"But what if I hadn't come back from my meeting in time? Who would have gotten it to the client?"
Richard:	"I didn't really think about that, to be honest."
Me:	"Do you now see the problem with that kind of approach?"
Richard:	"Yes."
Me:	"And do you understand that this can't happen again?"
Richard:	"Absolutely."
Me:	"Great. So, what are you going to do in the future?"

Richard:	"I'll wait until you've had time to review the document, and take responsibility for making it right and getting it to the client on time."
Me:	"Good. OK, now, aside from leaving the document for me to deal with, do you think this is really the best work you can do?"

At this point Richard can only admit that he didn't put the effort in (he really can't say that it is "the best he can do," if he has any self-respect). With luck, he'll also figure out that his lack of commitment is not acceptable, and can't be allowed to rear its head again.

By using this approach, the person can usually be made to acknowledge his own error, and with the right prompting will usually offer the solution. Obviously, this method only works when you have some idea how the other person is likely to respond. If his response is defiant, the discussion may indeed turn into a "blood on the carpet" situation.

■ *Give the person a position of prestige.* Giving someone a position to live up to can motivate her to fulfill it. EXAMPLE: "Julie, you have always done excellent work, and this is why I give you some of the more complicated projects. Because of all your thorough analysis on past occasions, I was surprised that you didn't develop your research here as extensively as you normally do." This can then be followed by the question, "Do you feel that this work meets your usual standards?"

When we give someone a position to live up to, we're implementing what has been termed the "Pygmalion effect." (Pygmalion was a mythical Greek sculptor who carved a beautiful female statue, which he then believed was alive. His belief became self-fulfilling when the goddess Aphrodite took pity on him and brought the statue to life.) This same concept—that we get what we expect—can be applied to people management. In fact, a notable *Harvard Business Review* article, "Pygmalion in Management" by J. Sterling Livingston, documents this concept.

Similarly, a fascinating study many years ago in the U.S. school system exemplified the power of expectation. Three teachers were told that, due to their exceptional abilities, they had been chosen to teach classes of very gifted children and that the experiment was designed to find out how these gifted children would perform without being told that they were special. At the end of the year the students' performance was outstanding—in fact, at the levels expected of gifted students. But these students were in reality *not* gifted, and both they and the teachers involved had been randomly selected. The research concluded that the Pygmalion effect (the law of positive expectancy) had caused the remarkable performance. The teachers' high expectations had helped the students believe in themselves and match those high levels. Other studies have similarly revealed that people perform in line with expectations.

Probably another factor in the students' success was the self-confidence exuded by the teachers, in light of their having been told that they had been chosen for their abilities. Remember, when the leader/teacher exemplifies confidence it affects the collective self-efficacy of the team—in this case, the students.

As seen in the chapter on self-belief (Chapter 7, "Thinking"), when building up the team's confidence, it's important that you structure situations that allow them to generate incremental wins. Demonstrating their abilities will mitigate fear and cultivate self-efficacy, while winning automatically inspires enthusiasm and deepens commitment.

One of the best ways to do this is to make sure that team members are working within their areas of strength; this will both maximize their confidence and build up the neural network that feeds such abilities. We all tend to waste most of our feedback time helping people attack their weaknesses when we should really be encouraging them to push themselves where they excel. If you are a parent, think about your reaction to a child's report card containing, for the sake of argument, four As, two Bs, and an F. What area do you spend the most time discussing—the As or the F? It really should be the As. Ask questions like, "Why do you like this subject? What makes you so good at it? How can you develop/expand your talents in this area?" (Which doesn't mean that you *can't* ask, "Hey, what went wrong in Physics, then?" but do it within the parameters of instilling confidence!)

Remember, discovering the "sweet spot" in others is to discover their motivators and strengths.

THE OBVIOUS

Here are a few more thoughts about the way a leader might best manage a team.

- *Give credit.* Leaders always give credit where credit is due and ensure that everyone knows exactly who has accomplished what. Leaders tell their clients, often in front of the relevant person, what a great job he or she has done. How the team performs reflects directly on you, so when you give credit, you lose nothing and gain loyalty.

- *Be accountable.* When things go wrong, leaders take the rap. How they deal with it behind the scenes might be a very different story(!), but to the outside world leaders should graciously accept responsibility, because in the long run this garners respect and loyalty from colleagues and clients. (Always praise in public and criticize in private. Public criticism is—by definition—degrading.)

- *Everyone makes mistakes.* People have limitations; leaders accept this and deal with it appropriately. Realizing and understanding the strengths and weaknesses of each team member can prevent this from becoming an issue.

- *Shared purpose.* Leaders have a shared purpose with their team. There should be no "me and you" or "us and them" mentality; instead, there's only "us."

- *Forget orders.* Nobody enjoys being given orders, and astute leaders avoid anything that can be interpreted as such. Instead, they use all their people skills and leadership tools to motivate their team to perform. (You may have had a boss who used the old-fashioned "command-and-control" management method, but today's generation of leaders has figured out that, long-term, it just doesn't work.)

CREATING A VISION AND A SHARED PURPOSE

Throughout this book, I have consistently encouraged you to understand your own personality traits, strengths, and motivators so that you can set appropriate goals. Responsible and effective leaders take exactly this role in relation to their team: In essence, they encourage team members to achieve the goals of this book—to become leaders themselves. When this happens, the original leader attains quintessential leadership—leading other leaders. Too often lawyers (even law firms) fail to grasp the obvious fact that they can only meet the future needs of their clients by replicating their own leadership. As leaders, they care for their clients and promise them an uplifting experience, and their team delivers on that same assurance. Yet if the team itself lacks leadership skills, they will convey an inconsistent (and often damaging) message, potentially undermining client relationships.

Further, a high-performing team demands that its members act as leaders among themselves. They stimulate each other to challenge assumptions and generate new ideas (*leading through challenge*) so as to powerfully motivate their colleagues (*leading through enthusiasm*). Everyone must *lead through example*, acting in accordance with the role-model behaviors that support the goals of the group. Finally, a successful team means that everyone is coaching, teaching, and facilitating each other, and that all members support each other empathetically (*leading through empowerment*).

Communication as the Foundation of Leading a Team

We only create a team of leaders by engaging in real dialogue with the team and discovering each individual's personal vision—including his or her aspirations, values, strengths, and motivators. By getting to know these things about your team, you can (a) help them breathe life into their talents; (b) become better aware of how to motivate and reward them, thus inspiring stronger performance; and (c) increase your ability to align their goals with the greater goal of a shared purpose.

This level of communication helps reveal your vision and inspire others to engage in the shared purpose, but it also demonstrates your commitment to the team as individuals. Your team does not exist merely to mirror your vision as leader; each member also wants to realize his or her own aspirations. A leader who operates without bearing this in mind is an unimaginative leader with—at best—short-term goals.

Developing a team purpose and strategy is beyond the scope of this book, but there are several principles worth considering:

■ Everyone in the team must "buy into" the vision and understand the steps needed for its achievement.

■ In most cases, team ambitions will relate to client development: Typical goals might be to increase revenue, to be recognized as the top practice group, or to reach out to a new client base. As discussed in Chapter 12 ("Brand Creation"), achieving these goals must be based upon delivering unique value; otherwise you risk competing against other lawyers on the same legal aspects, thus undermining your chances of success.

■ The shared purpose must shape the behaviors of the team, meaning that each individual's brand must support the unique value promised.

■ The vision, goals, and strategy must be worked out with the whole team in mind. Everyone must know how each team member's individual skills fit into the goal-oriented team framework. Ideally, each team member's contribution should be aligned with his unique strengths and values; this is the most effective way to arouse the inner motivation and passion that secures success.

■ The team's shared purpose must unite every team member's individual vision. Each member must appreciate the team's purpose, what his (or her) contribution is to be (which must be in line with what he *wants* to be doing), and how his contribution will further his personal goals. For example, if the shared purpose is growth for the practice group, the impact on a senior associate (currently up for partnership) and the impact on a newly qualified lawyer could be very different—especially if the strategy includes hiring a lateral partner.

■ The leader must inspire collaboration among the team by demonstrating how working together will achieve more for everyone than any individual could possibly have achieved alone.

If these things have not been communicated (and understood), team members won't be individual owners of the shared vision. A shared purpose is essential, not only to enlist everyone's commitment to perform but also to give each person a stake in the result. People only *really* care (as opposed to "going with the flow") when the outcome affects them personally.

BUILDING THE PERSONAL VISION	BUILDING THE SHARED PURPOSE
1. What is the **vision?** (What are my long-term aspirations?)	1. What is the **vision?** (What are the team's long-term aspirations?)
2. What are my **goals** toward achieving that vision? *(Both are likely to include client development ambitions.)*	2. What are the **goals** required to achieve that vision? *(Both are likely to include client development ambitions.)*
3. What's my **strategy** to achieve those goals? ■ Does my strategy include delivering a unique value (as opposed to competing on the same dimension as most other lawyers)? If so, what is that unique value? ■ Does my brand help me achieve my strategy and deliver on the value I promise?	3. What's our **strategy** to achieve those goals? ■ Does the strategy include delivering a unique value (as opposed to competing on the same dimension as most other lawyers)? If so, what is that unique value? ■ Does the behavior of the team help to achieve the strategy and deliver on the value promised?
Pursuing the vision, goals, and strategy should ■ leverage my strengths ■ spark my inner motivators, thus generating the inspiration and the inner fire needed to succeed (resulting in job satisfaction).	Pursuing the vision, goals, and strategy should ■ leverage the strengths of the team ■ spark each individual's inner motivators, generating the inspiration and inner fire needed to succeed (job satisfaction) ■ UNITE EVERY MEMBER'S PERSONAL VISION. The leader must inspire collaboration and enable others to perform to the best of their ability.

Shared Values Create a Shared Brand

The shared purpose ideally stands upon shared values: *How do the team members need to behave for the shared purpose to be achieved?* At a minimum, the team values must incorporate not only the five characteristics of a leader, but also anything else required to specifically support the joint goal.

Ideally, team values go beyond credentials and technical expertise. Think back to Guy Savoy, of my favorite Paris restaurant (Chapter 17). Guy Savoy, with his long-established three Michelin stars, could rely on his credentials and exceptional food (his area of technical expertise) as his brand, but Guy chooses to do more than that. Yes, an evening at Guy Savoy is an exquisite culinary event, but it's also an extravaganza of entertainment and warm hospitality. It is this that evokes the loyalty of his customers and, for my husband and me, differentiates his restaurant from other three-Michelin-star establishments. Underlying the Guy Savoy brand is Guy's core value of wanting to create something personal for his guests (beyond the food). Similarly, our core values should extend to the experience we want to give our clients. (At the end of the day, the only brand we *really* have is the experience our clients receive.)

Most law firms have a set of core values that they espouse ("collegiality" or "teamwork culture" being common choices, though unluckily both are championed more often than delivered!). In Chapter 5 ("Motivators"), I noted that the things we believe in only qualify as values when we are dissatisfied without them and when we are willing to make actual sacrifices to achieve them (i.e., when the value itself becomes a priority). In short, values only support the team when *every* team member buys into them unconditionally and when the values drive individual behavior. (What values drive the behavior of the lawyers on your team?)

When expressed values shape the team's behavior (exemplified first by the leader), the outside world expects—and trusts—the team to deliver on them. In essence, the shared purpose is supported by a shared brand, which unites and distinguishes the team.

SHARED
PURPOSE
WHICH
SUPPORT THE

CREATE
LEADING   SHARED
(A TEAM!)   AND   VALUES
ADOPTED

LEADER'S VALUES
Trustworthiness
Self-awareness
People-focus
Positivity
Vision

WHEN
VALUES ARE
EXEMPLIFIED

Leadership (influence) through
example
enthusiasm
challenge
empowerment

TEAM VALUES

Just as you developed a personal brand statement in Chapter 12, you should also create a mission statement for your team that encapsulates your shared purpose and its supporting values. Remember, any shared brand is only as credible as its demonstration by each individual. When I am at Guy Savoy, I don't receive a personal experience because Guy declares it as a value; I receive it because *every* person employed by the restaurant has adopted it as his or her value and then delivers on it!

Because it's the individuals who build the team brand, any single team member also—unluckily!—has the potential to destroy it. And that analysis necessarily includes *everyone*. For example, our secretaries and receptionists, as key client interfaces, are important components to our team brand, not optional extras.

CREATING A FIRM-WIDE BRAND

While most large law firms possess formal values statements, I am skeptical about whether they *really* drive individual behavior; most of these statements are, frankly, more about marketing than about deeply endorsed values. (Can you even list your firm's values? And—if you can—do they actually drive your daily behavior?) Granted, it's not easy to herd a firm of strong-willed lawyers in one direction. And firms do try. Most big firms spend time, resources, and money on creating and promoting their values—with the curious result that these values are generally interchangeable from one firm to the next: client commitment, excellence (yawn), teamwork (zzzzz)...

Some go further. Realizing that values need to move from management and marketing statements to the attention of their lawyers, Clifford Chance rotates its eight values onto the screensavers of its lawyers each month, while Addleshaw Goddard has created a catchy slogan ("The AG Way") intended to resonate its values with its lawyers. These efforts surely increase awareness, but I'm not convinced that they motivate behavior.

Turning firm value statements from lip service into credible codes of behavior requires a minimum of three things:

1. The values must be *expressly* exemplified from the top. (If role models aren't demonstrating values, how can we be expected to follow them?)

2. The values need to be *explicitly* taught—and taught on an ongoing basis. (Even common sense needs continual reinforcement.) Simply scheduling a one-off seminar does not create new habits!

3. The performance of individual lawyers should be monitored and measured against the values. I've yet to hear of any firm that does this, but doesn't it send an inconsistent message to young lawyers to *teach* values but *measure* performance against billable hours and business generation? On what basis is your team measured? Are they the things that drive the *right* behaviors?

To demonstrate these principles in action, I give you three outstanding non-law-firm examples: McKinsey & Company, Goldman Sachs, and Starbucks.

Exemplifying and Teaching the Values

McKinsey is a firm with strong values. Marvin Bower, its former managing director (often called "the soul of McKinsey"), knew that the firm would only truly succeed through reliance on solid, guiding principles. Rajat Gupta, a subsequent managing director, has written of Bower (see the McKinsey website), "Convinced that behavior and conduct are every bit as important as skills and expertise, Marvin sought to build the firm into an enduring, values-based institution." In short, Bower didn't just preach about his values, he also practiced them, arguably with more commitment than anyone else in the history of management consulting. He then ensured that those values were drilled into new hires and experienced employees alike through a firm-wide training program. And what do you think was at the core of those values? Elizabeth Haas Edersheim (a former McKinsey partner and the author of *McKinsey's Marvin Bower: Vision, Leadership and the Creation of Management Consulting*) wrote, "Bower's values [the ones he lived, taught, and made integral to everyone in the firm] are synonymous with leadership."

I experienced McKinsey's values first hand when, as a young associate, I traveled to India with a client and a McKinsey consultant to conduct due diligence. Our trip involved a week's travel between Bangalore, Mumbai (then Bombay), and Delhi. It was a fabulous experience—in more ways than one—as throughout the trip I watched this McKinsey consultant work his relationship with the client. I remember thinking at first that it was a bit presumptuous of this youngster straight from college to think that the client, an older and well-established Indian businessman, would be interested enough in him to want to bond. But during the week that's what they seemed to do, even though I couldn't quite put my finger on how it happened.

A few years later, when our paths crossed again, I asked the consultant how he had managed it. He told me that he had benefited from intense preparation and training at McKinsey on how to work with this particular client—including how to deal with his personality and how to communicate most fruitfully. He had even had a crash course in Indian culture! In addition, the core values of leadership (and knowing how to influence) had already been ingrained in him. By contrast, my only preparation had been several 15-hour workdays on the necessary documentation for the trip!

That conversation led to further discussion about our two, very different, training programs. His had included systematic, ongoing coaching on how to develop trusting relationships, influence people, and become a leader; mine had only taught me how to become a technically accomplished lawyer.

Another example of McKinsey's excellent training occurred many years later when I was leading a team involved in a high-profile outsourcing deal. My group of associates was working alongside a group of consultants. One evening I had dinner with the client (with whom I had a long-standing relationship), during which he complimented me on my team but singled out one of the consultants as "brilliant." Now it so happened that this particular consultant was a relative novice to outsourcing who had only recently joined the niche practice engaged on the project; I had even been forced to override some of his advice—discreetly, of course. So I was at first puzzled about how he had so dazzled my client! Then I remembered that, just like that consultant in India long ago, he had previously been with McKinsey. When working at the client site, he had skillfully demonstrated his leadership skills, thus elevating himself in the client's eyes. My associates were all more technically knowledgeable than he (at least on these particular issues, and at that point in time), but it was this consultant who had stood out.

It was also instructive to realize that, with regard to my own associates, it was *my* fault that they had not been similarly singled out. I should have been better at exemplifying and teaching the importance of leadership—that critical, but often overlooked, aspect of being a lawyer and dealing with clients!

Like McKinsey, Goldman Sachs invests substantial resources in a structured leadership training program, recognizing that its executives' leadership behavior and the integrity of the Goldman brand are ineluctably intertwined. The Harvard Business School case study "Leadership Development at Goldman Sachs" by Boris Groysberg, Scott Snook, and David Lane details how Goldman's formal training program emerged: In 1999, a group of Goldman's elite leaders were chosen to form the Leadership Development Advisory Committee, and for six months this group assessed the firm's leadership development needs (and, specifically, the need for a structured leadership program) to better empower their managing directors. When presenting their recommendations, the committee recognized three potential obstacles (law firms take note!):

1. Leaders of the firm to that point had not used a leadership program to assist in their own development and success. Why would the next generation need one?

2. Goldman's bankers—not surprisingly—were already extremely busy. Could they be persuaded to leave their desks? Would they commit themselves to such a program?

3. Would the benefits outweigh any possible loss of revenue while Goldman's bankers invested in the program instead of in client work?

Despite these doubts, management determined that the traditional Goldman methods—apprenticeship and "learning on the job"—were increasingly unsatisfactory. Further, Goldman recognized that its most productive employees (in short, those doing the deals) were not necessarily intuitive, or good, leaders, and needed a more formal approach to their development. Lastly, Goldman had traditionally promoted a teamwork culture but recognized that it needed to develop a "leadership culture" instead. In the words of one Goldman vice president, "[there was] a recognition that everything really starts with outstanding leadership."

Both Goldman Sachs and McKinsey understand that leadership and the individual brand cannot be separated—and that leadership must drive everyone's brand. Moreover, leadership *must* be every individual's core interface with both colleagues and clients.

I wish that more law firms would invest in legitimate leadership training programs like these. If they did, and if they consciously intertwined leadership, business development, and brand-building (based on *real* firm values), then partners would tend to be better role models and juniors would probably better exemplify the values of the firm. The result would be a firm of lawyers demonstrating a powerful and unified brand.

Client Values and Their Leadership Development

In common with McKinsey and Goldman Sachs, many of our clients are similarly developing their people through formal leadership and values-based programs—and expecting their lawyers to demonstrate equivalent principles and behaviors. Furthermore, how can we expect to lead our clients (who are very likely leaders themselves) without a firm grasp of what leadership is all about?

Measuring and Monitoring the Values

Howard Schultz, the founder of Starbucks, wrote an autobiography entitled *Pour Your Heart Into It*. In it, he says that a mission statement was extremely important to him: In fact, his took months to develop, and he tried to involve everyone in the company in the process. From the beginning the Starbucks values were reviewed and reinforced on a regular basis, and everyone's behavior was routinely measured against those values, especially in the early days. The mission statement has been vital to the organization's success, because employees consistently communicate and deliver on the promise of the Starbucks brand, both among themselves and in their attitudes toward their customers (one of those particular brand values being "to develop enthusiastically satisfied customers all the time"). There is currently much debate about whether the Starbucks business model is sustainable in today's economy;

Starbucks recently had to close 600 of its U.S. stores. However, this setback may be due less to its business model than to the likelihood that—as an enormous public company—Starbucks can no longer monitor the implementation of those values that made it so successful in the first place.

As a side note, it is interesting that Starbucks' mission statement includes the following: "Recognize that profitability is essential to our future success." Not every law firm is quite so honest and upfront! Maybe if we were, young lawyers would have a better understanding about how their own firm's values work together, or how those values affect day-to-day workplace issues (for example, questions about promoting teamwork versus seeking credit for new business).

I encourage you to constantly monitor your own performance in relation to the goals of this book. After all, doesn't success in almost anything come down to our daily commitment toward making it happen? What if firms required the same of their lawyers, with respect to the firm's values? What if our peers and clients rated us on that basis? Maybe the values would come to the forefront of our minds just a little more often—and we'd certainly take the trouble to learn *exactly* what they are.

THE CRITICAL QUESTIONS

The leader's ultimate team objective must be for *every* member of the team to realize the goals of this book as an individual, attaining self-awareness, self-discovery, inner motivation, and confident enthusiasm, along with the skills and competencies that generate success. The best leaders work closely with their team members so that those individuals can answer the following statements positively about their own careers:

■ **I know what is expected of me** *Transactional leadership*

YES, and it is...

■ **I have had recent feedback on my performance**

YES, and it tells me...

■ **I have the resources (talents, skills, training, support) to perform what is expected of me**

YES, these are... *Leadership through enthusiasm*

■ **I am motivated and enthused by my job**

YES, by/because... *Leadership through challenge*

■ **I am intellectually stimulated and challenged by my job**

YES, an example of this is...

■ **I am part of a team that has a shared purpose**

YES, which my leader calls...

■ **The shared purpose stands on a set of core values that are conveyed by my leader**

YES, these are... *Leadership through example*

■ **I have adopted those core values and they are intrinsic to my own brand**

YES, as exemplified by...

- My vision is supported by my personal growth (e.g., my leader coaches, teaches, or otherwise empowers me to succeed—or there is some other form of positive enablement) ⟵

  YES, an example of which is... ⟋ (*Leadership through empowerment*)

- My contribution to the shared purpose leverages my strengths and is acknowledged, celebrated, and rewarded ↗

  YES, by... (*Everyone wants appreciation*)

- My goals/contributions in relation to the shared purpose further my own personal vision

  YES, by... (*Alignment of goals = socialized power and most effective leadership!*)

Being able to answer "yes" to these questions *optimally happens* when the respondent is being effectively led, but it also occurs when the respondent self-leads and uses the tools of transformational influence for self-motivation.

Only when you ensure that your team members can positively answer each of these questions can you be confident that they are on the path to achieving *their* personal visions—one of your most important leadership responsibilities.

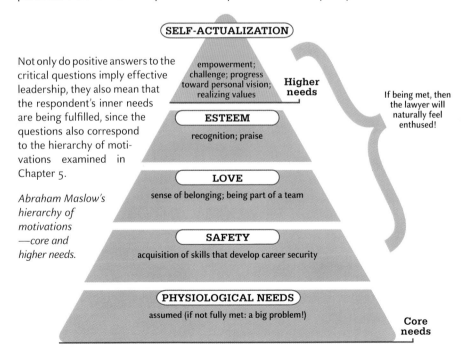

Not only do positive answers to the critical questions imply effective leadership, they also mean that the respondent's inner needs are being fulfilled, since the questions also correspond to the hierarchy of motivations examined in Chapter 5.

Abraham Maslow's hierarchy of motivations —core and higher needs.

SELF-ACTUALIZATION

empowerment; challenge; progress toward personal vision; realizing values

Higher needs

If being met, then the lawyer will naturally feel enthused!

ESTEEM

recognition; praise

LOVE

sense of belonging; being part of a team

SAFETY

acquisition of skills that develop career security

PHYSIOLOGICAL NEEDS

assumed (if not fully met: a big problem!)

Core needs

A TEAM OF GENERATION Y

Empowering your team members is especially important if they are from Generation Y. (See below for a definition of this group.) In the past, lawyers "signed on" without question to the unspoken rules of law-firm hierarchy. They accepted that hard work and personal sacrifice were necessary components to advancement and that the journey to partnership was more about *give* than *take.*

Generation Y does not accept these conditions; they want to receive as much as they give, and they want to receive it NOW. Since toddlerhood, this generation has been indulged, nurtured, and programmed—with activities, technology, information, choice, social awareness, and the mindset of entitlement. This makes them "high maintenance," but they are also high-performing, and they thrive in the midst of collaboration—ideal members of any team, *if* they feel empowered! They want to be challenged and enthused by worthwhile projects, and personally developed and empowered; they don't just *want*, but *demand,* to be part of a vision that has value.

Older generations may be offended by Generation Y's confidence and expectations, but Gen Y holds the key to the ongoing success of our teams and law firms. So it's up to today's leaders to understand Generation Y and provide the foundation they demand. After all, it's not that unreasonable, is it? We should all be so empowered.

Who is Generation Y?

The flood of Generation Y employees (those born in 1978–1998) into the workforce has caused a shift in workplace dynamics. Generation Y demand more from their employers than their predecessors did. Flatter hierarchies, sophisticated technology, and strong values are driving changes in how employers successfully attract and develop this new group of workers.

In a step away from the traditions and attitudes of generations past, members of Generation Y are resolutely loyal, not to their employers, but to their profession and to themselves. They are defined by what they do, not whom they work for. They "value their values" and work hardest not for extrinsic reward, but for a cause, or an end result by which their abilities and potential can be measured. Generation Y can also be defined by their radical working values and their 24/7 connectivity to the outside world.

The labor market dynamics are changing, and today's 20-somethings have multiple options in the workplace; therefore, it is common practice among this generation to leave jobs when their needs are not being satisfied. The new world of work and the influx of Gen Y into a traditionalist workplace have sparked a dynamic debate, and the onset of a generational collision is commonplace in many organizations.

—Emma Reynolds, Co-founder, e3 Unlimited and Ask Gen Y

THE POWER OF HUMILITY

Previously, within the context of building relationships, I mentioned that leaders ideally balance their own personal weaknesses with the strengths of their team members. Depending on the situation, this may mean calling on different people to lead different challenges—and daring to (temporarily) become a follower! If you are afraid, through pride or neurosis, to acknowledge that someone else may be better suited than you are to a given task, you automatically undermine your shared purpose.

Sadly, this is exactly what happens in most law firms: Lawyers lead from the front, only asking colleagues for help with abstruse technical issues. Just imagine what would happen if lawyers leveraged each other's strengths, leading or following according to circumstance rather than seniority! If lawyers with strengths in each area chose to collaborate, the leadership would be exceptional, and the result powerful. In fact, this is the definition of a truly great leader: one who is aware of the nature of the challenge and the makeup of the individuals available to achieve it. Consider the following scenarios:

- The leader may (of course) be leading, including those who are more senior in the firm.

- The leader may be following someone else, even someone more junior.

- The leader may be co-leading, giving a younger team member the chance to spread his or her wings and to feel empowered by collaborating as an equal.

Remember, the leader should develop the relationships that support leadership in every direction—upward, downward, and sideways. This enables the leader to leverage the talents at his command in the most efficient way, toward accomplishing the shared purpose.

You only attain this level of leadership when you have the self-knowledge to realize that you're not necessarily the best choice for the job, and the humility to act on this knowledge. This may at first seem rather counterintuitive. You could be thinking, "Wait a second. Leaders *aren't* humble. They're head-honcho, master-of-the-universe types!" I would argue that that might be the case in some scenarios (because leadership is, to a large degree, situational), but to sustain a shared purpose leaders must channel their personal motives into whatever is best for the team. This means not only controlling their own egos (incredible as this may seem in a lawyer!), but accessing socialized power, which inevitably trumps personal power.

Jim Collins, co-author of *Built to Last: Successful Habits of Visionary Companies*, asserts this principle in his *Harvard Business Review* article, "Level 5 Leadership." The term "Level 5" refers to the highest position in the hierarchy of executive qualities, which Collins believes is "humility combined with professional will." When a leader mobilizes others toward a shared purpose using these qualities, he leads with the highest level of capabilities and has the greatest ability to transform and elevate the team to "sustained excellence."

Back in Chapter 4 ("Personalities"), I mentioned that sometimes the most successful of all the personality types is the mild-mannered Moderate, and that part of this success derives from his natural humility and his tendency to put the shared purpose above his own status. Unfortunately, I have seen too many lawyers—young and old, inexperienced and experienced—signally fail in this regard (including myself!). I now realize that the most confident leaders are also the most self-effacing. You will recall the brilliant but arrogant tax lawyer from Chapter 2 who was busy developing a brand completely inadequate to the support of a flourishing legal career. His actions were driven by his lack of humility, and unless he makes significant changes, this will always prevent him from achieving real success as a leader.

Seriously, though, humility can feel inconsistent with our role as lawyers. After all, we are paid to advocate, to know all the answers, and to take charge. However, there is nothing intrinsically contradictory about having confidence and demonstrating humility. Humility enables you to lift (and thus motivate) others, to prioritize the shared purpose above your own personal agenda, to give your team credit for successes, and to take personal responsibility for mistakes—all crucial leadership attributes. It also reinforces the authenticity of your brand, as no one can *really* "know it all." On top of all this, humility simply makes a leader more likeable, which is vital in every aspect of your career!

Joe's charismatic leading style motivated his team members and helped them succeed.

But Jan's humility enabled her to lift others and empower them, and this made her team even more successful.

RECAP AND SUMMARY

Leading a team starts with imparting vision, followed by devising (and then implementing) a strategy to achieve a certain goal, which is then supported by the following:

- The leader employs the transformational tools of influence (leading through example, enthusiasm, challenge, and empowerment) with the objective of helping everyone on the team be his (or her) very best and discover his (or her) special talents. The leader does this by:

  - Being trustworthy, self-aware, positive, people-focused, and visionary (the five leadership characteristics!), and by encouraging everyone on the team to adopt those same values. These values are the foundation of the team's core brand.

  - Developing a compelling vision that fuels his or her passions and building on strengths that cultivate inner confidence— and assisting each team member to do the same.

  - Helping team members leverage their own talents.

  - Employing simple but effective methods to encourage others, including caring, looking out for the interests of team members, showing respect and appreciation, celebrating accomplishments (preferably on the spot!), giving regular feedback (i.e., not relying on arcane or tedious law-firm review procedures), expecting the best (scientifically proven to result in better performance), and maximizing confidence through focusing on strengths.

- The team should be composed of talented individuals with complementary strengths who together can optimally meet the goal.

- To inspire real commitment, the shared purpose must support the individual goals of every member. If a particular team member is not engaged, the fault lies with the leader for not sufficiently inspiring him or otherwise confirming his alignment with the team's purpose. (If a team member is just completely useless or self-focused, the leader must either inspire him or get rid of him.)

- Team strategy always includes supplying unique value to the client. The questions to ask are, "What important client need can we fulfill?" and "Does this add value and thus set us apart from the competition?" If you encourage your team to compete on the same level as the firm across the street, you immediately undermine your chances of success.

- Ideally, the team will have adopted a set of values that drives everyone's behavior. This is the team's core brand, and should be formalized in a mission statement.

- The "critical questions" must be asked of everyone on a regular basis, even if only informally. (Actually, informal discussions are usually more effective than conventional review systems!) This is a critical part of team morale.

- The leader must put the goals of the team and the success of the individuals he is leading above his own status.

As you begin to develop as a leader, your focus must necessarily shift from your own success to what best achieves the goals of the group. If you naïvely prioritize your own immediate success at the expense of the team, you will only succeed in undermining yourself. At best you will compromise the team's individual attempts at leadership (necessary for your own success); at worst you will lose their loyalty—and deservedly so.

Furthermore, you may think that you must at least *appear* to know everything (or inhabit some crazy ideal of a team leader!), but to rise to the most effective level of leadership, you must be strong enough to acknowledge when someone else might be better suited to lead. Only then are you equipped to achieve the best result for your team, which is your ultimate responsibility.

Chapter 22: Streamlining the Juggling Act

Conclusion

Chapter Twenty-Two
Streamlining the Juggling Act

In this concluding chapter I am going to deliver on the final part of the three-part promise I set out in Chapter 3 ("The Secret Knowledge of the Master Juggler"). Of course, that was some chapters ago, so allow me to jog your memory:

■ First, I promised to *help you develop an awareness of yourself and a way of thinking and interacting with others that will enable you to face most challenges of your career with optimism, confidence, and the right set of tools.* We have achieved this by working through the early chapters of the book—the "awareness building blocks."

■ I also undertook to give you insight into the dynamics of the three "balls": *brand, business,* and *leadership.* The second half of this book has, I hope, accomplished that objective.

■ Finally, I promised to show you how to *handle and leverage the different balls to achieve your objectives,* ultimately handling these essential factors of your career with ease—and achieving the status of a Master Juggler.

By now I hope that you have discovered that our juggling act as lawyers is not really so difficult after all. In fact, by building some simple skills on top of the right foundation, it can be achieved by each of us.

BRAND IS THE BEGINNING

Awareness ⟶ **Vision**

With the knowledge of the awareness building blocks, the first and critical step is to develop a personal vision, which must capture both the business you want to achieve and your leadership destination. It has to be the right vision that will leverage your unique strengths, ignite your passions, and inspire you to go the distance. Only by setting your personal vision can you begin to work with your three "balls."

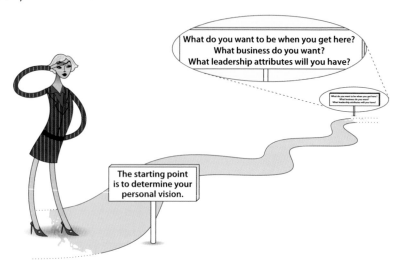

Since developing business and becoming a leader are contingent on demonstrating an authentic, distinct, and superior brand, you must understand what that means for you as an individual and how you can use it to achieve your goals. Your brand must reflect your authentic self and demonstrate the unique value you bring to clients and colleagues.

Awareness ⟶ *Vision* ⟶ **Leadership**

In addition, it's critical to integrate, as part of your brand, those things that demonstrate your confidence and professionalism—such as communicating well, handling emotions, dealing with conflict, and all the other issues addressed in Chapter 11 ("Adopting the Core Traits of a Superior Brand"). Most important, you must adopt the five leadership characteristics—trustworthiness, self-awareness, people-focus, positivity, and vision—as integral to your leadership brand. The path to success starts with your mindset, and these attitudes will give you the right tools.

Awareness $\longrightarrow$ *Vision* $\longrightarrow$ *Leadership* $\longrightarrow$ **Self-leading**

Vision is only useful if there is a strategy and a realistic plan to make that vision reality. In terms of your brand, this means that you must first have an ideal in mind that leverages your strengths and talents; then you must work to become that person. I recommend a *written* plan. It is not an overnight process and it requires unswerving self-belief and persistence, especially when you are outside your comfort zone or when (the inevitable!) obstacles cross your path. At these moments it is crucial to motivate and lead yourself and to overcome those forces (internal or external) that urge you to "stay as you are."

This process will be easier if you have been using your mental program to your advantage by imprinting your success (and your positive self-beliefs) into your subconscious. Keep your focus on *becoming your ideal brand*.

Awareness $\longrightarrow$ *Vision* $\longrightarrow$ *Leadership* $\longrightarrow$ *Self-leading* $\longrightarrow$ **Self-promoting**

Being (and becoming) a brand is not enough! To gain the necessary benefit, you must promote your brand so that you're noticed and so that you can make connections with people who will support you in your business development and your pursuit of leadership.

You can promote your brand through formal marketing initiatives, such as writing articles, speaking in public, and being active in professional organizations, but remember that routine daily activities are also an opportunity to promote your confident, professional, and distinct self. And the more authentic your brand, the easier it becomes for you to follow through with what that brand promises.

Awareness $\longrightarrow$ *Vision* $\longrightarrow$ *Leadership* $\longrightarrow$ *Self-leading* $\longrightarrow$ *Self-promoting* $\longrightarrow$ **Connecting**

Marketing and self-promotion are important to building your brand's reputation, but they do not directly generate business or leadership. Only building relationships accomplishes these goals! So meet as many people as possible and make connections with them, so that they become interested in you and are favorably impressed with your brand.

By now you know how to make those connections—by using your well-honed people skills and the simple tools of being interested and making others feel important. And don't forget about the feel-good factors, such as being positive, energetic, and smiling! People skills must be an integral part of your brand.

Awareness ⟶ *Vision* ⟶ *Leadership* ⟶ *Self-leading* ⟶ *Self-promoting* ⟶ *Connecting* ⟶ **Developing trust**

With each connection you make, your goal is to move the relationship forward by networking and fostering bonds. (Remember the definition of networking: taking an interest in others and being generous with your time, energy, resources, and actions while expecting nothing in return.) You are "building bridges." Over time you must authenticate your brand (by proving it reliable and trustworthy) and work to achieve mutually beneficial relationships that are based on principles similar to friendship—meaning that the priority is the ongoing relationship, as opposed to any short-term gain. This means that clients are not only satisfied with your services but rely on you for providing a unique value. Their loyalty is derived from their confidence in you, but (equally important) they also know that you have a genuine interest in them. The same principles, of course, apply to your colleagues.

In short, you develop trust. When you achieve that with your clients and colleagues, you can accomplish your goals in business development and leadership because you are in the best position of influence.

Awareness ⟶ *Vision* ⟶ *Leadership* ⟶ *Self-leading* ⟶ *Self-promoting* ⟶ *Connecting* ⟶ *Developing trust* ⟶ **Leading**

Becoming your ideal brand inevitably involves the support of others, so if your motivation is only personal achievement or power, you can still fall flat at this point in the process. If you need the help of clients, colleagues, or others, you must be as concerned with their success as with your own. In essence, the goal must be about the collective best, and your success cannot be separated from others'. This is the basis for a shared purpose.

Although the previous chapters discussed a shared purpose in the context of leading a team, the same principles apply whether you are dealing with clients or colleagues: You must enlist support by showing others a clear benefit from your purpose and then inspiring them to want to achieve it with you. This isn't accomplished by using position or authority, but instead by showing appreciation, motivating, and creating enthusiasm.

Specifically, you influence as a transformational leader in the four ways you are by now familiar with:

- Be a role model of confidence and competence, and commit to your goals and values; inspire others to emulate and follow you (influence through example).

- Passionately communicate a clear and compelling vision, energizing others with purpose and meaning (influence through enthusiasm).

- Encourage others to think creatively, and stimulate them to seek goals that support your vision (influence through challenge).

- Teach and coach others, and celebrate their strengths and individual contributions. In the process you empower them, and their talents then synergize with your own, fueling and supporting your vision (influence through empowerment).

The bottom line is that *no one can succeed without support*. Surround yourself with a network of people who will share in your goals and passions and who, in the process, will help you become who you aspire to be. Thus, the steps listed above are designed to give you the insight, skills, confidence, and focus to generate the relationships that will be at the core of your success.

By using the knowledge gained in the first chapters—the awareness building blocks of personalities, motivators, people skills, healthy thinking, and positive impact—you are equipped to pursue each one of the steps. In fact, the key concepts from those five chapters flow directly into the process. Each step relies on the successful completion of the previous one, and by working through the process in sequential order you build the foundation (awareness, skills, and the creation of your network) that enables you to move to the next step with ease and with a better assurance of ultimate success.

Once you reach the final step—leveraging relationships to foster and further your personal vision (leading)—the process still doesn't end! You must continually be working toward your vision and refining it, repeating the process over and over again. Always maintain self-awareness and use the building blocks to reach your goals.

As the process repeats, your network and your relationships are reinforced and the steps become easier and less protracted, to the point that each one becomes so ingrained and natural that it flows just like a ball!

In essence, your "ball" of brand-building looks something like this:

THREE BALLS BECOME ONE!

As you begin working with your brand, you have to reach into your leadership behaviors (which drive your brand) and continually refine your brand on the basis of the business that you want. Further, your brand is the interface to the relationships you build, and your success (as a leader and a business generator) is dependent on it. In other words, the three facets of your career overlap, and no one facet can be accomplished in isolation from the others.

What is even more interesting is that the development process for each facet is the same, and follows the identical sequence of steps. So by understanding and proactively pursuing those steps (rather than by simply reacting), you can achieve all three goals simultaneously.

BALLS & STEPS	BRAND	BUSINESS	LEADERSHIP
Gain Awareness	Cultivate the foundation that will support my goals: ■ Know how to work with the personalities around me—including my own ■ Understand my motivators so they can fuel my goals ■ Learn how to connect with other people ■ Know how to optimize my thinking to generate self-belief and confidence ■ Know how to make a positive impression on others	Cultivate the foundation that will support my goals: ■ Know how to work with the personalities around me—including my own ■ Understand my motivators so they can fuel my goals ■ Learn how to connect with other people ■ Know how to optimize my thinking to generate self-belief and confidence ■ Know how to make a positive impression on others	Cultivate the foundation that will support my goals: ■ Know how to work with the personalities around me—including my own ■ Understand my motivators so they can fuel my goals ■ Learn how to connect with other people ■ Know how to optimize my thinking to generate self-belief and confidence ■ Know how to make a positive impression on others
Determine Personal Vision	Determine my personal vision, which leverages my personality strengths, speaks to my needs and values, and ignites my passion. In light of that vision, develop my ideal brand.	Determine my personal vision in regard to the business I want to achieve and my target clients—again, ensuring that this part of my vision leverages my personality strengths, speaks to my needs and values, and ignites my passion.	Determine my ultimate leadership vision—what is my ultimate goal, and what support do I need to achieve it?—again, ensuring that this part of my vision leverages my personality strengths, speaks to my needs and values, and ignites my passion.

BALLS & STEPS	BRAND	BUSINESS	LEADERSHIP
Adopt Leadership Character-istics	Adopt the leadership characteristics as part of my brand: trustworthiness, self-awareness, people-focus, positivity, and vision.	Adopt the leadership characteristics as part of my brand: trustworthiness, self-awareness, people-focus, positivity, and vision. This is the driving force of my brand that will interface with clients.	Adopt the leadership characteristics as part of my brand: trustworthiness, self-awareness, people-focus, positivity, and vision. This is the driving force of my brand that will interface with others to build my leadership.
Self-Lead	Develop (and write down) my strategy and plan for becoming my ideal brand. Take action and work toward achieving that goal. Support my endeavors with positive self-belief and advantageously use my mental program to help me succeed.	Develop (and write down) my strategy and plan for client development. Take action and work toward acquiring the attributes that will achieve the business I envision. Support my endeavors with positive self-belief and advantageously use my mental program to help me succeed.	Develop (and write down) my strategy and plan for leadership, including the support that is needed to achieve my goals. Take action and work toward acquiring the attributes that will help my efforts. Support my endeavors with positive self-belief and advantageously use my mental program to help me succeed.
Self-Promote	Promote my brand formally through marketing activities and informally by being my brand at all times—so that people know and recognize it.	Promote my brand formally through marketing activities and informally by being my brand at all times—so that potential and current clients know and recognize it.	Promote my brand formally through marketing activities and informally by being my brand at all times—so that others (including colleagues) know and recognize it and are inspired to support me.

BALLS & STEPS	BRAND	BUSINESS	LEADERSHIP
Make Connections	Connect with people through my authentic, positive, and leadership-focused brand. Make the best impression by using my people skills and understanding of personalities.	Connect with potential clients through my authentic, positive, and leadership-focused brand, and take care to demonstrate my unique value. Make the best impression by using my people skills and understanding of personalities.	Connect with people through my authentic, positive, and leadership-focused brand, and take care to demonstrate my unique value and willingness to collaborate. Make the best impression by using my people skills and understanding of personalities.
Build Trusting Relationships	From my connections, bond and authenticate my brand so that clients and colleagues trust it.	From my connections, bond and authenticate my brand to build trusting client relationships.	From my connections, bond and authenticate my brand (to my colleagues and others) to build trusting relationships. This is the basis for inspiring followers to share in my personal vision.
Leverage (Lead) Relationships	Leverage trusting relationships to further develop my own personal brand, and also create a shared brand with my team.	Leverage trusting relationships to win and increase business.	Leverage trusting relationships and motivate others to share in my personal vision, creating a shared purpose.

As we pursue the steps of each ball—brand, business, and leadership—our underlying awareness, mindset, and people skills support each of them, enabling us to juggle the balls so well that it's hard to see where one ball begins and another one ends. In fact, we can streamline the process with such proficiency that the three balls effectively become one, yet again. And as we all know, one ball is much easier to juggle than three!

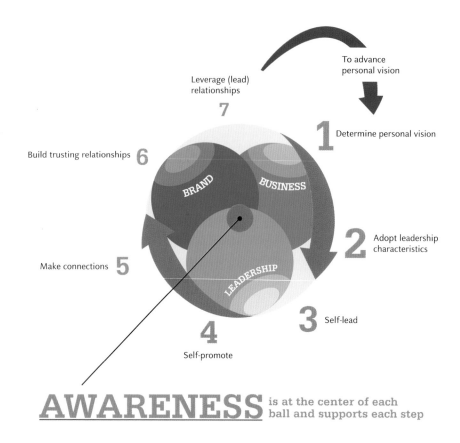

Leverage (lead) relationships **7**

To advance personal vision

Determine personal vision **1**

Build trusting relationships **6**

BRAND

BUSINESS

Adopt leadership characteristics **2**

Make connections **5**

LEADERSHIP

Self-lead **3**

4 Self-promote

AWARENESS is at the center of each ball and supports each step

CONSISTENT AND DELIBERATE PRACTICE

Awareness of the process is the first critical step. At this point in the book you have acquired the necessary awareness, but *knowing* and *doing* are two very different things! It's up to you to take action, set your vision, and determine your strategy. The strategy must include a proactive routine of learning and growing. By this I mean...

■ Prioritizing personal development (and all those quadrant 2 activities!);

■ Challenging behaviors that may be ineffective or even destructive to your goals, and then deliberately engaging in better ones;

■ Moving toward situations and relationships that challenge and support personal growth (i.e., moving outside your comfort zone), avoiding stagnation or retreat; and...

...doing all this in alignment with the steps outlined above.

This task requires you to practice the right habits every day. Merely reading this book—or any book—is not enough! The bottom line is that *what we practice is what we become*. Let's take tennis as an example. Reading a book about tennis techniques is unlikely to improve my serve. If I read such a book *and* hit a bucket of tennis balls once a week, I might see some benefit; but if I go out every day and practice 50 serves, focusing on *overcoming* my wobbly toss and *hitting* the ball in a particular spot, and if I then reflect on each success and failure and make adjustments, my serve *will* improve—because I have consistently and *deliberately* practiced!

Current research demonstrates clearly that there is no substitute for practice. Scientists worldwide have conducted loads of studies, some focused on areas in which performance is easy to measure (such as sports, music, and chess), some in other fields, and some in the world of business. They all conclude that high performance is dependent upon consistent and deliberate practice. Vladimir Horowitz, widely regarded as the 20th century's greatest pianist, is said to have remarked, "If I don't practice for a day, I know it. If I don't practice for two days, my wife knows it. If I don't practice for three days, the world knows it." I suppose the pertinence of this statement is what has caused it to be recycled and attributed to other world-class performers ever since.

And it is no different for us as lawyers. If we are really committed to our goals, we practice—every day! If we don't put in the practice, we simply set ourselves up for failure. Further, each time we repeat a new skill, behavior, or way of thinking, we change the neural pathways in our brains. Through practice, we

foster new synapses that support our desired outcomes, even to the point of transforming our natural inclinations, mindsets, and behaviors.

In fact, German researchers, studying the brains of people who have mastered juggling (real juggling, in the circus sense!), have shown that the process of learning increases the amount of gray matter in those areas of the brain that handle and store visual information. This increase is reckoned to be the direct result of stronger neural interconnections (synapses) created during the acquisition of the skills—while it's assumed that the increased brainpower then assists the juggler's progression through still trickier routines. Our "master juggling" skill set is no different: As we practice our skills, we transform ourselves by transforming the patterns in our brains.

Ways of practicing are wide and varied, and (of course) depend upon the goal and the person involved. But I'll give you a simple example of one habit I established that helped me incorporate practicing into my daily routine. Since every (tedious) time sheet entry, billable or non-billable, corresponded to an activity in which I had the opportunity to develop myself, practice a skill, or demonstrate my brand, I used filling out my time sheets as a tool of self-audit. For example, when entering a telephone conversation, I might think about how I had used my people skills. If the activity included meeting a fierce deadline, the question might be, "Did I keep my cool and motivate (rather than demoralize) my team?" Over time, this period of reflection affected my behavior and helped me to improve.

I know all too well how burdensome time sheets can be, and the thought of adding more administration to that responsibility is definitely unappealing, but reflecting each day on these things will bring them to the forefront of your mind, which is the first step in consciously implementing the skills. (Obviously, this ritual only works if you do your time sheets on a daily basis. Luckily for me, as described in Chapter 17 ["Winning and Developing Business"], early in my career I was forced to do mine on that basis, and it became a habit I never outgrew.)

It's fascinating to note that the researchers I mentioned previously who studied the brains of people learning to juggle found that after three months of not juggling, the participants lost their increased brain size, and some of them even forgot how to perform their newly acquired skill set. So if we want to retain our juggling synapses, we have to *keep* practicing.

Facebook, 274, 367
FEAR (Face Everything and
Recover), 170, 291, 409
Feedback, getting, 254–257, 421
Feedback, giving, 488–493
Feel the Fear and Do it Anyway
(Jeffers), 171
Feel-good factors, 139–146, 342,
520
Firm-wide brand, creating a,
500–503
The Five Love Languages
(Chapman), 465
Flow, 445
Freshfields, x

Gates, Bill, 452
Generation Y, 508–509
Generous, being, 138–139, 310,
317–319
Goldman Sachs, 278, 501,
502–503
Golf My Way (Nicklaus), 176
Google, 203, 217
Gore, Al, 207, 436
Grandmother Fox, 138
Grandmother Mattingly, 139
Gupta, Rajat, 501
Guy Savoy, 405–406, 497–499

Handshake as core to your
brand, 221
Hepburn, Audrey, 208
Higher needs, 102–103, 105.
See also Motivators
Hill, Napoleon, 30, 182
Horowitz, Vladimir, 527
Humility
begets admiration, 132–133
the power of, in a leader,
509–510

Image as core to your brand,
209, 218–220
Important, people want to feel,
125–126, 314
Impression(s), 29, 185–190
factors that make an, 185–188
image affecting, 187–188, 209
importance of first, 188–189,
209, 342
making a consistent, 257

Influence, 462–480, 481. *See also
Leading within relationships*
anger doesn't, 474
making others feel needed to,
472–473
showing you care to, 486
understanding others'
motivations to, 473
Ingham, Harry, 254
Intuition, 171–174
It's Not About The Bike
(Armstrong), 453

James, William, 439
Jeffers, Susan, 171
Jobs, Steve, 452
Johari window, 254–255
"The Johari Window:
A Graphic Model of
Interpersonal Awareness"
*(NTL Reading Book for Human
Relations Training News)*, 254
Jung, Carl, 172

K & L Gates, 275, 439
Kennedy, John F., 187
Kimberley, Christine, 293

Lazar, Dr. Sara, 449
Leader
characteristics of a, 218,
419–424, 426–427, 454, 519
definition of a, 16, 197, 217
ultimate objective of a, 506–507
Leadership, 16–17, 196–
198, 217–218, 417–431,
433–455, 457–513
as core to your brand, 217–218
three dimensions of, 417–419,
424, 429
transactional, 462, 479–480, 506
transformational, 425–429,
463–468, 479–480, 495,
506–507, 512, 521
Leadership (Burns), 425
The Leadership Challenge
(Kouzes & Posner), 420
"Leadership Development
at Goldman Sachs" *(Harvard
Business Review)*, 502
Leading a team, 17, 417–418,
424–426, 429, 481–513
Leading upward, 475–479

Leading within relationships,
16–17, 417, 418, 424–426, 429,
457–480
Ledoux, Joseph, 146, 223
Legal OnRamp, 367
"Level 5 Leadership" *(Harvard
Business Review)*, 510
Lincoln, Abraham, 458
LinkedIn, 367
Listening, 127–129, 345,
392–393
Luft, Joseph, 254

Madonna, 203, 208
Maltz, Maxwell, 182
Marketing yourself, 261–285,
519
diverse interests as a support
for, 278–279
Maslow, Abraham, 100, 101,
102, 109, 125, 507
Maslow's hierarchy of needs,
100–103, 109–110, 507
Massachusetts Institute of
Technology (MIT) Sloan
School of Management, 29
Master Juggler, 18, 23, 25–27,
32, 531
attitude of a, 22
needs strengths from all
personality types, 63
process for becoming, 517–530
Matrix of important versus
unimportant activities, 20, 22
McClelland, David, 469
McGaugh, James, 223
McKinsey & Company, vii,
501–503
McKinsey's Marvin Bower
(Edersheim), 501
Meetings, 21, 237–238
Mehrabian, Albert, 185
Mentor, finding one, 263–267
Miraval Spa, 529
Mirroring (of neurons/emotions),
139–140, 141–142, 153, 180,
223, 482
Mistakes, learning from,
452–453
Moderate, 47–48, 50–56, 59,
66–67, 209, 234, 385, 389, 467,
469, 471, 473, 484
Moderate boss, 92
Moderate client, 95

Morris, Manning & Martin, x, 281, 318
Motivation and Personality (Maslow), 100
Motivators, 28, 68, 99–121
  assessing whether out of alignment with career and goals, 108, 111–113
  assessing your, 109–113
  list of, 114–115
  Rebecca's example of her, 117–121

Names, using and remembering, 137–138, 363–364
Network, leveraging your, 398–408
  getting organized for, 404–408
  tips for, 401–404
Networking, 277–278, 307–339, 341–370, 398–409. *See also Working the room*
  benefits from commonality, 319–320
  creating opportunities for, 320–321
  definition of, 310–313, 520
  diverse interests as a support for, 278–279
  following up on, 322–323
  is not selling, 323–326, 354–355
  misperception about, 308–311
  on-line social, 274, 367
  people skills as the basis for, 314–16
  preparation for, 353–354
  requires committing to the success of others, 317–318
  tips, 326–336
Networking chart, developing your, 398–401
Nicklaus, Jack, 176
Nike, 203, 143
Nixon, Richard M., 187

O'Connor, Mike, 278
Obama, Barack, 188, 223
"Ockham Technologies: Living on the Razor's Edge" *(Harvard Business Review)*, 318
Olivier, Laurence, 292
The One Thing You Need to Know (Buckingham), 422

Organizations
  creating your own, 280–281
  getting involved in, 279–280

Parallel circuitry of the brain. *See Mirroring*
Peale, Norman Vincent, 182
People skills, 28–29, 123–153, 314–323, 519
Perfectionist, 43–46, 50–56, 59, 66–67, 101, 234, 385, 388, 467, 471, 473, 484
Perfectionist boss, 91–92
Perfectionist client, 94–95
Personal brand, 9–13, 193–200, 203–285, 435, 444, 518–522
  as the starting point for generating business, 193–196, 198, 384, 518
  as the starting point for leadership, 196–198, 518
  authentic, 197, 207, 241–242
  core traits of a superior, 217–240
  determining your, 205–206, 207, 242–260
  enhancing your, 257, 261–285
  exercise for developing your, 254–257
  experience and achievements reflected in your, 210–211
  lifestyle synching with your, 210
  list of, attributes, 215–216
  winning an award as beneficial to your, 267–268
Personal introduction, 355–358
Personal vision, 197, 433–447, 481–488, 497, 519
  generating passion and satisfaction, 99, 436–437, 517–518
Personality type(s), 27, 35–98
  attracted to your own, 59
  attraction to opposite, 57–58
  developing the latent traits of your, 63–67
  extroverted versus introverted, 49–50
  frameworks of, 37
  greatest opposites of, 52–54
  importance of understanding, 28, 36–37
  judgments of, 56–57
  leading a team by their, 96–98, 483–485

managing projects, priorities of different, 51–52
  patterns of, 54–56
  persuading clients from an understanding of, 385–389
  planning and organization, priorities of different, 50–51
  practical application: managing behaviors in relation to, 89–98
  synergizing with opposite, 58–59
  and transformational leadership, 464–468
  your core, 67–68
Personalizing, 137–138, 315–316
Pillsbury Wintrop Shaw Pittman, xi
Pitching for work. *See Selling*
Positive
  people want to feel, 140–142
  thinking. *See Thinking*
Posture as core to your brand, 220
Pour Your Heart Into It (Schultz), 504
Press releases, 273–274
Proactivity, the mindset of, 19–22, 526–528
Public speaking, 287–304
  benefits of, 289
  fear of, 288–289, 290
  learning, 289, 291
  practicing, 292–293
  preparing for, 294–295
  tips, 295–302
Published, getting, 269–274
Pygmalion effect, 491–493
"Pygmalion in Management" *(Harvard Business Review)*, 491

Questionnaire: Preferred Behaviors, 70–77

Reagan, Ronald, 187–188
The Relaxation Response (Benson), 448
Résumé, 276–277, 282–284
Retton, Mary Lou, 176
Reynolds, Emma, 509
Rizzolatti, Giacomo M.D., 139
Rockefeller, John D., 30
Roosevelt, Theodore, 373

Salk, Jonas, 172
Schultz, Howard, 504
Schwab, Charles, 30
Self-actualization, 101–103,
   110, 507
Self-leading, 16, 417, 418,
   424–426, 428–429, 433–455,
   519
Self-promotion, 274–276, 519,
   524. *See also Marketing yourself*
Self-talk, 165–166
Seligman, Martin, 182
Selling, 193–196, 381–398
   benefits from passionate brand,
      384
   common mistake in, 394
   compared with networking, 383
   from an innate understanding of
      personalities, 385–390
   listening as key to, 392–393
   sequence of steps for, 390–392
   successful legal career
      contingent on, 384
   three stages of, 382–384
*The 7 Habits of Highly Effective
   People* (Covey), 20, 22, 439
Shared purpose, 17, 418,
   494–500, 520
Shaw Pittman, x, xi, 262, 263,
   267
Shoes, stand in other people's,
   131–132
Small talk, 359–360, 401
Smile, affecting your own
   emotions, 143
Socialized power, 470, 480, 510
Soft skills, need for, 29–30
Southeastern Software
   Association, 281
Specialty, developing a, 211–214,
   261–263, 268–269
Sponsorship, 276
Starbucks, 203, 501, 502,
   504–505
Straight From the Gut (Welch),
   172
Strengths, building on your,
   60–67, 211, 421, 433, 445, 497
Stress, managing, 446–449
The Success Principles (Canfield),
   178
Suin, Richard, 180
Symbolic learning theory,
   179–180

Synaptic Self (LeDoux), 146

Team. *See also Leading a team*
   appreciating the, 487–488
   creating a spirited, 481–483
   looking out for the, 486
   values, 500–506
   vision, 494–497
Thatcher, Margaret, 207, 227
A Theory of Human Motivation
   (Maslow), 102
Theresa, Mother, 474
Think and Grow Rich (Hill), 30,
   182
Thinking, 143, 155–183
   as your mental program,
      156–160
   athletes using, for performance,
      176–177
   attitudes and feelings derived
      from, 161–164
   beliefs created by, 160–167
   generating confidence through
      your, 29, 157–171
   manifesting results, 174–180
   negative and toxic, 155,
      169–170, 287, 301
   results dependant on, 163–164
   subconscious versus conscious,
      157–160
Toastmasters, 291
Trump, Donald, 452
Trusting client relationships,
   creating, 371–381
   by building bridges, 323–326,
      354, 520
   sequence of steps for, 371–372
   showing you care as basis for,
      373–380
Twain, Mark, 125, 292
Twitter, 367

Uniqueness, competing on, 12,
   242, 258–259, 263, 383, 441
Ustinov, Sir Peter, 292

Valley of Death, 9–10, 450
Value add, creating a, 268
Values, 105–106, 497–503.
   See also Motivators
Vision. *See Personal vision.*
Visualization, 176–178, 179–180,
   301, 438–439
Voice, 185, 226–227

Volunteering in your firm, 280

Wants, 103–105. *See also
   Motivators*
Welch, Jack, 29, 172
Whitehall Wellbeing Working
   Group, 182
Who Moved My Cheese?
   (Johnson), 452
Williams, Venus, 438
Winfrey, Oprah, 203
Winning (Welch and Welch), 172
Women
   and mentors, 267
   and networking, 336–338
   and sponsorship, 276
Woods, Tiger, 176
Woodward, Sir Clive, 177
Working the room, 341–370
   attitude for, 342–344
   conversation sequence for,
      366–367
   conversation skills for, 344–352
   practicing, 352–353
   preparing for, 353–360
   tips for, 361–367
Writing articles. *See Published,
   getting*
Wrong, it's okay to be, 133–134

Yates, John, 281, 318–319

Bibliography

Armstrong, Lance, *It's Not About The Bike* (Great Britain: Yellow Jersey Press, 2001).

Barr and Barr, *The Leadership Equation* (Eakin Press, 1989).

Bear, Mark F., Barry W. Connors, and Michael A. Paradiso, *Neuroscience—Exploring The Brain* (United States: Lipincott Williams and Wilkins, 2007).

Begley, Sharon, *Train Your Mind Change Your Brain* (United States: Ballantine Books, 2007).

Benson, Herbert, with Miriam Z. Klipper, *The Relaxation Response* (United States: Harper Collins, 2000).

Boyatzis, Richard, and Annie McKee, *Resonant Leadership* (United States: Harvard Business School Publishing, 2005).

Buckingham, Marcus, *The One Thing You Need To Know* (Great Britain: Pocket Books, 2006).

Burns, James M., *Leadership* (United States: Perennial, 1978).

Burns, James M., *Transforming Leadership* (New York: Grove Press, 2003).

Canfield, Jack, *The Success Principles: How to Get from Where You Are to Where You Want to Be* (New York: HarperCollins, 2005).

Carnegie, Dale, *How To Win Friends And Influence People* (Ebury Press, 1998).

Chapman, Gary, *The Five Love Languages* (United States: Northfield Publishing, 1992).

Collins, Jim, "Level 5 Leadership: The Triumph of Humility and Fierce Resolve," *Harvard Business Review*, July 1, 2005.

Covey, Stephen R., *The 7 Habits Of Highly Effective People* (Great Britain: Simon and Schuster, 2004).

Cozalino, Louis, *The Neuroscience Of Human Relationships* (United States: W.W. Norton and Company, 2006).

Csikszentmihalyi, Mihaly, *Flow: The Classic Work On How To Achieve Happiness* (Rider, 1992).

Danksepp, Jaak, *Affective Neuroscience* (Great Britain: Oxford University Press, 1998).

Demarais, Ann, and Valerie White, *First Impressions* (Great Britain: Hodder and Staughton, 2004).

Doige, Norman, *The Brain That Challenges Itself* (United States: Penguin Group, 2002).

Ebersheim, Elizabeth Haas, *McKinsey's Marvin Bower* (John Wiley and Sons Inc, 2004).

Gawain, Shakri, *Creative Visualization* (Bantau Books, 1978).

Goleman, Daniel, *Emotional Intelligence* (Great Britain: Bloomsbury Publishing, 1995).

Goleman, Daniel, Richard Boyatzis, and Annie McKee, *Primal Leadership* (United States: Harvard Business School Press, 2002).

Groysberg, Boris, Scott Snook, and David Lane, "Leadership Development at Goldman Sachs," *Harvard Business Review,* November 3, 2005.

Hill, Napoleon, *Think and Grow Rich* (North Hollywood, CA: Wilshire Book Company, 1999).

Hill, Napoleon, and W. Clement Stone, *Success Through A Positive Mental Attitude* (United States: Prentice Hall Inc, 1960).

Iacocca, Lee, with William Novak, *Iacocca: An Autobiography* (United States: Bantam Books, 1984).

Jeffers, Susan, *Feel The Fear And Do It Anyway* (Great Britain: Vermillion, 1987).

Keirsey, David, *Please Understand Me II* (Prometheus Nemesis Book Company, 1998).

Kouzes and Posner, *The Leadership Challenge* (Jossey-Bass, 2007).

Kroeger, Otto, with Janet M. Thuesen and Hile Ruteledge, *Type Talk At Work* (Dell Publishing, 2002).

LeDoux, Joseph, *The Emotional Brain* (Great Britain: Weidenfield and Nicholson, 1998).

LeDoux, Joseph, *Synaptic Self—How Our Brains Become Who We Are* (United States: Viking Penguin, 2002).

Littaver, Florence and Marita Littaver, *Personality Puzzle* (Fleming H. Revell, 1992).

Livingston, J. Sterling, "Pygmalion in Management," *Harvard Business Review,* January 1, 2003.

Luft, Joseph, "The Johari Window: A Graphic Model of Interpersonal Awareness," *NTL Reading Book for Human Relations Training News,* 1982.

Maslow, Abraham H., *Motivation And Personality* (Wesley Education Publishers, 1987).

Maslow, Abraham H., "A Theory of Human Motivation," *Psychological Review,* 1943.

Montoya, Peter, with Tim Vandehey, *The Brand Called You* (United States: Personal Branding Press, 2002).

Murphy, Joseph and Ian Mc Mechan, *The Power Of Your Subconscious Mind* (Pocket Books, 2000).

Nicklaus, Jack, *Golf My Way* (United States: Simon and Schuster, 1998).

Owen, Jo, *How To Lead* (Great Britain: Pearson Education Limited, 2005).

Schultz, Howard, And Dori Jones Yang, *Pour Your Heart Into It* (United States: Hyperion, 1997).

Schwartz, David J., *Maximise Your Mental Power* (Great Britain: Thorsons, 1986).

Seligman, Martin E. P., *Learned Optimism: How To Change Your Mind And Your Life* (First Vintage Books Edition, 1990).

Siegel, Daniel J., *The Developing Mind—How Relationships And The Brain Interact To Shape Who We Are* (Guildford Press, 1999).

Siegel, Daniel J., *The Mindful Brain* (United States: W.W. Norton and Company, 2002).

Sullivan, George, *Mary Lou Retton* (Wanderer Books, 1985).

Wasserman, Noam, "Ockham Technologies: Living on the Razor's Edge," *Harvard Business Review,* February 10, 2004.

Weinbert, Robert S., and Daniel Gould, *Foundations Of Sport And Exercise Psychology* (Human Kinetics, 1995).

Welch, Jack, with John A. Byrne, *Straight From The Gut* (Warner Books Inc, 2001).

Welch, Jack, with Suzy Welch, *Winning* (Harper Collins, 2005).